Schroeders Negativ Praxis

Published by LABOR PARTNER GmbH
Geesthacht / Hamburg, GERMANY

Author
Hartmuth Schroeder

Graphics & Conceptions by
Paul Mohr

Design by
Thomas Schroeder

Translations by
Hans Einar Johannessen, Norway
Felix Bielser, Italy
Thomas Wollstein, Germany

Printing by
schulzdialog
Hamburg, Germany

First edition
– 3.000 –

Year of first publication
– 2002–

ISBN 3-00-010072-5

Contents

LABOR PARTNER Information

LABOR PARTNER Fotovertrieb GmbH, Geesthacht/ Hamburg, begann 1984 mit der Produktion von Schwarzweiß-Fotochemikalien. Gegründet wurde das Unternehmen durch Hartmuth Schroeder.
Der Gründer ist seit 1965 in der Fotobranche tätig, u.a. bei einem der führenden deutschen Fotochemiehersteller und bei einem traditionellen Fotopapierhersteller.
Die Absicht, die der Firmengründung zugrunde lag, war vor allem, den Anwendern weniger umweltbelastende und weniger gesundheitsgefährdende Fotochemie zur Verfügung zu stellen.
Die Produkte sollte möglichst weitgehend biologisch abbaubar sein, die Belastung der Atemwege minimieren und in wieder verwendbaren Flaschen angeboten werden.
Aus kleinsten Anfängen wurde zwischenzeitlich ein Unternehmen mit einem nennenswerten Marktanteil in Mitteleuropa. Seit einigen Jahren werden LABOR PARTNER Fotochemikalien weltweit erfolgreich exportiert.

Es begann 1984 mit dem Erfolg von drei ideal aufeinander abgestimmten Erzeugnissen: dem Entwickler LP-BROM 3, dem Stoppbad LP-CITRIN und dem geruchlosen Fixierbad LP-FIX NEUTRAL. Mit dieser Produktreihe wurden den Anwendern neue Fotochemikalien mit vergleichsweise geringer Atemwegsbelastung geboten, also besser für die Gesundheit der Laboranten. Die Lebenserwartung hochwertiger Geräte, vor allem auch der Objektive wurde verbessert. Die SO^2-Emission vom Fxierbad kann die Objektiv-Vergütung verblassen lassen. Der Wasser-verbrauch wurde minimiert, dies zeigte sich bei der Verarbeitung von Barytpapieren (engl. FB, für Fibre Based) sogar sehr drastisch.

Ein Produkt liegt dem Firmengründer ganz besonders am Herzen. Dies ist ›nur‹ ein Hilfsmittel, dem man in der Branche normalerweise keine erhebliche Bedeutung beimisst: LP-MASTERPROOF. Alle Vorstellungen, die den Firmengründer bereits seit der Firmengründung vor rund 20 Jahren bewegten, konnten mit diesem Produkt auf eine vorbildliche Weise realisiert werden. Bitte sehen Sie sich die Erläuterungen zum LP-MASTERPROOF in diesem Buch an, Sie werden dann unschwer erkennen, warum es in diese Bucheinführung Eingang gefunden hat.

Info di LABOR PARTNER

LABOR PARTNER Fotovertrieb GmbH, Geesthacht/ Hamburg, inizia la propria attività nel 1984 con la produzione di chimici fotografici per il bianco/nero. L'impresa è stata fondata da Hartmuth Schroeder. Il fondatore è attivo nel campo fotografico dal 1965, dapprima presso un importante produttore foto-chimico poi presso un produttore tradizionale di carta fotografica, entrambe tedeschi. L'intento, posto alla base della creazione dell'azienda, era soprattutto la volontà di mettere a disposizione dell'utilizzatore dei chimici fotografici a basso impatto ambientale. I diversi prodotti dovevano essere spiccatamente biodegradabili, gravare minimamente sulle vie respiratorie e essere confezionati in bottiglie riutilizzabili. Dai tempi dei primi passi, ora l'azienda vanta una quota di mercato ragguardevole nel bacino Mitteleuropeo. Da qualche anno i fotochimici LABOR PARTNER ven gono esportati con successo a livello mondiale.

Tutto iniziò nel 1984 con il successo di tre produzioni intonate idealmente fra loro: Lo sviluppo carta LP-BROM 3, il bagno d'arresto LP-CITRIN e il bagno di fissaggio inodore LP-FIX NEUTRAL. Grazie a questa linea di prodotti l'utilizzatore poteva contare su foto-chimici innovativi con un carico minimo sulle vie respiratorie, ovvero migliori per la salute degli operatori di laboratorio. Anche la vita media di apparecchiature di alto livello, soprattutto di obiettivi, è stata allungata. L'emissione di SO^2 dei bagni di fissaggio può far sbiadire i trattamenti sulle lenti. Il consumo dell'acqua è pure stato minimizzato, soprattutto nella lavorazione delle carte baritate (FB).

C'è però un prodotto preferito al fondatore dell'azienda. Si tratta ›solo‹ di un prodotto ausiliario, al quale nel settore non si riserva normalmente la dovuta considerazione: LP-MASTERPROOF. Tutte le aspettative, che hanno mosso il fondatore a partire dalla creazione dell'azienda vent'anni fa, sono state realizzate in questo prodotto in modo esemplare. Non perdere le delucidazioni su LP-MASTERPROOF presenti in questo libro, e capirai senza difficoltà il motivo dell'acceso a questa introduzione al libro stesso. Se d'un canto i prodotti chimici fotografici della LABOR PARTNER hanno conquistato un posto fisso presso i fotografi e stampatori grazie al loro alto livello qualitativo, d'altro canto

LABOR PARTNER Informasjon

LABOR PARTNER Fotovertrieb GmbH, i Geesthacht/ Hamburg, startet produksjonen av sort/hvitt fotokjemi i 1984.
Det ble grunnlagt av Hartmuth Schroeder. Han har vært virksom i fotobransjen siden 1965, bl.a hos en av Tysklands førende fotokjemi-produsenter og hos en tradisjonell fotopapir produsent.Hensikten med firmaet var å kunne tilby brukerne fotokjemi som var mindre belastende for miljøet.Produktene skulle så langt det var mulig være biologisk nedbrytbare, skulle ha mindre belastning på luftveiene og tilbys i gjennbruksforpakninger. Fra en forsiktig begynnelse er det nå blitt en bedrift med en betydelig markedsandel i sentraleuropa. I den senere tid blir LABOR PARTNER fotokjemi eksportert i hele verden.

Det hele begynte i 1984 med suksessen til tre ideelt avstemte produkter: Framkalleren LP-BROM 3, stoppebadet LP-CITRIN og det luktfrie fikserbadet LP-FIX-NEUTRAL. Med disse produktene fikk forbrukeren tilgang til kjemikalier som er forholdsvis lite belastende for luftveiene, alså bedre for helsen til fotolaboranten. Videre ble belastningen til labutstyret, fram for alt objektivene, redusert. SO^2 emisjonen fra fikserbad kan ødelegge overflatebehandlingen på objektiver.Vannforbruket blir også redusert, spesielt ved bruk av barytt-papir (fiberbase).

Et av produktene som ligger grunnleggeren spesielt på hjertet, er LP-MASTERPROOF. Dette er et hjelpemiddel som en ikke har lagt særlig vekt på i bransjen til nå. Alle intensjonene son lå til grunn for firmaets drift de siste 20 årene kunne virkeliggjøres på en eksemplarisk måte med dette produktet. Derfor ber vi om at kapittelet om LP-MASTERPROOF blir lest grundig. Det vil da blir klart hvorfor vi har vektlagt dette allerede i innledningen.På den ene side har LABOR PARTNER Fotochemikalien fått en fast plass hos fotografer og hos fotolaboranter på grunn av det svært høye kvalitetsnivå de garanterer. På den annen side er de økonomiske i bruk, selv om det ikke alltid er helt innlysende ved første blikk. Ved siden av prisen for en flaske med konsentrat er det også andre faktorer som spiller en rolle, noe vi vil gå nærmere inn på, og som har ført til at vi har fått stadig flere stamkunder for produktene til LABOR PARTNER.

ON LABOR PARTNER

LABOR PARTNER Fotovertrieb GmbH, Geesthacht/ Hamburg, Germany, took up its production of black-and-white photo chemicals in 1984. The company was founded by Hartmuth Schroeder.
The founder has been working in the photo industry since 1965, being employed, among others, by one of the leading German photo chemistry manufacturers, and by a traditional photographic printing-paper manufacturer.
The principal intention when founding the company was to provide the users with photo chemicals with less of a harmful impact on the environment and less of a health hazard. Products were devised to be biologically de-gradable to the furthest possible extent, to minimise the exposure of the respiratory system to fumes, and to be offered in reusable bottles. Since then, what started on a very small scale, has evolved to become a company holding a significant share of the Central European market. For some years new, there is a successful world-wide export of LABOR PARTNER chemicals.

It all started in 1984 with the success of three products which were an ideal match: The developer LP-BROM 3, the stop bath LP-CITRIN, and the odourless fixer LP-FIX NEUTRAL. This series of products offered the photo laboratory worker new photo chemicals affording relatively little stress to the respiratory tract, photo chemicals therefore, which are better for the lab worker's health. The life of expensive hardware, above all of the lenses, was improved, too, as the emission of SO^2 from the fixer may damage lens coatings. Water consumption was reduced, which becomes most apparent when fibre-based (FB) paper is processed.

There is one product, of which the founder is particularly fond. It is ›just‹ an accessory not normally regarded by the branch as very important: LP-MASTERPROOF.
All of the concepts of concern to the founder since the establishment of the company approximately 20 years ago, could be realised in an ideal way in this product. Please have a look at the information on LP-MASTERPROOF in this book, and you will understand just why it deserved a place in this introduction. On the one hand, it is because they ensure a high level of quality that LABOR PARTNER photo chemicals have found their way into the toolbox of photog-

MACO ORT 25clear, Leica Summicron, developed in LP-DOCUFINE LC, exposed with WA40 mm, exposure time 9s, 5.6 – on MACO expo RF2, graded baryta paper, glossy, grade 2.
© Valsasnini

Einerseits haben LABOR PARTNER Fotochemikalien bei den Fotografen und Laboranten einen festen Platz eingenommen, weil sie ein sehr hohes Qualitätsniveau sicherstellen. Andererseits sind sie preiswert, auch wenn nicht jeder Anwender dies auf den ersten Blick erkennen mag. Neben dem Preis für eine Flasche Konzentrat spielen letztlich viele weitere Parameter eine Rolle, von denen wir nur einige aufführen, die aber dazu geführt haben, dass die Nachkäuferrate (Stammkunden) für LABOR PARTNER Erzeugnisse einzigartig hoch ist.

▪

Qualität der Produkte: Gleichbleibend hohes Qualitätsniveau über lange Zeiträume, auch bei Nachbestellungen. Wiederverwendbare Verpackung bei den 1 l Flaschen mit Füllstandsanzeige. Einzigartig hohe Ergiebigkeit, der Gebrauchslösungen.
Im Vergleich sehr lange Haltbarkeit der Gebrauchslösungen. Der Versuch, auch biologisch abbaubare Fotochemie einzuführen. Ständige Weiterentwicklung der Rezepturen, Anpassung an Emulsionsveränderungen. Hohe Lieferbereitschaft, ständige Warenverfügbarkeit. Attraktives Preis-Leistungsverhältnis durch hohe Konzentration der Chemie. Der Versuch, mit emissionsreduzierter Fotochemie die gesundheitliche Belastung der Laboranten zu minimieren.

▪

Die Schwarzweiß-Fotografie besitzt einen Reiz, der einzigartig faszinierend ist. Wie die seit einigen Jahren wieder stark ansteigenden Verkaufszahlen bestätigen, besitzen für Fotografen die verschiedenen Schwarzweiß-Techniken einen hohen Stellenwert. Dies zeigt sich vor allem durch die Verwendung anspruchsvoller Filme, dort vor allem Roll- u. Planfilme, sowie der entsprechenden Fotochemie. Auch bei Kleinbild-Filmen ist ein Trend hin zu sehr hochauflösenden Filmen zu erkennen, die zwar vergleichsweise teuer sind und sogar Spezialentwickler voraussetzen, die jedoch ein Qualitätsniveau bieten, das bis dahin eigentlich dem Mittelformat vorbehalten war.
Billigprodukte haben bereits erhebliche Marktanteile verloren und wie es aussieht, gehen die Rückgänge aufgrund technologischer Veränderungen vor allem zu Lasten der ›Massenware‹.

▪

Die Tatsache, dass Sie dieses Buch lesen, zeigt dass Sie sich für hochwertige Foto-Erzeugnisse interessieren. Dies freut uns und wir sichern Ihnen zu, dass LABOR PARTNER weiterhin alles zu unternehmen wird, um Ihnen die Freude an sehr hochwertigen Foto-Erzeugnissen zu erhalten und noch zu vergrößern.

sono competitivi, anche se al primo impatto l'utilizzatore potrebbe anche non accorgersene. Insieme al prezzo di un litro di prodotto concentrato molti altri fattori, dei quali daremo conto, hanno determinato una rata di riacquisto del prodotto (clienti abituali) LABOR PARTNER particolarmente alta.

▪

Qualità dei prodotti: Un alto livello qualitativo costante nel tempo, ordine dopo ordine. Confezione riutilizzabile con le bottiglie da 1 litro con indicatore del livello. Alta capacità, le prestazioni della soluzione d'uso sono uniche.
La conservazione della soluzione d'uso in confronto è molto lunga. Il tentativo di introdurre anche chimici fotografici biodegradabili. La continua ricerca atta a migliorare le formulazioni e ad adattarsi sempre alle modifiche delle emulsioni. Grande potenzialità nella fornitura, costante disponibilità di merce. Rapporto prezzo/prestazioni grazie all'alta concentrazione chimica. Il tentativo di minimizzare l'impatto salutare sugli utilizzatori abituali, grazie ad una foto-chimica a basse emissioni dannose.

▪

La fotografia in bianco/nero vanta uno stimolo unico nel suo fascino. Per numerosi fotografi le diverse tecniche della fotografia in bianco/nero rappresentano un'alta considerazione nella scala dei valori. Possiamo osservare ciò, soprattutto nell'uso di pellicole impegnative, quali i rollfilm o le pellicole piane, e di una chimica fotografica adatta. Anche nel campo delle pellicole di piccolo formato assistiamo ad un trend per materiali ad alta definizione, che pur richiedendo sviluppi speciali e relativamente costosi, riescono ad offrire un livello qualitativo, che poteva essere raggiunto solo con il medio formato. I prodotti a basso prezzo hanno ormai perso una grande fetta di mercato e in base ai mutamenti tecnologici, questi stanno via, via scomparendo.

▪

Partiamo dal presupposto, che come lettore di questo libro, tu sia interessato a prodotti foto-chimici di alto livello. Naturalmente ciò ci rallegra e possiamo assicurarti, che LABOR PARTNER continuerà a mettercela tutta, per farti mantenere il piacere di reperire prodotti fotografici di alto livello.

Produktenes kvalitet: Svært høy kvalitet og stabil produksjon over lang tid. Høyverdige plastflasker med måleskala, kan brukes til så mangt. Enestående høy utnyttelsesgrad av kjemikaliene, også av bruker-blandingene. Lang holdbarhet på brukerblandingene. Så langt mulig bruk av biologisk nedbrytbare kjemikalier. Kontinuerlig videreutvikling av oppskrifter for å ta høyde for videreutvikling av film / papir. Kort leveringstid, stort lager (i Tyskland) Attraktivt forhold mellom pris og ytelse bl.a gjennom høy konsentrasjon av kjemien. Forsøk på stadig å minske emisjonen for å redusere den helsemessige belastningen i mørkerommet.

▪

Sort/hvitt fotografi har en fasinasjon som er enestående. Som de stadig økende salgstallene viser, er de forskjellige sort/hvitt-teknikkene viktige for fotografene. Dette blir tydelig i valg av spesielle filmer, spesielt rull og planfilm, og tilsvarende kjemi. Også 35mm film med svært høy oppløsning, som er dyrere og som krever spesialframkallere, men som da gir en kvalitet som tilsvarer mellomformat, øker sterkt. Billigprodukter taper markedsandeler og det teknologiske framskrittet synes å gå spesielt på bekostning av ›massevare‹.

▪

Vi forutsetter at leseren av denne boken interesserer seg for high-end fotoprodukter. Dette gleder oss og vi forsikrer at LABOR PARTNER også i framtiden vil gjøre alt for å opprettholde gleden ved høyverdige fotoprodukter.

raphers and laboratory workers. On the other hand, they are affordable, even if all users may not see this at first sight. In addition to the price to be paid for a bottle of concentrate, many other parameters played a part in establishing a uniquely high percentage of regular buyers of LABOR PARTNER products. We shall list just a few:

Quality of the products: High level of consistent quality over long periods, including subsequent orders. Reusable packaging in the case of the one-litre bottles with level indicator. Unrivalled capacity of the working solutions. The life of working solutions is very long when seen in relation to other products. The attempt to introduce biologically degradable photo chemicals. Permanent updating of formulations, adaptation to emulsion changes. Good readiness for delivery, products are always available. Attractive value for money due to high concentration of the chemicals. The attempt to reduce health hazards to the lab worker through low-emission chemicals.

There is a uniquely fascinating appeal in black-and-white photography. For several years, sales are going up. This shows the importance of the different black-and-white techniques for photographers. It is particularly evident in the use of specialised films, mainly medium-format roll film and sheet film, and the corresponding photo chemicals. Even in the 35-mm range, one can see a trend to high-resolution films which, while being relatively expensive and even requiring special developers, offer a level of quality previously reserved to medium format photography. ›Mr. Cheap‹ products have already lost considerable shares of the market, and it looks as though the decline of the market as a consequence of technological development will largely affect ›mass products‹.

By reading this book, so we shall assume, you show that you are interested in high-quality photo products. We are glad to see this, and we assure you that LABOR PARTNER will continue to do everything to preserve and enhance your delight in high-quality photo products.

MACO UP 100plus, Canon 50 mm f1.8, 1/60, developed in LP-SUPERGRAIN, exposed with WA40 mm, exposure time 12s, 5.6 – on MACO expo RF3, graded baryta paper, glossy, grade 3.
© Valsasnini

Fragen & Antworten

Ein Schlusswort, gleich zu Beginn, es handelt sich um ein Zitat: Heiner Henniges, ein anerkannter deutscher Foto-Fachredakteur, schreibt:
„Das Negativformat hat zwar einen entscheidenden Einfluss auf die Art des Fotografierens, die Anmutung der Bilder, ihre technische Qualität und somit auch auf die Aussagekraft des Ergebnisses, allerdings ist seine Größe ein Stilmittel, nicht mehr und nicht weniger und kein Kriterium für den künstlerischen Wert eines Bildes. Nichts gegen Fotografen, die oftmals nahezu asketisch als Puristen eine Stilrichtung vertreten. Nicht selten jedoch sind es gerade die Bilder, die gegen ›alle Regeln der Kunst‹ verstoßen, diejenigen die den Betrachter am stärksten in ihren Bann ziehen. Regeln, Vorurteile und Traditionen dürfen nicht einschränken."
Schwarzweiß-Magazin 11/1997

1. ***Warum stellt die Industrie so viele unterschiedliche Filmsorten her?*** Das hat mit der Tradition zu tun. Alles fing mit sehr niedrigempfindlichen Filmen an, die dann, im Laufe der Zeit, immer empfindlicher wurden. Heute bilden die 100 und 400 ISO Filme das Rückgrat des Marktes.

Einige ausgewählte Beispiele für ›normale Filme‹ für die ›bildmäßige Fotografie‹ sind:
- AGFA APX-Filme
- KODAK PLUS- X / TRI-X / T-MAX
- ILFORD FP4 / HP5 / Delta
- MACO UP25 / UP64 / UP100 / UP400 / CUBE400

Die Spezialfilme für sehr, sehr feines Korn und hohe Abbildungsqualität sind:
- KODAK TECHNICAL PAN
- MACO ORT25
- MACO Technical Pan TP64

Daneben gibt es den interessanten Bereich der Infrarot-Filme:
- ILFORD SFX
- KODAK HIE
- KONICA IR
- MACO IR 750
- MACO IR 820
- MACO CUBE 400

Für Verfremdungen, Kontaktkopien, grafische Anwendungen stehen zur Verfügung:
- AGFA LITHFILM & GRAPHIC FILM
- KODAK LITHFILM & GRAPHIC FILM
- MACO GENIUS film (Lithfilm)
- MACO GENIUS PRINT film (Photo-Type-Setting-Film)

Domande & Risposte

Una parola finale, proprio all'inizio; si tratta di una citazione: Heiner Henniges, un rinomato redattore tedesco nel campo fotografico, scrive:
„Il formato del negativo ha certamente un influsso determinante sul modo di fotografare, sull'impatto delle immagini, sulla qualità tecnica e così pure sull'espressività del risultato, però la sua dimensione è un mezzo stilistico, né più né meno, e nessun criterio per il valore artistico dell'immagine. Nulla contro quei fotografi, che spesso rappresentano una scuola di pensiero da puristi, in modo pressoché asettico. Non accade però di rado che proprio quelle immagini, che si scontrano con ›tutte le regole dell'arte‹, riescono a sbloccare nel modo più forte chi le guarda. Regole, pregiudizi e tradizione non devono essere riduttivi."
Schwarz-Weiss-Magazin 11/1997

1. ***Perché l'industria del settore produce una varietà di pellicole così ampia?*** Ha qualcosa a che fare con la tradizione. Tutto iniziò con pellicole a bassa sensibilità, poi man mano con il passare del tempo diventarono sempre più sensibili. Oggi le pellicole ISO 200/21 e 400/27 rappresentano la fetta maggiore.

Le pellicole ›normali‹ per ›la fotografia pittorica‹ sono (un semplice estratto di ciò che il mercato offre):
- AGFA Serie APX
- KODAK PLUS-X / TRI-X / T-MAX
- ILFORD FP4 / HP5 / Delta
- MACO UP 25 / UP64 / UP100 / UP400 / CUBE400

Le pellicole ›speciali‹ per una grana molto, molto fine ed alto potere risolvente sono:
- KODAK TECHNICAL PAN
- MACO ORT25
- MACO Technical Pan TP64

Accanto a queste esistono delle interessanti pellicole nella fascia delle pellicole infrarosso:
- ILFORD SFX
- KODAK HIE
- KONICA IR
- MACO IR 750
- MACO IR 820
- MACO CUBE 400

Per Elaborazioni creative, contatti, usi grafici esistono:
- AGFA LITHFILM & GRAPHIC FILM
- KODAK LITHFILM & GRAPHIC FILM
- MACO GENIUS film (Lithfilm)
- MACO GENIUS PRINT film (Photo-Type-Setting-Film)

Spørsmål og Svar

Helt i begynnelsen , et sluttord. Den annerkjente tyske fotofag-redaktøren Heiner Hennings skrev:
„Negativformatet har riktignok en avgjørene effekt på måten en fotograferer på, hvordan bildene blir, deres tekniske kvalitet og dermed også på uttrykkskraften til resultatet, men formatet er likevel et stilmiddel, ikke mer eller mindre og ikke noe kriterium for den kunstneriske verdien til bildet.
Ikke noe vondt sagt om fotografer som forfekter en asketisk puritanisme som stilretning. Ofte er det nettopp bilder som bryter med ›alle kunstens regler‹ som gir mest til den som betrakter det og som tiltrekker seg oppmerksomhet. Regler, fordommer og tradisjoner må ikke få lov til å virke innskrekende."
(Schwarz-Weiss-Magazin 11/ 1997)

1. ***Hvorfor produseres det så mange forskjellige filmer?*** Dette har bl.a med tradisjon å gjøre. Det hele begynnte med lavfølsomme filmer, som etter hvert fikk stadig høyere følsomhet. I dag utgjør filmer med 100 og 400 ISO hoveddelen av markedet.

›Normale filmer‹ for billedmessig fotografi er bl.a:
- AGFA APX FILMER
- KODAK PLUS-X / TRI-X / T-MAX
- ILFORD FP4 / HP5 / Delta
- MACO UP 25 / UP 64 / UP 100 / UP 400 / CUBE 400

Spesialfilmer med ekstremt fint korn og høy oppløsning er bl.a:
- KODAK TECHNICAL PAN
- MACO ORT 25
- MACO TECHNICAL PAN TP 64

Det finnes også interesante filmer for det infrarøde området:
- ILFORD SFX
- KODAK HIE
- KONICA IR
- MACO IR 750
- MACO IR 820
- MACO CUBE 400

For eksprimenter, kontaktkopier og grafik framstilling finnes:
- AGFA LITHFILM & GRAPHIC FILM
- KODAK LITHFILM & GRAPHIC FILM
- MACO GENIUS film (Lithfilm)
- MACO GENIUS PRINT film (Photo-Type-Setting-Film)

Questions & answers

A conclusion, right at the beginning, a quotation:
Heiner Henniges, a well-known German photography editor, writes:
„The format of the negative does have a decisive impact on the way photographs are made, the impression made by the images, and thus also on the expressiveness of the result, but its size is just a stylistic device, no more and no less. It is not a criterion by which the artistic value of an image can be judged. I do not mind photographers favouring their style as purists, in an often almost ascetic way. The case is not rare, however, that the viewer is most fascinated by just those images violating ›all acknowledged rules of the art‹. Rules, prejudices, and traditions must not confine.“
Schwarz-Weiss-Magazin 11/1997

1. ***Why does the photographic industry manufacture so many different types of films?*** This has to do with tradition. Everything started with films with very low speed, which, over time, became faster and faster.
Nowadays, 100 and 400 speed films are the ›backbone‹ of the market.
A few examples (There are many many others.) of ›normal‹ films for ›pictorial photography‹ are:
- AGFA APX films,
- ILFORD FP4/HP5/Delta,
- KODAK PLUS-X/TRI-X/T-MAX,
- MACO UP25/UP64/UP100/UP400/CUBE400.

Special-purpose films for ultra-fine grain and high imaging quality are, among others:
- KODAK TECHNICAL PAN,
- MACO ORT 25,
- MACO Technical Pan TP64.

There is also the interesting range of infrared films:
- ILFORD SFX,
- KODAK HIE,
- KONICA IR,
- MACO IR 750,
- MACO IR 820,
- MACO CUBE 400.

For abstractions, contact prints, graphical applications, there are, among others:
- AGFA LITHFILM + GRAPHIC FILM,
- KODAK LITHFILM + GRAPHIC FILM,
- MACO GENIUS film (lith film),
- MACO GENIUS PRINT film (photo typesetting film).

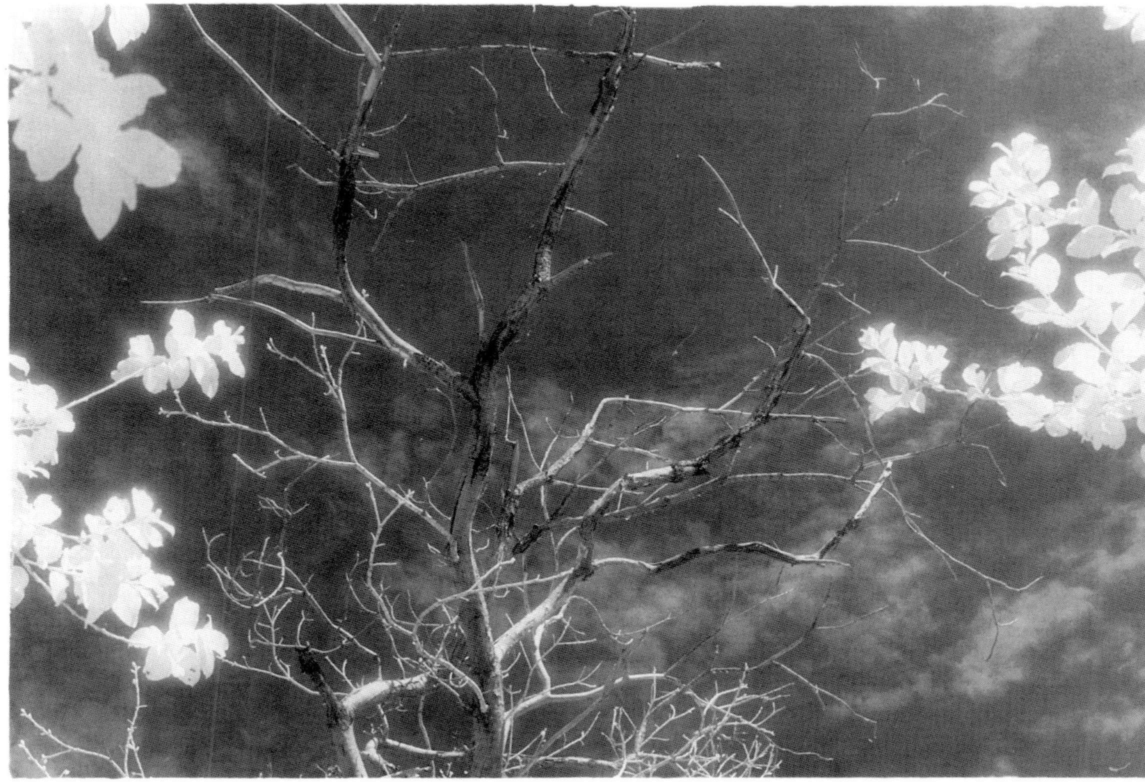

KODAK HIE, Leica Summicron 50 mm, 1/15 + 4, developed in LP-SUPERGRAIN, exposed with WA40 mm, exposure time 11s, 5.6 – on MACO expo RF, graded baryta paper, glossy, grade 4. © Valsasnini

2. ***Was sind Sensibilisierungsfarbstoffe?*** Silberhalogenide sind ›unbehandelt‹ nur für Violett, Blau und Grün empfindlich. Durch Anfärben der Kristalle mit Sensibilisierungsfarbstoffen werden sie auch für die übrigen Spektralfarben ›empfänglich‹. Es handelt sich um unechte, fluoreszierende Farbstoffe, die das Silberbromidkorn unmittelbar anfärben und ihm dadurch ein Absortionsvermögen für bestimmte Spektralfarben verleihen.

3. ***Was sind panchromatische Filme?*** Nahezu alles, was heute als Kleinbild- und Rollfilm angeboten wird, ist panchromatisch sensibilisiert. Der Bereich umfasst etwa von 400 bis 700 Nanometer (nm).
Panchromatische Filme sind für rote Farben etwas zu stark sensibilisiert, daher werden beim Positiv rote Farbtöne etwas zu hell wiedergegeben. Gelbgrüne Farben werden tonwertrichtig dargestellt, dagegen blauviolette Farben in etwas zu helle Grautöne übersetzt.

4. ***Was sind orthochromatische Filme?*** Nur wenige Filmsorten, z.B. Planfilme für die Lithtechnik, Spezialfilme für die Reproduktion, Elektronen-Mikroskopie u.a. liegen im Bereich von etwa 380 nm bis 600 nm. Dem Verfasserteam sind heute noch zwei Hersteller dieser Gattung bekannt: ILFORD ORTHO als Planfilm, MACO ORT 25clear als Kleinbild- Roll-und Planfilm. Die beiden Planfilm-Fabrikate unterscheiden sich erheblich im Gradationsverlauf.
Neben Blau werden die gelben und grünen Farben nahezu tonwertrichtig wiedergegeben. Dies macht diese Filme für Landschaftsfotografen so interessant.
Lediglich für Orange und Rot sind nicht genügend sensibilisiert, Rot wird daher als Schwarz auf den Vergrößerungen abgebildet.

5. ***Was sind orthopanchromatische Filme?*** Diese Filme werden auch Rectepanfilme genannt. Die bei der panchromatischen Emulsion überbetonte Rotempfindlichkeit wird hier durch besondere Sensibilisierungsfarbstoffe zurückgedrängt und damit ist die Schicht normal rotempfindlich geworden. Auch die übrigen Farben werden in nahezu richtiger gegenseitiger Helligkeitsabstufung wiedergegeben. Die orthopanchromatische Schicht stellt damit das Universalmaterial dar, das bereits ohne Gelb- oder Gelbgrünfilter tonwertrichtig arbeitet.
Dem Autor ist heute nur ein Film dieser Spezialgattung bekannt:
MACO PO 100clear. Früher waren u.a. der AGFA ISOPAN F, der PERUTZ PERPANTIC und der KODAK PANATOMIC Vertreter dieser Gattung.

2. ***Cosa sono le sostanze coloranti di sensibilizzazione?*** Gli alogenuri d'argento ›non trattati‹ sono sensibili solo al viola, blu e verde. Colorando i cristalli con coloranti di sensibilizzazione questi diventano ›ricettivi‹ anche per i rimanenti colori spettrali. Si tratta di coloranti non resistenti, fluorescenti, che tingono direttamente il granulo di bromuro d'argento e gli conferiscono in tal modo le bande di assorbimento per determinati colori spettrali.

3. ***Cosa sono le pellicole pancromatiche?*** Pressoché tutte le pellicole che vengono oggi proposte, sia nel piccolo che medio formato, sono sensibilizzate pancromatiche. La fascia racchiude ca. da 400 a 700 Nanometri (Nm).
Le pellicole pancromatiche sono sensibilizzate un po' troppo per le tonalità di colore rosso, per questo motivo le tonalità dei rossi nella stampa risulteranno un po' troppo chiare. I colori dal giallo/verde vengono riprodotti correttamente, le tonalità blu/viola in grigi leggermente troppo chiari.

4. ***Cosa sono le pellicole ortocromatiche?*** Solo pochi tipi di pellicole, p. es. pellicole piane per la tecnica lith, pellicole speciali per repro, pellicole speciali per microscopi elettronici, ecc., che si collocano in una fascia di sensibilità da 380 a 600 Nm.
Al nostro team al momento sono a conoscenza solo ancora due produttori: ILFORD ORTHO come pellicola piana e MACO ORT 25 clear sia come pellicola di piccolo formato e rollfilm, che pellicole piane. Altre grandi case come AGFA e KODAK, sembra abbiano interrotto la loro produzione. I due tipi di pellicole piane si distinguono fra loro in modo sostanziale in ambito di andamento della gradazione.
Accanto al blu, i colori dal giallo al verde vengono riprodotti in modo pressoché corretto nella resa tonale.
Questa peculiarità le rende particolarmente interessanti per la fotografia di paesaggio. Solamente per le tonalità dall'arancione al rosso la sensibilizzazione risulta insufficiente, il rosso verrà pertanto riprodotto sulla stampa, come nero.

5. ***Cosa sono le pellicole pancrortocromatiche?*** Anche materiale Rectepan. Grazie a particolari coloranti di sensibilizzazione la iper-sensibilità al rosso dell'emulsione pancromatica viene tamponata, cosicché lo strato diventa normalmente sensibile al rosso.
La riproduzione dei rimanenti colori rimane pressoché fedele nella gradazione delle rispettive tonalità.
L'emulsione pancrortocromatica rappresenta pertanto un materiale universale, che lavora anche senza filtro giallo o giallo/verde. Al nostro team ad oggi è conosciuto un solo materiale disponibile sul mercato:
MACO PO 100clear. In passato AGFA ISOPAN F, PERUTZ PERPANTIC e KODAK PANATOMIC rappresentavano questa tipologia di pellicola.

2. ***Hva er egentlig sensibilieringsfarvestoffer?*** Sølv halogenider er i sin grunnform bare følsomme for fiolett, blått og grønnt. Ved å benytte sensibiliseringsfarger blir krystallene følsomme for resten av spektralfargene. Dette er da uekte fluoriserende fargestoffer som gir sølvbromidkorn muligheten til å absorbere en spesiell spektralfarge.

3. ***Hva er pankromatiske filmer?*** Så godt som alle filmer som i dag selges i 35mm og i rullfilm er panchromatisk sensibilisert. Området går fra ca 400 til 700 nanometer. Panchromatiske filmer har øket følsomhet for rødt, slik at rødtoner blir gjenngitt litt for lyst i positiv. Gulgrønnefarger blir gjenngitt rett men blåfiolette farger blir omsatt til litt for lyse gråtoner.

4. ***Hva er orthochromatiske filmer?*** Det finnes bare noen få filmer av denne typen f.eks planfilmer for lithteknikk, spesialfilmer for reproduksjon, spesialfilmer for elektromikroskopi og noen andre. Disse er følsomme for området fra 380 til 600 nanometer.
Forfaterne kjenner bare til to produsenter av slik film: ILFORD ORTHO som planfilm og MACO ORT 25clear som 35mm, rullfilm og som planfilm. Disse to produktene skiller seg sterkt fra hverandre hva gjelder gjenngivelse av gråtoner.I tillegg til blått blirgult og grønnt gjenngitt tilnærmet riktig. Dette gjør disse filmene aktuelle for landskapsfotografering.Bare orange og rødt mangler i senisibiliseringen, rødt blir derfor gjenngitt som svart i papirkopien.

5. ***Hva er pan -orthochromatiske filmer?*** Disse blir også kalt rectepanmaterial. Den forhøyede følsomheten for rødt som oppstår ved panchromatisk sensibilisering blir her kompensert ved andre senibiliseringsfargestoff som gjør at nesten alle farger blir gjenngitt med riktig gråtone. Pan-orthchromatiske filmer er derfor et universalmaterial som ikke trenger gul eller orange filter for å gi rette gråtoner. Så hvidt forfatterne kjenner til finnes det i dag bare en slik spesialfilm nemlig MACO PO 100 clear, Tidligere fantes det filmer som AGFA ISOPAN F, PERUTZ PERPANTIC og KODAK PANATOMIC.

6. ***Hva er halvtone fotografi?*** Dette er filmer og fotopapir, som, med flest mulig grånoner, kan gjenngi hele spekteret fra helt hvitt til det dypeste sorte.

7. ***Hva er strek fotografi?*** For det meste dreier dette seg om såkalte dokument eller mikro filmer. Dette er sort/hvitt filmer med en mer eller mindre bratt gardasjonskurve og ekstrem høy oppløsning. Disse filmene blir benyttet til reproduksjon / avfotografering / mikrofotografering av dokumenter, strek orginaler og dokumenter.

2. ***What is a sensitising dye?*** When ›untreated‹, silver halides are only sensitive to violett, blue, and green. Dyeing the crystals using sensitising dyes makes them ›susceptible‹ for the other colours of the spectrum. The dyes used are false, fluorescent dyes which stain the silver bromide grain proper, thus making it capable to absorb certain colours of the spectrum.

3. ***What is a panchromatic film?*** Nowadays, almost any film offered as 35-mm or medium-format roll film has a panchromatic sensitisation. The spectrum ranges approximately from 400 to 700 nanometers. The sensitisation for red light is somewhat strong in panchromatic films, which means that red tones are rendered a bit too light in a positive reproduction. Yellow/green tones are rendered properly, the greys corresponding to blue/violet tones, however, appear a bit too light.

4. ***What is an orthochromatic film?*** Only a few types of film are limited to the range of 380 to 600 nm. Examples are sheet films for lithographic techniques, specialised document films, films for electron microscopy, etc. The authors are aware of two current manufacturers in this field: ILFORD ORTHO sheet film, MACO ORT 25 clear 35-mm and medium-format roll film and sheet film. These two makes of sheet film differ considerably in their gradation curves.
In addition to blue, yellow and green tones are rendered approximately correctly. This is what makes these films so interesting for scenic photography.
Only for orange and red is their sensitisation insufficient, which means that red is rendered black in prints.

5. ***What is an ortho-pan-chromatic film?*** This material is also called rectepan material. The exaggerated sensitisation for red light is subdued by special sensitisation dyes, and the emulsion's sensitivity to red is normal. The tonal rendition of all other colours is approximately correct, too. The orthopanchromatic emulsion is, therefore, the universal material, with proper tonal rendering already without a yellow or yellow/green filter. Currently, the authors are only aware of one film of this type: MACO PO 100 clear. Former examples of orthopan films, all of them discontinued, are AGFA ISOPAN F, PERUTZ PERPANTIC, and KODAK PANATOMIC.

6. ***Halftone photography – what does that term mean?*** This term subsumes all films/papers serving to reproduce the entire range from white to the deepest black, with the greatest possible number of shades of grey in between.

7. ***Line photography – what does that term mean?*** This is primarily an application for document films

The spectral-lines of MACO-B&W films

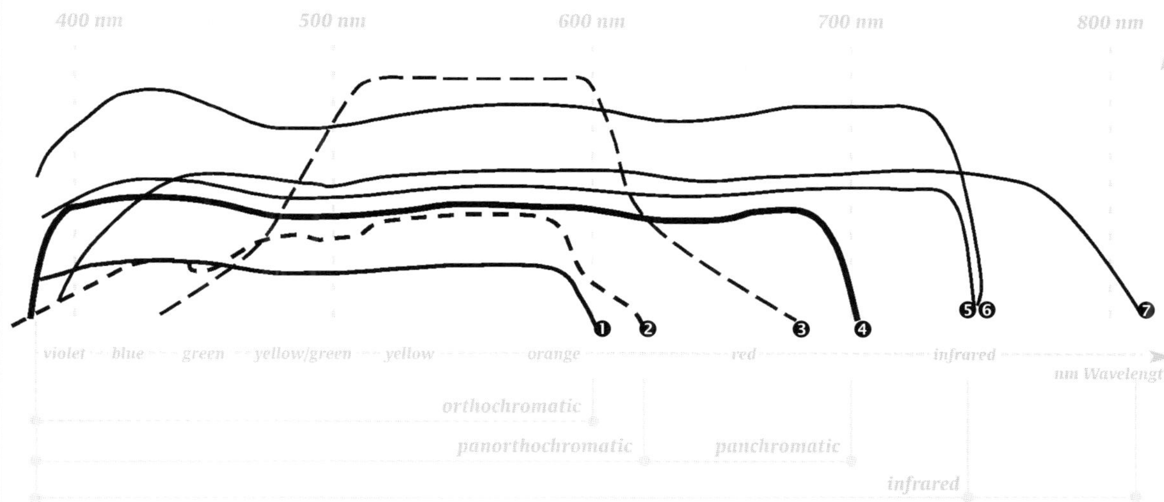

❶ MACO ORT 25

❷ MACO PO 100clear

❸ *Eyecurve*

❹ MACO UP 100plus & MACO UP 400plus

❺ MACO IR 750clear

❻ MACO CUBE 400clear

❼ MACO 820clear

6. **_Halbtonfotografie, was bedeutet das?_** Damit sind die Filme/Papiere beschrieben, die dazu dienen, das möglichst komplette Spektrum vom Weiß bis zum tiefsten Schwarz mit möglichst vielen dazwischen liegenden Grauabstufungen wiederzugeben.

7. **_Strichfotografie, was ist das?_** Meist handelt es sich um Dokumentenfilme (Mikrofilme). Man versteht darunter gering empfindliche Schwarzweiß-Filme mit mehr oder weniger steiler Gradation und extrem hoher Auflösung. Diese Filme finden Anwendung bei der Reproduktion oder Mikroverfilmung von Dokumenten, Schriftstücken usw. Eine Besonderheit sind Filme, wie KODAK TECHNICAL PAN, MACO ORT 25clear und MACO TECHNICAL PAN TP 64clear, die mit dem Spezialentwickler LP-DOCUFINE LC fein abgestufte Halbtöne bei praktisch kornloser Struktur und höchster Schärfe leisten. Die Negative erlauben sehr starke Vergrößerungen.

8. **_Lithfilm, was ist das?_** Lithfilme sind Filmmaterialien mit maximalem Kontrast und extrem hoher Maximaldichte (=4). Die extrem steile Gradation (Gamma =6) lässt bei der korrekten Belichtung nur eine Entweder-Oder-Funktion zu: Entweder ist die Belichtung ausreichend, die Schwärzung wird maximal, oder sie ist ungenügend, der Film bleibt ungeschwärzt. Beispiel: MACO GENIUS film (GF) auf 100 Mikron Polyesterbasis, transparent, zu verarbeiten in LP-LITH oder LP-DOCUFINE HC.

9. **_Infrarotfilme, was macht man damit?_** Bei der militärischen Aufklärung, bei der Polizeiarbeit, bei Sachverständigen in Museen finden IR-Filme Anwendung.
Daneben sind seit vielen Jahrzehnten, vor allem im englischsprachigen Raum, auch Anwendungen in der bildmäßigen Fotografie bekannt, z. B. für Landschaft und Akt. Der Empfindlichkeitsbereich dieser Filme reicht je nach Fabrikat von etwa 400 nm bis 750, 820 bis oder gar 900 nm. Mit dem KONICA IR 750 steht ein ortho-IR-Film zur Verfügung. Im panchromatischen Bereich der ILFORD SFX200, der KODAK HIE und die MACO IR 750clear, sowie MACO IR 820clear und neuerdings MACO CUBE 400 clear.

10. **_Was versteht man unter Farbtemperatur?_** Die Farbtemperatur ist nicht die Charakterisierung der vorherrschenden Lichtfarbe als ›warmes‹ oder ›kühles‹ Licht, sondern die Temperatur, die ein imaginärer ›Glühfaden‹ haben müsste, um Licht mit einer bestimmten spektralen Zusammensetzung zu erzeugen. Mit ›warmem‹ Licht meinen wir umgangssprachlich meist solches mit hohem Rot-und Gelbanteil, aber das hat gerade eine niedrige Farbtemperatur. Je höher die Farbtemperatur, desto höher der Blauanteil, denn ein heißerer Glühfaden (Halogenlicht) glüht bläulicher als ein kälterer (normale Glühlampe).

6. **_Fotografia a mezzi toni, cosa significa?_** Si definiscono così pellicole e carte che offrano uno spettro sufficientemente ampio dal bianco al nero profondo, con una gamma tonale dei grigi assai estesa.

7. **_Fotografia al tratto, cosa significa?_** Prevalentemente si tratta di pellicole per documenti (microfilm). Si caratterizzano tali pellicole con una gradazione più o meno ripida e una risoluzione estremamente alta. Queste pellicole trovano utilizzo nelle riproduzioni o microfilmati di documenti o scritte, ecc. Una caso particolare è rappresentato da pellicole quali KODAK TECHNICAL PAN, MACO ORT 25clear e MACO TECHNICAL PAN TP 64 clear, che grazie allo sviluppo speciale LP-DOKUFINE LC, risaltano i mezzi toni finemente differenziati con una struttura praticamente priva di grana e con una estrema nitidezza. Queste pellicole negative permettono di ottenere ingrandimenti anche di grandi dimensioni.

8. **_Pellicole lith, cosa sono?_** Pellicole lith sono materiali fotosensibili con un contrasto massimale e una massima densità estremamente alta (= 4). La gradazione estremamente ripida (Gamma = 6) alla corretta posa, permette solo un risultato aut-aut: O l'esposizione è sufficiente, la densità del nero diventa massima, oppure è insufficiente, e la pellicola rimarrà priva di annerimento. Esempio: MACO GENIUS film (GF) su base di poliestere di 100 micron, trasparente, da trattare in LABOR PARTNER Sviluppo Lith oppure LP-DOKUFINE HC.

9. **_Pellicole infrarosso, cosa sono?_** L'utilizzo classico delle pellicole IR è da ricercare nella ricognizione fotografica militare, della polizia e presso i periti nei musei. Da qualche decennio, soprattutto a partire dai paesi anglosassoni, questo tipo di pellicole viene utilizzato anche nella fotografia tradizionale.
La fascia di sensibilizzazione è posta fra 400 fino 750, 820 fino 900 Nanometri (Nm), a seconda del fabbricato. Con la KONICA IR 750 è a disposizione una pellicola orto-IR. In ambito pancromatico sono disponibili: ILFORD SFX200, KODAK HIE e le MACO IR 750clear e IT 820clear.

10. **_Cosa si intende per temperatura colore?_** Una bassa temperatura colore segna un alto contenuto di rosso, un'alta temperatura colore invece un alto contenuto di blu nella radiazione.
- Sole pieno di mezzogiorno in cielo azzurro: 6000 K
- Sole di mattina e di sera: 5200 K
- Lampade Nitraphot, Argaphot: 3200 K
- Lampadine ad incandescenza 1000 W 3100 K
- 500 W 2900 K
- 100 W 2700 K

Più basso è il valore Kelvin, più adatta è l'illuminazione per

Spesielt for filmer som KODAK TECHNICAL PAN, MACO ORT 25clear og MACO TECHNICAL PAN TP 64clear er at de kan oppnå fantastiske gråtoner samtidig som de er tilnærmet kornløse, når de framkalles i LP-DUCOFIN LC. Slike negativer tillater svært store forstørrelser.

8. **_Lithfilm, hva er det?_** Lithfilmer er filmmaterialer med maksimal kontrast og ekstrem tetthet / sværtning (dmax 4). Gammaverdi 6 gir en svært hard gradasjon som bare tillater en enten eller funksjon ved eksponering: Enten rett eksponering og gardasjon, eller et ubrukbart, resultat, uten sværtning. F.eks MACO GENIUS film (GF) på 100 mircon polyesterbasis, helt transparent, for framkalling i LABOR PARTNER lith framkaller eller i LP-DOCUFINE HC.

9. **_Hva brukes infrarød film til?_** Militær etterertning, politi og museumssakkyndige, benytter IR filmer i sitt arbeid for å gjøre "usynlige_ spor synlige. Parallelt til dette har de i en årrekke, fram for alt i det engelskspråklige område, blitt benyttet som uttrykksmiddel i den billedmessige fotografien.Følsomhetsområdet strekker seg fra 400 til 750, 820 og 900 nanomete, alt etter hvilket fabrikat filmen har.KONICA IR 750 er en ortho-IR film. Panchromatiske filmer er ILFORD SFX 200, KODAK HIE, MACO IR 750clear og MACO IR 820 clear.

10. **_Hva forstår en med ›farvetemperatur‹?_** Lav fargetemperatur kjennetegnes ved høyt innhold av rødt lys, høy fargetemperatur kjennetegnes ved høyt innhold av blått lys.
- Sollys ved middagstid og blå himmel: 6000 K
- Sollys om morgen og kveld: 5200 K
- Nitraphotlamper: 3200 K
- Elektrisk lys 1000 Watt ca 3100 K
- Elektrisk lys 500 Watt ca 2900 K
- Elektrisk lys 100 Watt ca 2700 K

Jo lavere Kelvingrad, om så bedre egnet for sort/hvittfilmer. Ved denne lille listen blir det klart at sort/hvitt IR fotografi ikke er bundet opp mot sommerdager med mye sollys. Studioopptak uten blitz, men med enkle Nitraphotlamper gir fantastiske IR effekter, som kan gjenntas under kontrolerte forhold.

(microfilms). These are understood to be slow b&w films with more or less contrasty gradation and extremely high resolution. Such films are used to reproduce, or make microfilm copies of documents, etc. Films like KODAK TECHNICAL PAN, MACO ORT 25 clear, and MACO TECHNICAL PAN TP 64 clear, giving a fine gradation of halftones with practically no grain and extreme sharpness with special developers like LP DOCUFINE LC, are special cases. Negatives made on these films allow for very great enlargement factors.

8. ***Lith film – what's that?*** Lith films are films with maximum contrast and an extremely high maximum density (= 4). Assuming correct exposure, their extremely contrasty gradation (Gamma = 6) allows for a yes-or-no decision only. Exposure is either sufficient and density is maximal, or it is insufficient and the film remains clear. Example: MACO GENIUS film (GF) on a 100-micron transparent polyester support, to be processed in LP-LITH developer or LABOR PARTNER DOCUFINE HC.

9. ***What do you do with an infrared film?*** IR films are used for military reconnaissance, for forensic work, and by experts in museums. For many decades, however, pictorial applications, e.g. for landscape and nude photography, have also been known, mainly among English-speaking photographers. The spectral range is that from 400 to 750, 820, up to 900 nanometres, depending on make.
KONICA IR 750 is an ortho IR film. In the panchromatic range, there are ILFORD SFX 200, KODAK HIE, MACO IR 750 clear, MACO IR 820 clear, and, recently, MACO CUBE 400 clear.

10. ***What is understood by colour temperature?*** Colour temperature is not what we mean when we talk about ›warm‹ light or ›cool‹ light. It is the temperature that an imaginary lamp filament would have to have to radiate light with a specified spectral distribution. By convention, we understand ›warm‹ light to contain a lot of red and yellow, but this is light with a low colour temperature. The higher the colour temperature, the greater the blue content, because a hotter filament (halogen lamp) emits more blue radiation than a cooler one (conventional tungsten bulb). Colour temperatures are expressed as so-called ›absolute‹ temperatures, in Kelvins (K).

- Bright sun in a blue sky at noon: 6,000 K
- Morning and evening sun: 5,200 K
- Nitraphot lamp: 3,200 K
- Tungsten lamp 1,000 W: around 3,100 K
- Tungsten lamp 500 W: around 2,900 K
- Tungsten lamp 100 W: around 2,700 K

The lower the value in Kelvins, the better the light is suited for IR films. This short list shows that b&w IR photography

MACO UP 100plus, Canon FD 135-mm, f2.8, 1/60, developed in LP-CUBE XS, conformably to instruction, exposed with WA40 mm, exposure time 10s, 5.6 – on MACO expo RF, graded baryta paper, glossy, grade 3. © Valsasini

Farbtemperaturen werden als so genannte ›absolute‹ Temperaturen in Kelvin (K) angegeben.

- Helle Mittagssonne bei blauem Himmel: 6000 K
- Sonne morgens und abends: 5200 K
- Nitraphotlampe: 3200 K
- Elektrische Glühlampe 1.000 Watt um 3100 K
- 500 Watt um 2900 K
- 100 Watt um 2700 K

Je niedriger der K-Wert, desto besser ist das Licht für IR-Aufnahmen geeignet. Durch diese kleine Aufstellung wird bestätigt, dass die Schwarzweiß-IR-Fotografie nicht unbedingt an schöne Sonnentage im Sommer gebunden ist. Studioaufnahmen ohne Blitz mit ›einfachen‹ Nitraphotlampen ermöglichen fantastische IR-Effekte, bei unter wiederholbaren Aufnahmebedingungen.

11. ***Gibt es einen idealen Film?*** Eine Regel zu den drei Forderungen an einen Schwarzweiß-Film, eine Aussage zu Empfindlichkeit, Korngrösse und Schärfe:

- Feinstkörnigkeit ist nur auf Kosten der Empfindlichkeitsausnutzung,
- Empfindlichkeitsausnutzung nur auf Kosten der Feinstkörnigkeit zu erreichen,
- Für den jeweiligen Zweck müssen der Film und der Entwickler aufeinander abgestimmt werden.

So wird auch der beste Feinkornfilm, entwickelt in einem Metol-Hydrochinon-Entwickler (stellt LABOR PARTNER nicht her) grobes Korn liefern. Umgekehrt wird ein höchstempfindlicher Film durch Feinkornentwicklung nicht feinkörnig (!) Diese Zusammenhänge muss man kennen. Die Frage nach ›dem besten Entwickler‹ ist daher müßig, weil jede Film/Entwickler-Kombination ihren besonderen Zweck erfüllt.

12. ***Wie sind die Filmschichten aufgebaut?***

12A ***Die Emulsion*** besteht aus Gelatine und lichtempfindlichen Silberhalogenid-Kristallen, nämlich:

- AgCl = Silberchlorid
- AgBr = Silberbromid
- AgJ = Silberjodid

Durch dosierte Lichteinwirkung wird den Halogeniden Energie zugeführt, die sie latent speichern. Die Entwickler sollen nur die Kristalle zu Silber reduzieren, die das latente Bild enthalten. Die Zusammensetzung der Entwickler und die Entwicklungszeit sind daher von entscheidender Bedeutung. Die reinen reduzierten Silberkörnchen sind die schwarzen Pünktchen im Film.

Viele übereinander liegende Pünktchen verdichten die Filmschicht so, dass bei Vergrößern kein Licht mehr durchgelassen wird und auf dem Papier weiße Flächen hinterlassen. Es sei denn, die Silberkörnchen reichen in der Menge nicht aus und haben Lücken in der Schicht hinterlassen,

le pellicole bianco/nero. Grazie a questo piccolo schema si conferma, che la fotografia b/n-IR non è necessariamente legata al belle giornate di sole estivo.

Riprese in studio senza flash, bensì con “semplici” lampade tipo Nitraphot, fanno ottenere effetti IR fantastici, in condizioni di ripresa ripetibili in ogni momento.

11. ***Esiste la pellicola ideale?*** Una regola sulle tre richieste ad una pellicola bianco/nero, e una dichiarazione su sensibilità, grossezza della grana e nitidezza (acutanza)?

- Grana estremamente fine è ottenibile solo a scapito dello sfruttamento della sensibilità, e viceversa.
- Per il rispettivo scopo pellicola e sviluppo devono essere sintonizzati fra loro.
- In questo modo anche la pellicola più finegranulare, sviluppata in uno sviluppo a base di Metolo-Idrochinone (non prodotto da LABOR PARTNER), produrrà una grana grossa.

Al contrario una pellicola ad alta sensibilità sviluppata in uno sviluppo a grana fine, in verità non lo sarà(!)

Bisogna conoscere queste correlazioni. La domanda ›del migliore sviluppo‹ diventa imperativa, in quanto ogni combinazione pellicola/sviluppo adempie ai tuoi scopi.

12. ***Mi spieghi la costruzione degli strati della pellicola?***

12A ***Lo strato fotografico*** (emulsione fotografica) è composto da gelatina e cristalli ad alogenuri d’argento sensibili alla luce.

- AgCl = Cloruro d’argento
- AgBr = Bromuro d’argento
- AgJ = Joduro d’argento

Grazie all’influenza dosata della luce viene trasmessa energia agli alogenuri, che questi accumulano in latente. Gli sviluppi hanno il compito di ridurre i cristalli in argento, che contengono l’immagine latente. La composizione degli sviluppi ed i tempi di sviluppo sono pertanto determinanti. I puntini neri nella pellicola rappresentano i granuli d’argento puri ridotti. Numerosi puntini posti l’uno sopra l’altro addensano lo strato della pellicola, fino al punto che durante la stampa non viene più trasmessa luce, con la conseguenza di zone bianche sulla stampa.

Ciò non avviene invece qualora la quantità dei granuli d’argento fosse insufficiente e hanno lasciato dei vuoti nello strato, o qualora fossero grossi, o qualora si fossero agglomerati durante lo sviluppo. Questi ›vuoti‹ si traducono in grana sulla stampa positiva. Si ›assegna la razza‹ delle caratteristiche del materiale fotografico con la grandezza della grana degli alogenuri d’argento e con la consistenza dello strato di emulsione.

La misura della grana e la quantità nello strato determinano la sensibilità alla luce della pellicola. Infine lo sviluppo determina ›la formazione grana-vuoti‹.

11. ***Finnes det en ideal film?*** En regel for de tre kriteriene som gjelder for sort/hvitt- film og som dekker følsomhet, kornstørrelse og skarphet?Ekstremt fint korn får en bare på bekostning av følsomhet, høy følsomhet gir grovt korn. For et hvert formål må film og framkaller tilpasses hverandre. Da vil selv den mest finkornete filmen gi grove korn hvis den framkalles i en Metol-Hydrochinon framkaller (LABOR PARTNER lager ikke slike framkallere). En høyfølsom film blir ikke til en finkornet film ved bruk av en finkornframkaller. Sammenhengene er derfor viktig å kjenne fordi enhver film/framkallerkombinasjon gir et eget resultat som derfor kan velges utifra hvilket mål som vil oppnås.

12. ***Forklar hvordan en film er bygd opp?***

12A ***Fotografisk skikt:*** Det fotografiske skiktet, emulsjonen, består av gelantine og lysfølsomme sølvhalogenidkrystaller.

- AgCl = sølvchlorid
- AgBr = sølvbromid
- AgJ = sølvjodid

Ved en kontrollert lyspåvirkniing blir det tilført energi tilhalogenidene, som lagrer denne latent (dvs ikke synlig). Framkalleren skal så redusere krystallene til metallisk sølv for å synliggjøre det latente bildet. Framkallerens sammensetning og framkallingstiden er derfor avgjørende for resultatet.De sorte prikkene i en framkallt film ersølvhalogenider som er redusert til sølvkorn. Mange slike sølvkorn overhverandre vil fortette seg slik at lys ikke kan trenge gjennom og det vil igjen gi et hvitt område på fotopapiret ved kopiering. Hvis det ikke er tilstrekkelig sværtning på filmen, eller det er blit svært grove kornsamlinger pga framkallingen, vil lys trenge gjennom mellomrommene mellom sølvkornene og vil gi et kornete positiv. Det er avstanden mellom sølvkornene i filmen som gir et grovkornet positiv og ikke sølvkornene i seg selv. Ut i fra størrelsen på sølvhalogenidene og tykkelsen av emulsjonen blir filmens egenskaper bestemt.Kornstørrelsen og mengden av korn i emulsjonsskiktet bestemmer lysfølsomheten i filmen. Framkalleren og framkallingsmetoden, bestemmer forholdet mellom korn og kornmellomrom.

12B ***Beskyttelses-skiktet*** skal minske muligheten for mekaniske skader på emulsjonen. En hver skade virker som en ekstra eksponering og fører til sværting av filmen. Også belastninger ved innføring i framkallerspolen fører til sværtning som kan strekke seg inn i motivet.

12C ***Filmbase:*** Ved siden av acetat (triacetat) blir stadig mer polyester benyttet til dette. Vanligvis blir rullfilmer og lith-planfilmer støpt på 100 my filmbase, 35 mm filmer blir laget på 135 my, planfilmer på 100, 135, 155 og 180 my. Det

is not necessarily limited to fine sunny days in summer. Studio shots taken without flash, just in the light of a ›simple‹ Nitraphot lamp, allow for fantastic IR effects, under reproducible lighting conditions.

11. ***Is there an ideal film?*** Is there a rule concerning the three requirements to be met by a b&w film, a statement concerning speed, grain, and sharpness? There is: Ultra-fine grain can only be achieved by sacrificing speed, exploiting speed means accepting more grain.

Match film and developer considering the desired results. Even the best fine-grain film, when developed in a metol-hydroquinone developer (something that LABOR PARTNER does not manufacture) will give coarse grain.
An ultrahigh-speed film, on the other hand, cannot be made a fine-grain film by just using a fine-grain developer. You must be aware of these ›laws‹. Asking for ›the one and only best developer‹ is, therefore, futile, as every combination of film and developer serves its special purpose.

12. ***Explain the structure of the layers of a film.***

12A ***The emulsion layer*** consists of gelatine plus light-sensitive silver-halide crystals. These are

- AgCl = silver chloride
- AgBr = silver bromide
- AgI = silver iodide

When the halides are exposed to a dose of light, they save it in latent form. Developers are supposed to convert only those silver halide crystals to silver, which contain the latent image. Developer composition and developing time are, therefore, of utmost importance.
The grains of pure, reduced silver are the little black dots in the film. Many such overlapping dots increase the optical density of the emulsion in such a way as to block the transmission of any light when the negative is printed, leaving white areas on the paper. This is not the case if there are not enough silver grains, and gaps are left, either because the grains are very coarse, or grains have clumped during development. It is the gaps that result in grain showing in the print. The size of the silver halide grains and the thickness of the emulsion layer determine the characteristics of negative material.

12B ***The supercoat*** protects the emulsion from mechanical damage. Mechanical pressure applied to the emulsion has the same effect as exposure to light and will, therefore, leave black marks on the film. Buckling of the film while it is fed into the reels of the developing tank results in black marks (the well-known ›moon sickles‹).

12C ***The Film support*** holds the film together. Polyester,

ISO 25 / 64

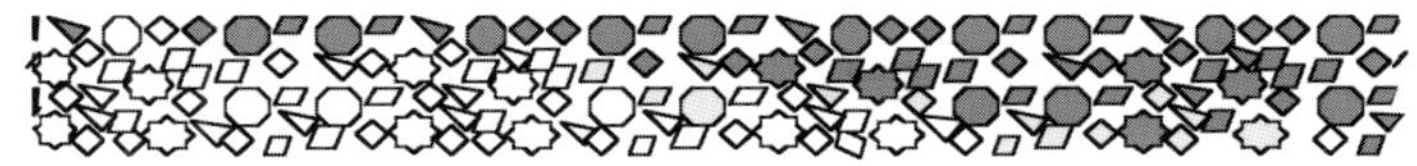

ISO 100

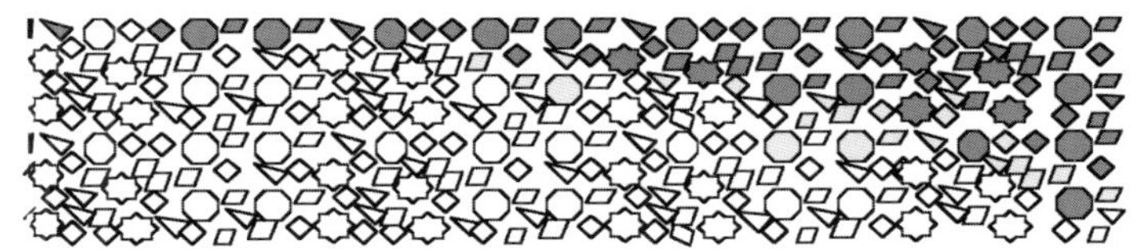

ISO 400, 800 and 1600

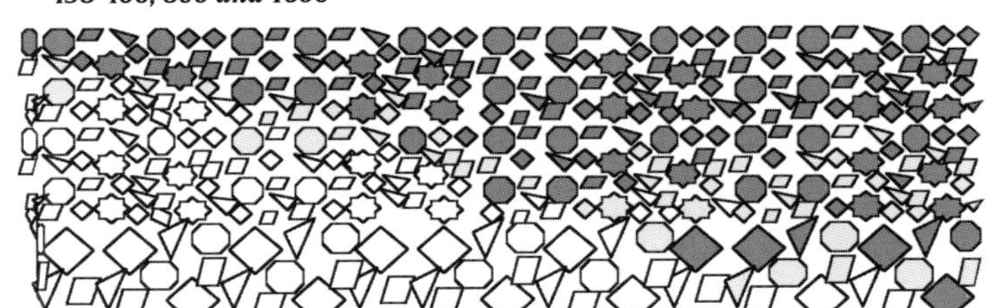

weil sie sehr grob sind, oder sie haben sich bei der Entwicklung zusammengeballt. Diese Lücken bilden die Körnung auf dem Positiv ab. Mit der Korngrösse der Silberhalogenide und der Dicke der Emulsions-Schicht werden die Eigenschaften des Film-Materials ›geprägt‹.
Die Korngrösse und die Menge in der Schicht bestimmen die Lichtempfindlichkeit des Films. Letztlich bestimmt der Entwickler die ›Korn-Lücken-Bildung‹.

12B ***Die Schutzschicht*** schützt die Emulsion vor mechanischen Beschädigungen. Jede mechanische Verletzung der Emulsions-Schicht reagiert wie eine Belichtung und führt zur Schwärzung. Auch Knickungen beim Einfädeln des Films in die Spirale der Film-Entwicklungs-Dose reagieren mit Schwärzungen (die berüchtigten ›Schwalbenschwänze‹).

12C ***Die Filmbasis*** hält den Film zusammen. Neben Azetat (Triazetat) wird wegen seiner besseren Beständigkeit verstärkt Polyester verwendet.
- Normalerweise werden Rollfilme und Lith-Planfilme auf 100 Mikron Filmbasis gegossen.
- Kleinbildfilme auf 135 Mikron, Planfilme auf 100; 135; 155 bis 180 Mikron. Ausnahmen sind möglich, die besondere Ausnahmen: MACO CUBE 400clear, bei dem es gelungen ist, auch 100 Mikron bei Kleinbild-Patronen zu verwenden, ohne dass es zu Lichteinfall kommt.

MACO ORT 25clear als 35 mm Meterware, nicht als Kleinbild-Patrone steht ebenfalls auf 100 Mikron zur Verfügung.

12D ***Der Lichthofschutz*** verbessert die Schärfe des Bildes. Die sicher auch wegen des günstigen Preises übliche Variante, ist die graue Einfärbung der Filmbasis.
Filme, wie AGFA APX 25 und APX 100 sind eine Besonderheit: Hier wird zwar die Lichthofschutz-Schicht *auf* die Film-Basis gegossen, trotzdem wirken die Filme grau und sind daher nicht transparent.
Filme, wie der AGFA SCALA sind vollkommen transparent. In diese Gattung gehören seit einigen Jahren auch die ›clear-Filme‹ von MACO. Diese Gattung basiert auf einer glasklarenr Filmbasis, Acetat und auch Polyester, je nach Sorte, die Lichthof-Schutzschicht befindet sich allerdings auf der Rückseite der Filmbasis.
Ausnahme: MACO CUBE 400clear. Dort befindet sich, wie bei den genannten AGFA-Filmen, die Lichthof-Schutzschicht *auf* der Filmbasis, löst sich jedoch anders als bei den AGFA-Filmen während der Entwicklung rückstandsfrei auf.
Man erhält so einen transparenten Film mit einer leichten Blaufärbung, die keine Verlängerung der Belichtungszeiten während des Vergrößerns verursacht.
Die Einfärbung der Lichthofschutzschicht ist vom jeweiligen Film-Hersteller so gewählt, dass die Lichtfarbe des

12B ***Lo strato di protezione*** protegge l'emulsione da sollecitazioni meccaniche. Qualsiasi ferimento meccanico dello strato dell'emulsione reagisce come una esposizione alla luce e porta all'annerimento della zona interessata.
Anche pieghe dovute al caricamento della pellicola sulla spirale della tank di trattamento reagiscono come annerimenti (le purtroppo fin troppo conosciute ›code di rondine‹).

12C ***La base della pellicola:*** Si utilizza particolarmente il poliestere accanto ad acetato (triacetato).
- Normalmente le pellicole in rullo e le pellicole piane lith vengono stese su supporti di 100 mm.
- Pellicole di piccolo formato su 135 mm, pellicole piane su 100, 135, 155 fino 180 mm. Sono possibili eccezioni, fra le quali citiamo: MACO CUBE 400clear, dove è riuscito utilizzare 100 mm in caricatori 35 mm, senza che ciò provocasse infiltrazioni di luce.

MACO ORT 25clear in metraggio 35 mm (non in caricatori) è pure disponibile in 100 mm.

12D ***Lo strato protettivo antialone:*** La variante più comune, sicuramente più economica, è la colorazione grigia della base della pellicola.
Pellicole come AGFA APX 100 sono un caso particolare: Viene sì steso uno strato antihalo sul supporto, ma le pellicole mantengono una base grigia e non sono pertanto trasparenti. Pellicole come AGFA SCALA sono perfettamente trasparenti. Nella medesima categoria si collocano anche le pellicole ›clear‹ della MACO.
Questa famiglia si basa su un supporto chiaro-trasparente, in acetato o poliestere, a seconda del tipo, e lo strato antialone viene però apportato sul retro del supporto base. Eccezione: MACO CUBE 400clear. In questo caso, come AGFA, lo strato protettivo antihalo viene apportato s u l supporto base della pellicola, si dissolve però completamente durante la fase di sviluppo. Si ottiene così un negativo trasparente con una leggerissima colorazione base azzurrina, che però non provoca alcuna interferenza nei tempi di posa durante la fase di stampa.
La colorazione base dello strato antialone viene scelta da parte del produttore in funzione al colore di luce trasmesso della luce riflessa attraverso la sensibilizzazione della pellicola, passandoci attraverso senza provocare alcun annerimento. Esiste una barriera contro gli aloni di luce?
Proprio per evitare aloni provocati dalla riflessione le pellicole fotografiche vengono munite di uno strato antialone (antihalo). Le pellicole trasparenti, con il supporto base n o n colorato di grigio, offrono indubbi vantaggi di nitidezza dei negativi. Questo tipo di pellicola si presta anche per produrre diapositive a contatto. Le pellicole a strato sottile attuali evitano oltretutto aloni di diffusione di luce.

finnes unntak f.eks: MACO CUBE 400 clear, hvor det har vært mulig å benytte en 100 my i en småbildekassett uten at det oppstår lysinnfall. MACO ORT 25 clear i 35 mm metervare lages også på 100 my (Ikke ferdig i kassett pga faren for lysinnfall.)

12D ***Antihalogenasjonbeskyttelse:*** Den vanligste, og billigste metoden for å oppnå dette er å farge filmbasen grå. Filmer som AGFA APX 25 og APX 100 er et unntak da antihalogenasjonsskiktet er lagt oppå filmbasen, men likevel virker filmene grå og er ikke transparente.Filmer som AGFA SCALA et helt transparente, eller "glassklare_. Til denne gruppen hører også "clear_ filmene fra MACO. Denne gruppen filmer har en glassklar base på acetat eller polyesterbase hvor antihalogenasjonsskiktet er på baksiden av filmbasen. Unntak MACO CUBE 400 clear. Der er antihalogenasjonsskiktet på filmbasen, som hos AGFA, men løser seg fullstendig opp under framkalling. En får da en transparent film med en lett blåfarging som ikke påvirker kopieringen.Hver filmprodusent velger en farge på antihalogenasjonsskiktet som ikke samsvarer med filmen senibilisering og derfor ikke kan sværte filmen. Hvor for det hele? Uten antihalogenasjonsskikt kan det opptre ›lysglorier‹ og dermed uskarpe bilder. Glassklare negativer, uten gråfarget base, gjør det betydelig lettere å stille skarpt ved forstørrelser. De er også bedre egnet til å produsere diapositiver som kontaktkopier. Moderne filmer med tynne emulsjoner unngår antihalogenasjonsskikt som blir permanent i filmen.

with its improved permanence, is increasingly used to replace acetate (tri-acetate).
Medium format roll films and lith film sheets are usually coated onto a 100-micrometer support.
135 micrometers are common for 35-mm, 100, 135, and 155, up to 180 for sheet film. Exceptions are possible, one noteworthy exception being MACO CUBE 400 clear where a 100-micrometer support was successfully used for 35-mm film, and there is still no light leaking into the cartridge. MACO ORT 25 clear as 35-mm bulk film, but not in cartridges, is also available on a 100-micrometer support.

12D ***The Anti-halation layer*** improves sharpness. Dyeing the film support grey is the typical way of providing an anti-halation layer, probably not the least because this is an inexpensive way of doing it.
Films like AGFA APX 25 and APX 100 are special: Here, the anti-halation layer is coated onto the film support, but the films still appear grey and they are not transparent for this reason.
Films like AGFA SCALA are completely transparent. It is since a few years ago that the ›clear‹ films produced by MACO are also of this type. This type of film uses a support that is as clear as glass and which, depending on the sort of film, is either acetate or polyester. However, the anti-halation layer is coated as a backing onto the back of the film support. Again, MACO CUBE 400 clear is an exception: Here, as with the above AGFA films the anti-halation backing is coated as an underlayer onto the film support, but, other than with the AGFA films, it is resolved during development, leaving no residue at all. As a result, one obtains a slightly bluish transparent film whose colour will not prolong printing exposure times.
The film manufacturer selects the colour of the anti-halation layer in such a way that colour of the light it reflects lies outside the sensitisation spectrum of the film, which means it will not expose the silver halides.
Clear negative material, where the support is not grey, is very favourable when it comes to focusing negatives. Also, clear negatives are better suited to produce transparencies by means of contact printing.
Because of the small thickness of the emulsions, halation by irradiation due to scattering within the emulsion are less of a problem in today's thin-emulsion films.

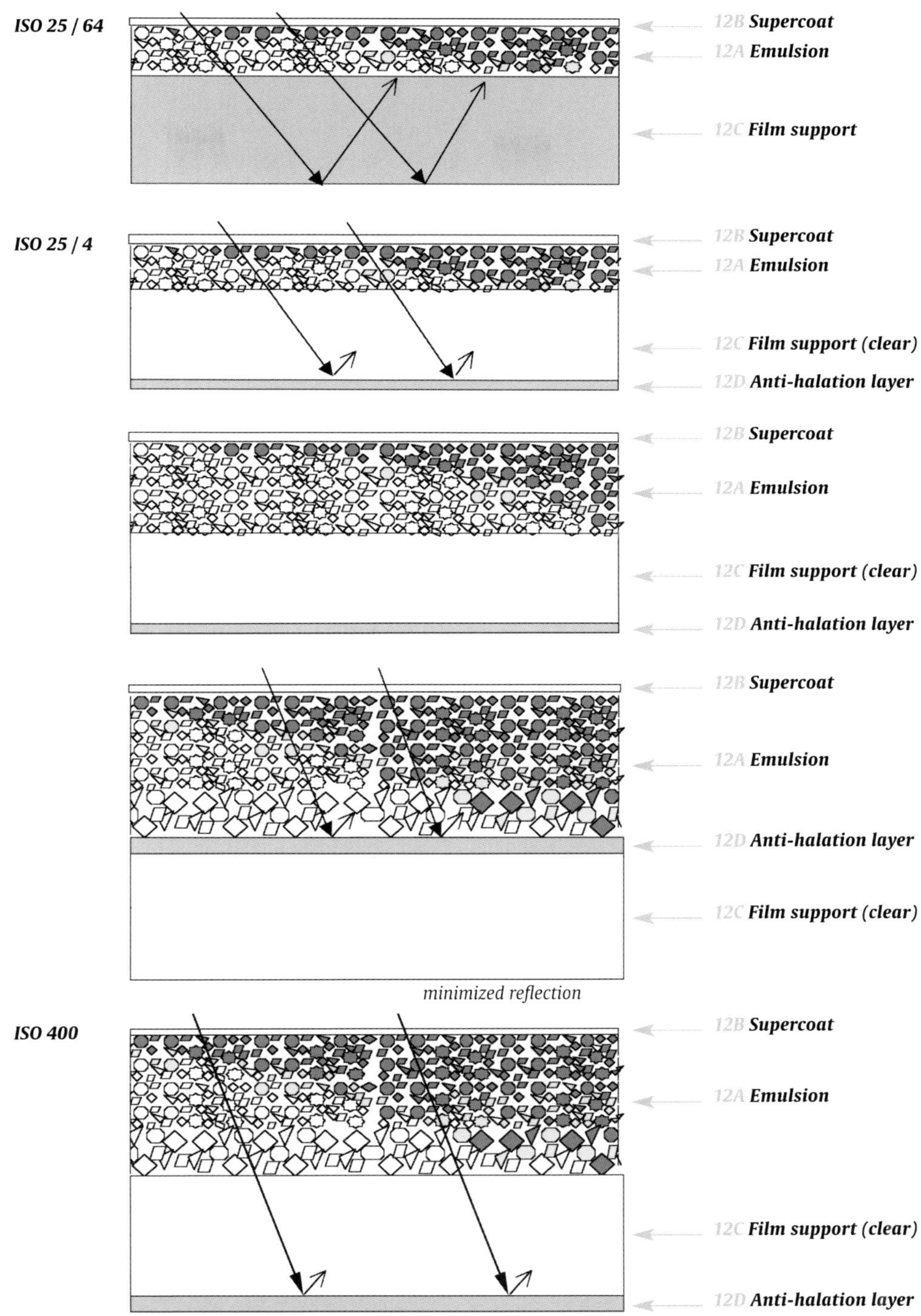

reflektierten Lichts an der Sensibilisierung des Films ›vorbeigeht‹ und keine Schwärzung verursacht.
Glasklares Filmmaterial mit nicht grau eingefärbter Filmbasis bietet erhebliche Vorteile beim Scharfstellen der Negative. Auch eignen sich glasklare Negative besser dazu, im Kontakt Dias zu produzieren. Diffusionslichthöfe, die durch Streuung des einfallenden Lichts in der Emulsion entstehen, sind aufgrund der geringen Schichtdicke bei den heute üblichen Dünnschichtfilmen ein geringeres Problem.

13. ***Schwarzschild-Effekt:*** Eine mit hoher Lichtintensität kurz belichtete Silberhalogenidschicht zeigt nach dem Entwickeln eine stärkere Schwärzung als eine mit sehr geringer Lichtintensität entsprechend länger belichtete Schicht.
Das heißt, dass bei Belichtungszeiten, die 1 Sekunde überschreiten, nicht mehr die Gesetzmäßigkeit gilt, dass eine Stufe Abblendung bei Verdopplung der Belichtungszeit dieselbe Schwärzung liefert. Wenn Ihnen Ihr Belichtungsmesser Belichtungszeiten von 1Sekunde und mehr vorschlägt, müssen Sie korrigieren. Die nötige Korrektur variiert von Film zu Film, aber die folgenden Korrekturwerte können Sie als Anhaltspunkt verwenden:

Belichtungszeit nach Messung	*korrigierte Belichtungszeit*
1 Sekunde	1 bis 2 Sekunden
2 Sekunden	4 Sekunden
5 Sekunden	10 bis 15 Sekunden
10 Sekunden	20 bis 30 Sekunden
20 Sekunden	60 bis 80 Sekunden
50 Sekunden	150 bis 300 Sekunden

Zusätzlich führt der Schwarzschild-Effekt zu verstärktem Kontrast zwischen Lichtern und Schatten, den Sie ggf. durch verkürzte Entwicklung kompensieren sollten.

14. ***Was bedeutet Auflösungsvermögen?*** Das Auflösungsvermögen eines fotochemischen Materials wird durch die Angabe einer bestimmten Zahl von Linien bestimmt, die bei der Wiedergabe eines Linienrasters auf 1 Film-mm scharf erkennbar sind. Das Auflösungsvermögen reicht von etwa 90 Linien bei 400 ISO über 180 Linien bei 25 ISO bis zu 500 Linien bei 6 ISO.
Je höher die Empfindlichkeit, desto geringer ist das Auflösungsvermögen. Daneben hängt das Auflösungsvermögen auch von der Wellenlänge des einfallenden Lichts ab.
Je kürzer die Wellenlänge, desto höher das Auflösungsvermögen.

13. ***Spiega brevemente che cos'è l'effetto Schwarzschild?*** Uno strato al bromuro d'argento esposto per breve tempo ad un'alta intensità luminosa, dopo lo sviluppo mostra un annerimento maggiore rispetto ad un'esposizione più lunga, ma ad una intensità luminosa inferiore.

14. ***Cosa significa potere risolutivo, MTF, RMS grandezza del granulo?*** La capacità di risoluzione di un materiale fotosensibile viene determinato dall'indicazione di un certo numero di linee, che sono poi riconoscibili in modo nitido previo riproduzione di un retino di linee su base di 1mm/Film. Il potere risolvente va da ca. 90 linee/mm con ISO 400/27° a ca. 180 linee/mm con ISO 25/15° a, fino 500 linee/mm con 6 ISO.
Più è alta la sensibilità della pellicola, più bassa è la capacità di risoluzione.
Il potere risolutivo dipende anche dalla lunghezza d'onda della luce incidente. Più corta è la lunghezza d'onda, più alto è la capacità risolutiva.

15. ***Quali requisiti caratterizzano l'idoneità riproduttiva di una pellicola?***
15A ***Gradazione:*** Esistono emulsioni delle pellicole a gradazione normale, per le quali lo sviluppo non intraprende alcuna regolazione della gradazione.
Esistono invece emulsioni ›tecniche‹ delle pellicole, per le quali lo sviluppo ha il compito di piegare ed appiattire la gradazione. Queste pellicole speciali ricevono un conferimento di attitudine alla resa tonale tradizionale, con una finezza di grana ed una nitidezza senza eguali.
Esempio: MACO ORT 25clear; MACO TECHNICAL PAN TP 64clear e KODAK TECHNICAL PAN in combinazione al rivelatore LABOR PARTNER LP-DOKUFINE LC.

15B ***La densità:*** Spesso e volentieri viene conferita una densità eccessiva a determinati tipi di pellicola. Esempio: MACO UP 25plus, che grazie a diverse diluizioni dello sviluppo raggiunge risultati ragguardevoli.
Esempio: LP-SUPERGRAIN a diluizione 1+15 anziché 1+7.

15C ***La trasparenza:*** Si pone in stretta correlazione con la densità e viene spesso scambiata erroneamente. La trasparenza di un negativo dipende anche dalla colorazione base, grigia, del supporto della pellicola. Diversi produttori colorano appunto la base della pellicola, risparmiando così un ciclo di produzione supplementare, evitando l'applicazione di uno strato antialone.
A causa della colorazione base, grigia, o la mancata dissoluzione dello strato antihalo, le pellicole mantengono sempre un velo base. Questo fenomeno può disturbare nella messa a fuoco. D'altro canto queste pellicole con base grigia non sono adatte a produrre delle diapositive. Un'alta trasparenza (clear base) è sinonimo di qualità.

13. ***Kort forklaring av Schwarzschildeffekten.*** Et sølvbromidskikt som utsettes for høyintenst lys over kort tid har etter framkalling en høyere sværtning enn om det var eksponert tilsvarende lenger med et lavintenst lys.

14. ***Hva betyr oppløsningsevne?*** En films eller et annet fotokjemisk materiales oppløsningsevne blir bestemmt ved å oppgi evnen til å skille et gitt antall linjer fra et linjeraster pr mm. Denne evnen går fra ca 90 linjer ved 400 ISO til180 linjer ved 25 ISO til 500 linjer ved 6 ISO. I utgangspunktet vil høy følsomhet gi lav oppløsning og omvendt. I tillegg er bølgelengden til lyset viktig, kort bølgelengde gir høy oppløsning.

15. ***Hva kjennetegner en films kopieringsevne?***
15A ***Gradasjon:*** Det finnes filmer med en normal gardasjon, hvor framkalleren ikke påvirker resultatet. Det finnes tekniske filmer, hvor en spesiell framkaller kan endre gradasjonskurven betraktelig slik at disse filmene kan nyttes til billedmessig fotografi.F.eks: MACO ORT 25clear, MACO TECHNICAL PN TP 64 clear og KODAK TECHNICAL PAN når disse framkalles i LABOR PARTNER LP-DUCOFINE LC (Low Contrast)

15B ***Tetthet:*** Ofte får filmer en stor tetthet/ høy sværtning. F.eks. MACO UP 25plus, som først ved bruk av en spesiell framkallerfortynning oppnår ekselente resultater i LP-SUPERGRAIN benyttes fortynning 1 + 15 i stedet for standard 1+ 7.

15C ***Transparens:*** Dette står i sammenheng med filmens tetthet og blir derfor ofte forvekslet med denne. Transparensen er avhengig av hvorvift filmbasen er farget grå. Mange filmprodusenter gjør dette for å spare et steg i produsjonen, som det er å legge på et antihalogenasjonsskikt. Ved gråfarging av basen, eller ved at antihalogenasjonsskiktet ikke kan fjernes helt vil slike filmer alltid ha en grunntetthet, et slør. Dette kan påvirke skarpstillingen ved kopiering på en negativ måte. Dessuten er filmer med en grå base ikke optimale for å framstille diapositiver. Høy transperens (clear base) er derfor et kvalitetsmerke.

16. ***Hvordan unngår man stress under framkallingen?*** Fotografen Burkhardt Kiegelland har skrevet: Jeg passer alltid på, ved alle oppskrifter og fortynninger, at jeg har en framkallingstid på minimum 7 minutter. Jo kortere frankallingstid, jo større rolle spiller tiden det tar å fylle og å tømme framkallertanken, eller tiden det tar å få en planfilm i skålen. Dette gir unødvendig stress. Lengre framkallingstider fører derfor ikke bare til mindre stress, men også til mer gjevn framkalling.

13. ***Could you give a brief explanation of reciprocity failure?*** When developed, a silver halide emulsion exposed to high-intensity light for a short time will exhibit a higher density than an emulsion that has been exposed to very low intensity light for a proportionately longer time. This means that for any exposure time exceeding 1 s, the reciprocity law, stating that closing the aperture by one f-stop while doubling exposure time will give equivalent results in term of density, will fail. So when your exposure meter suggests exposure times of 1 s and more, you have to correct these times. The correction required depends on the film in question, but the following values can be used for reference:

Exposure time as suggested by meter	*corrected exposure time*
1 s	1 to 2 s
2 s	4 s
5 s	10 to 15 s
10 s	20 to 30 s
20 s	60 to 80 s
50 s	150 to 300 s

In addition, reciprocity failure will result in stronger contrast between the lights and shadows. You may wish to correct this by curtailing development.

14. ***What does the term ›resolving power‹ mean?*** The resolving power of photographic material is determined in terms of the number of lines of a grid which can be sharply discerned on 1 mm of film. Typical resolving powers range from about 90 lines at ISO 400 to 180 lines at ISO 25 up to 500 lines at ISO 6. The faster the film, the lower its resolving power. Resolving power also depends on the wavelength of the light. The shorter the wavelength the better the resolving power.

15. ***What characterises printability?***

15A ***Gradation:*** There are film emulsions with normal gradation, where the developer does not control the gradation. There are also technical film emulsions where the developer must control, or rather flatten, the gradation. This allows using such very fine-grained and sharp (but not fast) films for pictorial photography.
Examples: MACO ORT 25 clear, MACO TECHNICAL PAN TP64 clear, and KODAK TECHNICAL PAN in combination with LABOR PARTNER DOCUFINE LC.

15B ***Density:*** Quite often, films are developed to too high a density. Example: MACO UP25 plus will only give excellent results when developed at particular dilutions, e.g. in LP-SUPERGRAIN 1 + 15 instead of 1 + 7.

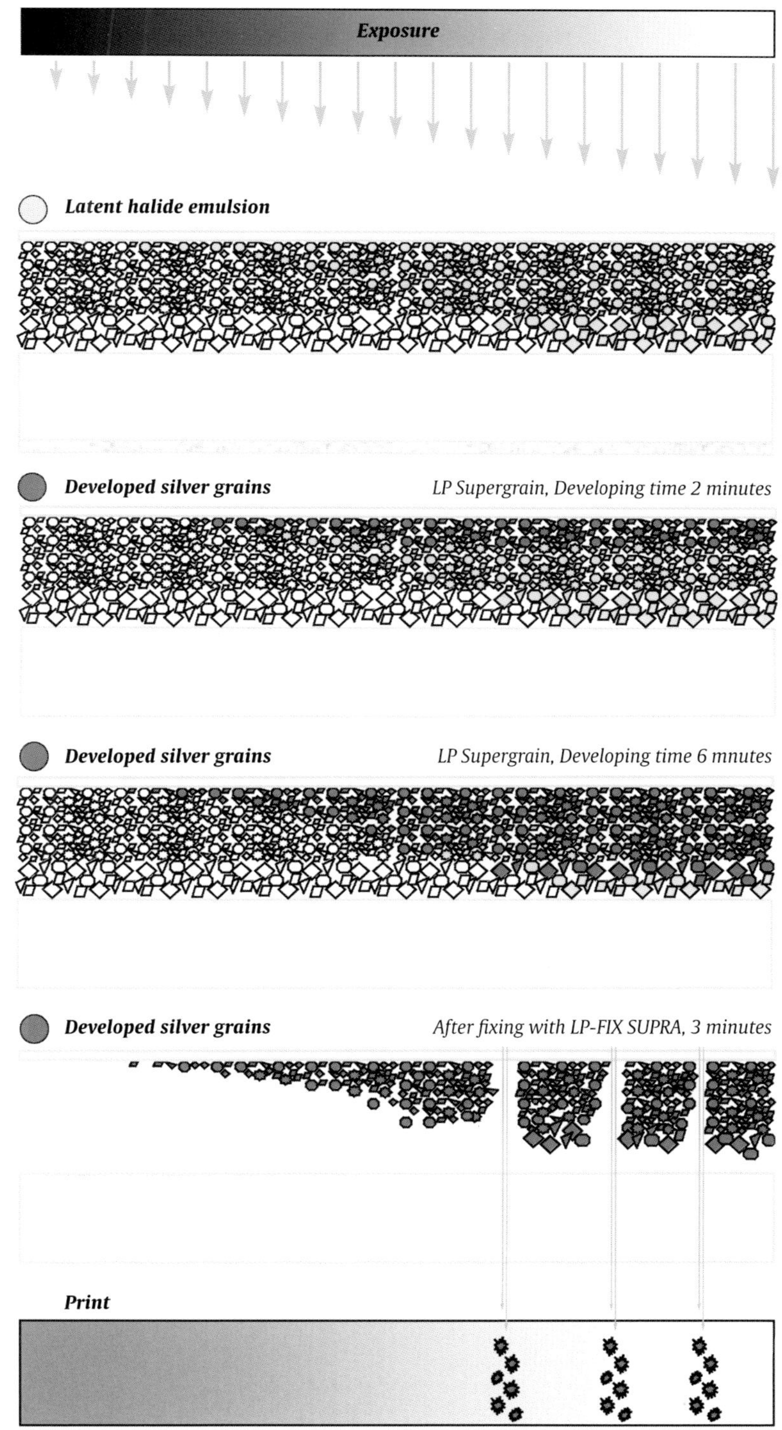

15. Welche Merkmale kennzeichnen die Kopierfähigkeit eines Films?

15A ***Die Gradation:*** Es gibt normal graduierte Filmemulsionen, bei denen der Entwickler keine Gradationssteuerung vornimmt. Es gibt technische Filmemulsionen, bei denen der Entwickler die Gradation zu beugen, abzuflachen hat. Damit wird es möglich, diese sehr feinkörnigen und scharfen (nicht empfindlichen) Filme für die bildmäßige Fotografie zu erschließen. Beispiele:
■ MACO ORT 25clear ■ MACO TECHNICAL PAN TP 64clear
■ KODAK TECHNICAL PAN in Kombination mit LABOR PARTNER LP-DOCUFINE LC.

15B ***Die Dichte:*** Oft werden Filme durch die Entwicklung zu dicht. Beispiel: MACO UP 25plus, der erst durch spezielle Entwickler-Verdünnungen zu exzellenten Resultaten gelangt: LP-SUPERGRAIN Verd. 1+15, anstatt 1+7.

15C ***Die Transparenz*** steht in engem Zusammenhang mit der Dichte und wird oft damit verwechselt. Die Durchsichtigkeit eines Filmnegativs hängt auch mit der Einfärbung (grau) des Filmträgers zusammen. Manche Filmproduzenten färben die Filmbasis ein und sparen sich dadurch den extra Arbeitsgang des Aufbringens einer Lichthofschutzschicht.
Durch die Graufärbung oder das nicht restlose Entfernen der Lichthofschutzschicht behalten diese Filme immer eine höhere Grunddichte. Diese kann sich beim Scharfstellen unter dem Vergrößerer nachteilig auswirken. Außerdem sind grau gefärbte Filme nicht optimal geeignet, um sie als Dia auf Transparentfilm umzukopieren. Eine hohe Transparenz (clear base) ist daher ein Qualitätsmerkmal.

16. ***Wie vermeidet man Stress während der Entwicklung?*** Der Fotograf Burkhardt Kiegelland schreibt: „Ich achte bei allen Rezepturen und Verdünnungen auf eine Entwicklungszeit von wenigstens 7 Minuten. Je kürzer die Entwicklungszeit, desto mehr Gewicht bekommt die Dauer des Füllens und Entleerens der Dose oder das Einlegen der Planfilmblätter in die Schale – das macht unnötigen Stress. Längere Entwicklungszeiten tragen also nicht nur zur Entspannung, sondern auch zu einer gleichmäßigen Entwicklung bei.“

17. ***Schichtoberflächen-Entwickler (Ausgleichsentwickler)*** fangen sofort nach dem Benetzen der Filmemulsion an zu entwickeln. Zuerst die groben Kristalle, dann die feineren. Die Ausentwicklung aller belichteten Kristalle wird durch Inhibitoren verhindert. Dieser ›Bremser‹ hat kontraststeuernde Wirkung (Ausgleichsvermögen). Oberflächen-Entwickler sind schnelle Entwickler, die sich durch Abbruch der der Entwicklung in der Eindringtiefe und damit im Kontrast oder Gradation gut steuern lassen.

16. ***Come si evita lo stress durante lo sviluppo?*** Il fotografo Burkhard Kiegelland scrive: „Faccio attenzione in tutte le combinazioni e diluizioni di ottenere un tempo di sviluppo di almeno 7 minuti.
Più breve è il tempo di sviluppo, maggiormente acquisiscono importanza, la durata del tempo di riempimento e svuotamento della tank, oppure l'immersione della pellicola piana nella bacinella, e ciò provoca frettolosità e stress inutili.
Tempi di sviluppo più lunghi non conferiscono solo una maggiore rilassatezza, ma migliorano qualità e omogeneità nel risultato finale.“

17. ***Sviluppo di superficie dello strato (Sviluppo compensatore)*** Iniziano *subito* la loro azione nell'immediatezza del contatto con lo sviluppo, dapprima i cristalli grossi, poi quelli più fini. Lo sviluppo a fondo di tutti i cristalli esposti viene tamponato da inibitori.
Questi ›freni‹ possiedono un potere di regolazione del contrasto (potere compensatore). Sviluppi rapidi, che dopo l'inibizione provocata nello strato profondo, si lasciano controllare perfettamente in materia di contrasto o gradazione. L'interruzione dell'azione dello sviluppo è rappresentata dalla componente temporale.
Più a lungo i cristalli d'argento risultano ›liberi‹ di muoversi nello sviluppo, più hanno la possibilità di agglomerarsi e pertanto di formare granuli più grossi.

18. ***Sviluppo di profondità dello strato (Sviluppo finegranulante)*** Sviluppi di profondità implicano un maggiore tempo di esposizione. Lavorando in modo particolarmente finegranulante ed emergono per la loro eccezionale tonalità. (LP-CUBE XS).
Dapprima penetra nell'emulsione senza attivarsi, raggiunge tutti i cristalli esposti, prima che subentrino i cosiddetti ›freni‹, e poi li sviluppa tutti. I ›freni‹ che ora riescono ad inibire l'azione di sviluppo inutilizzato in arrivo: l'effetto dello sviluppo può essere definito ›a fondo‹. L'azione dello sviluppo porta ad una grana estremamente fine ed allo stesso tempo riduce lo sfruttamento della sensibilità.

19. ***Sviluppo compensatore a grana fine (Falso sviluppo fine-granulante)*** Si tratta di una simbiosi fra i due tipi di sviluppo 17 + 18. Si ottiene una grana fine senza perdita di sensibilità e si lascia ben calibrare con il tempo di sviluppo. Poiché la profondità di penetrazione viene regolata dal tempo, si ottiene una sviluppata a compensazione del contrasto.

20. ***Sviluppi ad incremento della sensibilità:*** Anche sviluppi di superficie dello strato (18). Con l'aggiunta di idrossilamina o idrazina (diammide) si riesce ad ottenere un incremento della sensibilità, senza peraltro

17. ***Overflateframkaller / utgjevnende framkalling.*** Denne begynner straks, etter at filmen er kommet i kontakt med vesken, å virke. Først tar den de grovere krystallene, etterpå de finere. En overframkalling blir hindret av en inhibiator som virker som en bremse. På denne måten reguleres kontrasten. Hurtige framkallere kan derfor, ved å stoppe prosessen, kontrollere hvor dypt den virker og dermed påvirke gradasjonen og / eller kontrasten. Avbrudd i prosessen er tidskomponenten. Jo lengre sølvkrystallene kan bevege seg ›fritt‹ jo mer grovkornet blir resultatet.

18. ***Dybdeframkaller / ekstrem finkornframkaller.*** Denne typen framkaller krever noe lengre eksponering. De arbeider svært finkornet og gjenngir hele gråtoneskalaen på en fremragende måt. (LP-CUBE-XS)De trenger først inn i fotoskiktet uten å begynne å framkalle. De kommer derfor i kontakt med alle belyste sølvkrystaller, og framkaller alle krystallene likt uten at inhibitatoren kan bremse og forskyve resultatet. Det som så skjer er at inibitatoren som oppstår under framkallingen hindrer fersk framkaller å nå fram, prosessen stopper opp. Framkallingsprosessen fører til ekstremt fint korn, med lav utnyttelse av følsomheten i filmen.

15C ***Transmittance*** is closely related to density, and often confused with it. The degree to which a negative is transparent is also related to dyeing (grey) of the film support. Some manufacturers of film dye the film support in order to save the process of applying an anti-halation layer.
The grey dye, or an anti-halation layer that is not removed completely increase base density. This can be a disadvantage when it comes to focusing under the enlarger. Also, films with a grey base are not optimal for copying on transparent film to produce slides. High transmittance (clear base) is, therefore, an aspect of quality.

16. ***How do you avoid stress during development?*** Photographer Burkhardt Kiegelland writes: „With all formulations and dilutions, I favour a developing time of at least 7 minutes. The shorter the developing time the more significant will the effects of filling the tank or submerging the sheets of film will be—this causes unnecessary stress. So longer development will not only contribute to relaxed working, but also to uniform development.“

17. ***Emulsion-surface developers (high-definition compensating developers)*** will start developing the film immediately upon making contact with its surface, big grains being developed first, fine ones last. Restrainers prevent all exposed crystals from being developed. This ›brake‹ controls contrast (compensating action). These are fast developers whose penetration into the emulsion can be controlled by curtailing development, allowing good control of contrast and/or gradation. Curtailing development is the time component of the development process. The longer the time the ›liberated‹ silver crystals have to move about freely in the developer, the better their chances to clump together, forming bigger grains.

18. ***Depth developers (high-definition, non-solvent, ultrafine-grain developers):*** These developers effect a slight reduction in film speed. They allow for very fine grain and excellent tonality. LP-CUBE XS is an example of this type.
They will first penetrate into the emulsion without developing it. This means that they find all exposed crystals before restrainers can stop them, so all exposed crystals are developed. Restrainers formed during development inhibit the supply of fresh, unused developing agent, so developments comes to a halt. However, this process gives very small grains while the full speed of which the film would be capable is not used.

KODAK T-Max 100 NEW (120), Rolleiflex Tessar, 1/60, orange filter (see the sky), developed in LP-CUBE XS exposed with WA40 mm, exposure time 11s, 5.6 – on MACO expo RF, graded baryta paper, glossy, grade 2.
© Valsasnini

Der Abbruch ist die Zeitkomponente des Entwicklungsvorgangs. Je länger sich die ›befreiten‹ Silberkristalle im Entwickler frei bewegen können, um so mehr haben sie Gelegenheit, sich zusammen zu ballen und bilden größere Körner.

18. **Schichtiefen-Entwickler (Feinstkornentwickler):** Schichttiefen-Entwickler bewirken eine etwas verringerte Filmempfindlichkeit. Sie arbeiten sehr feinkörnig und zeichnen sich durch eine hervorragende Tonalität aus. Ein Beispiel ist LP-CUBE XS. Dringt zunächst in die Schicht ein, ohne zu entwickeln. Kommt dadurch an alle belichteten Kristalle heran bevor die ›Bremser‹ stören und entwickeln alle belichteten Kristalle. Die bei der Entwicklung nun entstehenden ›Bremser‹ behindern den Nachschub von unverbrauchtem Entwickler, die Entwicklung steht. Der Entwicklungsvorgang führt aber zu sehr kleinem Korn bei geringer Empfindlichkeitsausnutzung.

19. **Feinkorn-Ausgleichs-Entwickler (Unechter Feinkorn-Entwickler):** Eine Symbiose aus den beiden Entwickler-Typen 17 und 18. Bringt feines Korn ohne Empfindlichkeitverlust, lässt sich über die Entwicklungs-Zeit gut steuern. Da die Eindringtiefe über die Zeit gesteuert wird, ergibt das eine kontrastausgleichende Entwicklung.

20. **Empfindlichkeitsteigernde Entwickler:** Auch Schicht-Oberflächen-Entwickler (18). Durch Zusatz von Hydroxylamin oder Hydrazin lässt sich eine Steigerung der Empfindlichkeit erreichen, ohne den Kontrast zu steigern. Entwickler dieses Typs stellt LABOR PARTNER nicht her. Beim LP-SUPERGRAIN wird die höhere Empfindlichkeits-Ausnutzung durch eine verlängerte Entwicklungszeit erreicht. Bei zu langen Zeiten leidet der Tonwertumfang, er ›reisst‹. Eine wirklich höhere Empfindlichkeits-Ausnutzung erreicht ein klassischer empfindlichkeitssteigernder Entwickler ohne Verlängerung der Entwicklungszeiten (TETENAL NEOFIN BLAU und ROT). Früher waren diese Entwickler nicht nur beliebt, sondern notwendig, heute bietet die Industrie Filme bis 1.600 ISO Nennempfindlichkeit an, die Notwendigkeiten haben sich daher hin zu Entwicklern mit Fähigkeiten im Bereich Schärfe und Auflösungsvermögen verschoben.

21. ***Was ist Entwickler-Härtung?*** In der Literatur findet man den Begriff ›Tropenentwicklung‹. Wenn in südlichen Ländern mit Temperaturen über 25°C gearbeitet wird, dann ist es notwendig, die mit zunehmender Temperatur immer verletzlicher werdende Filmgelatine zu härten. Das gilt ebenfalls bei besondern frischen Filmen oder flüssigen Fotoemulsionen.
Früher war es üblich, dem Entwickler NATRIUMSULFAT contribuire ad aumentare il contrasto. LABOR PARTNER non produce questo tipo di sviluppo.
Nel caso del LP-SUPERGRAIN l'alto sfruttamento della sensibilità viene ottenuto con un tempo di sviluppo allungato. Con tempi troppo lunghi ne soffre l'ambito della resa tonale, ›strappa‹. Un tradizionale sviluppo ad incremento della sensibilità riesce a conferire un aumento della sensibilità senza dover incrementare il tempo di sviluppo (TETENAL NEOFIN BLU e ROSSO). In passato questo tipo di sviluppo non solo era ricercato, ma anche necessario. Oggi l'industria propone pellicole fino 1600 ISO di sensibilità nominale, e la necessità si è spostata verso sviluppi che possiedono attitudini in campo di nitidezza e capacità risolutiva.

21. ***Cos'è lo sviluppo induritore?*** Nella letteratura tecnica si trova la definizione *Sviluppo tropico*. Nei casi di trattamento delle pellicole nei paesi caldi, sopra 1 25°C, è necessario indurire la gelatina della pellicola assai delicata. Ciò vale anche per emulsioni liquide o pellicole di fresca produzione.
In passato era consuetudine aggiungere solfato sodico. C'era però il pericoloso rischio che i tempi di sviluppo si riducevano in modo assai differenziato.
Consiglio: LP-GELADUR, si tratta di un moderno INDURITORE DI SVILUPPO, che non provoca alcuna modifica dei tempi di sviluppo.

22. ***Cosa accade durante la fase di sviluppo?*** Gli alogenuri d'argento dapprima sono ›la memoria dell'immagine‹ della POSA durante la ripresa. I cristalli vengono caricati in modo latente da quantità di luce (immagine latente). Come ciò accade è rimasto un mistero fino ad oggi. Grazie alla carica dei cristalli , questi possono essere ›aggrediti‹ da parte della chimica di sviluppo. Poiché il negativo deve essere un supporto trasparente per trasferire l'immagine, nelle luci può avere solo una certa densità, che deve essere sufficientemente ›trasparente‹ da trasmettere anche minime sfumature di contorno del bianco.
A differenza dello sviluppo del positivo, lo sviluppo del negativo è un procedimento che viene interrotto, regolato in un determinato lasso di tempo. Non sono necessari tutti i cristalli di alogenuri esposti per la densità ›trasparente‹, altrimenti nelle luci si addurrebbe alla trasparenza.
La conseguenza di lunghi anni di ricerca hanno portato a diversi sviluppi, che vengono descritti qui di seguito:
L'esposizione simula il perimetro di contrasto dell'oggetto fotografato.
Senza prodotto chimico non accade proprio nulla.. Gli sviluppi richiamano dapprima la memoria latente dell'immagine verso luci e ombre. La diversa intensità luminosa della luce di ripresa implica una profondità di penetrazione diversa nell'esposizione latente dei cristalli al bromuro d'argento. Si ottiene cioè una tonalità finemente graduata. In

19. ***Finkornframkaller med utgjevning (uekte finkornframkaller)*** Dette er en symbiose av typene 17 + 18. Denne gir fint korn uten tap av lysfølsomhet. Den kan i stor grad kontrolleres via tid. Da dybdepåvirkningen kontrolleres med hjelp av tiden, så kan en kontrast-utgjevning oppnås.

20. ***Framkaller for høyere utnyttelse av følsomhet (pressing).*** Denne virker på samme måte som beskrevet i nr 18. Ved å tilsette hydroxylamin eller hydrazin, kan det oppnås en bedre utnyttelse av følsomheten, uten at kontrasten blir endret. LABOR PRTNER produserer ikke slik framkaller. Ved LP-SUPERGRAIN kan en oppnå øket følsomhetsutnyttelse ved å forlenge tiden. Ved for lange tider, vil tonegjengivelsen kunne lide. En virkelig økning i den effektive følsomheten oppnår en ved bruk av klassiske framkallere for ›pressing‹ (TETENAL NEOFIN BLAU + ROT). Tidligere var disse framkallerne en nødvendighet, men i dag framstilles filmer med en ISO-verdi inntil 1600. Det er derfor blitt mer nødvendig med framkallere som er rettet mot oppløsning og skarphet.

21. ***Hva er framkaller-herding?*** I faglitteraturen vil en konne finne ordet *tropeframkalling*. Når det blir arbeidet med temperaturer over 25°C, blir det nødvendig å beskytte filmgelantinen, dvs å herde denne. Dette gjelder spesiellt for helt ferske filmer og for flytende fotoemusjoner. Tidligere var det vanlig å tilsette natruimsulfat til framkalleren. Dette medførte en stor risiko da framkallingstidene forandret seg forskjellig fra film til film.Derfor anbefales i dag LP-GELADUR som er en moderne framkaller-herder som ikke endrer framkallingstidene.

22. ***Hva skjer under framkallingen?*** Sølvhalogenidene er først og fremst ›minnet‹ av opptaket som skjer under eksponeringen. Krystallene blir latent ladet av lyskvanter og vi får et latent bilde. Hvordan dette skjer er ennå ikke helt klart. Denne latente ladningen gjør krystallene mottakelige for framkalleren. Da negativet skal være et transparent for omkopiering på papir, kan høylysene bare ha en tetthet som fortsatt tillater at de fineste nyansene kan avtegnes i det hvite på papiret. I motstening til positivframkallingen er filmframkallingen en tidavhengig styrt prosess. Ikke alle sølvhalogenidene, som er eksponert, trenges for å få et godt og transparent negativ. I høylysene ville det, som beskrevet, ellers gro igjen. Reslutatet av mange års utvikling er forskjelige framkaller typer som vil bli beskrevet her.Eksponeringen simulerer fotoobjektes kontrastomfang. Uten kjemi skjer det ikke noe. Framkalleren er det som omvandler det latente bildet til lys og skygge. Opptakslysets forskjellige verdier resulterer i forskjellig oppbygning av det latente bildet i sølvbromidkrystallene. Blandingen av forskjellig store korn er det som gjør det

19. ***Fine-grain compensating developers (false fine-grain developers):*** These are hybrids of developer types 17 and 18. The result is fine grain without a loss in speed, good control via developing time. Depth of penetration being controlled by controlling the time, development is compensating.

20. ***Speed-increasing developers:*** These are also emulsion-surface developers. (See 18.) Adding hydroxylamine or hydrazine to the developer allows to increase film speed without affecting contrast. LABOR PARTNER does not produce developers of this type.
When using LP-SUPERGRAIN the increase in speed is effected by prolonged development. When the time is too long, the tonality suffers, tearing up. A classical speed-increasing developer (TETENAL NEOFIN BLAU and ROT) will effect an increase in true speed without prolonged development. Formerly, developers of this type were not only favoured, they were in fact a necessity, but today, with industry offering films with nominal speeds up to ISO 1,600, developers improving sharpness and resolution are needed.

21. ***What is hardening during development?*** You might find the term *tropical development* in photographic literature. Working in the south, at temperatures in excess of 25°C (77 °F), calls for a hardening of the gelatine which gets softer with increasing temperature. This is also true for very fresh film and liquid photo emulsions.
Adding SODIUM SULPHATE to the developer used to be common practice. However, this involved some risk for the laboratory worker, as development times tend to be shortened to varying degrees.
Recommendation: LP-GELADUR, a modern HARDENER FOR THE DEVELOPER not effecting any change in developing time.

22. ***What happens during development?*** First, silver halides are the ›eidetic memory‹ of the film. Crystals receive a latent ›charge‹, the latent image, from light quanta. The exact process has not been fully explained to date. This charge makes the crystals susceptible to the ›attack‹ of developing chemicals. The negative being supposed to be ›transparent‹ for printing, its density in the densest areas, the lights, must still let enough light pass to allow for fine nuances of off-white to register. Contrary to print development, film development is a time-controlled, terminated process. All exposed crystals are not needed for the still ›transparent‹ density, or the highlights would ›block up‹. Therefore, different types of developers have evolved over the years.
Nothing happens without chemistry. It is the developer that makes the latent memory of light and shadow visible.
The subject brightnesses lead to varying depths of pene-

A1

without filter 1/15, f16

A2

yellow/green filter 1/10, f16, + 1/2

A3

orange filter (22) 1/10, f16, + 1/2

A4

red filter (25A) 1/6, f16, + 1

These images were taken on a Canon camera with a 35-mm lens, using MACO IR 750clear infrared film, rated at ISO 100, developed in LP-SUPERGRAIN
© Valsasnini

zuzusetzen. Dies bedeutete jedoch für den Laboranten ein erhebliches Risiko, denn die Entwicklungszeiten verringern sich dabei unterschiedlich.
Empfehlung: LP-GELADUR, ein moderner ENTWICKLER-HÄRTER, der keine Veränderungen der vorgegebenen Entwicklungszeiten bewirkt.

22. ***Was geschieht während der Entwicklung?*** Die Silber-Halogenide sind bei der Belichtung zunächst das ›Bildgedächtnis‹ der Aufnahme. Die Kristalle werden durch Lichtquanten latent ›aufgeladen‹ (das latente Bild). Wie das geschieht, ist bis heute immer noch nicht völlig geklärt. Die Ladung macht die Kristalle ›angreifbar‹ für die Entwickler-Chemie. Da das Negativ ein Transparent zum Umkopieren sein soll, darf es in den Lichtern nur eine Dichte haben, die noch ›tranparent‹ genug ist, kleinste Nuancen von Weiß hellen Grauwerten, fast weiß, fein abgestuft abzubilden.
Im Gegensatz zur Positiventwicklung ist die Filmentwicklung ein zeitgesteuerter, abgebrochener, Vorgang. Nicht alle Halogenid-Kristalle, die belichtet sind, werden gebraucht, um die noch ›transparente‹ Dichte aufzubauen. In den Lichtern würde die Transparenz vielmehr ›zulaufen‹, wenn tatsächlich alle entwickelt würden. Das Ergebnis der langen Entwicklungsjahre sind daher unterschiedliche Entwicklertypen.
Ohne Chemie passiert nichts. Entwickler rufen erst die latente Speicherung des Bildes zu Licht und Schatten hervor.
Die unterschiedliche Leuchtdichte des Aufnahmelichtes ruft eine unterschiedliche Eindringtiefe der latenten Belichtung der Silberhalogenidkristalle hervor. Mischstrukturen verschiedener Korngrössen ermöglichen erst das unterschiedliche Ansprechverhalten der Halogenide auf den Entwickler. Das ergibt feingestufte Tonalität.
Eigentlich müssten zur Abstufung des Ansprechverhaltens die kleinen Kristalle alle oben in der Schicht liegen und mit zunehmender Größe immer tiefer (Prinzip: MACO CUBE 400clear mit zwei Emulsionsschichten).

23. ***Kennen Sie Schwarzweiß-Mehrschicht-Filme?*** Nach dem aktuellen Wissensstand des Autors bieten heute nur wenige Schwarzweißfilme zwei aufeinander liegende unterschiedliche Emulsionsschichten:

- AGFA APX25
- APX100
- MACO CUBE 400clear

Diese Filme verfügen (vereinfacht gesagt) über eine Emulsionsschicht mit groben Silberhalogeniden, die vor allem für die Empfindlichkeit zuständig ist. Dazu kommt eine weitere Emulsionsschicht mit feinkörnigen Silberhalogeniden. Diese extra Schicht ist zuständig für das feine Korn.

effetti per la gradualità nel comportamento della reazione i cristalli di piccole dimensioni dovrebbero essere posti tutti in alto e man mano a seconda della grandezza orientarsi verso il basso.

23. ***Conosce le pellicole in bianco/nero multi-strati?*** Secondo le conoscenze del team di autori si offrono oggi solo poche pellicole bianco/nero con due strati di emulsione sovrapposti :

- AGFA APX 25
- APX 100
- MACO CUBE 400clear

Queste pellicole si avvalgono (detto in modo semplicistico) di uno strato di emulsione con alogenuri d'argento grossi, competenti per la sensibilità + Un ulteriore strato di emulsione con alogenuri più fini. Questo extra-strato è competente per la grana finissima.

24. ***Sviluppare, arrestare, fissare, lavare, imbibente – in breve:***
La soluzione di sviluppo viene irrorata nell'emulsione della pellicola e riduce dapprima i grandi e poi i cristalli più piccoli. I bromidi così ricavati ritardano l'attacco dello sviluppo in profondità (inibitori, prodotti ritardanti). Questo è il decorso chimico-meccanico dell'azione di sviluppo.
A seconda della durata del tempo di sviluppo non tutti i cristalli latenti vengono attivati. L'azione dello sviluppo viene così interrotta. I ›latenti‹ non sviluppati sono inutili in quanto provocherebbero nel negativo una densità troppo elevata. Questo ›lasciare indietro‹ dei cristalli inutilmente

mulig at sølvhalogenidene kan reagere forskjellig i framkalleren. Slik oppnås fine gråtoner. Egentlig burde alle små korn ligge øverst i skiktet, for så å blir større jo lengre ned de kommer for å tilpasses reaksjonsevnen for de enkelte kornstørrelsene.

23. ***Finnes merskikts sort/hvitt filmer?*** Så vidt forfatterne kjenner til finnes det bare svært få sort/hvitt filmer som har to eller flere emusjonsskikt.AGFA APX 25, APX 100 og MACO CUBE 400 clear. Disse filmene har, forenklet sagt, et skikt med grove sølvhalogenider som bestemmer følsomheten og ett med de fineste sølvhalogenidene som er grunnlaget for ekstremt fint korn.

tration of the latent exposure of the silver halide crystals. Mixtures of silver grains of different sizes allow for the differentiated response of the silver halides to the developer. The result of this process is a finely graduated tonal rendition. Actually, for controlling the response all small crystals should lie at the surface, and crystal size should grow with depth.

23. ***Do you know double-coated black-and-white films?*** The authors are aware of only a few current films with two different emulsion layers:
AGFA APX 25, APX 100 and MACO CUBE 400 clear (In simple terms). These films have one emulsion layer with coarse-grained silver halides, whose principal task is to increase film speed. Another layer with ultrafine-grain silver halides is added. This makes for ultrafine grain.

B1

without filter 1/15, f16

B2

yellow/green filter 1/10, f16, + 1/2

B3

orange filter (22) 1/10, f16, + 1/2

B4

red filter (25A) 1/6, f16, + 1

These images were taken on a Canon camera with a 35-mm lens, using MACO IR 750clear infrared film, rated at ISO 100, developed in LP-SUPERGRAIN
© Valsasnini

24. Entwicklen, Stoppen, Fixieren, Wässern, Netzmittel – in Kurzform:

- Die Entwicklerlösung ist in die Film-Emulsion eingeschwemmt und reduziert zuerst die großen und danach die kleineren Kristalle. Die dabei anfallenden Bromide verzögern den Angriff des Entwicklers in der Tiefe (Reaktionsprodukte, Inhibitoren). Das ist der physikalisch-chemische Ablauf der Entwicklung.

Je nach Entwicklungsdauer sind nicht alle latenten Kristalle entwickelt. Die Entwicklung wird danach abgebrochen. Die nicht entwickelten Latentbildkeime werden nicht benötigt, sie würden eine zu große Dichte im Negativ erzeugen. Dieses Übriglassen der zuviel belichteten Kristalle ermöglicht erst die Reduzierung des großen Motivkontrastumfangs zu noch kopierbaren Negativdichten.

- Nach dem Unterbrechen werden die belichteten und nicht entwickelten, dazu die nicht belichteten Silberhalogenidkristalle mit dem Fixierbad wasserlöslich gemacht, anschließend ausgewaschen. Der Film wird dann mit LP-MASTERPROOF vor Trockenflecken und Lagerungsschäden geschützt.

25. Haben Sie ein Rezept zur Umkehr-Entwicklung?

25A ***Nicht optimal geeignete Filme:*** Grundsätzlich kann man jeden ›normalen‹ Schwarzweiß-Film zu einem Dia-Film umkehren.

Filme mit einem grau gefärbten Filmbasismaterial (grey base) oder einer grau färbenden Lichthofschutzschicht sind leider nicht gut geeignet, Beispiele sind da etwa: AGFA APX 25, ILFORD Pan F.

25B ***Geeignete Filme:*** Optimal sind eigentlich die Filme, die über ein transparentes Filmbasismaterial verfügen. Beispiele sind hier:

- AGFA SCALA
- MACO UP 64clear

als Standard Aufnahmefilme. Der AGFA SCALA ist hochempfindlich bis zu 200 ISO, der MACO UP 64clear weist dagegen eine besonders hohe Maximalschwärzung auf. Diese macht ihn ideal zum Gebrauch als Druckvorlage oder zum Scannen.

Um Dias für Vorträge anzufertigen suchen Fotografen häufig nach einem steilen Film. Hier bietet MACO mit dem

- ORT 25clear

eine optimale Lösung an. Hierbei sollte der Erstentwickler geändert werden. Dazu später mehr.

Das Prinzip der Umkehrentwicklung bietet eine Methode an, bei der nach der Entwicklung unmittelbar ein tonwertrichtiges Positiv vorliegt. LABOR PARTNER bietet die Möglichkeit, unter Zusatz von einigen Rohchemikalien, diesen Prozess im eigenen Labor durchzuführen.

Die Grundlage bietet eine seit Jahrzehnten bewährte AGFA-Vorschrift, basierend auf 20°C, 30 Sekunden Rhythmus:

esposti consente proprio la riduzione dell'ampio spettro di contrasto, in densità di negativo ancora riproducibili.

- Dopo l'arresto i cristalli degli alogenuri d'argento esposti e non sviluppati e inoltre quelli non esposti, con il fissaggio vengono resi idrosolubili. Il lavaggio finale e il trattamento in LP-MASTERPROOF rendono il negativo resistente all'archivio.

25. Avete una ricetta per lo sviluppo invertibile?

25A ***Concettualmente*** qualsiasi ›comune‹ pellicola bianco/nero può essere invertita a pellicola dia.

Pellicole con un supporto base colorato in grigio (gray-base) o con uno strato antialone colorato di grigio purtroppo non sono particolarmente adatte. Esempi:

AGFA APX 25, ILFORD PAN F.

25B ***Danno risultati ottimali*** solo quelle pellicole che dispongono di un supporto base trasparente. Esempi:

- AGFA SCALA
- MACO UP 64clear

come pellicole da ripresa standard. L'AGFA SCALA è di medio-alta sensibilità di 200 ISO nominali, e la MACO UP 64clear, di medio-bassa sensibilità vanta densità massime dei neri assai elevate. Questa peculiarità la rende particolarmente adatta a campioni di stampa o per la scansione.

Per preparare dia per conferenze i fotografi cercano spesso una pellicola relativamente ripida.

Qui MACO propone con la

- ORT 25clear

una soluzione ottimale. In questo caso il primo sviluppo dovrebbe essere modificato. Questo più avanti.

Il principio dello sviluppo invertibile propone un metodo, con il quale si ottiene un positivo con una corretta resa tonale. LABOR PARTNER offre la possibilità, con l'aggiunta di alcuni chimici di base, di effettuare questo procedimento nel proprio laboratorio. La base viene offerta da una descrizione AGFA acquisita ormai da decenni a 20°C, ad un ritmo di agitazione di ogni 30 secondi.

25C ***Ricetta:***

- ***Passo 1:*** 1. Sviluppo di ca. 5-8 minuti Aggiungere 3 grammi di solfocianuro (solfocianato o rodanato di potassio) per litro di soluzione d'uso al LP-BROM 4 (sviluppo carta) alla diluizione 1+7 Se si devono ottenere alti contrasti, utilizzare LP-DOKUFINE HA alla diluizione da 1 + 4 a 1 + 7
- ***Passo 2:*** Lavaggio in acqua corrente di ca. 5 minuti
- ***Passo 3:*** Bagno di sbianchimento di ca. 5 minuti

BICROMATO DI POTASSIO	5 gr
ACIDO SOLFORICO conc.	5 ml
ACQUA a	1 litro

(Prima l'acqua, poi gli acidi) (!)

24. Framkalling, stoppebad, fiksering, spyling, skyllemiddel i kortform:

Framkalleroppløsningen trenger inn i filmemulsjonen og reduserer først de groveste og så de fineste krystallene. Avfallsproduktet bromid bremser framkallerens evne til å trenge inn i dybden (Avfallsproduktet er inhibitorer). Framkallining er en kjemisk- mekanisk prosess.Alt etter hvilken framkallingstid som er valgt vil ikke alle latente krystaller være framkallt. Framkallingen blir avbrudt. De ikkeframkallte latente krystallene trenges ikke, de ville føre til en forstor tetthet i negativet. Bare på denne måten, ved å ikke bruke alt av det latente bildet, blir det mulig å redusere den store lyskontrasten til et kopierbart negativ.etter et stoppebad blir de eksponerte,men ikke framkallte og de ueksponerte sølvhalogenidkrystallene gjordt vannløslige i et fikserbad. Etter en grundig spylig blir negativene gjordt arkivfaste ved hjelp av LP-MASTERPROFF.

25. Oppskrift på på omvenderframkaller.

25A ***I prinsippet*** kan en hver ›normal‹ sort/hvitt-film omvender framkalles (til lysbilde). Filmer med grå base (grey base) eller med grått antihalogenasjonsskikt er dessverre ikke spesiellt godt egnet, f.eks: AGFA APX 25 og ILFORD Pan F.

25B ***Optimalt*** er egentlig bare filmer som har en transparent filmbase. F.eks:

- AGFA SCALA 200
- MACO UP 64clear

AGFAs variant har høy følsomhet 200 ISO, mens MACO UP 64clear kan vise til en spesielt høy maksimalsværtning. Dette gjør den spesiellt godt egnet for skanning og som utgangspunkt for trykk. For å framstille lysbilder til foredrag ønskes ofte en film med hardere gradasjon.

- MACO ORT 25clear er den optimale filmen for dette. Da må førsteframkalleren endres, men mer om det senere.Prinsippet for omvenderframkalling er å gi en metode for å framskaffe toneriktige positiver direkte etter prosessen. LABOR PARTNER gir deg muligheten, ved bruk av noen ekstra råkjemikalier, til å gjøre dette i ditt eget mørkerom. Grunnlaget for denne prosessen er en kjennt oppskrift fra AGFA som forutsetter 20°C ved 1 aggitasjon hvert 30 sek.

25C ***Oppskrift:***

- ***Steg 1:*** Førsteframkaller ca 5 til 8 min LP-BROM 4 (papirframkaller) blandes 1+7 og tilsettes 3 gram kaliumrhodanid pr liter. Ønskes svært høye kontraster benyttes LP-DOCUFINE HC (high contrast) i fortynning 1 + 4 til 1 + 7.
- ***Steg 2:*** Spyling ca 5 min.
- ***Steg 3:*** Blekebad ca 5 min.

Kaliumbichromat	5 gram
Svovelsyrekonsentrat	5 ml
vann opp til	1000 ml (Først vann så syre!)

24. Developing, stopping, fixing, washing, wetting agent – in brief:

■ The developing solution has soaked the film emulsion, reducing the big crystals first, and then the small ones. Bromides released in this process retard the effect of the developer deep in the emulsion (reaction products, restrainers). This is the physico-chemical process of development. Depending on the duration of development, all crystals are not developed. Development is then stopped. Latent centres not developed so far are not needed as they would result in excessive negative density. It is only this process of ›leaving a few‹ that allows to reduce the wide range of subject brightnesses to printable negative densities.
Following stopping, exposed, but undeveloped, and also unexposed silver halide crystals are made water-soluble and removed by the fixer. Fixer residues are then washed out, and the film is protected from drying marks and damage during storage using LP-MASTERPROOF.

25. Have you got a recipe for reversal processing?

25A ***Basically,*** every ›normal‹ b&w film can be reversal-processed to become a slide film.
Unfortunately, films with their supports dyed grey (grey base) and films with a remaining grey anti-halation layer, are not very suitable. Examples are AGFA APX25, ILFORD PAN F.
25B ***Actually,*** only those films are optimal where the support is clear. Examples of such films are
■ AGFA SCALA
■ MACO UP64 clear
as standard recording films. AGFA SCALA is fast, up to ISO 200, while MACO UP64 clear features a particularly high maximum density. This makes it the ideal film for pre-printing or scanning.
Photographers often look for contrasty films to prepare slides for presentations. Here,
■ MACO ORT 25 clear is the optimal solution. In this case, the first developer bath should be modified, more details to follow.
The principle of reversal processing offers a method which, upon development, immediately produces a positive with correct tonal rendition.
LABOR PARTNER gives you the opportunity to carry out this process in your own lab, using a few raw chemicals. The process is based upon an AGFA recipe which has been known for decades to perform well, for 20°C (68°F), with inversion every 30 s.
25C ***Recipe:***
■ ***Step 1:*** First development about 5 to 8 minutes. Add 3 grams of potassium rhodanide to one litre LP-BROM 4 paper developer 1+7. If you want very stark contrast, use LP-DOCUFINE HC, diluted 1+4 to 1+7.

C1

without filter 1/20, f16

C2

yellow/green filter 1/15, f16, + 1/2

C3

orange filter (22) 1/15, f16, + 1/2

C4

red filter (25A) 1/8, f16, + 1

These images were taken on a Canon camera with a 35-mm lens, using MACO IR 750clear infrared film, rated at ISO 100, developed in LP-SUPERGRAIN

25C **Rezeptur / Zeiten:**

- ***Schritt 1:*** Erstentwicklung ca. 5-8 Minuten
  Dem LP-BROM 4 Papierentwickler Verdünnung 1+7 werden 3 Gramm KALIUMRHODANID pro Liter zugesetzt. Sollen sehr kräftige Kontraste erreicht werden, dann ist der LP-DOCUFINE HC, Verdünnung 1+4 bis 1+7 zu verwenden.
- ***Schritt 2:*** Wässerung ca. 5 Minuten
- ***Schritt 3:*** Bleichbad ca. 5 Minuten
  KALIUMBICHROMAT 5 Gramm
  SCHWEFELSÄURE konz. 5 ml
  WASSER auf 1 Liter
  (zuerst das Wasser, dann die Säure) (!)
- ***Schritt 4:*** Wässerung ca. 5 Minuten
- ***Schritt 5:*** Klärbad ca. 3 Minuten
  NATRIUMSULFIT 50 Gramm
  WASSER auf 1 Liter
- ***Schritt 6:*** Wässerung ca. 5 Minuten
- ***Schritt 7:*** ZWISCHENBELICHTUNG
  500 Watt Lampe, 2 Meter Abstand,
  jede Spiralseite mindestens 90 Sekunden
- ***Schritt 8:*** Zweitentwicklung ca. 3-5 Minuten
  Den LP-BROM 4 Papierentwickler Verdünnung 1+7 ohne Zusätze verwenden.
  Werden kräftigeren Dias angestrebt, dann auch hier den LP-DOCUFINE HC Verdünnung 1+4 oder 1+7 verwenden.
- ***Schritt 9:*** Wässerung ca. 5 Minuten
- ***Schritt 10:*** Fixierung ca. 3 Minuten
  LP-FIX-SUPRA, Verdünnung 1+7.
- ***Schritt 11:*** Wässerung ca. 10 Minuten
- ***Schritt 12:*** Netzmittel ca. 2 Minuten
  LP-MASTERPROOF Verdünnung 1+100

Im Bleichbad (Schritt 3) wird das negative Silberbild zu wasserlöslichem Silbersalz.
Im Klärbad (Schritt 5) wird die durch das Bleichen entstandene Gelbfärbung entfernt.
Die physikalische Belichtung ist einer chemischen Umkehrung vorzuziehen. Sie ist wirklich kein Problem, wenn man sich überwunden hat, mit einer hellen Lampe den noch nicht fertigen Film zu bestrahlen.

25D ***Die Belichtung des MACO UP 64clear Films für die Umkehrentwicklung:*** Im Gegensatz zur Belichtung von Filmen für die Negativentwicklung (wo man bekanntlich auf die Schatten belichtet) legt man für die korrekte Belichtung des MACO UP 64clear (alle MACO ›clear‹ Filme sind vom Hersteller speziell auf die Umkehr-Entwicklung eingestellt) für die Umkehr-Entwicklung bei selektiver Belichtungsmessung den Messpunkt mehr in die Nähe der Lichterpartien. Verwendet man zur Belichtung eine integral arbeitende Belichtungsautomatik, muss eine entsprechend höhere Empfindlichkeit eingestellt werden.
50 ISO als ›normaler‹ Negativ-Film, 64 ISO als Dia-Film.

- ***Passo 4:*** Lavaggio in acqua corrente di ca. 5 minuti
- ***Passo 5:*** Bagno chiarificatore di ca. 3 minuti
  SOLFURO DI SODIO 50 gr
  ACQUA a 1 litro
- ***Passo 6:*** Lavaggio in acqua corrente di ca. 5 minuti
- ***Passo 7:*** 2a ESPOSIZIONE ALLA LUCE Con lampada da 500 W a 2 metri di distanza Minimo 90 secondi per lato della spirale
- ***Passo 8:*** 2. Sviluppo di ca. 3-5 minuti
  LP-BROM 4 a diluizione 1+7, senza alcun additivo
  In caso vengano richieste dia più intense, utilizzare:
  LP-DOKUFINE HC da 1+4 a 1+7
- ***Passo 9:*** Lavaggio in acqua corrente di ca. 5 minuti
- ***Passo 10:*** Fissaggio di ca. 3 minuti LP-FIX SUPRA, diluizione 1+7
- ***Passo 11:*** Lavaggio finale in acqua corrente di ca. 10 minuti
- ***Passo 12:*** Bagni imbibente di ca. 2 minuti
  LP-MASTERPROOF, diluizione 1+100

Nel bagno di sbianchimento (passo 3) l'immagine d'argento negativa si muta in sale d'argento idrosolubile.
Nel bagno chiarificatore (passo 5) viene eliminata la colorazione giallastra provocata dal bagno di sbianca.
L'esposizione fisica è da preferire all'inversione chimica. Non c'è veramente alcun problema, se non quello di convincersi a dover esporre nuovamente alla luce una pellicola già in parte trattata.

25D ***L'esposizione della pellicola MACO UP 64 clear per lo sviluppo invertibile:***
A differenza dell'esposizione di pellicole per il trattamento quale negativo (dove è risaputo che si misura nelle ombre) per la corretta esposizione della MACO UP 64clear quale diapositiva si pone il punto di lettura della misurazione esposimetrica vicino alle parti nelle luce. (Tutte le pellicole MACO ›clear‹ sono regolate dal produttore in particolare sul trattamento invertibile). Qualora si disponga di un automatismo di esposizione integrale, bisogna necessariamente regolare una sensibilità superiore. ISO 50/18° come ›normale‹ negativa, 64/19° come dia bianco/nero.

- ***Steg 4:*** Spyling ca 5 min
- ***Steg 5:*** Klarebad ca 3 min
  Natrium sulfitt 50 gram
  vann opptil 1000 ml
- ***Steg 6:*** Spyling ca 5 min
- ***Steg 7:*** Eksponering / etterbelysning
  500 Watt, ca 2 meter avstand hver side av spiralen minimum 90 sek. NB ikke stålspiral.
- ***Steg 8:*** Annenframkaller ca 3 – 5 min
  LP BROM 4 papirframkaller 1 + 7 uten tilsetninger
  Ønskes kraftige lysbilder kan også her
  LP-DOCUFINE HC 1 + 4 til 1 + 7 benyttes
- ***Steg 9:*** Spyling ca 5 min
- ***Steg 10:*** Fiksering ca 3 min LP SUPRA 1 + 7
- ***Steg 11:*** Spylig ca 10 min
- ***Steg 12:*** Spylemiddel ca 2 min LP-MASTERPROFF 1 + 100

I blekebadet blir det negative sølvbildet omgjordt til vannløslig sølvsaltI klarebadet blir gulfargen som oppstår under bleking fjernet. Den fysiske eksponeringen (Steg 7) er å foretrekke framfor en kjemisk eksponering bare en klarer å overvinne seg selv og belyse en film som ennå ikke er ferdig. (Fra steg 6 kan lyset være på).

Step 2: Washing about 5 minutes
Step 3: Bleach bath about 5 minutes

POTASSIUM BICHROMATE	5 grams
SULPHURIC ACID, conc.	5 ml
WATER to make	1 l

(Remember: Water first, then the acid!)
Step 4: Washing about 5 minutes
Step 5: Clearing about 3 minutes

SODIUM SULPHITE	50 grams
WATER to make	1 l

Step 6: Washing about 5 minutes
Step 7: INTERMEDIATE EXPOSURE
500-Watt lamp, distance about 2 metres, each side of the reels should be exposed for at least 90 s.
Step 8: Second development about 3 to 5 minutes
Use LP-BROM 4 paper developer at 1+7, no additives.
Where denser slides are required,
Use LP-DOCUFINE HC at 1+4 or 1+7 in this case, too.
Step 9: Washing about 5 minutes
Step 10: Fixing about 3 minutes
LP-FIX SUPRA, 1+7
Step 11: Washing about 10 minutes
Step 12: Wetting agent about 2 minutes
LP-MASTERPROOF 1+100

In the bleach, the negative silver image is converted to a soluble silver salt.
Clearing removes the yellowish cast caused by bleaching.
Physical exposure to light is preferred over chemical reversal. It is actually not a problem at all once you collect your nerve to expose an unfinished film to the light of a strong lamp.
25D ***How to expose MACO UP 64 clear for reversal processing:*** When measuring in a selective mode, other than for negative processing (where exposure is determined for the shadows), use an area closer to the highlights to determine the correct exposure of a frame to be reversal-processed. (All MACO films with the ›clear‹ suffix have been adapted by the manufacturer for reversal processing.)
When using an integrating automatic meter, set an appropriately higher speed.
Use ISO 50 for ›conventional‹ negative processing, ISO 64 for use as slide film.

KODAK T-Max 100 NEW (120), Rolleiflex Tessar, 1/125, f16, developed in LP-CUBE XS, exposed with WA40 mm, exposure time 14s, 8 – on MACO expo RF, graded baryta paper, glossy, grade 2.
The quality of the KODAK T-MAX 100 NEW gains well owing to the use the LP-CUBE XS. In relation to the KODAK PLUS-X Pan the KODAK T-MAX 100 NEW is much as smoother. © Valsasnini

26. ***Was bedeutet Route Mean Sqare (RMS)?*** Körnigkeit meint die Korngröße der unentwickelten Halogenidkristalle, das sind die Körner, die dem Betrachter im Positiv als störend erscheinen.
Die entwickelten Silberkörner häufen sich durch Ballung und Überlappung zusammen und hinterlassen in der Schicht ›Lücken‹, die beim Vergrößern das Licht durchlassen und auf dem Positiv schwarze Pünktchen ergeben.
In den Schatten gehen die Pünktchen unter, aber in den Lichtern, z.B. dem Himmel führen sie zu einer Punktierung in Flächen, die einheitlich hell erscheinen sollten. Diese ›Lücken‹ in der dunklen Schicht kann man mit einem Mikro-Fotometer oder Mikro-Densitometer ausmessen. Dabei wird die Durchlässigkeit des Negativs mit einer Messblende von 48 Mikrometer, das entspricht einem Vergrößerungsfaktor 12 x, ausgemessen. Die Proben haben eine mittlere (oder Makro-) Negativdichte von lg D 0,7. Je größer die ›Lücken‹, desto mehr Licht kommt bei der Messzelle an und signalisiert eine größere Dichte-Abweichung. Den Wert könnte man im übertragenen Sinne als Delta lg Mikrodichte ansehen. In der Praxis können wir subjektive Vergleiche anstellen, wobei unsere Werte sehr stark vom verwendeten Filmentwickler abhängig sind:

- ***Gattung 1 = RMS 17***
  Hochempfindliche Filme um 400 ISO
  (HP5p, UP400p,Tri X;T-MAX 400, Neopan 400)
- ***Gattung 2 = RMS 9***
  Mittelempfindliche Filme um 100/125 ISO
  (FP4p, UP100p, Plus X, T-Max 100, Neopan 100)
- ***Gattung 3 = RMS 5***
  Niedrigempfindliche Filme um 25 ISO
  (Agfapan 25, UP 25p)
  Für die Umsetzung dieser Werte in die tägliche Praxis können folgende Anhaltswerte dienen, wobei der Betrachtungs-Abstand jeweils 40 cm und kein Korn erkennbar ist.
- ***Gattung 1*** = Vergrößerungsfaktor ca. 5,5-fach
- ***Gattung 2*** = Vergrößerunfsfaktor ca. 8-fach
- ***Gattung 3*** = Vergrößerunfsfaktor ca. 12-fach

Natürlich sind diese Bewertungen vom Beleuchtungs-System des Vergrößerers abhängig. Die Auswahl des Materials für bestimmte Aufgaben sollte aber immer die bestmögliche Tonalität sein und nicht die Körnigkeit. Für praktisch kornfreie Vergrößerungen gibt es Spezialfilme in Kombination mit dem LP-DOCUFINE LC.
Dies sind KODAK TECHNICAL PAN, MACO ORT 25clear, MACO Technical Pan TP 64clear.

26. ***Cosa significa Route Mean Sqare (RMS)?*** La grana indica la grandezza dei granuli dei cristalli di alogenuri non sviluppati, e sono quei grani, che creano disturbo nell'osservazione di una stampa positiva.
I granuli d'argento sviluppati si accumulano sovrapponendosi ed agglomerandosi, lasciando nello strato.
Dei ›buchi‹, che in fase di stampa lasciano passare luce che lascia sul positivo tanti puntini neri.
Nelle ombre questi puntini sprofondano, ma nelle luci punteggiano p.es. i cieli. Questi ›buchi‹ nello strato scuro possono essere misurati con un Micro-Foto-(Densito)-Metro. Viene così misurata la trasparenza del negativo con un diaframma di 48 mm, che corrisponde ad un fattore d'ingrandimento di 12 x. Le prove hanno una densità del negativo pari a lg 0,7. Maggiori sono i ›buchi‹, più luce raggiunge la cellula di misurazione e segnala una maggiore differenza di densità. Il valore in senso lato, potrebbe essere visto come microdensità Delta lg.
Nella pratica possiamo invece fare confronti soggettivi, Anche se dipendono moltissimo dal tipo di sviluppo per pellicole utilizzato:

- ***Famiglia 1 = RMS 17***
  Pellicole ad alta sensibilità intorno a ISO 40/27°
  (HP5 Plus, UP 400 Plus, Tri-X. T-Max 400, Neopan 400)
- ***Famiglia 2 = RMS 9***
  Pellicole a media sensibilità intorno a ISO 100-125/21-22°
  (FP4 Plus,UP100 Plus, Plus-X, T-Max 100, Neopan 100)
- ***Famiglia 3 = RMS 5***
  Pellicole a bassa sensibilità intorno a ISO 25/15°
  (APX 25, UP 25 Plus)

Per il trasferimento di questi dati alla pratica giornaliera possono servire i seguenti valori di riferimento, dove ad una distanza di visione di 40 cm non si riesce a riconoscere alcuna grana.

- ***Famiglia 1*** = Fattore d'ingrandimento di ca. 5,5 x
- ***Famiglia 2*** = Fattore d'ingrandimento di ca. 8 x
- ***Famiglia 3*** = Fattore d'ingrandimento di ca. 12 x

Naturalmente questa valutazione dipende sia dal sistema di illuminazione che dall'ingranditore. La scelta del materiale per adempiere ai rispettivi compiti dovrebbe sempre mettere in primo piano la tonalità e non la grana. Per ingrandimenti in pratica privi di grana esistono pellicole speciali, che in combinazione allo sviluppo LP-DOKUFINE LC danno inoltre stampe nitide e ad ampia resa tonale: KODAK TECHNICAL PAN, MACO ORT 25clear, MACO Technical Pan TP 64clear.

25A ***Eksponering*** av MACO UP 64clear for sort/hvitt lysbilder. I motsetning til eksponering av filmer for negativframkalling, hvor en tar hensyn til skyggepartiene, skal en ved eksponering av MACO UP 64clear (alle MACO clear filmer er egnet for lysbildeframkalling) ta mer hensyn til høylysene. Ved integral lysmåling benyttes en høyere EI. 50 ISO som negativ og 64 ISO for lysbilder.

26. ***Hva betyr Route Mean Square (RMS)?*** Med korn menes kornstørrelsen av uframkallte sølvhalogenider, dedtte er da korn som virker forstyrrende ved forstørrelse.De framkallte sølvkornene samler seg og overlapper hverandre og det oppstår ›hull‹ i skiktet som slipper igjennom lys ved forstørrelse og det dannes da små sorte prikker. I skyggepartier forsvinner disse prikkene, men i høylys virker de forstyrrende. Disse ›hullene‹ i det mørke partiene kan måles med et micro-foto-densitometer.
Da blir gjennomskinnligheten til negativet målt gjennom et hull med 48 um, noe som tilsvarer en forstørrelsesfaktor på 12 x. Prøvene har en negativtetthet på lg D 0,7. Jo større ›hull‹ det er i negativet, jo mer lys kan trenge igjennom og komme til målecellen. De indikerer da et større avvik i tetthet. Denne verdien kan en overført se som Delta lg mikrotetthet. I praksis kan vi gjøre subjektive sammenlikninger. Valget av framkaller vil kunne påvirke vårt inntrykk.

- ***Gruppe 1 = RMS 17***
  Høyfølsomme filmer på ca 400 ISO
  (Ilford HP5p, MACO UP 400plus, KODAK Tri X og T-MAX 400, FUJI Neopan 400)

Gruppe 2 = RMS 9
  Mellomfølsomme filmer med ca 100 ISO (ILFORD FP 4, MACO UP 100plus, KODAK PLUS X og T-MAX 100, FUJI Neopan 100)

Gruppe 3 = RMS 5
  Lavfølsommefilmer med ca 25 ISO (AGFA APX 25 og MACO UP 25plus)

For praktisk bruk kan følgende verdier tjene som utgangspunkt, når betraktningsavstanden en 40 cm og korn ikke skal være synlig.

- ***Gruppe 1*** = forstørrelsesfaktor ca 5,5
- ***Gruppe 2*** = forstørrelsesfaktor ca 8
- ***Gruppe 3*** = forstørrelsesfaktor ca 12

Dette er naturligvis avhengig av hvilket lyssystem forstørrelsesapparatet har. Viktig for valg av material burde alltid være best mulig tonegjenngivelse og ikke kornethet. Det finnes spesielle filmer som i kombinasjon med LP-DOCUFINE LC praktisk er kornløse. (KODAK TECHNICAL PAN, MACO ORT 25clear, MACO TECHNICAL PAN TP 64clear)

26. What does Root Mean Square (RMS) mean?

›Graininess‹ refers to the size of the developed silver halide crystals, i.e. those grains that look unpleasant in the print.
Developed silver grains gather, clumping and overlapping, leaving ›gaps‹ in the emulsion. During printing, these gaps let the light pass, which means they register as black dots in the print.
These black dots ›drown‹ in the shadows, but in lighter areas which ought to be rendered as areas of uniform density, e.g. the sky, they lead to mottling. The ›gaps‹ in the photographic emulsion can be measured using a microdensitometer. The transmittance of the negative is measured using a 48-micrometer aperture, which corresponds to 12 times linear enlargement. Samples have a macroscopic negative density of 0.7 log D. The larger the ›gaps‹, the more light the photometric cell will detect, and the greater the deviation from macrodensity that will be indicated. In a sense, one could see this value as a delta log micro-density.
In practice, we may compare results subjectively, the values varying significantly with the developer used:

Type 1 = RMS 17
High-speed films around ISO 400 (HP5p, UP400p, Tri X, T-Max 400, Neopan 400)
Type 2 = RMS 9
Medium-speed films around ISO 100 (FP4p, UP100p, Plus X, T-Max 100, Neopan 100)
Type 3 = RMS 5
Slow films around ISO 25 (Agfapan 25, UP25p)

As to the practical application of these values: The following reference values give the enlargement factor at which no grain is visible when the print is viewed at a distance of 40 cm (16 in):

- ***Type 1 =*** approx. enlargement factor 5.5 times
- ***Type 2 =*** approx. enlargement factor 8 times
- ***Type 3 =*** approx. enlargement factor 12 times

The evaluation is obviously influenced by the lighting system of the enlarger used. When selecting a material for a specific task, however, the best possible tonality, rather than graininess, should be the criterion. For practically grainless enlargements, there are special films in combination with LP-DOCUFINE LC.
These are KODAK TECHNICAL PAN, MACO ORT 25clear, MACO TECHNICAL PAN TP 64clear.

MACO UP400plus, Canon FD 50-mm, 1/15 + 2, f1.4, developed in LP-CUBE XS, exposed with WA40 mm, exposure time 14s, 5.6 - on MACO expo RF, graded baryta paper, glossy, grade 4.
© Valsasnini

27. Was bedeutet Auflösungs-Vermögen oder Modulations-Übertragungs-Funktion (MTF)?

Das Maß für die Schärfewiedergabe kleinster Details wurde bisher durch das *Auflösungsvermögen in Linienpaaren je Millimeter* ausgedrückt, die auf dem entwickelten Film noch getrennt wiedergegeben werden.
Dieses Verfahren ist ohne Einschränkungen noch bei Lith- und Halbtonfilmen sinnvoll.
Halbtonfilme wurden bisher auch so miteinander ›verglichen‹. Dies entspricht jedoch nicht der Praxis, dem täglichen Leben eines Fotografen (!). Die Vergleiche werden mit Mikroskopie-Objektiven mit höchstem Auflösungsvermögen durchgeführt.
Im Gegensatz dazu schaffen die in der ›normalen‹ bildmäßigen Fotografie eingesetzten Objektive allenfalls bis zu 50 Lp/mm. Schärfe oder Unschärfe kann besser an einer Lichtkante mit ihrem nun mal nicht vermeidbarem Diffusionslichthof beurteilt werden. Der Diffusionslichthof ist abhängig vom Lichthofschutz des Filmmaterials und geht daher unmittelbar in die Kantenschärfe ein.
Die MTF-Kurven sind im unteren Frequenz-Bereich 110 %-tig, d.h. der Kontrast an der Kante bei 3-15 Lp/mm wird vom Film ›überhöht‹ wiedergegeben.
Das ist abhängig vom ›Kanteneffekt‹ des Entwicklers. Im Kantenbereich treten von der nicht belichteten Zone, wo der Entwickler nur wenig beansprucht wird, noch reichlich vorhandene frische Entwicklersubstanzen innerhalb der Schicht in die belichteten Kanten Bereiche ein, wo der Entwickler ›arbeiten‹ muss und schon mehr oder weniger stark verbraucht ist und bewirken die Ausentwicklung der belichteten Kristalle. Es kommt zu einer ›überhöhten‹ Schwärzung im Bereich der Kante. Im stark belichteten Bereich werden andererseits mehr Inhibitoren (Bromide) freigesetzt, die sich über die Hell-Dunkel-Grenze hinweg in den wenig belichteten Bereich ausbreiten und dort die ohnedies geringe Dichte durch Verlangsamung der Entwicklung weiter herabsetzen. Dadurch wird der Helligkeitssprung hell nach dunkel an der Kante noch verstärkt, was den Schärfeeindruck verbessert.

Bewertung der MTF-Kurven:
Die Schärfe ist abhängig vom Verlauf der Kurve 3 - 20 Lp/mm, wie weit die Überhöhung der Kantenschärfe reicht. Von da ab sackt die Kurve je nach Modulation prozentual ab. Wir empfehlen den Bereich von 20 - 35 Lp/mm als Bewertungskriterium zu verwenden. Hier sind die Kurven der Hersteller am besten unterscheidbar.

Wie bei der RMS-Messung werden aufbelichtete Raster mit einem Mikro-Densitometer in ihrer Übertragungsfunktion ausgemessen. Die Kantenschärfe ist von der Kristallform, der Wirksamkeit des Lichthofschutzes und der Entwicklergattung abhängig.

27. Cosa significa potere risolutivo / Funzione di trasmissione e modulazione (MTF)?

La misura per la riproduzione della nitidezza di minimi dettagli veniva fin ad oggi espressa in *potere Risolvente per Millimetro* e vengono riprodotte ancora separatamente rispetto alla pellicola sviluppata. Questa procedura è significativa senza limitazioni ancora con le pellicole Lith- e a mezza tinta.
Le pellicole tradizionali sono fino ad ora state ›confrontate‹ fra loro con questi criteri. Questi però non corrispondono alla pratica della vita giornaliera di un fotografo (!). Questi confronti vengono eseguiti con obiettivi da microscopio caratterizzati dal massimo potere risolvente. Al contrario i ›normali‹ obiettivi da ripresa utilizzati per la fotografia tradizionale raggiungono ›appena‹ 50 Lp/mm. Nitidezza o sfuocatura può essere meglio giudicata ad un taglio di luce con l'inevitabile alone di luce diffusa. L'alone di luce diffusa dipende dallo strato antialone del materiale fotosensibile e la capacità di nitidezza a taglio.
Le curve MTF nel campo di frequenza inferiore è del 110 %, ovvero il contrasto al taglio a 3-15 Lp/mm viene riprodotto dalla pellicola in modo ›eccedente‹. Questo dipende dall'effetto-taglio dello sviluppo. Nel campo di taglio affiorano lateralmente sostanze di sviluppo fresco dalle zone non esposte verso le zone di taglio esauste però esposte e provocano lo sviluppo a fondo dei cristalli esposti. Si provoca un ›eccessivo‹ annerimento della linea di taglio e conferisce un'impressione di nitidezza.

Valutazione delle curve MTF:
La nitidezza dipende dall'andamento della curva 3 - 20 Lp/mm, fino a dove arriva il superamento della nitidezza di taglio. Da questo punto in poi la curva crolla a seconda della modulazione in %tuale. Consigliamo di prendere quale criterio di valutazione la fascia da 20 - 35 Lp/mm. Qui le curve dei produttori sono meglio differenziate.

Come nella misurazione RMS i retini esposti vengono misurati con un micro-densitometro nella loro funzione di trasmissione. La nitidezza dei bordi dipende dalla forma del cristallo, dalla efficacia dello strato antialone e dalla famiglia di sviluppo. Più nella prova si avvicinano i bordi del retino, maggiormente lo strato antialone di diffusione copre gli interspazi, non vengono più dissolti.
La nitidezza dei bordi è una funzione del modello di retino, anche in linee/mm, verso l'effettiva risoluzione misurabile del materiale sviluppato. La funzione di trasmissione viene inserita in % al disopra della frequenza del diagramma del modello in Lp/mm.

27. Hva betyr oppløsningevne / modulasjons overførings funksjon (MTF)?

Måleenheten for skarphet av minste detaljer ble inntil nydlig uttrykt ved oppløsning pr mm av linjer som ble gjennigtt adskilt. Denne metoden er fortsatt hensiktsmessig for lith og halvtonefilmer. Halvtonefilmer er til nå blitt sammenliknet på denne måten. Dette passer ikke med praksis hos en fotograf, da testene blir gjordt med høyoppløslige mikroskopluper. I motsetning til slike objektiver har normale objektiver en oppløsning på 50 linjepar pr mm. Skarphet eller uskarphet kan måles bedre ved en lysbrytningskant som jo også bestemmes av diffusjonsskiktet som igjen er avhengig av antihalogenasjonsskiktet i filmen ogsom derfor direkte påvirker lysbrytningskanten.
MTF- kurvene er i det nedre frekvensområdet 110% ige, dvs, kontrasten ved lysbrytningskanten ved 3 til 15 linjepar/mm blir gjenngitt overproposjonalt. Dette er avhengig av kanteffekten til framkalleren. I lysbrytningskantområdet kommer frisk framkaller fra det ubelyste området over det området som er blii belyst, noe som fører til en sterkere framkalling av krystallene her. Denne overdrevne sværtningen gir inntrykk av skarphet.

Forstå en MTF kurve: Skarpheten er avhengig av hvordan kurven som beskriver 3-20 linjepar/mm forløper, og hvor langt den overdrevne kantskarpheten rekker. Etter dette synker kurven i forhold til modulasjonen prosentvis. Vi anbefaler området 20-35 linjepar/mm som kriterium for en bedømmelse. Her er det lettest å skille kurvene fra hver enkelt produsent. Som ved RMS målingen blir et kopiert raster målt med det mikro-foto-densitomenter for å finne overføringsfunksjonen. Kantskarpheten er avhengig av krystallformen, virkningen av antihalogenasjonsskiktet, og den valgte framkallertypen. Jo nærmere kantene på prøven komme, jo mer dekker diffusjonskiktet mellomromene, og oppløsningen synker. Kantskarpheten er derfor en funksjon av det kopierte rasteret, også i linjepar/mm, til den virkelig målbare oppløsningen av det framkalte materiale. Denne overføringsfunksjonen blir uttrykt i prosent av den målte frekvensen til orginalen gjenngitt i linjepar/mm.

27. What do the terms ›resolving power‹ (resolution) and ›modulation transfer function‹ (MTF) mean?

To date, the measure for the sharpness of very fine detail was the RESOLVING POWER given as the number LINE PAIRS per MILLIMETER resolved, i.e. recognisable as separate lines, in the negative.
The method does make sense for lith films.
Even halftone films were ›compared‹ on these terms, although this is not realistic, i.e. not related to the photographer's routine. Comparisons are made using microscope lenses with very high resolving powers. Contrary to this practice, lenses used in ›normal‹ pictorial photography will not resolve beyond 50 lp/mm. Sharpness is better judged by evaluating the boundary between a light and a dark area with its unavoidable halation. Halation depends on the anti-halation treatment and is thus of immediate concern to border sharpness.
In the low-frequency range, MTF curves are at 110 per cent, meaning that border contrast in the range between 3 and 15 lp/mm is exaggerated. This depends on the acutance, or adjacency, or border, effect of the developer. In the vicinity of the border, fresh developer diffuses from the unexposed area, where there is not much silver halide to reduce, and not much developer is depleted, into the exposed area to replace depleted developer there, carrying on development of the exposed crystals. Density at the border is thus raised. On the other hand, more restraining reaction products (bromides) are released in the exposed area, which wander across the border into the less exposed area and restrain development there, reducing the already low density further. In total, the density step in enlarged, enhancing the impression of sharpness.

Evaluation of MTF curves:

Sharpness depends on what a curve does in the range between 3 to 20 lp/mm, on how far the exaggerated acutance, or border sharpness, reaches. From there onwards, the curve falls off, its slope depending on modulation. We recommend to make the range between 20 and 35 lp/mm the basis of your evaluation. This is where the curves of different manufacturers can best be distinguished. As with the RMS measurement, line grids are printed, and the MTF function is measured using a microdensitometer. Acutance depends on the shape of the crystals, the effectiveness of the anti-halation treatment, and the type of developer. The closer the lines of the grid lie together, the more the gaps between them will be smoothened out by halation, and they are not resolved any more. Acutance is a function of the grid pattern printed, also in lines per millimetre, over the actual resolution of the developed material, which can be measured. The transfer function is plotted as percentage over the spatial frequency, in lp/mm, of the test pattern.

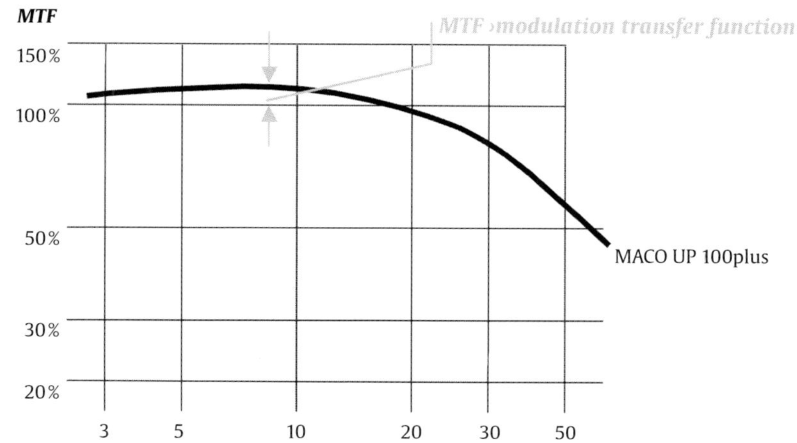

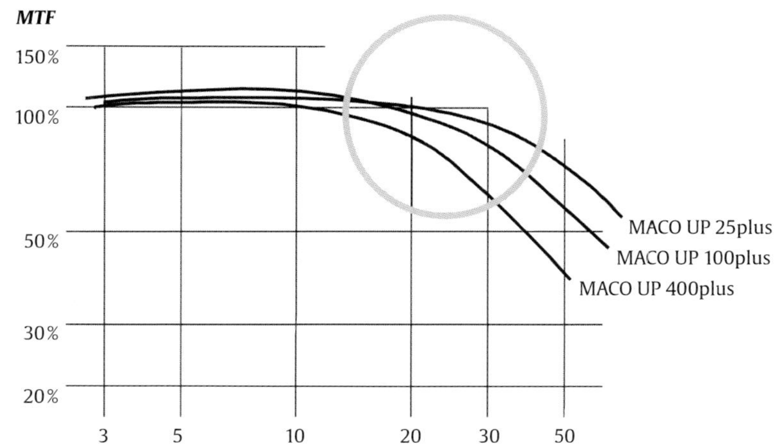

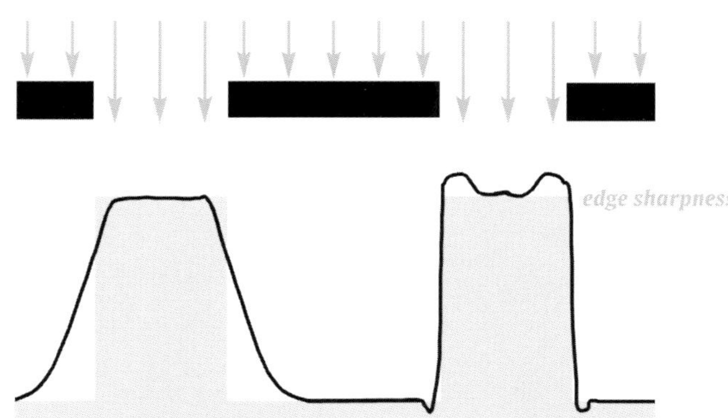

Je näher sich die Kanten des Rasters bei der Probe kommen, um so mehr deckt der Diffusionslichthof die Zwischenräume zu, sie werden nicht mehr aufgelöst. Die Kantenschärfe ist eine Funktion der aufbelichteten Rastervorlage, auch in Lp/mm, zu der tatsächlichen messbaren Auflösung des entwickelten Materials. Die Übertragungs-Funktion wird in % über der Ortsfrequenz der Vorlage in Lp/mm aufgetragen.

27A ***Erwin Puts:***
In der deutschen Fachzeitschrift SCHWARZWEISS schrieb der niederländische Fotograf zu der Frage:
„Was bedeutet es, wenn man 400 Lp/mm auf dem Negativ abbildet?“ (Anlass für diesen Artikel war die Anwendung des AGFA COPEX PAN Mikrofilms in Kombination mit einem low contrast Spezialentwickler.)
„Das Auge kann aus 25 cm Entfernung bestenfalls 10 Lp/mm wahrnehmen, in der Regel sogar nur 5 Lp/mm (!). Um 400 Lp/mm tatsächlich sehen zu können, brauchen wir die vierzig- bis achtzigfache Vergrößerung, also einen Abzug mit einer Breite von 1,5 bis drei Metern. Die Mehrzahl der Leistungsbeispiele hat das Format 30 x 40 cm, also einen Vergrößerungsfaktor von etwa zwölf. Das bedeutet, dass man überhaupt nur feine Strukturen mit dem blossen Auge wahrnehmen kann, die um 120 bis 160 Lp/mm liegen. In der Praxis wird man sich schwer tun, 80 Lp/mm zu registrieren. Wenn man sich auf dieser Hochleistungsebene bewegt, gibt es eine Unmenge von Störeinflüssen, die das Ergebnis verfälschen können. Die Qualität der Aufnahme- und Vergrößerungs-Objektive, die Filmplanlage, eine genaue Belichtung und Fokussierung, die Wahl des Entwicklers, die Erschütterung des Kamera-Gehäuses beim Auslösen und derlei mehr. Wenn jemand nun versucht, die sagenhaften 400 Lp/mm zu erreichen und er bekommt auf dem Negativ ›nur‹ 50 Lp/mm zustande, dann gibt es eine Menge Ausreden, warum er die erhofften feinsten Details nicht sieht.“
(Anmerkung: Diese Argumentation, wiewohl scheinbar plausibel, ist anfechtbar. Ctein (Post Exposure) hat in verschiedenen Artikeln gezeigt, dass Schärfe und Auflösung nicht dasselbe sind, und dass der Schärfeeindruck von Ortsfrequenzen bestimmt wird, die um den Faktor 3 (!) über dem Auflösungsvermögen liegen. Man kann auch wie folgt argumentieren: Die besten Augen sehen bei den bewussten 25 cm 10 lp/mm im Papierbild. Nach den schlechtesten wollen wir uns ja wohl nicht richten. Für den Schärfeeindruck sind also die Kennwerte bis 30 Lp/mm im Papierbild wichtig. 30 Lp/mm im Papierbild bei einem Print 20x25 cm verlangen rund 250 Lp/mm im Negativ, also so weit sind wir nicht von den sagenhaften 400 Lp/mm entfernt!)

27A ***Erwin Puts:***
Nella rivista tecnica tedesca ›SCHWARZWEISS‹ il fotografo olandese Erwin Puts scriveva:
„Cosa significa se si illustrano 400 Lp/mm su un negativo?“ (Il motivo di questo articolo era l'utilizzo della pellicola AGFA COPEX PAN Mikrofilms in combinazione ad uno sviluppo speciale ›low contrast‹.)
„L'occhio umano riesce a percepire 10 Lp/mm da una distanza di 25 cm, in regola solo 5 Lp/mm. (!) Per essere in grado di vedere effettivamente 400 Lp/mm, abbiamo bisogno di un ingrandimento da quaranta a ottanta volte, ovvero una stampa di una larghezza di 1,5 fino 3 metri. La maggior parte degli esempi di prestazioni sono del formato 30x40 cm, ovvero un fattore d'ingrandimento di ca. dodici volte. Ciò significa, che ad occhio nudo si riescono a percepire solo fini strutture, che si aggirano a 120 fino 160 Lp. In pratica si faticherà a recepire 80 Lp/mm.
Quando ci si muove su un livello così alto, esiste un enorme quantità di fattori di disturbo, che possono falsificare il risultato: La qualità degli oggetti ripresi ed ingranditi, la planearità della pellicola, l'esatta esposizione e la messa a fuoco, la scelta dello sviluppo, le vibrazioni dell'apparecchio durante la posa, ed altri ancora. Se ora qualcuno prova a raggiungere i fatidici 400 Lp/mm e poi sul negativo riesce a trasmettere ›solo‹ 50 Lp/mm, questi, con molte scusanti cerca di spiegare perché non vede i dettagli più fini.“

27A ***Erwin Puts:***
I det tyske fagtidsskriftet ›SCHWARZWEISS‹ skrev den nederlandske fotografen Erwin Puts følgende:
„Hva betyr det når man har 400 linjepar/mm på negativet?“
(Grunnen til artikkelen var bruken av AGFA COPEX PAN Mikrofilm i kombinasjon med en spesial lavkontrast fremkaller.)
„Øyet kan, på 25 cm avstand i bestefall skille 10 linjepar/mm, som regle er det 5 linjepar/mm(!). For virkelig å kunne se 400 linjepar/mm trenger vi førti til åttigangers forstørrelse, alså en kopi på 1,5 x 3 meter. De fleste eksemplene har formatet 30 x 40 cm, dvs en forstørrelsesfaktor på 12. Dette betyr at en kun kan oppfatte fine strukturer mellom 120 til 160 linjepar/mm med det blotte øye. I praksis er det vanskelig å oppfatte noe over 80 linjepar/mm. Når en gir seg inn på dette ekstremnivået er det en uendelig mengde med feilkilder som vil kunne forfalske resultatet. Kvaliteten på opptaks og forstørrelses objektivene, filmen planhet, en nøyaktig eksponering og fokusering, valget av framkaller, bevegelsene i kamera ved utløsing etc. Hvis noen nå forsøker å få til disse fantastiske 400 linjeparene/mm og det ›bare‹ blir 50 linjepar/mm på negativet, så finnes det alså mange unnskyldninger på hvorfor man ikke ser de fineste detajene som man håpet på.“

27A **Erwin Puts:**
In the German b&w photography journal SCHWARZWEISS, Dutch photographer Erwin Puts wrote:
„What does it mean when you image 400 lp/mm in your negative?“ (The article was dedicated to the use of AGFA COPEX PAN microfilm in combination with a special low-contrast developer. Note by the editor.)
„From a distance of 25 cm (10 in), the eye can resolve 10 lp/mm at its very best, most eyes will only resolve 5 lp/mm. In order to be able to actually see 400 lp/mm, we need a 40 to 80 times enlargement, a print, thus, whose side measures between 1.5 and 3 metres. The majority of examples of film performance are 30 by 40 cm (12 by 16 in) prints, which means enlargement is roughly 12 times. This, in turn, means that the eye can only perceive fine detail at 120 to 160 lp/mm. Practically, 80 lp/mm are already a challenge. When working at this level of high performance, there are many interfering effects which can affect the results: the quality of taking and enlarging lenses, film flatness, precise exposure, and focusing, the selection of the developer, camera shake when the shutter is released, and more. For someone trying to reach the elusive 400 lp/mm, who will not get beyond 50 lp/mm, there are lots of excuses why the fine detail hoped for is not visible.“

MACO PO 100clear , Canon FD 50-mm, 1/30 + 2, f1.4, developed in LP-CUBE XS, exposed with WA40 mm, exposure time 18s, 5.6 – on MACO expo RF, graded baryta paper, glossy, grade 3.
© Valsasnini

28. *Fixage und Wässerung:*

28A ***Filmfixierzeiten:*** In alten und aus unserer Sicht überholten Foto-Lehrbüchern werden Fixierzeiten von bis zu einer Stunde empfohlen. Diese Zeiten basieren meist auf der Verwendung von Natriumthiosulfat als Fixiersubstanz in Fixierbädern.
Heute haben praktisch nur noch Fixierbäder auf Basis von Ammoniumthiosulfat eine Bedeutung. Diese benötigen nur noch kurze Fixier- und Wässerungszeiten.
Nach dem Fixieren ist gründlich zu wässern. Damit werden das Fixiersalz und die übrigen Salze aus der Gelatineschicht gewaschen. Frische Fixierbäder sind unproblematisch. Gebrauchte Fixierbäder müssen erst einmal geprüft werden. Dafür nimmt man einen nicht entwickelten Filmstreifen. Diesen hält man in das Fixierbad. Die Zeit, die der Film benötigt, um klar zu werden, nennt man die Klärzeit.
■ ***Die Fixierzeit*** ist die doppelte Klärzeit, bei Filmen mit speziellen Kristallformen (KODAK T-MAX, ILFORD DELTA) die dreifache. Ein gebrauchtes Fixierbad sollte durch ein frisches ersetzt werden, wenn die Klärzeit mit einem gegebenen Film doppelt so lang ist wie mit demselben Film bei frischem Bad.
■ ***Facit:*** Lange Fixierzeiten gehören jetzt der Vergangenheit an (!). Heute sind lange Fixierzeiten sogar schädlich, denn dabei kann das Fixierbad die geringen Dichten angreifen.
Das soll jedoch kein Anlass sein, wieder zum ›guten alten‹ Natriumthiosulfat zurückzukehren. Sobald man es sich angewöhnt hat, die Stopp- und Fixierzeiten genau so gewissenhaft, wie die Entwicklerzeiten zu beachten, gibt es mit der modernen, Wasser und Zeit sparenden Technologie kein Problem, oder?
Das Fixierbad ist kein Ort, um Bilder ›zwischen zu lagern‹. Derartige Verhaltensweisen gelten als nicht fachgerecht. Die Ausführung in 28A beziehen sich ausschließlich auf das Fixieren von Filmen. Bei dem Fixieren von Papierbildern gelten teilweise hiervon abweichende Bedingungen (dazu mehr in dem Buch ›Schroeders Positiv Praxis‹).

28B ***LABOR PARTNER*** empfiehlt Kaskaden-Wässerung: Bei Filmen und bei Papieren, auch Barytpapieren, ist heute die Kaskadenwässerung ein fester und bewährter Bestandteil der modernen Schwarzweiß-Verarbeitung.
■ ***Das bedeutet:*** Der Inhalt der Filmdose oder der Wässerungsschale wird 8 x vollkommen durch Frischwasser ersetzt. Jede Frischwasserbehandlung dauert 2 (Film) bis 5 (Barytpapier) Minuten bei permanenter Bewegung. So kommt man heute auf Wässerungszeiten von 8 x 2 und bis zu 5 Minuten. Längere Wässerungszeiten sind nicht umweltverträglich.

28. *LABOR PARTNER consiglia il lavaggio a cascata.*

28A ***Tempi di fissaggio:*** Da un vecchio punto di vista di indicazioni di pubblicazioni fotografiche, superate dal nostro punto di vista, tempi di fissaggio di fino ad un ora erano la norma. Questi tempi si basano spesso su bagni di fissaggio a base di tiosolfato quale sostanza di fissaggio. Oggigiorno hanno importanza in pratica solo bagni di fissaggio a base di tiosolfato di ammonio. Questi ultimi implicano solo ancora dei tempi brevi di fissaggio e di lavaggio.
Dopo il fissaggio bisogna lavare per bene. Solo in questo modo si lavano via dallo strato di gelatina i sali di fissaggio e di altri sali.
Bagni di fissaggio freschi non creano problemi. Bagni di fissaggio usati devono essere prima di tutto testati.
Per questa prova si prende uno spezzone di pellicola non sviluppato e lo si immerge nel fissaggio. Il tempo necessario alla pellicola nel diventare trasparente si chiama tempo di chiarificazione. Il tempo di fissaggio necessario è del doppio del tempo di chiarificazione. Se da questo test il tempo di chiarificazione è di oltre 2 minuti, significa che il bagno di fissaggio è da sostituire con un bagno fresco.
■ ***Conclusione:*** I lunghi tempi di fissaggio appartengono al passato (!). Attualmente possiamo dire che lunghi tempi di fissaggio si dimostrano perfino dannosi, in quanto il fissaggio può danneggiare le luci della pellicola. Tutto ciò non deve però indurre a ritornare ai ›vetusti‹ fissaggi a base di tiosolfato. Non appena ci si è abituati ad osservare tempi di arresto e fissaggio con lo stesso scrupolo come quelli di sviluppo, grazie alle nuove tecnologie, si risolvono tutti i problemi risparmiando acqua e tempo.
Il bagno di fissaggio non è semplicemente il luogo dove ›mettere in attesa‹ le immagini. Tali modi comportamentali non fanno parte della professionalità!

28. *LABOR PARTNER anbefaler kasskadespyling:*

28A ***Fikseringstider:*** I gamle, og etter vår sikt uaktuelle fotolærebøker, oppgis fikseringstider med inntil en time. Disse tidene baserer seg på bruk av natriumthiosulfat som fikseringsmiddel. I dag finnes det nesten bare fikserbad som bruker ammuniumthiosulfat. Disse trenger bare korte fiksertiden og korte spyletider. Etter fiksering skal en spyle grundig. Da blir fiksersaltene og øvrige salter fjernet fra gelantinskiktet. Frisk fikser er uproblematisk. Brukte fikserbad bør testes. Til dette formålet brukes uframkalte filmbiter. Disse blir lagt i fikserbadet. Tiden som film bruker på å bli helt klar blir kalt klarningstid. Fikseringstiden er det dobbelte av denne. Overstiger klaringstiden 2,5 min, bør en lage et nytt fikseringsbad. Fasit: Lange fikseringstider tilhører historien. I dag er lange tider til og med skadelige, da høylysene i filmen vil bli skadet. Dette er ikke en grunn til å gå tilbake til gammel-dagse natriumthiosulfat fikserer. Hvis en venner seg til å passe på stoppebad og fikser tidene på samme måte som en er nøyaktig med framkallertider, så er det ingen problem å bruke dn moderne fikser teknologien. Fikserbadet er ikke noe sted å oppbevare bilder før spylig. Det ville ikke hensiktsmessig.

28B ***Kaskadespyling:*** Ved film og papir (også barytt papir) framkalling er kaskadespyling i dag en viktig del av moderne sort/hvitt framkallings metodikk. Dette betyr: Vannet i framkallingsboksen eller i spyleskålen byttes helt med rent vann 8 x. Slik kan en få spyletiden på 8 x 2 min for film og helt ned i 5 min for barytpapir. Lange spyletider er ikke gunstige for miljøet.

28. *Film fixing times:*

28A ***Recommendations*** in old – and, if you ask us – outdated books teaching photography mention fixing times of up to one hour. These recommendations are mostly based on the use of sodium thiosulphate as fixing agent. Nowadays, only ammonium thiosulphate fixers have any practical relevance. They only require short fixing and washing times.
Wash thoroughly after fixing. This removes the fixing agent and any other residual salts from the emulsion.
Fresh fixing baths are not a problem. Used fixer must be checked first. Use an undeveloped strip of film for this purpose. Dip it in the fixer. The time it takes the film to become clear is called the clearing time. The fixing time is twice the clearing time, or three times the clearing time in case of films with special crystal shapes (KODAK T-MAX, ILFORD DELTA). When the clearing time for a given film is twice as long as it is for the same film with fresh fixer, replace the fixer by a fresh bath.
So: Long fixing times are history. Nowadays, long fixing times are even harmful as the fixing bath may bleach away the low densities.
This, however, should not be the reason to return to "old-fashioned" sodium thiosulphate. As soon as you get accustomed to observing stopping and fixing times with the same precision as developing times there is no problem with modern, water- and time-saving technology. Is there?
The fixing tray is not an intermediate storage for prints. Such a practice is not considered as "state of the art".

28B ***LABOR PARTNER*** recommends cascade washing for films and papers, even FB papers, cascade washing has become proven routine practice in modern b&w processing.
What does it mean? Use 8 washing cycles of 2 (for film) to 5 (for FB paper) minutes each, with permanent agitation, completely replacing the water in the tank or tray by fresh water each time. This makes for washing times of 8 times 2 minutes up to 8 times 5 minutes. More than this is not environmentally acceptable today.

MACO ORT 25clear , Leica Summicron 50-mm, 1/30 + 4, f1.4, w/ filter, developed in LP-DOCUFINE LC, exposed with WA40 mm, exposure time 6s, 5.6 – on MACO expo RF, graded baryta paper, glossy, grade 3. © Valsasnini

29. Darf man mit den Fingern in die Entwickler fassen? Nein. Das ist unter allen Umständen zu vermeiden. Im Jahr 2002 muss in der Europäischen Union u.a. Hydrochinon in Entwicklern als krebserregender Bestandteil durch die Hersteller von Fotochemikalien ausgewiesen werden.
Daher sollte spätestens jetzt jeder Laborant diesen Ratschlag ernst nehmen:
■ ***Niemals*** mit ungeschätzten Fingern in Entwickler- oder Tonerlösungen greifen! Durch die ungeschützte Haut können chemische Substanzen direkt in die Blutbahn gelangen (perkutane Aufnahme) und den Laboranten gesundheitlich schädigen. Also achten Sie bitte als Laborant auf Ihre eigene Gesundheit. Wenn Sie als Lehrer oder Ausbilder tätig sind, dann achten Sie bitte darauf, dass die Ihnen Anvertrauten sich entsprechend schützen.

30. Was bedeutet Tonalität oder Tonwert-Differenzierung? Wir finden sehr viele Begriffe für die Beschreibung von Fotos, die aus der Musik stammen. Differenzierung will folgendes ausdrücken: So wie wir kleinste Tonhöhen-Unterschiede wahrnehmen können, wenn jemand falsch singt, so können wir auch feinste Grau- und Farbwert-Unterschiede erkennen. Die Klaviatur der Fotografie ist die Tonwertskala.
Eine Verdoppelung der Lichtmenge entspricht bei einer Zone oder Blende, wie bei der Tonleiter eine Verdopplung der Frequenz einer Oktave.

Eine Zone = eine Oktave

29. Si può inserire un dito nello sviluppo? No. Bisogna evitare a tutti i costi. Dal 2002 in tutta la Comunità Europea anche le componenti di idrochinone presenti nello sviluppo devono essere indicati da parte dei produttori di fotochimica come cancerogeni.
Ecco il motivo per il quale al più tardi ora gli utilizzatori devono prendere sul serio questo consiglio:
■ ***Mai immettere le dita non protette in soluzioni di sviluppo e viraggio (!).***
Sostanze chimiche possono raggiungere direttamente le vie sanguigne attraverso la pelle non protetta (assorbimento percutaneo) e danneggiare la salute degli addetti di laboratorio. Allora riguardi la sua salute!
Docenti e istruttori facciano attenzione di controllare le persone a loro affidate e di sensibilizzarle a riguardo.

30. Cosa significa tonalità, ovvero differenziazione del valore tonale? Troviamo molte definizioni per il giudizio fotografico che provengono dalla musica. Differenziazione vuole definire, come riusciamo a recepire minime differenze di acutezze di suono, quando qualcuno stona; allo stesso modo siamo in grado di riconoscere minime differenze o sfumature di valori nei grigi e nei colori. La tastiera in musica è la scala tonale. Il raddoppio del numero della frequenza di oscillazione corrisponde ad una zona o diaframma, come la scala tonale di un'ottava.

UNA ZONA = UNA OTTAVA

29. Kan en ta med fingrene ned i framkalleren? Nei! Det må i alle fall ungåes. I EU må en, fra 2002, merkes på forpakningene hvis framkalleren innholder det kreftframkallende stoffet hydrochinon. Derfor må den som arbeider i mørkerommet ta dette rådet alvorlig: ALDRI ta ned i framkaller eller tonerbad uten beskyttelse. Gjennom ubeskyttet hud kan kjemiske substanser komme i direkte kontakt med blodet (perkutant opptak) og medføre helseskader. Sett din egen helse i høysete. Som lærer må en sørge for at de en har ansvar for bruker rett beskyttelse.

30. Hva betyr tonalitet hhv gråtonedifferensiering? Det finnes mange begrep i fotografien som stammer fra musikken. Differensiering vil beskrive at vi kan skille de minste tonene fra hverandre, og mensvi merker hvis noen synger falskt, så kan vi også merke de fineste nuanser i gråtoner og fargevarianter. Klaviaturet er i musikken en toneskala. Fordobbles svingningene kommer en til neste sone, i foto vil dette si en blender i musikken en oktav.

En Sone = En Oktav

29. ***Can I dip my fingers in the developer?*** No. Avoid this by all means. As of 2002, photochemistry manufacturers within the European Union, among others, are obliged to declare the hydroquinone contents of developers as carcinogenic. So at least now, every lob worker should take this advice seriously.

■ ***Never*** put unprotected fingers in developer or toner solutions!

Chemical agents may be taken in through unprotected skin and immediately penetrate into the blood vessels (percutaneous ingestion). This may impair the lab worker's health. So please mind your health when working in the laboratory. When working as a tutor or instructor, please make sure that your students protect themselves properly.

30. ***What does ›tonality‹, or ›tonal separation‹ mean?*** Many terms used to describe photographic images originated in music. Separation means that we can distinguish very fine shades of grey and other colours just as we may perceive very fine differences in pitch when a singer misses a note. In music, the keyboard is an image of the pitch.

Just as a doubling of quantity of light corresponds to a zone or f-stop, a doubling of the acoustic frequency corresponds to one octave.

ONE ZONE = ONE OCTAVE

MACO CUBE 400clear, Hasselblad Planar 80-mm, yellow filter, developed in LP-SUPERGRAIN exposed with WA40 mm, exposure time 9s, 5.6 – on MACO expo RF, graded baryta paper, glossy, grade 4.

© Valsasnini

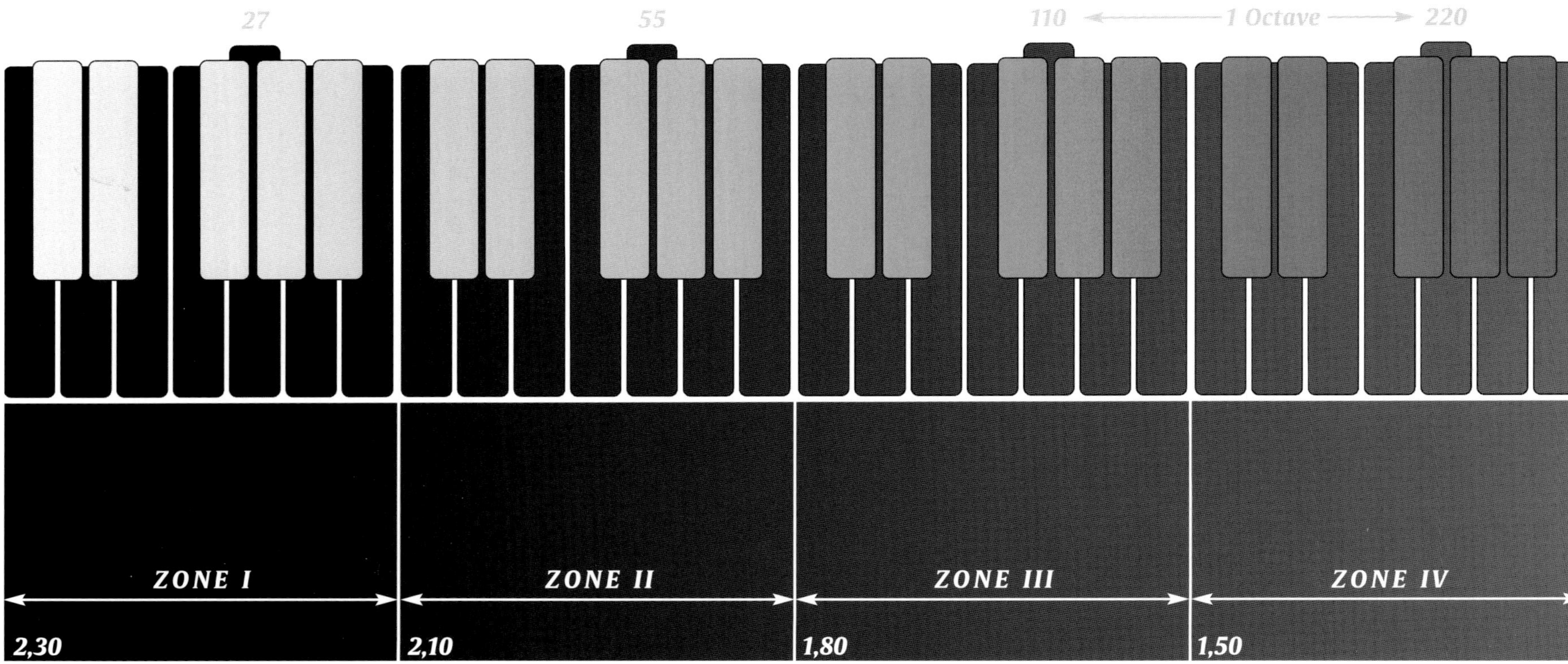

Eine Zone = Eine Oktave.

Low key Bilder sind Fotos mit tiefen, schwarzen Tönen, Low key wie ein Bassschlüssel. High key mit hellen Weißtönen wie entpricht dem Violinschlüssel.
Es ist sicher kein Zufall, dass viele große Fotografen auch anerkannt gute Musiker sind. Herr Richard Müller, der 1917 die ›Argenta fotochemische Werke‹ in München gründete, war ein sehr angesehener bayerischer Komponist und Musiker.
In der Fotografie treffen wir höchste Tonalität bei Diapositiven und im Kino an. Ein Diapositiv kann Kontraste von lg D 0 bis 4,5 übertragen. Dies ist in der Schwarzweißfotografie nur dann möglich, wenn von hervorragenden Negativen die Vergrößerungen anstatt auf Papier, auf dem GENIUS PRINT film angefertigt werden. Es sind dann (und nur dann) ähnlich exzellente Tonwertumfänge zu erreichen. Fotopapiere, spiegelglänzend und auf Barytkarton, schaffen es gerade einmal, auf maximal 2,3 zu kommen. Matte

Una Zona = Una Ottava

Immagini ›Low kay‹ sono foto con toni neri profondi, Low kay come una chiave di basso.
›High kay‹ sono foto con toni bianchi, chiari come una chiave di violino. Non è certo un caso, che grandi fotografi siano anche musicisti rinomati.
Il Signor Richard Mueller, che nel 1917 fondò la ›ARGENTA fotochemische Werke‹, era un compositore e musicista bavarese assai rinomato.
Nel campo fotografico incontriamo tonalità estreme nelle diapositive o al cinema. Una diapositiva può trasmettere contrasti da lgD 0 fino a 4,5. Nella fotografia in bianco/nero ciò è possibile solo se si producono ingrandimenti da negativi eccellenti su GENIUS PRINT film anziché su carta. In quel caso e solo in quel caso si possono ottenere valori tonali eccellenti, paragonabili.
Le carte fotografiche, extra-lucide o su cartoncino baritato riescono a raggiungere al massimo i 2,3, cartoncinio opachi

En Sone = En Oktav

Low key bilder er fotografier med dype svarte toner, Low key er som bass (F)- nøkkelen. High key med lyse hvite toner er som fiolin (G)- nøkkelen. Det er ikke noen tilfeldighet at store fotografer også er gode musikere.
Richard Müller, som grunnla ›Argenta fotochemische Werke‹ i München i 1917, var en annerkjent bayersk musikker og komponist.
I fotografien finner vi den største tonaliteten i lysbilder og på kino. Et lysbilde kan gjenngi kontraster fra lgD o til 4,5. Dette er i sorthvittfotografien bare mulig , hvis et framragende negativ blir forstørret på MACO GENIUS PRINT film i steden for på papir. Bare da kan tilsvarende tonalitet oppnås. Fotopapir, speilblanke og på barytt oppnår maksimalt lgD 2,3, matte papir maksimalt lgD 1,7. Og det er det beste en kan få til. Adams og Weston, forbildene for generasjoner av landskapsfotografer, hadde i sin tid , problemer med å overføre alle gråtonene. De hadde bare faste papir-

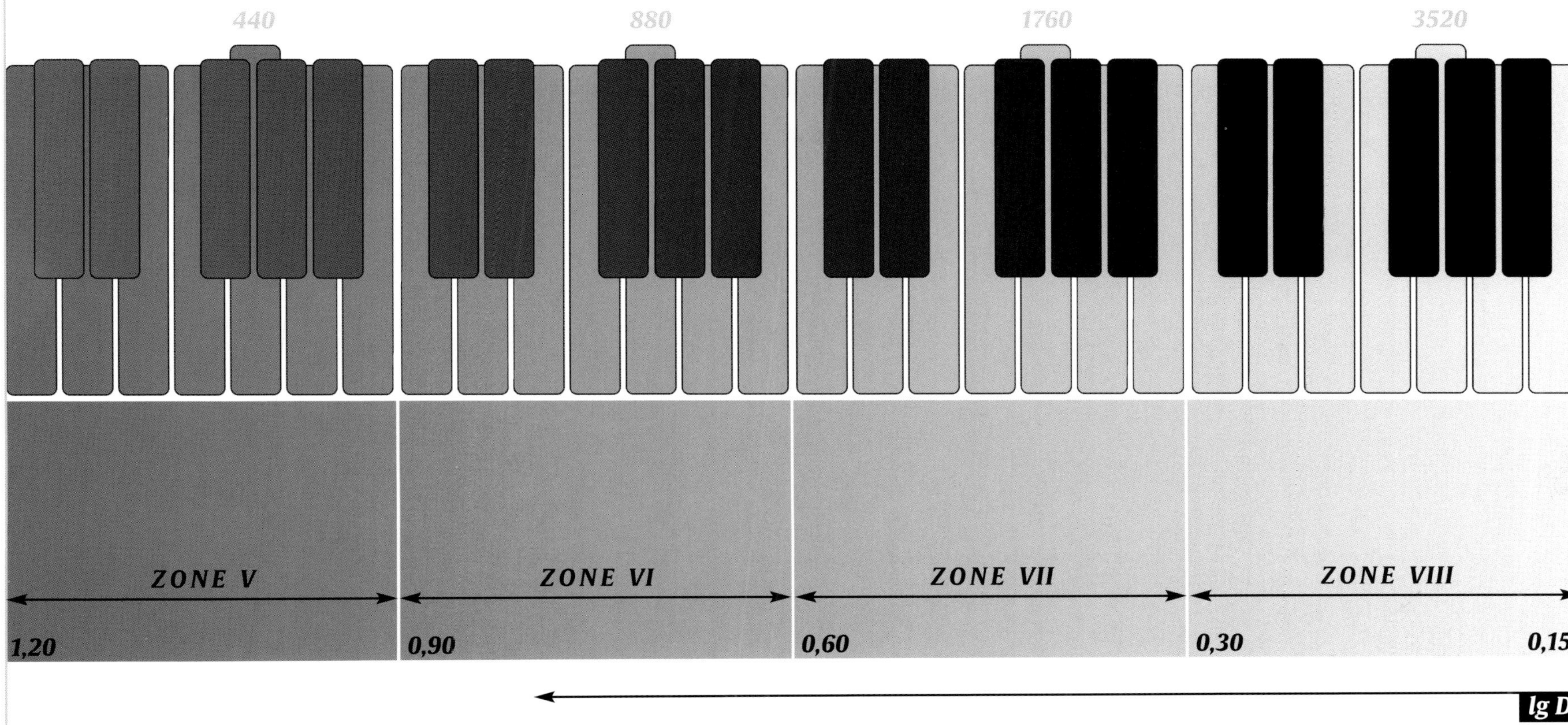

One Zone = One Octave

Low-key images are images with rich blacks, low-key corresponding to a bass clef. High-key, with bright highlights, corresponds to a violin clef.
It is certainly not pure chance that many great photographers are also recognised as proficient musicians.
Richard Müller who, back in 1917, founded ›Argenta Fotochemische Werke‹ in Munich, was a respected Bavarian composer and musician.
In photography, the greatest tonality is found in slides and cinemas. A slide is capable of rendering brightness ranges between log D = 0 and 4.5. In b&w photography, this will only be possible if GENIUS PRINT film is used instead of paper to make prints of excellent negatives. Then (and only then) will tonal ranges of similar excellence be possible.
Photographic papers, glazed and fibre-based, achieve a mere 2.3. Matte papers level off at 1.7.
Adams and Weston, paragons for generations of landscape

Papiere machen bei etwa 1,7 Schluss.
Adams und Weston, die Vorbilder für Generationen von Landschaftsfotografen, hatten es seinerzeit schwer, die vollen Tonwerte zu übertragen.
Es stand seinerzeit ja nur eine Papiergradation zur Verfügung. Diese Meister ihrer Zunft waren daher gezwungen, immer ausgeglichene Negative zu erzeugen. Nur damit waren sie in der Lage, meisterlich die Belichtung und die Entwicklungszeit dem Motivkontrast anzugleichen. Diese tonwertrichtigen Bilder sind großformatige Glasplatten mit viel Silber in der Schicht, die dann im Kontakt auf Chlorbromsilberpapier belichtet wurden. Am Prinzip hat sich nichts geändert, es stimmt immer noch.
Nicht ohne Grund steigt der Verkauf von Großbildformatkameras ständig an. Ein Bild, im Kontakt von einem großformatigen Planfilmnegativ erzeugt, ist von einzigartiger Kraft.

30A ***Tonalität ist nicht gleich Tonalität:*** Die oben bereits angeführten Low key und High key Beispiele zeigen in ihrem begrenzten Kontrast-Umfang zarteste Tonalität, jeweils nur 2-3 Zonen/Oktaven. Die totale Tonalität meint die sanften Abstufungen im gesamten Kontrastumfang, also 7-8 Zonen/Oktaven. Dies ist vom Können des Fotografen, des verwendeten Filmmaterials, vom Können des Laboranten, des verwendeten Papiermaterials und der Fotochemie abhängig.
Im Idealfall passt das Negativ genau zur Normal-Gradation des Papiers, abgestimmt auf die Lichtführung des Vergrößerers. Durchgezeichnete Lichter und Schatten vom reinsten Weiß bis zum tiefsten Schwarz streben alle diejenigen an, die sich mit der anspruchsvollen Schwarzweiß-Fotografie befassen.

30B ***Wie sind die realen Kontrastverhältnisse, abseits der Aufnahmetheorie?*** Es ist üblich, Kontraststufen nur noch im doppelt-logarithmischen Maßstab zu betrachten. In der linearen Darstellung entsprechen log D 0 - 2,3 ein Kontrast von fast 1 : 128. Dies will sagen: Das Weiß ist fast 128 x so hell wie das Schwarz. Im ›normalen Leben‹ kommen kaum Kontrastunterschiede bis 1 : 1.000 vor. Das bedeutet eine brutale Reduzierung der Kontrastverhältnisse. Das menschliche Auge kann das eigentlich nicht überbrücken. Unsere Pupille blendet ab, wenn wir ins Helle schauen. Nicht jeder Fotograf hat den Anspruch, eine Tonalität wie Adams, Weston oder Weidner zu erreichen.
Die 35 mm Filme lassen so etwas sowieso kaum zu, mit Rollfilmen und 4 x 5 Zoll-inch Formaten nähert man sich dem Ziel zumindest. Jeder sucht für sich das ›beste‹ Filmmaterial, den ›idealen‹ Entwickler und ein Papier mit höchstem Silbergehalt bei weißestem Weiß und schwärzestem Schwarz.
■ ***Jeder*** sollte aber auch wissen, das alles das, was er unter-

ca. 1,7 e il dado è tratto!
Adams e Weston, i miti per generazioni di fotografi di paesaggio avevano vita dura nel trasmettere i valori tonali in pieno. Ai tempi solo una gradazione di carta era a disposizione. Questi maestri erano pertanto costretti di produrre sempre negativi compensati. Solo in tal modo erano in grado di adattare in modo magistrale, il tempi di esposizione e il tempo di sviluppo, al contrasto del soggetto. Queste immagini a resa tonale corretta sono su lastre di vetro di grandi dimensioni, con molto argento, poi stampate per contatto su carte al cloro-bromuro d'argento. Nulla di questo principio è mutato , è tutt'oggi giusto, basti pensare al successo che ancora oggi hanno gli apparecchi di grande formato. Una foto stampata a contatto da una pellicola piana di grande formato possiede un impatto ed una forza unica.

30A ***Tonalita' non e' uguale a Tonalita':*** Gli esempi ›Low kay‹ e ›High kay‹ sopra illustrati mostrano nel loro perimetro di contrasto circoscritto delle tonalità delicatissime, solo 2-3 zone/ottave.
Per la tonalità totale si ritiene la graduazione delicata nell'intero ambito di contrasto, cioè 7-8 zone/ottave.
Tutto ciò dipende dalle capacità del fotografo, dal materiale (pellicola) utilizzato, dalle capacità dello stampatore, dal materiale fotosensibile e dalla chimica. Nel caso ideale il negativo si adatta perfettamente alla gradazione normale della carta, fatta quadrare con la regolazione luminosa dell'ingranditore.
Luci e ombre con dettagli dal bianco puro al nero profondo fanno parte delle aspirazioni di tutti coloro che si occupano di esigente fotografia in bianco/nero.

30B ***Cosa sono i reali rapporti di contrasto, a parte la teoria di ripresa?*** E' consuetudine di osservare i gradini di contrasto solo in doppia scala logaritmica. Nella rappresentazione reale 0 – 2,3 log D sono un contrasto di quasi 1 : 128. Ciò vuol dire: Il bianco è quasi 128 x così chiaro rispetto al nero. Nella ›vita normale‹ accade difficilmente una differenza di contrasto fino 1 : 1000.
Ciò significa una riduzione brutale dei rapporti di contrasto, allorché l'occhio umano non riesce a percepire né tantomeno a connettere. La nostra pupilla si comprime (chiude il diaframma), quando osserviamo verso il chiarore. Non tutti i fotografi hanno l'esigenza di ottenere una resa tonale come la intendevano rispettivamente Adams, Weston o Weidner. Le pellicole 35 mm in pratica non lo permettono comunque, con i rollfilm e le pellicole piane 4 x 5″ ci si avvicina quantomeno al traguardo. Ognuno ricerca per sé il "migliore" materiale su pellicola, lo sviluppo ›ideale‹ e la carta fotografica con il più alto contenuto d'argento con i bianchi più puri e i neri più densi.
■ ***Ognuno di voi deve però sapere,*** che tutto ciò che

gradasjoner. Disse kunstens mestre var derfor nødt til å lage negativer som var svært utgjevnte. Bare slik var de i stand til å frambringe sine mesterlig negativer, med en total kontroll over eksponeringstider og framkalling hadde de kontroll over motivkontrastene. Disse negativene, med rette gråtoner for storformat glassplater med mye sølv i skiktet som så ble kontaktkopiert på klorbrompapir. Dette prinsippet har ikke endret seg. Ikke uten grunn øker salget av storformatkamera. Et bilde, som kontakt fra et storformatnegativ har en enestående kraft.

30A ***Tonalitet er ikke lik tonalitet.*** De tidligere nevnte High-key og Low-key eksemplene med et begrenset gråtonespekter en sart tonalitet med 2 til 3 soner/oktaver. En total tonalitet er en varsom gjenngivelse av hele kontrasområdet ca 7 til 8 soner/oktaver. Disse er avhengig av fotografens kunnskap, av filmmaterialet, avkunnskaper om framkalling, av papir valget og av valget av fotokjemi. Ideelt sett så skulle negativet passe helt til normalgraden av papiret, når en tar hensyn til lyskilden i forstørreren. Gjennomtegnte høylys og skygger fra det reneste hvite til det dypeste sorte er det vi alle streber mot som bryr oss om høyverdig sort/hvitt fotografi.

30B ***Hva er de reele kontrastforholdene uavhengig av opptaksteorien?*** Det er vanlig å se kontrasttrinnene i en dobbelt-logaritmisk målestokk. I en real framstillig vil logD 0 -logD 2,3 ha et kontrastomfang tilnærmet 1:128. Dvs at hvitt er 128 x lysere en sort. I det normale livet forekommer skjelden kontrast større enn 1:1000. Dette medfører en brutal reduksjon av kontraster. Det menneskligе øye kan ikke klare slike kontraster. Pupillen lukker seg når vi ser på lyse områder. Ikke alle fotografer kan påstå at han oppnår samme tonalitet som Adams, Weston eller Weidner. Med 35mm film er dette også knappest mulig. Med rullfilm og 4 x 5 tommer kommer en noe nærmere målet. En hver leter etter den filmen som er det ›beste‹ for ham med en ›ideal‹ framkaller og ett ›idealt‹ fotopapir med høyt sølvinnhold og som gir det hviteste hvitt og det sorteste sort.
Alle bør vite at alt dette bare er et forsøk på å nå fram til IDEALET.

photographers, had their problems to represent the full tonal scale, having just one paper grade. These masters of their art were therefore always forced to produce balanced negatives. That was what enabled them to expertly adapt exposure and developing time to the subject brightness range. Their images, featuring a balanced tonal scale, were made on large-format glass plates with silver-rich emulsions and were contact printed on chloride/bromide papers. The principle has not changed. It still holds.
Sales figures of large-format cameras are rising steadily. There is a good reason for that. An image produced by contact-printing from a large-format sheet-film negative has a unique effect.

30A ***Tonality is not the same as Tonality:*** The above-mentioned examples of high-key and low-key photographs, within their limited brightness range, exhibit very subtle tonalities, 2 to 3 zones/octaves in each case.
Overall tonality refers to the subtle gradations over the entire range, i.e. 7 to 8 zones/octaves. This depends on the photographer's skills, the film used, the lab worker's skills, and the paper and chemistry used. Ideally, the negative density range will exactly match the range of the normal paper grade, adapted to the lighting system of the enlarger. All those engaging in fine-art b&w photography strive for detail in lights and shadows, from the brightest white to the deepest black.

30B ***What are the actual brightness ranges, leaving the theory of exposure aside?*** Brightness range is commonly considered on a log/log scale. In a linear representation, the brightness range between log D = 0 and log D = 2.3 is almost 1:128, meaning that white is almost 128 times as bright as black. In ›real life‹ brightness ranges of 1:1,000 are encountered. This implies a brutal reduction of brightness range. The human eye cannot really deal with this brightness range. When looking into a bright light, the pupil ›stops down‹.
All photographers do not claim to achieve a tonality like Adams, Weston, or Weidner. 35-mm film does not allow for it anyway, medium and 4 x 5 in formats are somewhat closer at least. Everybody is looking for the ›best‹ film, the ›ideal‹ developer, and the paper with the highest silver content, the whitest white and the blackest black.
Note, however, that whatever you do, you can always only try to reach an ›ideal‹.

MACO IR 820clear, Leica Summicron 50-mm, 1/15 + 4, filter Heliopan 715, developed in LP-SUPERGRAIN, exposed with WA40 mm, exposure time 14s, 5.6 – on MACO expo RF, graded baryta paper, glossy, grade 4.
© Valsasnini

nimmt nur ein Versuch sein kann, das ›Ideal‹ anzustreben.

31. ***Gibt es das Ideal, oder ›nur‹ Kompromisse?*** Wir von LABOR PARTNER setzen unsere Kraft daran, dem Fotografen und Laboranten möglichst perfekte Fotochemikalien zur Verfügung zu stellen, um das ›Ideal‹ zu erreichen. Wir lieben es jedoch auch, wenn sogenannte Verfremdungstechniken (z.B. die MLD-Technik, basierend auf LP-LITH Chemie) den Betrachter in den Bann ziehen, wenn Toner verfremden, wenn ein steiler Film nicht in steiler, sondern in weicher Chemie verarbeitet wird.
Hoffentlich verstehen wir uns richtig. Wir wollen auch dazu beitragen, dass neue Kreativfelder erschlossen werden und besonders kreative Fotografen die ›eingefahrenen Wege‹ verlassen können. Für Schwarzweiß Fotografen und Laboranten gilt es herzufinden, welches die optimalen Kompromisse für seine, z. T. auch wechselnden Aufgabenstellungen, sind.

32. ***Informationen zu ›optimalen‹ Film-Entwickler-Kombinationen:*** Der Autor hat viele Gespräche mit Fotografen, vor allem jedoch Laboranten geführt. Es wurde oft sehr deutlich, das viele Anwender davon überzeugt sind, ›ihren Entwickler‹ gefunden zu haben. Man hat wertvolle Zeit im Labor zugebracht, kennt ›seinen‹ Entwickler in- und auswendig.
Wir hoffen, diesen Fotografen, sowie Laboranten deutlich gemacht zu haben, dass es den ›einzig wahren Entwickler‹ nicht gibt, genau wie es den ›einzig wahren Film‹ nicht geben kann.

33. ***Aufgabe der ›Selbstbeschränkung‹*** Der Autor möchte mit diesem Buch auch erreichen, dass möglichst viele an der Schwarzweiß-Fotografie Interessierte die Selbstbeschränkung aufgeben und mit unterschiedlicher Chemie und ›normalen‹ wie ›technischen‹ Filmen Versuche anstellen. Diese werden dann dazu führen, dass sich ›neue Welten‹ erschließen und sich eine noch größere Freude an der von uns so geliebten Schwarzweiß-Fotografie einstellt.

intraprende, rappresenta solo un tentativo di raggiungere ›l'ideale‹.

31. ***Esiste l'ideale, oppure ›solo‹ compromessi?*** Noi della LABOR PARTNER ce la mettiamo tutta nell'offerta di chimici fotografici possibilmente perfetti per il fotografo, atti ad ottenere ›l'ideale‹. D'altra parte amiamo anche portare a conoscenza del fotografo di cosiddette tecniche alternative (p. es. la tecnica MLD, che si basa sulla chimica LP-LITH), viraggi che modificano i toni, pellicole ripide che vengono trattate in sviluppi morbidi e non ripidi..
Speriamo di essere capiti bene. Desideriamo pure contribuire ad aprire nuovi orizzonti di creatività e di condurre fotografi, che intendono sperimentare, di abbandonare ›la via maestra‹. Al fotografo e stampatore non resta altro di trovare quali siano i COMPROMESSI ideali, anche alla luce delle diverse e mutanti impostazioni del problema.

32. ***Informazioni sulle combinazioni ›ottimali‹ di sviluppi per pellicole:*** Gli autori coinvolti in questo libro hanno avuto dialoghi approfonditi con fotografi e stampatori. Spesso è risultato, che molti operatori sono convinti del fatto di aver trovato ›il proprio sviluppo‹. Si è trascorso tempo prezioso nel proprio laboratorio, e si conosce il ›proprio‹ sviluppo dentro e fuori.
Noi ci auguriamo di aver chiarito, a questi fotografi e stampatori, che ›l'unico vero‹ sviluppo non esiste, precisamente come ›l'unica vera‹ pellicola non può esistere.

33. ***Compito della ›autolimitazione‹*** Il team di autori, con questo libro, vuole anche ottenere, che il numero maggiore possibile di ›fan‹ della fotografia in bianco/nero ›depongano› l'auto-limitazione e sperimentino pellicole ›normali‹ e ›tecniche‹ con procedimenti chimici variegati. Questa sperimentazione permetterà di scoprire ›nuovi mondi‹ e di trovare piaceri ancora più grandi alla così amata fotografia in bianco/nero.

31. ***Finnes et ideal, eller bare kompromisser?*** Vi hos LABOR PARTNER gjør alt vi kan for å gjøre de best mulige kjemikalier tilgjenngelig for fotografer og fotolaboranter, slik at ›Idealet‹ kan nås. Vi elsker også å kunne tilby eksprimentelle teknikker (som MLD- teknikken som bygger på LP-LITH- kjemi), som trollbinner den som ser resultatet. Dette kan være når en benytter tonere, eller når en film med hard gradasjon blir framkallt i en spesiell myktarbeidene framkaller i stedet for en hard som den var tiltenkt. Forhåpentlig vis forstår du oss rett. Vi vil bidra til at nye kreative veier blir gjordt tilgjenngelige slik at noen viker fra den rette vei for å finne nye løsninger eller finne gamle på nytt. For en sort/hvitt fotograf og laborant gjennstår det bare å finne fram til hvilke optimale kompromisser som passer hans eller hennes vekslende behov og ønsker.

32. ***Informasjon om ›optimale‹ film framkaller kombinasjoner.*** Forfatterne av denne boken har hatt mange samtaler med fotografer og laboranter. Ofte ble det klart at mange var overbeviste om å ha funnet ›sinn‹ framkaller. Etter lang og verdifull tid i mørkerommet kunne de ›sinn‹ framkaller utenatt. Vi håper at vi har kunne gjøre det klart at det ikke finnes den ›eneste sanne‹ framkalleren, like så lite som det finnes den ›eneste sanne‹ filmen.

31. Does ›the ideal‹ exist, or are there just compromises? At LABOR PARTNER, we do everything within our power to offer the photographer and lab worker photo chemicals with the highest possible degree of perfection, to reach THE IDEAL. We also love the mesmerizing effect on the viewer of abstraction techniques (such as MLD technique, based on LP lith chemistry), of toners, of a contrasty film processed in a softening developer instead of a contrast-enhancing one.
So let there be no misunderstanding: We also wish to contribute to opening up new areas of creativity, allowing particularly creative photographers to leave old paths.
The b&w photographer must try to find the optimum COMPROMISE for his (sometimes varying) tasks.

32. Information on ›optimal‹ film/developer combinations: The authors contributing to this book have had many conversations with photographers, and even more with lab workers. These showed that many users are convinced that they have found ›their developer‹. Having spent a lot of time in the lab, one knows one's developer like the back of one's hand.
We hope we were able to persuade these photographers and lab workers that there is no such thing as the ›one and only‹ developer or the ›one and only‹ film.

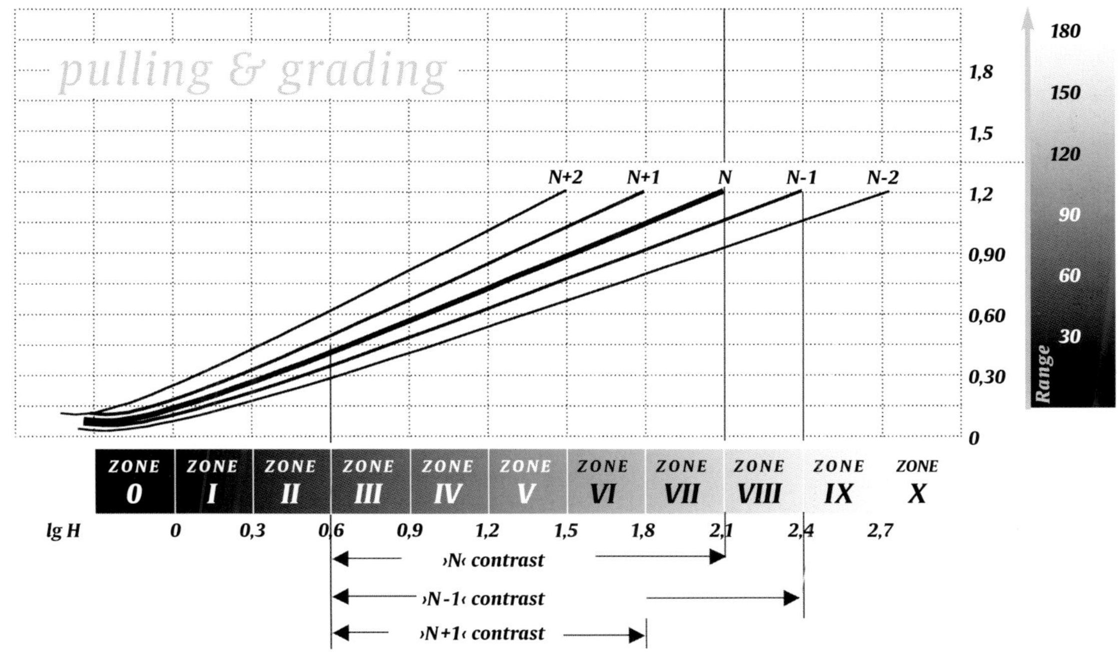

Example:
MACO UP400plus exposed with ISO 400. Normal developing time 6 minutes.
MACO UP400plus exposed with ISO 200. Normal developing time 4.5 minutes.

For pulling with reduced developing time 85% = 4.5 minutes.

N-1	***developing time 4.5 minutes -20% = 3.5 minutes***
N	***developing time 4.5 minutes***
N+1	***developing time 4.5 minutes +25% = 5 minutes***
N+2	***developing time 4.5 minutes +35% = 6 minutes***

34. **KODAK & MACO-Film mit LP-Entwicklern:** Bei den folgenden Vorschlägen beschränken wir uns auf KODAK + MACO Filme. KODAK weil sie weltweit problemlos verfügbar sind, MACO, weil das außerordentlich vielfältige Sortiment interessante Anwendungen ermöglicht.

- KODAK Technical Pan & LP-DOCUFINE LC:
  extrem feinkörnig, hohe Tonalität, mittlere Empfindlichkeit
- MACO UP 25plus & LP-CUBE XS:
  sehr feinkörnig, leistet 25 ISO, perfekte Nachfolgekombination für den AGFA APX 25
- MACO UP 25plus & LP-SUPERGRAIN:
  sehr scharf, leistet 50 ISO
- MACO TP 64clear & LP-DOCUFINE LC:
  extrem feinkörnig, hohe Tonalität, hohe Empfindlichkeit, transparent (perfekt zum Scannen)
- MACO TP 64clear & LP-DOCUFINE HC:
  steile Gradation, für Strich + Reproduktion
- MACO UP 64clear & LP-CUBE XS:
  sehr feinkörnig, leistet bis 50 ISO
- MACO UP 64clear & LP-SUPERGRAIN:
  sehr scharf, leistet von 64 bis 100 ISO
- MACO UP 64clear & Dia-Entwicklung:
  mittlere Empfindlichkeit, sehr hohe Maximalschwärzung , ideal als Druckvorlage, transparent (perfekt zum Scannen)
- KODAK PLUS-X & LP-CUBE XS:
  feinkörnig, hohe Tonalität, leistet bis 100 ISO
- KODAK PLUS-X & LP-SUPERGRAIN:
  scharf, leistet bis 125 ISO
- MACO UP 100plus & LP-CUBE XS:
  feinkörnig, hohe Tonalität, leistet bis 100 ISO
- MACO UP 100plus & LP-SUPERGRAIN:
  scharf, leistet bis 125 ISO, pushbar auf 200 ISO
- KODAK TMAX 100 & LP-CUBE XS:
  feinkörnig, hohe Tonalität, leistet bis 100 ISO
- KODAK TMAX 100 & LP-SUPERGRAIN:
  scharf, leistet bis 125 ISO, pushbar auf 200 ISO
- MACO IR 750clear & LP-CUBE XS:
  feinkörnig, hohe Tonalität, leistet bis 50 ISO ohne Filter
- MACO IR 750clear & LP-SUPERGRAIN:
  scharf, leistet bis 100 ISO ohne Filter
- MACO IR 820clear & LP-CUBE XS:
  feinkörnig, hohe Tonalität, leistet bis 50 ISO ohne Filter
- MACO IR 820clear & LP-SUPERGRAIN
  scharf, leistet bis 100 ISO ohne Filter
- KODAK TRI X 400 & LP-CUBE XS:
  feinkörnig, hohe Tonalität, leistet bis 200 ISO
- KODAK TRI X 400 & LP-SUPERGRAIN:
  scharf, leistet 400 ISO, pushbar auf 800 ISO
- MACO UP 400plus & LP-CUBE XS:
  feinkörnig, hohe Tonalität, leistet bis 200 ISO

34. **KODAK & MACO-Film – Combinazioni con sviluppi LABOR PARTNER:** Con le seguenti proposte ci limitiamo per ora alle pellicole KODAK e MACO. KODAK, perché sono ben conosciute in tutto il mondo, MACO, perché propone un assortimento variegato, che consente interessanti applicazioni.

- KODAK Technical Pan & LP-DOKUFINE LC
  grana extra-fine, ampia resa tonale, media sensibilità
- MACO UP 25 plus & LP-CUBE XS
  grana molto fine, nominale ISO 25/15°, ottima erede dell' AGFA APX 25
- MACO UP 25 plus & LP-SUPERGRAIN
  molto nitida, arriva a ISO 50/18°
- MACO TP 64clear & LP-DOKUFINE LC
  grana extra-fine, ampia resa tonale, alta sensibilità, trasparente
- MACO TP 64clear & LP-DOKUFINE HC
  gradazione ripida, per tratto + repro
- MACO UP 64clear & LP-CUBE XS
  grana molto fine, nominale ISO 50/18°
- MACO UP 64clear & LP-SUPERGRAIN
  molto nitida, arriva a ISO 64/19° fino 100/21°
  Sviluppo dia sensibilità media, alta densità massima dei neri, ideale per test di stampa, trasparente
- KODAK PLUS-X & LP-CUBE XS
  grana fine, ampia resa tonale, rende ISO 100/21°
- KODAK PLUS-X & LP-SUPERGRAIN
  nitida, arriva a ISO 125/22° fino 200/24°
- MACO UP 100plus & LP-CUBE XS
  grana fine, ampia resa tonale, nominale ISO 100/21°
- MACO UP 100plus & LP-SUPERGRAIN
  nitida, arriva a ISO 125/22° fino 200/24°
- KODAK T-MAX 100 & LP-CUBE XS
  grana fine, ampia resa tonale, nominale ISO 100/21°
- KODAK T-MAX 100 & LP-SUPERGRAIN
  nitida, arriva a ISO 125/22à fino 200/24°
- MACO IR 750clear & LP-CUBE XS
  grana fine, ampia resa tonale, rende fino ISO 50/18°
- MACO IR 750clear & LP-SUPERGRAIN
  nitida, sensibilità nominale ISO 100/21° senza filtri
- MACO IR 820clear & LP-CUBE XS
  grana fine, ampia resa tonale, rende fino ISO 590/18°
- MACO IR 820clear & LP-SUPERGRAIN
  nitida, sensibilità nominale ISO 100/21° senza filtri
- KODAK TRI-X & LP-CUBE XS
  grana fine, ampia resa tonale, rende fino ISO 200/24°
- KODAK TRI-X & LP-SUPERGRAIN
  nitida, sensibilità nominale ISO 400/27°, push 800/31°
- MACO UP 400plus & LP-CUBE XS
  grana fine, ampia resa tonale, rende fino ISO 200/24°
- MACO UP 400plus & LP-SUPERGRAIN
  nitida, sensibilità nominale ISO 400/27°, push 800/31°

33. **Oppgi selvpålagte begrensninger.** Forfatterne ønsker at fotointeresserte oppgir de begrensninger de har pålagt seg selv og at de gjør forsøk med ›normale‹ og ›tekniske‹ filmer i forskjellige fotokjemikalier. Nye verdener vil åpne seg og mer glede vil være resultatet i vår elskede sort/hvitt verden.

34. ***Kodak og Maco film med LP framkaller kombinasjoner.*** Vi har begrenset oss til KODAK og MACO filmer. KODAK da disse kan skaffes nærmest over alt og MACO da de har et svært interessant utvalg som gir mange muligheter.

- KODAK Technical Pan og LP-DOCUFINE LC
  ekstrem finkornet, høy tonalitet, middels følsom
- MACO UP 25plus og LP-CUBE-XS
  svært finkornet, 25 ISO, en perfekt etterfølger til AGFA APX 25
- MACO UP 25plus og LP-SUPERGRAIN
  svært skarp, ISO 50
- MACO TP 64clear og LP-DOCUFINE LC
  ekstrem finkornet, høy tonalitet, høy følsomhet, transparent
- MACO TP 64clear og LP-DOCUFINE HC
  hard gradasjon, for strek og reproduksjon
- MACO UP 64clear og LP-CUBE XS
  svært finkornet 50 ISO
- MACO UP 64clear og LP SUPERGRAIN
  svært skarp 64 ISO Lysbilde framkalling: moderat følsomhet, høy maksimalsværtning. Ideal som utgangspunkt for trykk, transparent.
- KODAK PLUS-X og LP-CUBE XS
  finkornet, høy tonalitet inntil 100 ISO
- KODAK PLUS-X og LP-SUPERGRAIN
  skarp 125 ISO
- MACO 100 plus og LP-CUBE XS
  finkornet, høy tonalitet 100 ISO
- MACO 100 plus ogLP-SUPERGRAIN
  skarp 125 ISO ved pressing 200 ISO
- KODAK T-MAX 100 og LP-CUBE XS
  finkornet, høy tonalitet, 100 ISO
- KODAK T-MAX 100 og LP-SUPERGRAIN
  skarp 125 ISO pressing 200 ISO
- MACO IR 750clear og LP-CUBE XS
  finkornet, høy tonalitet 50 ISO uten filter
- MACO IR 750clear og LP-SUPERGRAIN
  skarp 100 ISO uten filter
- MACO IR 820clear og LP-CUBE XS
  finkornet, høy tonalitet 50 ISO uten filter
- MACO IR 820clear og LP-SUPERGRAIN
  skarp 100 ISO uten filter
- KODAK TRI X 400 og LP-CUBE XS
  finkornet, høy tonalitet 200 ISO
- KODAK TRI X 400 og LP-SUPERGRAIN
  skarp 400 ISO pressing 800 ISO

33. Stop ›limiting yourself‹: It is one of the authors' aims to encourage as many as possible of those interested in b&w photography to stop LIMITING THEMSELVES, and to experiment with different chemicals and ›normal‹ as well as ›technical‹ films. This will open up ›new worlds‹ to you, and even more pleasure from the b&w photography we love.

34. KODAK & MACO films with LP developers: The following suggestions are limited to KODAK and MACO films, KODAK because they are available everywhere in the world without problems, and MACO because the extremely wide spectrum allows for interesting applications.

- KODAK Techn. Pan & LP-DOCUFINE LC
  extremely fine grain, great tonality, medium-speed
- MACO UP 25plus & LP-CUBE XS
  very fine grain, ISO 25, perfect replacement for AGFA APX 25
- MACO UP 25plus & LP-SUPERGRAIN
  very sharp, ISO 50
- MACO TP 64 clear & LP-DOCUFINE LC
  extremely fine grain, great tonality, fast, transparent
- MACO TP 64 clear & LP-DOCUFINE HC
  steep gradient, for line and repro
- MACO UP 64 clear & LP-CUBE XS
  very fine grain, up to ISO 50
- MACO UP 64 clear & LP-SUPERGRAIN
  very sharp, ISO 64 to 100
  Reversal processing: medium speed, very high maximum density, ideal for print media, transparent
- KODAK PLUS-X & LP-CUBE XS
  fine grain, great tonality, up to ISO 100
- KODAK PLUS-X & LP-SUPERGRAIN
  sharp, up to ISO 125
- MACO UP 100 plus & LP-CUBE XS
  fine grain, great tonality, up to ISO 100
- MACO UP 100 plus & LP-SUPERGRAIN
  sharp, up to ISO 125, pushable to ISO 200
- KODAK T-MAX 100 & LP-CUBE XS
  fine grain, great tonality, up to ISO 100
- KODAK T-MAX 100 & LP-SUPERGRAIN
  sharp, up to ISO 125, pushable to ISO 200
- MACO IR 750 clear & LP-CUBE XS
  fine grain, great tonality, up to ISO 50 w/o filter
- MACO IR 750 clear & LP-SUPERGRAIN
  sharp, up to ISO 100 w/o filter
- MACO IR 820 clear & LP-CUBE XS
  fine grain, great tonality, up to ISO 50 w/o filter
- MACO IR 820 clear & LP-SUPERGRAIN
  sharp, up to ISO 100 w/o filter

AGFA APX 100, Leica M4, Summicron 50-mm, 1/15 + 4, f2.0, developed in LP-DOCUFINE LC, 8 minutes, conformably to instruction, exposed with WA40 mm, exposure time 12s, 5.6 – on MACO expo RF, graded baryta paper, glossy, grade 3. © Valsasnini

- MACO UP 400plus & LP-SUPERGRAIN:
  scharf, leistet 400 ISO, pushbar auf 800 ISO
- MACO CUBE 400 clear & LP-CUBE XS:
  sehr feinkörnig, hohe Tonalität, leistet bis 200 ISO
- MACO CUBE 400 clear & LP-SUPERGRAIN:
  sehr scharf, leistet 400 ISO, pushbar auf 800 ISO
- KODAK HIE & LP-CUBE XS:
  feinkörnig, hohe Tonalität, leistet bis 100 ISO ohne Filter
- KODAK HIE & LP-SUPERGRAIN:
  scharf, leistet bis 400 ISO ohne Filter
- KODAK TMAX 3200 & LP-CUBE XS:
  feinkörnig, hohe Tonalität, leistet bis 400 ISO
- KODAK TMAX 3200 & LP-SUPERGRAIN:
  scharf, leistet 800 ISO, pushbar auf 1600 ISO

35. Ratschläge zur Film- (Negativ-) Verarbeitung:

35A **Vorbereitung** mit einigen Tipps aus der Praxis, nicht nur für Anfänger: Die komplett belichteten Filme sollten unverzüglich entwickelt werden. Das Latenzbildverhalten ist bei Standard-Schwarzweiß-Filmen nicht so problematisch wie bei Farbfilmen. Bei hochempfindlichen und vor allem IR-Filmen sollte die Latenzzeit so knapp wie möglich bemessen sein.
Polyester-Filme sind nur mit einer Schere zu schneiden. Das Entnehmen aus der Metalldose ist schwierig, dies wird wirklich wichtig, wenn Polyester-Filme in lichtdichten Säcken eingespult werden.
Nur bei orthochromatischen Filmen ist die dunkelrote Laborbeleuchtung zulässig, bei panchromatischen Filmen: Totale Dunkelheit, Fremdlicht verursacht Schleier.
Bei der Fotochemie von LABOR PARTNER werden grundsätzlich Flüssigkonzentrate angeboten, diese können auch im Labor angesetzt werden. Werden noch Pulver verwendet, dann sind diese grundsätzlich außerhalb des Labors anzusetzen. Falls das Fotolabor nicht perfekt staubfrei ist, sollte der Raum für das Fotolabor rechtzeitig mit einem Blumenwassersprüher ›benebelt‹ werden. Wassertröpfchen binden den Staub.
Alle für den Entwicklungsvorgang benötigten Utensilien sollten sich immer an der gleichen Stelle befinden.

35B ***Vorwässerung:*** Einige Filmhersteller raten von der Vorwässerung mit klarem Wasser ab, andere empfehlen sie.
- Oberflächenentwickler können, müssen jedoch nicht vorgewässert werden.
- Tiefenentwickler sollten grundsätzlich vorgewässert werden.

Eine Vorwässerung bewirkt die Entfernung der Lichthof-Schutzschicht, das bestätigt die intensive blaue oder grüne Einfärbung dieses Bades.
Das kann ein Vorteil sein, muss es jedoch nicht. Ein sicherer Vorteil ist jedoch, dass die Gelatine gequollen wird, sich

- MACO CUBE 400clear & LP-CUBE XS
  grana molto fine, ampia resa tonale, rende fino ISO 200/24°
- MACO CUBE 400clear & LP-SUPERGRAIN
  nitida, sensibilità nominale ISO 400/27°, push 800/31°
- KODAK HIE & LP-CUBE XS
  grana fine, ampia resa tonale, rende fino ISO 100/21° senza filtro
- KODAK HIE & LP-SUPERGRAIN
  nitida, sensibilità nominale ISO 400/27° senza filtro
- KOKAK T-MAX 3200 & LP-CUBE XS
  grana fine, ampia resa tonale, rende fino ISO 400/27°
- KOKAK T-MAX 3200 & LP-SUPERGRAIN
  nitida, arriva a ISO 800/31° fino 1600/34°

35. Consigli sul trattamento delle pellicole

35A ***Preparazione:*** (Alcuni consigli dalla pratica, non solo riservata ai principianti!)
Le pellicole esposte dovrebbero essere sempre trattate entro il più breve tempo possibile. Il comportamento dell'immagine latente nel caso di pellicole bianco/nero standard non è così problematico come nel caso di pellicole a colori. Nel caso di pellicole di alta sensibilità e soprattutto nel caso di pellicole IR il tempo latente dovrebbe essere tenuto il più ridotto possibile. Pellicole su base di poliestere devono essere tagliate esclusivamente con le forbici.
L'asportazione della pellicola dal caricatore in metallo può risultare problematico.
E' particolarmente importante quando si caricano le pellicole su base in poliestere nei sacchi neri di caricamento (manicotti).
Solo nel caso di pellicole ortocromatiche è consentita una luce di sicurezza rosso-scura, nel caso di pellicole pancromatiche vale la regola: oscurità totale. Luci parassite provocano velature.
LABOR PARTNER propone prevalentemente chimici fotografici liquidi, questi possono essere preparati anche nella camera oscura. Qualora si utilizzino ancora prodotti in polvere, questi vanno preparati preferibilmente all'esterno della camera oscura.
Qualora la camera oscura non dovesse essere perfettamente priva di polvere è utile ›irrorare‹ l'ambiente con uno spruzzatore per fiori. Le goccioline di acqua amalgamano la polvere.
Fare attenzione di riporre tutto le componenti utilizzate per il trattamento sempre allo stesso posto.

35B ***Prelavaggio:*** Ci sono produttori di pellicole che sconsigliano, altri che consigliano il prelavaggio.
In linea di principio vale: Con sviluppi di superficie le pellicole possono, ma non devono essere prelavate.
Con sviluppi di profondità le pellicole dovrebbero essere prelavate.Un prelavaggio ha la funzione di asportare lo

- MACO UP 400plus og LP-CUBE XS
  finkornet, høy tonalitet 200 ISO
- MACO UP 400plus og LP-SUPERGRAIN
  skarp 400 ISO pressing 800 ISO
- MACO CUBE 400clear og LP-CUBE XS
  svært finkornet, høy tonalitet 200 ISO
- MACO CUBE 400clear og LP-SUPERGRAIN
  svært skarp 400 ISO pressing 800 ISO
- KODAK HIE og LP-CUBE XS
  finkornet, høy tonalitet 100 ISO uten filter
- KODAK HIE og LP-SUPERGRAIN
  skarp 400 ISO uten filter
- KODAK T-MAX 3200 og LP-CUBE XS
  finkornet, høy tonalitet 400 ISO
- KODAK T-MAX 3200 og LP-SUPERGRAIN
  skarp 800 ISO pressing 1600 ISO

35. Råd om filmframkalling:

35A ***Forberedelse*** (praktiske tips, ikke for nybegynnere): Ferdig eksponerte filmer bør framkalles straks (Latentbildet holder seg bedre enn ved fargefilmer. Høyfølsomme filmer og spesiellt IR filmer har betydelig kortere latens tid) Polyesterfilmer kan bare kuttes med saks. Å få filme ut av kassetten kan være vanskelig.
Det er viktig, å oppbevare polyesterfilmer i en lystett beholder. Bare med ortochromatiske filmer er en mørk rød belysning tilllatt, panchromatiske filmer må behandles i totalt mørke. Ellers vil filmene bli sløret.
Fra LABOR PARTNER tilbys bare flytende konsentrater, som enkelt kan blandes i mørkerommet.
Pulverkjemi MÅ blandes i et annet rom. Hvis mørkerommet ikke er helt støvfritt kan en ›fukkte‹ det med en blomstersprayflaske. Vann binder støv. Alle hjelpemiddler som benyttes i framkallingen må ha sin faste plass.

35B ***Forspyling:*** Noen filmfabrikanter frarår forspyling andre anbefaler dette.
Følgende gjelder: Ved bruk av overflateframkallere kan det forspyles, men det må ikke gjøres. Ved bruk av dybdeframkallere bør det alltid forspyles.
En forspyling fører til at antihalogenasjonskiktet fjernes, noe som merkes ved at spylevannet blir grønnt eller blått. Det kan være en fordel, men må ikke være det.
En fordel er i allefall at gelantinen svulmer opp slik at kapillarvirkningen øker.
Da kan framkalleren nå mer gjevnt fram til det lysfølsomme skiktet.

35C ***Tilberedning av framkaller:*** Vannet fra springen må tempereres. Vann kan inneholde en stor andel luft oh klor. For å unngå dette bør man tappe vannmengden som trenges dagen før, og la det stå over natten.

- KODAK TRI X 400 & LP-CUBE XS
  fine grain, great tonality, up to ISO 200
- KODAK TRI X 400 & LP-SUPERGRAIN
  sharp, ISO 400, pushable to ISO 800
- MACO UP 400 plus & LP-CUBE XS
  fine grain, great tonality, up to ISO 200
- MACO UP 400 plus & LP-SUPERGRAIN
  sharp, ISO 400, pushable to ISO 800
- MACO CUBE 400 clear & LP-CUBE XS
  very fine grain, great tonality, up to ISO 200
- MACO CUBE 400 clear & LP-SUPERGRAIN
  very sharp, up to ISO 400, pushable to ISO 800
- KODAK HIE & LP-CUBE XS
  fine grain, great tonality, up to ISO 100 w/o filter
- KODAK HIE & LP-SUPERGRAIN
  sharp, up to ISO 400 w/o filter
- KODAK T-MAX 3200 & LP-CUBE XS
  fine grain, great tonality, up to ISO 400
- KODAK T-MAX 3200 & LP-SUPERGRAIN
  sharp, ISO 800, pushable to ISO 1,600

35. ***Recommendations for FILM PROCESSING:***

35A ***Preparations:*** Some advice from a practitioner, not only for beginners. Exposed films should be processed as swiftly as possible. The stability of the latent image of standard b&w films is not as problematic an issue as that of colour films. The latent time of fast, and particularly of IR films should be kept as short as possible.

Polyester-based film can only be cut using a pair of scissors. Getting them out of the metal cartridge may prove difficult, particularly when polyester-based film is spooled into reels in a changing bag.

A red safelight is only permissible when orthochromatic film is processed. For panchromatic film, total darkness is required. Any light leads to fogging.

LABOR PARTNER exclusively offers liquid concentrates. These can be diluted in the laboratory. Where powder chemicals are to be used, these should be mixed outside the laboratory as a matter of principle.

If the darkroom is not absolutely dust-free, spraying the room with water is recommended. Water droplets act as dust scavengers.

All items needed should always be stored at the same places.

35B ***Prewashing:*** Some film manufacturers advise against prewashing, others recommend it.

The following is fact:

- Prewashing is permissible, but not necessary, with surface developers.
- With depth developers, prewashing is always recommended.

MACO UP 400plus, Canon 50-mm f1.4, 1/15 + 2, developed in LP-CUBE XS, exposed with WA40 mm, exposure time 11s, 5.6 – on MACO expo RF, graded baryta paper, glossy, grade 4. © Valsasnini

die Kapillarwirkung erhöht. Damit wird die Entwicklerlösung gleichmäßiger auf die lichtempfindliche Schicht einwirken.

35C ***Ansatz des Entwicklers:*** Das Leitungswasser ist vorzutemperieren.
Frisches Leitungswasser kann einen hohen Anteil von Sauerstoff und Chlor enthalten. Um diesen Nachteil zu vermeiden, sollte man *am Abend vorher* die benötigte Wassermenge bereits abfüllen und über Nacht stehen lassen.
Es ist zu entscheiden, ob mit oder ohne Entwicklerhärter LP-GELADUR gearbeitet wird. Zuerst wird das Wasser genau abgemessen. Dann das Entwicklerkonzentrat abgemessen und dem Wasser zugegeben. Ein Durchmischen sollte mit wenig Energie betrieben werden, denn das Einbringen von Luftbläschen ist unter allen Umständen zu vermeiden. Manche Laboranten stoßen die Entwicklerdose fest auf, um Luftbläschen, die sich auf dem Film als kreisrunde weiße Flecken zeigen können, zu vermeiden.

35D ***Entwicklung von Kleinbild- und Rollfilmen:*** Nachdem die Filmspirale eingesetzt und die Dose sicher verschlossen ist, wird die Entwicklergebrauchslösung eingefüllt. Auch hierbei wieder darauf achten, keine Luftbläschen entstehen zu lassen.
Die vorher eingestellte Zeitdauer auf der Laboruhr anstellen und dann die Dose etwa 30 Sekunden lang regelmäßig kippen. Danach alle halbe Minute einmal, solange, wie es der Film erfordert.
Sollte der Entwickler eine höhere Verarbeitungstemperatur erfordern, dann ist die Filmdose in eine Entwicklerschale mit vortemperiertem Wasser zu stellen. Dies ist auch dann zu empfehlen, wenn die Raumtemperatur erheblich von der Entwicklertemperatur abweicht.

35E ***Entwicklung von Planfilmen:*** Wir geben die Ratschläge des Fotografen Burkhard Kiegelland weiter, der regelmäßig eine sehr große Anzahl von Planfilmen, auch 8 x 10"Formate, innerhalb kurzer Fristen zu verarbeiten hat: „Ich finde es effektiv, zur guten alten Schalenentwicklung zurückzukehren und 6 Planfilme auf einmal zu entwickeln Nach dieser Methode kann ich in zwei Tagen rund 100 Planfilme entwickeln. Die Schalenentwicklung, richtig angewendet, garantiert prinzipiell für alle Planfilmformate gleichmässigegleichmäßige Ergebnisse.
Auf ein paar Dinge sollte geachtet werden: Eine geeignete Schale mit Noppen, nicht mit Rillen oder Stegen, reichlich Flüssigkeitsmenge, Negative mit Emulsions-Schicht nach unten (wichtig) und Handschuhe aus Latex.
Eine entscheidende Rolle spielt die Art des Umschichtens. Solange wir das unterste Negativ unseres Stapels immer gerade herausziehen, es so halten, dass die Ecken leicht

strato antialone, che provoca una colorazione del bagno in color blu o verde. Ciò può rappresentare un vantaggio, ma non necessariamente. Un vantaggio indubbio è però sicuramente il fatto che la gelatina viene gonfiata e di conseguenza aumenta l'azione capillare. La conseguenza è un effetto più omogeneo della soluzione di sviluppo sullo strato sensibile alla luce.

35C ***Sviluppo – Preparazione:*** L'acqua corrente è da preriscaldare. Acqua fresca può contenere una parte consistente di ossigeno e cloro. Per evitare questo svantaggio, è consigliabile prelevare la quantità d'acqua necessaria la sera prima e di lasciarla depositare l'intera notte.
E' utile decidere se si vuole lavorare con o senza induritore dello sviluppo LP-GELADUR. Dapprima si dosa con precisione l'acqua.
La miscelazione dovrebbe avvenire con poca energia per evitare a tutti i costi la formazione di bollicine d'aria.
Molti operatori danno un colpetto secco alla tank sul piano per togliere dall'emulsione della pellicola le bollicine d'aria che si possono fermare e provocare le odiate macchioline bianche rotonde.

35D ***Sviluppo (Piccolo e medio formato):*** Dopo aver inserito la spirale nella tank, apportato il coperchio si procede al riempimento della stessa con il liquido d'uso di sviluppo. Anche durante questa procedura si deve fare attenzione che non si possano formare bollicine d'aria. Far partire il timer con il tempo prestabilito e capovolgere a ritmo regolare la tank per ca. 30 secondi.
In seguito ciò deve avvenire una volta ogni mezzo minuto, fino a completamento della durata di sviluppo della pellicola.
Qualora lo sviluppo necessiti di una temperatura di trattamento più alta, porre la tank durante gli intervalli di agitazione a bagnomaria in una bacinella con acqua temperata. Questa procedura è consigliabile anche nei casi in cui la temperatura ambiente si discosta di molto dalla temperatura dei bagni di sviluppo.

35E ***Sviluppo (Pellicole piane):*** Condividiamo i consigli del fotografo Burkhard Kiegelland, che deve trattare nel più breve tempo possibile numerose pellicole piane, anche in 8 x 10":
„Trovo molto razionale di ricorrere ad una tecnica ormai acquisita negli anni, ovvero il trattamento in bacinella di ben 6 pellicole piane alla volta. Grazie a questo metodo riesco a sviluppare fino a 100 pellicole piane i due giorni.
Il trattamento in bacinella, se eseguito correttamente, garantisce risultati omogenei per tutti i formati di pellicole piane. Bisogna però fare attenzione ad alcuni accorgimenti: Prima di tutto bisogna utilizzare una bacinella munita di protuberanze a bolla, non a scanalatura né a ponticello, e

En må bestemme seg for om en skal arbeide med eller uten framkaller herderen LP- GELADUR. Først måler en vannet nøyaktig. Så blandes framkallerkonsentratet med vannet. Det er viktig å unngå å bruke formye kraft på å blande for å unngå luft i framkalleren. Noen laboranter støter målebegeret mot bordet for å løsne eventuelle luftbobbler.
Ellers kan det dannes små hvite flekker på filmen
der framkalleren ikke når fram.

35D ***Framkalling (35 mm og rullfim)***
Etter at filmspolen er satt inn i tanken og denne er forsvarlig lukket, helles framkallerblandingen inn itanken. Også nå er det viktig å bli kvitt alle luftbobbler. Start klokken og pass nøye på tiden. Agiter i 30 sek.
Etter dette agiteres en gang hvert 30 sek til den foreskrevne tiden er oppnådd. Kreves en høyere temperatur kan framkallingstanken plasseres i en skål med temperert vann. Dette anbefales også når romtemperaturen ligger langt under prosesstemperaturen.

35E ***Framkalling av planfilm:*** Vi videreformidler her rådene til fotograf Burhard Kiegelland, som regelmessig framkaller store mengder planfilm også 8 x 10". Jeg synes det er mest effektivt å gå tilbake til den gamle metoden med skålframkalling for slik å kunne framkalle inntil 6 filmer på en gang. Med denne metoden kan jeg framkalle inntil 100 planfilmer på to deger. Skålframkallingen gir, når den er utført på rett måte, garantert et prinsipiellt gjevnt rersultat for alle størrelser av planfilm. Det er viktig å passe på følgende:
Best egnet er skåler uten riller og fordypninger, best er skåler med små nupper. Viktig er nok framkaller og latex hansker. Filmen legges alltid med emulsjonen ned (dette er svært viktig).
Avgjørende er måten filmen blir ›bladd‹ i . Så lenge vi alltid tar det nederste negativet forsiktig opp, bøyer det forsiktig for så å legge det øverst og trykke det forsiktig ned i framkalleren ; da kan ikke mye gå galt. Farlig blir det først når en framkaller med emulsjonen opp; denne følsomme siden er svært sårbar og ville ta skade hver gang et nytt negativ blir lagt oppå. Når jeg, etter å har forspylt negativene, har lagt dem i framkalleren følger jeg alltid denne rutinen: Mens jeg teller trekker jeg langsomt negativene ut med høyre hånd mot høyre, neste runde med høyre hånd oppover, så tredje gang med venstre hånd mot venstre. Etter dette starter en ny syklus med høyre hånd.
Når en framkaller etter sikt, så er denne metoden ikke bare for store formater svært effektiv, den tillater at hvert enkelt negativ kan tas over i stoppebadet når det har oppnådd ønsket tetthet. Mest konfortabel er kontroll ved hjelp av IR lys (ca 1000 nm), dyr er også bruken av desenibilisatorer som Pinakryptol, som blandes i framkalleren og som tillater at en etter et par minutter kan benytte et gulgrønnt

Prewashing removes the anti-halation backing as can be seen from the blue or green colour of the water. This may, or may not, be an advantage. The swelling of the gelatine, however, is an advantage, as capillary action is enhanced. The action of the developing solution on the emulsion becomes more uniform.

35C ***Preparation of developer:*** Bring tap water to the proper temperature. Fresh tap water may contain large quantities of oxygen and chlorine. This disadvantage is avoided by leaving the required quantity of water to stand for a night.
Decide on whether or not you intend to use the developer hardener LP-GELADUR. First prepare precisely the required quantity of water.
Then measure the required quantity of developer concentrate, and add it to the water.
Mixing should not be too vigorous, as the generation of air bubbles shall be avoided at any rate.
Some lab workers tap down the developing tank to dislodge any air bubbles from the film, which might otherwise register as circular white spots.

35D ***Development of 35-mm and medium format roll films:*** The film reels having been inserted and the tank safely closed, the developer working solution is poured in. Try to avoid generating air bubbles during this step, too. Start counting down the selected time on the lab timer, and regularly invert the tank for 30s.
Later, invert once every 30s for as long as the film takes.
Where the developer requires working at elevated temperature, let the tank sit in a developing tray filled with water at the right temperature.
This is also recommended where room temperature significantly deviates from the processing temperature.

35E ***Development of sheet films:*** We pass on the advice of photographer Burkhard Kiegelland who regularly processes a large number of sheet-film negatives, even 8 x 10in, within short periods of time:
„I find it expedient to return to good old tray processing, developing all 6 sheets at a time. This method allows me to process up to 100 sheets of film in two days. As a matter of principle, tray development, when done properly, ensures uniform results for all sheet-film formats.
Mind the following:
The tray should have a knob pattern rather than grooves or lands, the volume of solution should be sufficient, slip in the negatives with the emulsion side down (This is important!), use latex gloves.
The method of shuffling the stack of negatives is decisive. As long as we pull out the bottom negative straight, then hold it slightly bend, with the edges upward, and place it

MACO CUBE 400clear, Leica M, Thambar 90 mm lens (soft working lens), 1/30, developed 24 minutes in LP-CUBE XS, exposure time 18s, 5.6 – on MACO MULTIBROM WA, warmtone baryta paper, matte
© Valsasnini

aufgebogen sind, es dann gerade zuoberst auf den Stapel legen und dabei mit den Fingerspitzen sanft unter die Flüssigkeit drücken, kann nicht viel passieren. Gefährlich würde es erst, wenn wir die Schicht nach oben entwickelten: die empfindliche Seite des jeweils untersten Negativs würde dann jedes Mal über die scharfen Kanten des darüber liegenden Stapels gezogen.
Sind meine Negative nach der Vorwässerung in der Entwicklerschale untergebracht, folge ich dieser Routine: Leise zählend ziehe ich in der ersten Runde die Negative mit der rechten Hand nach rechts heraus, in der zweiten mit der rechten Hand nach oben, und in der dritten mit der linken Hand nach links; dann beginnt der Zyklus von neuem mit der rechten Hand nach rechts.
In Verbindung mit Sichtkontrolle ist die Schalenentwicklung für große Formate nicht nur effektiv, sie erlaubt auch, jedes Blatt individuell aus dem Entwickler in das Unterbrecher-Bad zu befördern, wenn es genügend Dichte zeigt. Am komfortabelsten ist die Sichtkontrolle mittels IR-Lichtquellen (um 1.000nm), auch teuer sind Desensibilisatoren wie Pinakryptol, die dem Entwickler zugemischt wurden und nach ein paar Minuten das Einschalten des gelbgrünen Dunkelkammerlichts erlauben.
Die meisten Praktiker verwenden dunkelgrün Filter (AGFA 108) für die Entwicklung panchromatischer Filme. Nach 4-5 Minuten in völliger Dunkelheit schalte ich zum ersten Mal das Schutzlicht ein und betrachte kurz die Rückseite jedes Blattes. Was ist zu sehen? Die Reflexionen des Motivs auf der Rückseite des Films. Das Blatt ist ausentwickelt, wenn der Unterschied zwischen dem unbelichteten Filmrand und dem Bildfeld – also zwischen Grundschleier und belichteten Zonen – einen bestimmten Kontrast aufweist. Die genaue Beurteilung ergibt die Erfahrung.
Ich verwende kein Stoppbad, sondern kaltes, klares Wasser, weil die Entwicklungszeiten oft unterschiedlich sind. Ich würde beim Verfrachten einzelner Blätter in ein Stoppbad Spuren davon in den Entwickler zurückschleppen."

35F ***Unterbrechen oder Stoppen:*** Nachdem der alkalische Entwickler zügig abgegossen ist, wird entweder ganz kurz einmal mit Leitungswasser die Dose ausgespült oder gleich das saure Stoppbad eingefüllt. Das Stoppbad LP-CITRIN oder LP-CITRODUR wird zügig eingefüllt.
Es ist darauf zu achten, dass die Temperaturen der Folgebäder nicht erheblich von der Temperatur des Filmentwicklers abweichen. Die Stoppbad-Gebrauchlösung bleibt etwa eine halbe bis eine ganze Minute in der Filmdose. Die Dose diese Zeit über regelmässigregelmäßig kippen. Das Stoppbad ist so vergleichsweise preiswert, dass dieses Bad grundsätzlich frisch angesetzt werden sollte.

35G ***Fixieren:*** So wie beim Wechsel vom Entwickler zum

riempite con liquido abbondante; i negativi vanno rivolti con l'emulsione verso il *basso* (importante) ed utilizzare guanti in latex.
Una grande importanza viene riposta nel come si impilano le pellicole durante lo sviluppo. Finché estraiamo linearmente la pellicola in fondo alla pila, la teniamo in modo tale da tenere gli angoli leggermente inarcati, posizionandola in alto alla pila stessa, premendola con le punte delle dita sotto il livello del liquido di sviluppo, non può accadere nulla di spiacevole. La cosa sarebbe critica qualora sviluppassimo le pellicole con l'emulsione rivolta verso l'alto, in quanto, ogni volta che si effettua un passaggio verso l'alto della pellicola, la parte sensibile andrebbe a sfregare contro i brodi affilati della pila di pellicole poste sopra. Una volta immesse le pellicole da sviluppare nella bacinella, dopo aver effettuato il prelavaggio, seguo questa procedura: Conto sottovoce e tiro fuori la pellicola verso destra nel primo round, verso l'alto nel secondo round, sempre con la mano destra e nel terzo round verso sinistra; poi ricomincio con il ciclo con la mano destra verso destra.
Lo sviluppo in bacinella di pellicole di grande formato consente un controllo dello strato, permettendo inoltre di passare ogni singolo foglio dallo sviluppo al bagno d'arresto, individualmente, quando mostra la densità desiderata. Il modo più confortevole di controllare lo strato è una fonte di luce IR (intorno a 1.000 nm), oppure aggiungere allo sviluppo un desensibilizzatore, come p. es. pinacriptolo, che permette di accendere la luce giallo/verde di sicurezza pochi minuti dopo.
La maggior parte di addetti, per lo sviluppo di pellicole pancromatiche, utilizzano un filtro di sicurezza VERDE SCURO (AGFA 108).
Dopo 4-5 minuti in totale oscurità accendo per la prima volta la luce di sicurezza ed osservo brevemente il retro di ogni singola lastra di pellicole. Cosa vedo? La riflessione dell'immagine sul retro della pellicola. La lastra è sviluppata a fondo quando, la differenza del bordo non esposto con il campo dell'immagine - ovvero velo base grigio e zone esposte – mostra un determinato contrasto. Il giudizio preciso arriva con l'esperienza.
Normalmente non utilizzo un bagno d'arresto, bensì acqua pura, fredda, in quanto i tempi di sviluppo risultano spesso differenti fra loro. Utilizzando un bagno d'arresto acido rischierei di inquinare lo sviluppo quando sposterei pellicola per pellicola.“

35F ***Interrompere / Arrestare:***
Dopo aver fatto defluire con rapidità lo sviluppo, risciacquare un attimo con acqua corrente e riempire immediatamente la tank con il bagno d'arresto.
Riempire la tank con il bagno d'arresto LP-CITRIN o LP-CITRODUR. Fare attenzione che la temperatura di tutti i bagni seguenti allo sviluppo non si differenzino in modo

mørkeromslys.
De fleste benytter et mørkegrønnt filter (AGF 108) for framkalling av panchromatiske filmer. Etter 4-5 min i totalt mørke slår jeg førstegang på lyset og ser kort på baksiden av hvert negativ. Hva kan en da se? Refleksjonen av hvert negativ på baksiden av filmen. Filmen er ferdig framkalt når forskjellen mellom filmkanten, som ikke er belyst, og motivet , dvs mellom grunnslør og motiv,oppnår en bestemmt kontrast. Dette krever erfaring.
Jeg benytter ikke stoppebad, men friskt, kalt vann, dette siden framkallingstidenene kan variere mellom negativene og det lett kan komme til forurensning av framkalleren , når framkallingen fortsettes etter at et negativ er fraktet over i stoppebadet.

35F ***Stoppebad***: Etter at framkalleren er tømt ut, spyles det enten kort med vann i tanken, eller en tar stoppebadet rett oppi.
Stoppebadene LP-CITRIN eller LP- CITRODUR tømmes raskt i tanken. Det er viktig at temperaturen ikke avviker vesentlig fra framkallertemperaturen. Stoppebadet bør bare brukes en gang, da det er forholdsmessig gunstig i pris. Tanken aggiteres gjevnt mellom 30 sek og ett minutt.

35G ***Fiksering:*** Som ved framkaller og stoppebad er det viktig å tømme og å fylle tanken raskt. Aggiter de første 30 sek og så hvert 30 sek i den tid som er nødvedig for filmen du framkaller.
Fikserbadet er svært viktig for å få et perfekt resultat og framfor alt viktig for å oppnå maksimal holdbarhet på negativene.
Benytt aldri samme fikser for PE -papir og film!. Det eneste som går er å bruke filmfiks til PE-papir, men ikke omvendt.

35H ***Spyling***: La filmen bli på spolen, ikke ta den ut.
Nå er vi kommet til den delen av filmframkallingen som ofte har gitt frustrerende feil og som fører til skuffede laboranter. Når en ikke tar ›følgebadene_ like alvorlig som selv framkallingen kan dette få store konsekvenser. Spylingen er like viktig som resten av prosessen!
Ofte benyttes slanger rett fra springen. Det er å ta stor sjanser. Det kan komme til forskyvning av temperaturen som igjen kan føre til at emulsjonen løsner eller at den retikulerer. En kompromissløs og framforalt arkivfast spyling kan en gjøre slik:
Kvelden på forhånd fylles en bøtte med den nødvendige mengde vann. Vanne vil da ofte ha rett temperatur, romtemperatur, og hvis ikke kan store mengder lettere tempereres enn små.
Hvilken mengde trenges?
Etter at fikseren er tømt ut fylles samme mangde med vann i tanken (1 film 35 mm ca 260 ml). Aggiter i 1 min.
Hell ut vann og hell på nytt vann aggiter i 2 min. Gjenta

on top of the stack in line with the others, applying gentle pressure with our fingertips to keep it covered with solution, not much is likely to go wrong. Developing with the emulsion facing upward, however, is hazardous, as the vulnerable side of the bottom negative, each time it is pulled out from under the stack, is pulled over the sharp edges of the stack lying on top of it. As soon as I have arranged my negatives in the developing tray after prewashing, I follow this routine:
Counting silently, during the first round, I pull out the negatives to the right, using the right hand, upwards during the second round, again using the right hand, then left in the third round, using the left hand. This cycle is then repeated. Tray development in combination with visual inspection is not only efficient, it also allows to pull each sheet from the developer to put it in the stop bath when its density is sufficient. The most comfortable lights for visual inspection are IR light sources (around 1,000 nm). Desensitisers like Pinacryptol, which are added to the developer and allow switching on a yellow-green safelight after a few minutes, are expensive.
Most practitioners use DARK GREEN filters (AGFA 108) for the development of panchromatic films. Having developed in complete darkness for 4 to 5 minutes, I first switch on the safelight and briefly inspect the back of each sheet. What do I see? The mirror image of the subject on the back of the film. Development of a sheet is complete when the difference in the densities of the unexposed rebate and the frame proper, i.e. the difference between the film base and fog density and the density of the exposed zones shows sufficient contrast. Exact judgement comes with experience.
I do not use an acid stop bath, but cold, clear water, because development times often differ. I could hardly avoid carrying over traces of an acid stop bath back into the developing tray while transferring the individual sheets from there to the stop bath."

35F ***Stop bath:*** As soon as the developer has been swiftly poured out of the tank, either briefly rinse the tank, or immediately pour in the stop bath.
The stop bath, either LP-CITRIN or LP-CITRODUR is filled in swiftly. Make sure that the temperatures of the baths following the developer do deviate considerably from the developer temperature. The stop bath working solution remains in the tank for approximately half a minute, or a minute. Invert regularly during this time. Stop bath is relatively inexpensive, so it should be used one-shot.

35G ***Fixing:*** Just like the change from developer to stop bath, pour swiftly again. Here, too, invert permanently during the first 30s, then once every 30s, for as long as the film takes to fix.

MACO IR 820clear, without filter, ISO 100, 1/30, f13 © Valsasnini

MACO IR 820clear, filter HELIOPAN 715, ISO 100, 1/30 + 4, 1s, f13, developed in LP-SUPERGRAIN

Stoppbad, wird auch jetzt wieder zügig aus- bzw. eingegossen. Auch hier wird wieder in der ersten halben Minute die Dose regelmäßig gekippt. Danach alle halbe Minute einmal, solange wie es der Film erfordert.
Fixierbäder sind extrem wichtig für das Gelingen der Verarbeitung und die Haltbarkeit des fertigen Films (!).
■ Niemals Fixierer-Gebrauchslösungen sowohl für Filme als auch PE-Papiere verwenden. Wenn, dann ist wäre es zulässig, gebrauchte Film-Fixier-Gebrauchslösungen anschließend als PE-Papier-Fixierbad zu verwenden.

35H **Wässern:** Der Film verbleibt in der Filmspirale, nicht herausnehmen (!). Jetzt kommen wir zu dem Teil der Filmverarbeitung, der leider oft genug dazu führt, dass enttäuschte Laboranten Fehlresultate erhalten.
Diese Leute haben den ›Folgebädern‹ einfach nicht mehr genug Aufmerksamkeit gewidmet.
■ Das Wässern erfordert genau die gleiche Sorgfalt wie das Entwickeln und das Fixieren.
Oft werden Schläuche an die Filmdosen angeschlossen, die das Wasser frisch aus der Wasserleitung transportieren. Welch ein Wagnis (!). Es kann zu Über- oder Untertemperierung kommen, abgelöste Emulsionen oder Runzelkorn wären dann eine der Folgen.
Kompromisslos und für die archivfeste Aufbewahrung könnte wie folgt gewässert werden: Stellen Sie am Abend vorher einen Eimer mit der zur Wässerung benötigten Wassermenge bereit. Dieses Wasser hat dann oft schon die richtige Temperatur, wenn nicht, ist diese größere Wassermenge leicht zu temperieren bzw. auf Temperatur zu halten.
Welche Wassermenge ist vorzusehen?
Wir gehen von einem Film aus, der in 260 ml Gebrauchslösung verarbeitet wird.
■ Nachdem die Fixierbad-Gebrauchslösung ausgegossen ist, sollten zügig gut 260 ml vorbereitetes Wasser eingefüllt werden.
■ Die Filmdose ist dann 1 Minute regelmässigregelmäßig zu kippen. Wasser auskippen und neu einfüllen.
■ Erneut 2 Minuten regelmäßig kippen.
■ Diesen Wasseraustausch nehmen Sie insgesamt 8 x vor. Nach achtmaligem Wasserwechsel bei jeweils 2 Minuten Agitation, ist von einer optimierten, sprich: archivfesten Wässerung auszugehen.

35K **Netzmittel & Trocknen:** Der Film verbleibt in der Filmspirale, nicht herausnehmen (!). *Nach der Wässerung ist ein spezielles Netzmittelbad zwingend erforderlich.*
■ Der Laborant gießt als neuntes Wässerungsbad das speziell mit demineralisiertem Wasser (oder Aqua dest. oder Batteriewasser von der Tankstelle bzw. der Drogerie) in die Filmentwicklerdose.
■ Wieder eine halbe Minute regelmäßig kippen, wobei jede

sostanziale. La durata di permanenza del bagno di arresto nella tank ammonta a ca. mezzo a un minuto. La tank va agitata regolarmente durante questo periodo di tempo.
E' consigliabile preparare sempre bagno d'arresto fresco, non ultimo per la sua economicità.

35G **Fissaggio:** Come già avvenuto nel cambio di chimica fra sviluppo e arresto, anche in questo caso si procede rapidamente nel svuotamento, ovvero riempimento la tank, e anche in questo caso si capovolge regolarmente la tank durante i primi trenta secondi. In seguito si capovolge una volta ogni minuto fino allo scadere del tempo di fissaggio necessario.
I bagni di fissaggio sono particolarmente importanti per la riuscita del trattamento e per la durata nel tempo della pellicola finita (!).
Non bisogna mai utilizzare un bagno di fissaggio in soluzione pronto-uso sia per pellicola, che per carta fotografica. Qualora proprio non se ne potesse fare a meno, è concesso utilizzare un bagno di fissaggio per carta dopo averlo utilizzato per pellicole e non viceversa.

35H **Lavaggio:** La pellicola rimane avvolta sulla spirale, non scaricarla (!).
Ora arriviamo a quella parte del trattamento della pellicola, che spesso e volentieri porta purtroppo ad ottenere risultati negativi. Questa è la riprova del fatto, che non si sia dato sufficiente importanza ai bagni ›seguenti‹ allo sviluppo. Il lavaggio richiede tanta attenzione quanta viene data sia allo sviluppo che al fissaggio.
Spesso si allaccia un tubi dell'acqua alla tank, che apportano acqua fresca direttamente dalla tubatura. Quale affronto (!). La conseguenza è una sopra o sotto-temperatura, ciò che provoca stacchi o raggrinzimenti dell'emulsione. Senza compromessi e per una durata nel tempo si potrebbe procedere al seguente metodo di lavaggio:
Preparare la sera prima un secchio d'acqua in quantità sufficiente per il lavaggio. Quest'acqua raggiunge così la temperatura ambiente, e in caso di necessità si riesce a temperarla facilmente.
Quale quantità d'acqua è necessaria?
Non appena la tank viene svuotata dal bagno di fissaggio, la si riempie con la medesima quantità d'acqua (p.es. in una tank di capacità di 260 ml). La tank va poi capovolta regolarmente per 1 minuto. Svuotare la tank e riempirla nuovamente. Agitare nuovamente e regolarmente per 2 minuti. Questo ricambio di acqua va effettuato per 8 volte. Dopo questo lavaggio di 8 volte a 2 minuti cadauno, si può tranquillamente parlare di un lavaggio ottimale e perfino sicuro.

35K **Imbiente/Asciugatura:** La pellicola rimane avvolta sulla spirale, non scaricarla (!) Dopo il lavaggio è indispensabile uno speciale bagno d'imbibente. Si versa nella tank il

dette 8 ganger. Etter 8 ganger 2 min er filmen optimalt spylt dvs arkivfast.

35K ***Vetemiddel/ tørking:*** La filmen fortsatt være på spolen. Etter spyling må filmen behandles i et spesiellt vetemiddel. Fortrinnsvis blandet med destilert vann. Aggitert rolig i ca 30 sek for å unngå luftbobler som ablolutt må unngås.
Etter at vetemiddele er blitt tømt vekk, tas filmen med største forsiktighet av spolen og henges på et støv og trekkfritt sted med filmklemmer. Så må en klemme med vekt henges nederst på filmen, slik at denne kan tørke plant. Skal filmen tørkes i tørkeskap, må det ikke benyttes varme. Bare slik kan filmen tørke gjevnt og uten flekker. En hver mekanisk manipulering må unngås, også filmavstrykning , det være seg med fingrer, tenger, eller pusseskin. Slike ›hjelpemiddler‹ produseres av folk som aldri framkaller selv.
Spesiellt filmer på polyesterbase er vanskeligge å få plane, benytt derfor LP- MASTERPROOF for alle moderne filmer.

35L ***Arkivering:*** Vanligvis klippes den folkomment tørre filmen i striper. Bare polyesterfolie har den holdbarheten som en nødvendig for å kunne beskytte filmen over lang tid. Alle former for oppbevaring medfører risikoer, framforalt for fuktskader.
Acetat filmene som var vanlige før kan forvandles til støv..
Det er viktig ikke å oppbevare nye og gamle acetatfilmer omhverandre. I tilfelle det skulle komme til utsondring av eddiksyre-ethylester, kan også helt nye filmer bli ›smittet‹
Bare polyersterfilmer er helt sikre og derfor perfekte for langtidslagring.

35M ***Ripefri film som basis for forstørrelser Kjemisk løsning:*** Filmmaterialet er følsomfor riper, fingeravtrykk og fuktighet. Det finnes forskjellige måter å beskytte filmen på. De kjemiske er disse:
Herding av filmemulsjonen ved hjelp av den herdene framkaller. For mange fotografer er dette kanskje nytt, men denne metoden er gammel og ble før kalt tropesikker. Framforalt maskinframkallere burde alltid ha denne tilsetningen. Offte vet man ikke at det handler om en slik, da den bare er en av mange deler som danner en framkaller.
LP-GELADUR er ikke en inovasjon fra LABOR PARTNER, men gjennoppdagelsen av noe som har vært effektivt før.
I tillegg finnes det herdende stoppebad og fikserbad. Men hva hjelper det hvis filmen er blitt skadet i framkalleren? Alså benytt en framkaller herder.

Omkopiering- Det finnes forskjellig planfilmer i format 24 x 30 cm på markedet. Med hjelp av disse kan et helt kontaktark omkopieres , slik at en får lysbilder av hele filmen. Noen av disse planfilmene (MACO GENIUS FILM + GENIUS PRINT film) er på polyesterbase. En oppnår da en kvalitet som ikke kan oppnås ved kopiering på papir. Orgi-

Fixers are of utmost importance for the results, and for the permanence of the finished film.
Never use the same fixer working solutions for films and papers.
The only acceptable exception would be using film fixer for RC papers.

35H **_Washing:_** The film remains in the reels. Don't take it out of them. We are now approaching that stage of film processing which often gives disappointed lab workers faulty results. This is because the ›other baths‹ are not given the same attention as the developer. Washing requires as much attention as developing and fixing.
Rather often, tanks are connected to hoses by which fresh tap water is injected into the tank. A very daring method! Over- and undertemperature are possible, emulsion peeling or reticulation may be the consequence. For archival results, use the following washing procedure:
Prepare a bucket of water, as much as you may need, the day before you process a film. Often, the water will then have the right temperature when you need it, and if not, this larger quantity is much easier to get to, and hold at, the right temperature.
How much will you need?
Let us assume 260 ml of solution for one 35-mm film. The fixer working solution having been poured out of the tank, swiftly fill in 260 ml of the water prepared the evening before. The tank is then inverted regularly for one minute. Pour out the water, refill. The tank is then inverted regularly for two minutes.
8 changes followed by 2 minutes of regular agitation each ensure optimised, i.e. archival washing.

35K **_Wetting agent/drying:_** The film still remains in the reels. Don't take it out of them. Following the washing, a special wetting agent treatment is mandatory. As the ninth washing bath, pour the wetting agent solution, prepared with demineralised water (or Aqua Dest., or battery water from the gas station or drugstore), into the tank. Again, invert regularly, but not hectically.
When the wetting agent solution has been poured out of the tank (do not keep it, it's for one-shot use only), take the film out of the reels with utmost diligence, and attach a film hanger. The film should be hung in a dry, dust-free, and draught-free environment. Attach a weight to the bottom end for the film to dry flat. If you can dry the film in a drying cabinet, switch on the fan, but not the heating.
Only then will the film dry uniformly and without drying marks. Avoid any mechanical manipulation, squeegees, leather; pulling the film through your fingers is not a good

MACO UP 400plus, 1/15 +5, Canon FD 50-mm, f1.8, developed in LP-CUBE XS © Valsasnini

Hektik zu vermeiden ist. Diese würde erneut zu Luftbläschen führen, die es – wie beim Entwickler – 100 %ig zu vermeiden gilt.
■ Nach dem Ausgießen des Netzmittelbades (nicht aufbewahren – Einmalanwendung) wird der Film mit größter Sorgfalt der Filmspirale entnommen und an einer Filmklammer befestigt.
■ Diese wird an einem trockenen, staubfreien und zugfreien Ort sorgfältig befestigt. Dann muss eine Gewichtsklammer befestigt werden damit der Film plan trocknen kann.
■ Sollte der Film in einem Film-Trockenschrank getrocknet werden können, dann ist der *Ventilator ohne Wärme* zu betreiben. Nur so trocknet der Film gleichmäßig und ohne Streifen zu hinterlassen.
■ Jede mechanische Manipulation ist zu unterlassen, Film-Abstreifzangen, Ledertücher oder der Trick mit dem Durchziehen durch zwei Finger ist zu unterlassen. Derartige Gerätschaften sind sicher vor allem von Kaufleuten dem Markt angeboten worden, die wohl noch nie selbst einen Film ordentlich entwickelt haben.
■ Vor allem Filme auf Polyesterbasis sind nur schwer plan zu bekommen. Der Laborant sollte daher vor allem für diese modernen Filme das LP-MASTERPROOF anwenden.

35L ***Archivierung:*** Die vollkommen trockenen Filme werden zumeist in Streifen abgelegt. Nur Polyesterfolie hat die Beständigkeit, Filme für sehr lange Zeit ohne schädliche Einwirkungen zu schützen. *Jede andere Art der Aufbewahrung läuft Gefahr,* kurz oder lang, den Film zu schädigen, vor allem bei Feuchtigkeitseinwirkung.
Die über Jahrzehnte üblichen Acetatfilme bergen die Gefahr, zu Staub zu zerfallen. *Es ist zu vermeiden,* alte und neue Acetatfilme nahe beieinander zu lagern. Falls es bei alten Filmen zu einer Absonderung von Essigsäureethylester kommt, dann werden davon vielleicht auch ganz frische Filme ›angesteckt‹.
■ Nur Polyesterfilme sind vollkommen sicher und perfekt für die Langzeitarchivierung geeignet.

35M ***Kratzerfreier Film als Basis für Vergrößerungen:***
Chemischer Schutz: Das Filmmaterial ist empfindlich gegenüber Kratzern, Fingerabdrücken und Feuchtigkeit. Zum Schutz der Filme gibt es unterschiedliche Möglichkeiten, die chemischen sehen wie folgt aus:
■ Härtung der Emulsion durch einen Entwicklerhärter. Für viele Fotografen/Laboranten mag das vielleicht neu sein, aber diese Methode ist seit Jahrzehnten bewährt unter dem Begriff *Tropenentwicklung*. Vor allem den Maschinenentwicklern wurde eigentlich immer ein Zusatz beigefügt. Oft realisierte man nicht, dass es sich um einen Härtezusatz handelte, weil es einfach ein Part unter vielen war. Also LP-GELADUR ist keine innovative Neuentwicklung von LABOR

nono bagno d'acqua, preparato questa volta con acqua demineralizzata (acqua distillata reperibile dal benzinaio o in drogheria). Si capovolge regolarmente la tank per 30 secondi, senza enfasi.
Si provocherebbero nuovamente le tanto temute bollicine d'aria, come erano del resto da evitare al 100 % nel caso dello sviluppo. Dopo aver svuotato la tank dell'imbibente (bagno sempre fresco, usa e getta) si asporta la pellicola dalla spirale con la massima cura e si aggancia alla pinza per pellicole. Quest'ultima viene agganciata in un luogo asciutto e privo di polvere. Successivamente si aggancia anche la pinza con peso, affinché la pellicola si asciughi rimanendo piana. Se si fanno asciugare le pellicole in un armadio essiccatore si consiglia di attivare il solo ventilatore ve non il riscaldamento. Solo così si ha la garanzia che la pellicola si asciughi regolarmente e senza lasciare tracce o striature.
Qualsiasi manipolazione meccanica tipo le pinze tergi-film, la pelle di daino, o il vecchio trucco di far scorrere la pellicola attraverso le due dita, è da evitare anche se il trattamento è stato fatto con la massima cura.
Soprattutto le pellicole su base di poliestere sono difficilmente da tenere in piano. Proprio in questi casi è consigliabile utilizzare per questo moderno tipo di pellicole lo speciale imbibente LP-MASTERPROOF.

35L ***Archiviazione:*** Le pellicole perfettamente asciutte vengono normalmente archiviate in striscia. Solo il poliestere garantisce la stabilità di proteggere per lunghissimo tempo le pellicole da negativi influssi esterni. Qualsiasi altro tipo di conservazione, prima o poi rischia di danneggiare le pellicole, soprattutto per l'effetto dell'umidità.
Le pellicole in acetato utilizzate per decenni rischiano di decomporsi in polvere.
Bisogna evitare di archiviare le recenti e datate pellicole in acetato troppo vicine fra loro. Qualora da queste pellicole viene provocata la separazione di acetato di etile, anche pellicole recenti ne possono essere "contaminate" in modo irrimediabile.
■ Esclusivamente le pellicole su base di poliestere sono perfettamente sicure e adatte all'archiviazione a lungo termine.

35M ***Pelllicola priva di graffi quale base per ingrandimenti Chimicamente:*** Le pellicole sono particolarmente sensibili a graffi, impronte digitali ed umidità. Per la loro protezione sono possibili diverse possibilità, fra le quali quelle chimiche sono le seguenti:
■ Indurimento dell'emulsione con l'aggiunta di un induritore allo sviluppo. Per molti fotografi questo sistema rappresenterà una novità, ma questo metodo passa da decenni sotto la definizione: Tropicalizzazione.
Soprattutto negli sviluppi per sviluppatrici è praticamente sempre stato aggiunto un additivo. Spesso non veniva chia-

nalene kan beskyttes og lysbildene kan betraktes på en lysbord. Hvis en ikke lager bildene selv, så trenger en bare å gi fra seg kontaktarket og kan beholde orginalnegativene selv.

idea. Such items were probably thrown on the market by sales people who have never developed a film themselves. Flatness of the film after drying is particularly difficult to achieve with films on a polyester base.
Especially for these, the lab worker should use special LP-MASTERPROOF.

35L ***Archival/storage of processed film:*** When completely dry, films are mostly cut. Only polyester film possesses the necessary permanence to protect film for extended periods without harmful influences. Any other storage medium risks to damage the film sooner or later, particularly under humid conditions.
The acetate films which have been common for decades are in danger of disintegrating, leaving only dust.
Avoid storing old and new acetate films closely together. When old films start to release ethylacetate, they tend to ›infect‹ fresh films.
Only polyester film is absolutely safe and perfectly suited for archival storage.

35M ***Scratch-free film as the basis for prints:***
Chemical protection: Films are easily scratched, marked by fingerprints, or damaged by humidity. There are several means of protecting films. Chemical protection is achieved by hardening of the emulsion by means of a hardener to be added to the developer.
This may be news to quite a number of photographers/lab workers, but the method has been known under the heading *tropical developer* for a long time. An additive was mainly used for machine development, although it was not realised that it was a hardener, because it was just one part in many.
So LP-GELADUR is not a new development by LABOR PARTNER, but learning from history.
Hardening stop baths are also common.
Or hardening fixers.
But what's the use of protection at later processing stages if the emulsion is already damaged in the developer?
Scratch-free copy negatives: The market offers a fair number of sheet films in 24 x 30 cm (roughly 9 x 12in) format, allowing to contact print a complete film onto one sheet of film. Following development, all negatives are available as SLIDES. These contact prints mostly being made on polyester-based material (MACO GENIUS film and MACO GENIUS PRINT film), a quality is possible, which could never be achieved on printing paper, and the original negatives can be protected. The small slides can be judged perfectly on a light box. If you don't process in your own lab, but in a professional one, all you have to give them is the contact sheet. You don't have to part with your precious originals.

MACO IR 820clear, exposed ISO 100, + 4, mit Canon FD 35-mm, f16, developed in LP-Docufine LC © Valsasnini

PARTNER, sondern der Rückgriff auf Bewährtes.

- Daneben sind härtende Stoppbäder üblich.
- Oder auch härtende Fixierbäder.

Nur, was nutzt es, wenn die Emulsion bereits im Entwickler Schaden nimmt um dann in einem Folgebad geschützt zu werden?

Kratzerfreie Negative durch Umkopieren: Es stehen dem Markt verschiedene Planfilme im Format 24 x 30 cm zur Verfügung, auf die ein ganzer Film-Kontaktbogen 1 zu 1 kontaktet werden kann.

Nach der Entwicklung steht ein kompletter Film als *Dia* zur Verfügung. Da diese Kontakte zumeist auf Polyester abgezogen werden (MACO GENIUS film & MACO GENIUS PRINT film), *steht eine Qualität zur Verfügung, die mit einem Kontakt auf Fotopapier niemals zu erreichen ist*, die Originalfilme werden geschützt.

Die kleinen Dias lassen sich auf einem Leuchtkasten perfekt beurteilen. Sofern eine Verarbeitung nicht im eigenen Labor erfolgt, sondern ein professionelles Fachlabor damit beauftragt wird, dann könnte nur noch der Kontaktbogen aus der Hand gegeben werden, die kostbaren Filmoriginale verlassen nicht das eigene Haus.

rito, che si trattava di un additivo indurente, in quanto si trattava di una parte come tante altre.

LP-GELADUR non è pertanto una nuova, innovativa concezione, bensì una riappropriazione di una sostanza acquisita negli anni.

- Anche i bagni di arresto indurenti sono abbastanza diffusi, come pure i fissaggi induritori. Ma a cosa serve se l'emulsione viene danneggiata già nello sviluppo, per poi proteggerla nel bagno seguente?

Per Duplicazione: Sul mercato sono disponibili diverse pellicole piane nel formato 24 x 30 cm, sul quale si può stampare a contatto un intera pellicola in rapporto 1:1. Dopo il trattamento avremo la pellicola completa come DIA. Poiché questi contatti spesso e volentieri vengono stampati su pellicola in poliestere (prima su MACO GENIUS FILM poi su MACO GENIUS PRINT film) si ottiene una qualità, che a confronto di un contatto su carta fotografica, risulterà nettamente superiore e le pellicole originali rimangono protette.

Le piccole dia possono essere giudicate facilmente su un piano luminoso. Qualora le lavorazioni successive non dovessero essere effettuate nel proprio laboratorio, bensì da parte di un laboratorio professionale, si potrebbe consegnare la sola copia a contatto e le pellicole originali rimarrebbero nelle proprie mani.

KODAK Plus-X NEW, developed in LP-CUBE XS

© Valsasnini

36. Sortiment der LABOR PARTNER Fotochemie für die Negativ-Verarbeitung:

	Konfektionierung	Artikel-Nr.
Filmentwickler		
LP-SUPERGRAIN	1l	LPF11
LP-CUBE XS	250ml	LPF82
	1l	LPF81
LP-DOCUFINELC	250ml	LPF92
	1l	LPF91
LP-DOCUFINE HC	1l	LPP51
	5l	LPP55
LP-GELADUR	1l	LPF91
Stoppbäder		
LP-CITRIN	1l	LPS11
	5l	LPS15
LP-CITRODUR	1l	LPS41
	5l	LPS45
Fixierbäder		
LP-FIX SUPRA	1l	LPX21
	5l	LPX25
LP-FIX NEUTRAL	1l	LPX11
	5l	LPX15
Netzmittel		
LP-MASTERPROOF	2 x 250ml	LPH12
	1l	LPH11
Selentoner		
LP-SELENIA	2 x 250ml	LPH42
	1l	LPH41
Brauntoner		
LP-SEPIA	2 x 250ml	LPH52
	2 x 1l	LPH51
Blautoner		
LP-AZUR	2 x 250ml	LPH62
	2 x 1l	LPH61

36. Assortimento dei prodotti foto-chimici LABOR PARTNER

Sviluppi per pellicole		
LP-SUPERGRAIN	1l	LPF11
LP-CUBE XS	250ml	LPF82
	1l	LPF81
LP-DOCUFINELC	250ml	LPF92
	1l	LPF91
LP-DOCUFINE HC	1l	LPP51
	5l	LPP55
LP-GELADUR	1l	LPF91
Bagni d'arresto		
LP-CITRIN	1l	LPS11
	5l	LPS15
LP-CITRODUR	1l	LPS41
	5l	LPS45
Bagni di fissaggio		
LP-FIX SUPRA	1l	LPX21
	5l	LPX25
LP-FIX NEUTRAL	1l	LPX11
	5l	LPX15
Bagno imbibente		
LP-MASTERPROOF	2 x 250ml	LPH12
	1l	LPH11
Viraggio al selenio		
LP-SELENIA	2 x 250ml	LPH42
	1l	LPH41
Viraggio bruno		
LP-SEPIA	2 x 250ml	LPH52
	2 x 1l	LPH51
Viraggio blu		
LP-AZUR	2 x 250ml	LPH62
	2 x 1l	LPH61

36. Sortimentet av LABORPARTNER fotokjemi:

Filmframkallere		
LP-SUPERGRAIN	1l	LPF11
LP-CUBE XS	250ml	LPF82
	1l	LPF81
LP-DOCUFINELC	250ml	LPF92
	1l	LPF91
LP-DOCUFINE HC	1l	LPP51
	5l	LPP55
LP-GELADUR	1l	LPF91
Stoppebad		
LP-CITRIN	1l	LPS11
	5l	LPS15
LP-CITRODUR	1l	LPS41
	5l	LPS45
Fikserbad		
LP-FIX SUPRA	1l	LPX21
	5l	LPX25
LP-FIX NEUTRAL	1l	LPX11
	5l	LPX15
Vetemiddel		
LP-MASTERPROOF	2 x 250ml	LPH12
	1l	LPH11
Selentoner		
LP-SELENIA	2 x 250ml	LPH42
	1l	LPH41
Bruntoner		
LP-SEPIA	2 x 250ml	LPH52
	2 x 1l	LPH51
Blåtoner		
LP-AZUR	2 x 250ml	LPH62
	2 x 1l	LPH61

36. Product range of LABOR PARTNER photo chemicals for film development

Film developers		
LP-SUPERGRAIN	1l	LPF11
LP-CUBE XS	250ml	LPF82
	1l	LPF81
LP-DOCUFINELC	250ml	LPF92
	1l	LPF91
LP-DOCUFINE HC	1l	LPP51
	5l	LPP55
LP-GELADUR	1l	LPF91
Stop baths		
LP-CITRIN	1l	LPS11
	5l	LPS15
LP-CITRODUR	1l	LPS41
	5l	LPS45
Fixers		
LP-FIX SUPRA	1l	LPX21
	5l	LPX25
LP-FIX NEUTRAL	1l	LPX11
	5l	LPX15
Wetting agents		
LP-MASTERPROOF	2 x 250ml	LPH12
	1l	LPH11
Selenium toner		
LP-SELENIA	2 x 250ml	LPH42
	1l	LPH41
Brown toner		
LP-SEPIA	2 x 250ml	LPH52
	2 x 1l	LPH51
Blue toner		
LP-AZUR	2 x 250ml	LPH62
	2 x 1l	LPH61

KODAK Plus-X Pan NEW (120), Rolleiflex Tessar, 1/60, f1, developed 11 minutes in LP-CUBE XS © Valsasnini

Filmentwickler

LP-SUPERGRAIN

LP-SUPERGRAIN ist der moderne Hochleistungsentwickler. Es handelt es sich um einen sehr scharf arbeitenden Feinkornentwickler mit hohem Ausgleichsvermögen.
Wer mehr Wert auf ein extrem feines Korn legt, sollte den LABOR PARTNER LP-CUBE XS verwenden.

■

Der LP-SUPERGRAIN ist ehrlich.
Je nachdem, was der jeweilige Filmhersteller mit seiner Emulsionstechnologie zu leisten imstande ist, leistet der LP-SUPERGRAIN seinen Teil durch ein sehr großes Ausgleichsvermögen. Das bedeutet, Sie als Fotograf können davon ausgehen, dass der LP-SUPERGRAIN die vom Filmhersteller vorgegebene Empfindlichkeit um etwa eine volle Blende plus/minus auszugleichen imstande ist. Dies muss man bei Belichtungsreihen berücksichtigen, bei diesem Entwickler sind Schritte von jeweils 2 Blendenstufen sinnvoll.
Diese Eigenschaft ist auch dafür verantwortlich, dass die Negative nahezu optimal durchzeichnet werden, auch in den tiefsten Schattenpartien und den feinsten Lichtern. Diese Eigenschaft macht den LP-SUPERGRAIN auch für Fotografen interessant, die extreme Lichtverhältnisse zu bewältigen haben. Ein Beispiel:
Theaterfotografen haben es mit Schauspielern zu tun, deren vom Schweiß spiegelnde Gesichter mit Punktlicht angestrahlt sein können. Dort noch eine Durchzeichnung zu erreichen, gehört zu den schwierigsten Aufgaben eines Schwarzweiß-Fotografen. Die in diesem Fall verwendeten hochempfindlichen Filme zeichnen sich jedoch glücklicherweise durch eine hohe Tonalität aus. Die Kombination dieser Filme mit dem LP-SUPERGRAIN ist seit vielen Jahren sehr bewährt, deshalb gehören Theater- und Portrait/Aktfotografen seit der Verfügbarkeit des LP-SUPERGRAIN zu dessen treuesten Liebhabern.
Das hohe Ausgleichsvermögen ermöglicht es dem Laboranten ›alle‹ Schwarzweiß-Filme zwischen 25 ISO und 1.600 ISO, die mit der vom Hersteller vorgegebenen Empfindlichkeit belichtet sind, in einem Arbeitsgang gleichzeitig zu entwickeln. Ausnahmen sind spezielle Filme mit Besonderheiten (siehe Tabelle). Daher sind kleinere Fachlabors begeistert, durch diese besondere Eigenschaft, sicher und rationell Eigen- und Kundenaufträge optimiert und preiswert verarbeiten können.

Sviluppo per pellicole

LP-SUPERGRAIN

LP-SUPERGRAIN è un moderno sviluppo dalle alte prestazioni. Si tratta di uno sviluppo a grana fine con un'attitudine all'alta nitidezza e con grande potere compensativo.
Chi privilegia una grana particolarmente fine dovrebbe optare per il LP-CUBE XS.

■

LP-SUPERGRAIN è onesto.
A seconda di quali prestazioni è capace il rispettivo produttore di pellicole con la propria tecnologia di emulsione, LP-SUPERGRAIN assolve egregiamente la propria missione grazie al sua attitudine di compensazione. Ciò significa, che come fotografo puoi partire dal presupposto, che la sensibilità nominale indicata dal produttore della pellicola che utilizzi, viene compensata dal LP-SUPERGRAIN di ca. un diaframma pieno verso l'alto e verso il basso. Bisogna tenerne conto che nelle serie di esposizioni è necessario operare passi di 2 gradini di diaframma.
Questa caratteristica è pure responsabile della lucentezza ottimale, sia nelle alte che nelle basse luci. (effetto contorno). Questa sua peculiarità rende il LP-SUPERGRAIN interessante per quei fotografi, che devono superare problemi di ripresa in condizioni di luci estreme.
Un esempio: Fotografi di teatro hanno spesso a che fare con i visi grondanti di sudore degli attori, che possono essere illuminati da luci puntiformi e provocare riflessi fastidiosi. Di riuscire ad ottenere ancora un effetto bordo rappresenta una delle imprese più ardue. Le pellicole ad alta sensibilità utilizzate in questi casi, fortunatamente si caratterizzano da una grande tonalità. LP-SUPERGRAIN in combinazione a tali pellicole, è apprezzato da anni,
raccogliendo da parte di una larga fascia di fotografi di teatro, ritratto e glamour ampi consensi.

L'alto potere compensativo permette ai laboratori di trattare contemporaneamente agli stessi tempi ›tutte‹ le pellicole bianco/nero di a sensibilità compresa fra 25 e 1600 ISO, esposte secondo le sensibilità nominali indicate dai produttori. Alcune eccezioni sono rappresentate da alcune pellicole particolari (vedi tabella).
Soprattutto realtà di laboratori più piccoli sono entusiasti grazie a queste caratteristiche, di poter trattare con razionalità, con ottima qualità ed economicamente, le proprie pellicole e quelle dei loro clienti. Principianti, come pure

Filmframkaller

LP-SUPERGRAIN

LP- SUPERGRAIN er en moderne framkaller med toppyteevne. Dette er en svært skarptarbeidene finkornframkaller med høy evne til utgjevnende framkalling. Den som ønsker ennå finere korn burde benytte LP CUBE XS.

■

LP- SUPERGRAIN er en ærlig framkaller.
Alt etter hva filmemulusjonen til forskjellige produsenter er i stand til å yte, så yter LP- SUPERGRAIN sitt med sin utgjevnende virkning. Dette betyr at fotografen kan gå utfra at LP- SUPERGRAIN er i stand til å gjenngi den følsomhet som er oppgitt med en utgjevning på +/- en hel blender. Dette bør en ta hensyn til ved eksponeringsprøver. Skritt på 2 blendere er mest hensiktsmessig.
Denne utgjevnende egenskapen er også grunnen til at negativene er tilnærmet optimale i tegningen, både i høylys og i skyggepartier. Dette gjør LP- SUPERGRAIN interessant for fotografer som arbeider med ekstreme lysforhold.
F.eks: Teaterfotografer har ofte med skuespillere å gjøre som er badet i svette og som i tillegg er belyst med punktlys. Å få til tegning også i disse høylysene er noe av det vanskeligste en fotograf kan prøve på. De høyfølsomme filmene som ofte benyttes til dette har heldigvis en høy tonalitet. I kombinasjon med LP- SUPERGRAIN har fotografer i lang tid kunne oppnå det optimale både i teater, portrett og akt fotografi. Blandt disse fotografene finner vi også dem som virkelig elsker LP- SUPERGRAIN.

Den høye utgjevningen gjør at fotolaboranten kan framkalle ›alle‹ filmer mellom 25 ISO og 1600 ISO med den følsomheten som er oppgitt i en og samme framkaller og det i samme gjennomgang. Det finnes noen unntak (Se tabellen)
Derfor er mindre faglaboratorier begeistret for denne framkalleren. Da dette optimerer og rasjonalliserer arbeidet og det på en økonomisk gunstig måte. Både nybegynnere og fagfotografer, presse og politi sverger til LP- SUPERGRAIN.
Det er viktig at både klassiske filmer med kubiskkornstruktur og nyere filmer med T krystaller kan framkalles i LP SUPERGRAIN.

LABOR PARTNER presenterte denne framkalleren første gang i 1984. Oppskriften ble sterkt modifisert i 1992 og er siden den gang blitt stadig optimert for å ta høyde for utviklingen av filmemusjoner.

Negativ Developer
LP-SUPERGRAIN

LP-SUPERGRAIN is the modern high-performance developer. It produces very sharp negatives and is highly compensating.
If you want extremely fine grain, use LABOR PARTNER LP-CUBE XS.

LP-SUPERGRAIN is an honest developer.
Depending on the virtues with which the film manufacturer endowed his product, LP-SUPERGRAIN will contribute to high negative quality by relying on its compensating action. This means that when shooting photos, you can rely on LP-SUPERGRAIN to compensate the speed provided by the film manufacturer by plus/minus about one f-stop. Remember this when bracketing: steps of two f-stops are convenient with this developer.
It is this characteristic that provides for almost optimal detail, in the deepest shadows as in the most subtle highlights. It makes LP-SUPERGRAIN interesting for photographers who have to deal with extreme contrasts.
An example: Theatre photographers portray actors whose sweaty, reflecting faces may be illuminated by spotlights. Achieving detail in such areas is one of the most challenging tasks for a b&w photographer. Fortunately, however, the very fast films used in this field have a wide spectrum of tones. The combination of these films with LP-SUPERGRAIN has stood the test of time, so as soon as it became available, LP-SUPERGRAIN has won a lot of faithful friends among theatre and portrait/nude photographers.
The strongly compensating effect allows to simultaneously develop ›all‹ b&w films between ISO 25 and ISO 1,600 which were exposed at the manufacturer's rated speed.
The only exceptions are special films (see chart). This is why small laboratories are taken by this particular characteristic allowing them to safely and economically process their own films and customers' orders in an optimised way, and at low cost. The legendary reputation of LP-SUPERGRAIN is based upon these characteristics, which is why beginners and demanding experts alike, newspaper and police photographers swear by this developer. It should be noted that classical cubic-grain as well as recent T-grain films give equally good results when processed in LP-SUPERGRAIN. LP-SUPERGRAIN was first introduced to the market by LABOR PARTNER as a new development in 1984; in 1992,

Auf diesen Eigenschaften beruht der legendäre Ruf des LP-SUPERGRAIN. Darum ›schwören‹ Anfänger als auch anspruchsvolle Fachfotografen, Zeitungs- und Polizeifotografen auf diesen Entwickler.
Wichtig ist, dass sowohl die Filme mit der klassischen kubischen als auch der später verfügbaren T-Kristall-Technologie, mit gleich guten Ergebnissen zur Verarbeitung im LP-SUPERGRAIN geeignet sind.
1984 brachte LABOR PARTNER den LP-SUPERGRAIN als Neuheit erstmalig auf den Markt, die Rezeptur wurde 1992 erheblich modifiziert und wird seitdem in kleinsten Schritten dem technischen Fortschritt der Emulsionstechnologie kontinuierlich angepasst.

VERPACKUNG
1 Liter Polyethylenflaschen

ANSATZ DER CHEMIE
Es wird Leitungs- o. demineralisiertes Wasser verwendet. Nach der Zugabe des LP-SUPERGRAIN Entwicklerkonzentrates ist die Gebrauchslösung sofort gebrauchsfertig (siehe den Hinweis auf Ansatzwasser unter *Filmentwicklung*).

VERARBEITUNGSTEMPERATUR
Es sollte nicht unter 18°C und nicht über 25°C entwickelt werden. Bei höheren Temperaturen werden die Entwicklungszeiten zu kurz. Dann besteht die Gefahr von ›Wolkenbildung‹ aufgrund nicht optimal entwickelter Emulsionen. Entwicklungszeiten sollten im ›Normalfall‹ 5 Minuten nicht sehr unterschreiten, das zeigt sich in der Praxis immer wieder. Die Angaben in der Entwicklungszeitentabelle basieren auf 20°C, gemäß der folgenden Tabelle:

Gebrauchslösung	*Entwicklungszeitänderung:*
18°C	+ 20%
19°C	+ 10%
20°C	Standard
21°C	- 5%
22°C	- 10%
23°C	- 20%
24°C	- 30%
25°C	- 40%

EINMALENTWICKLER – MEHRFACHENTWICKLER
Alle Verdünnungen ab 1 + 9 sind grundsätzlich nur zur Einmalentwicklung geeignet.
Nur die Verdünnung 1 + 7 bietet die grundsätzliche Möglichkeit, die Gebrauchslösung erneut zu verwenden.

professionisti, fotoreporter ed in ambito della polizia ›giurano‹ su questo sviluppo.
Un altro dato importante è rappresentato dal fatto, che sia pellicole a tecnologia di cristalli cubici, che T-Grain possono essere trattate con LP.SUPERGRAIN con altrettanti ottimi risultati. Nel 1984 LABOR PARTNER immetteva per la prima volta sul mercato il LP-SUPERGRAIN, quale novità. Nel 1992 la ricetta è stata alquanto modificata e da allora viene costantemente adattata a piccolissimi passi al progresso della tecnologia delle emulsioni,

CONFEZIONE
Bottiglie da 1 litro in polietilene

PREPARAZIONE DEL CHIMICO
Si utilizza acqua di rubinetto o acqua demineralizzata. Una volta aggiunto il prodotto concentrato LP-SUPERGRAIN la soluzione d'uso è subito pronta all'utilizzo (Vedi i consigli in riguardo all'acqua di preparazione nel capitolo *SVILUPPO DELLE PELLICOLE*).

TEMPERATURA DI TRATTAMENTO
Si consiglia di sviluppare ad una temperatura compresa fra 18 e 25°C. A temperature più elevate i tempi di trattamento diventano troppo brevi e c'è pericolo di ›formazione di nuvole‹ dovuta all'emulsione non sviluppata a fondo. Nella pratica di tutti i gironi si conferma che non bisogna stare con tempi di sviluppo al disotto dei 5 minuti.
Le indicazioni dei tempi di sviluppo – tabella di sviluppo si basano sui 20°C.
Secondo la tabella seguente:

Soluzione d'uso:	*Compensazione del tempo di sviluppo:*
18°C	+ 20 %
19°C	+ 10 %
20°C	standard
21°C	- 5 %
22°C	- 10 %
23°C	- 20 %
24°C	- 30 %
25°C	- 40 %

SVILUPPO USA E GETTA – SVILUPPO PLURI-USO
Tutte le diluizioni a partire da 1 + 9 sono adatte al monouso. Solo da diluizione consente la possibilità di riutilizzare la soluzione d'uso, a condizione che la seconda sviluppata venga effettuata ›a ruota‹ dalla prima (entro ca. 30 minuti).

FORPAKNING
1 liter polythylenflasker

BLANDING AV KJEMI
Det benyttes vann eller deminiralisert vann. Etter at LP SUPERGRAIN er tilsatt vannet er løsningen klar for bruk (Se også punktet om *filmframkal!ling* og blanding av kjemi.)

BRUKSTEMPERATUR
Det kan arbeides mellom 18°C og maksimalt 25°C. Ved høyere temperaturer blir tidene for korte. Det er da fare for skydannelse fordi framkalleren ikke kan virke optimalt i emulsjonen. Praksis viser at tider under 5 min bør unngås.

TIDENE I FRAMKALLERTABELLEN BASSERER PÅ 20°C
Følgende gjelder:

Framkaller temp:	*Avvik:*
18°C	+ 20 %
19°C	+ 10 %
20°C	standard
21°C	- 5 %
22°C	- 10 %
23°C	- 20 %
24°C	- 30 %
25°C	- 40 %

ENGANGSFRAMKALLER – FLERBRUKSFRAMKALLER
Alle fortynninger over 1 + 9 er alltid for engangsbruk
Bare fortynningen 1 + 7 gir muligheten for gjenntatt bruk. Men også her bare hvis den blir benyttet med en gang (innen 30 min). Den opprinnelige tiden beholdes. Se også *UTNYTTELSE*.

FORTYNNING
Standard fortynning er 1 + 7.
Ved en framkallingstank som trenger 260 ml gir dette 1 + 7 32,5 ml LP SUPERGRAIN + 227,5 ml vann.
Kvaliteten blir ikke bedre med fortynning (Aminophenol effekt). Høyere fortynning gir lengre framkallingstider og sparer kjemi, noe som kan være interessant for private brukere.
Høyere konsentrasjon blir frarådt, det er da bedre å øke temperaturen.

the formulation was modified considerably, and since then it is continuously updated to accommodate progress in emulsion technology.

PACKAGING
1 l polyethylene bottles

PREPARATION OF THE SOLUTION
Use tap water or demineralised water. The working solution is ready for use as soon as the LP-SUPERGRAIN developer concentrate has been added (See note on water for photographic solutions under *FILM DEVELOPMENT*).

PROCESSING TEMPERATURE
Processing below 18°C (64°F) or above 25°C (77°F) is not recommended. Developing times will get too short at higher temperatures, which means there is a risk of ›clouding‹ due to faulty development of the emulsion. ›Normally‹, development times should not be considerably less than 5 minutes. This has been proven by practice over and over again.
The recommendations given in the following chart are based upon a temperature of 20°C (68°F).

Temperature of working solution:	*Change in developing time:*
18°C (64°F)	+ 20%
19°C (66°F)	+ 10%
20°C (68°F)	standard
21°C (70°F)	- 5%
22°C (72°F)	- 10%
23°C (73°F)	- 20%
24°C (75°F)	- 30%
25°C (77°F)	- 40%

ONE-SHOT DEVELOPER – DEVELOPER FOR REPEATED USE
All dilutions of 1 + 9 or higher are suited for one-shot use only.
Only 1 + 7 dilutions allow repeated use, this, however, only being possible if the second development ›immediately‹ follows the first (›immediately‹ meaning about 30 minutes). In this case, the working solution used once is kept in a sealed bottle. Development need *not* (!) be longer than for the first use. See also *CAPACITY*.

Dies nur in dem Fall, wenn ›unverzüglich‹ nach einem Entwicklungsvorgang ein zweiter folgen wird. (Innerhalb von etwa 30 Minuten). In diesem Fall wird die einmal verwendete Gebrauchslösung in einer verschließbaren Flasche aufbewahrt. Eine Verlängerung der ursprünglichen Entwicklungszeit ist nicht erforderlich (!). Siehe auch unter *Ergiebigkeit.*

VERDÜNNUNG

Die Standard-Verdünnung ist 1 + 7. Bei einer Standard-Entwicklerdose von 260 ml Inhalt wird wie folgt verdünnt:

1 + 7 =	32,5 ml LP-SUPERGRAIN-Konzentrat
	+ 227,5 ml Wasser

Die Qualität wird nicht besser durch höhere Verdünnungen (Aminophenol-Effekt). Höhere Verdünnungen bedingen längere Entwicklungszeiten und sparen Chemiekosten, das kann für den privaten Anwender interessant sein. Von höheren Konzentrationen zur Verkürzung von Entwicklungszeiten wird gewarnt, da ist es besser, die Temperaturen zu erhöhen.

ENTWICKLERHÄRTUNG

Jeder Film verträgt es, während der Entwicklung zusätzlich gehärtet zu werden. LABOR PARTNER rät dazu, den Entwicklerhärter LP-GELADUR der Entwicklergebrauchslösung wie folgt zuzugeben:

VERDÜNNUNGSTABELLE FÜR 260 ml GEBRAUCHSLÖSUNG

1 + 7 (Standard)	32,5 ml LP-SUPERGRAIN
	+ 138 ml Wasser
	+ 90 ml LP-GELADUR
1 + 9	26 ml LP-SUPERGRAIN
	+ 139 ml Wasser
	+ 95 ml LP-GELADUR
1 + 12	20 ml LP-SUPERGRAIN
	+ 144 ml Wasser
	+ 96 ml LP-GELADUR
1 + 16	15 ml LP-SUPERGRAIN
	+ 145 ml Wasser
	+ 100 ml LP-GELADUR
1 + 19	13 ml LP-SUPERGRAIN
	+ 147 ml Wasser
	+ 100 ml LP-GELADUR

Die Verdünnungen 1 + 16 und 1 + 19 werden nur dann angewendet, wenn ein Test die Eignung der jeweiligen Film-Entwicklerkombination bestätigt hat.

Anche in questo caso la soluzione d'uso già utilizzata una volta va conservata in una bottiglia chiusa e colma. Non è necessario un incremento del tempo di sviluppo (!). Vedi anche sotto il capitolo *CAPACITA'*

DILUIZIONE

La diluizione standard è 1 + 7.

Con una tank di sviluppo standard di 260 ml di contenuto si diluisce come segue:

1 + 7 =	32,5 ml LP-SUPERGRAIN
	+ 227,5 ml di acqua

La qualità non migliora con la maggiore diluizione (effetto amminofenolo). Diluizioni maggiori implicano dei tempi di sviluppo più lunghi e riducono i costi della chimica, un affare interessante per utilizzatori privati.

Si evitino concentrazioni più alte, è meglio cioè aumentare la temperatura.

INDURIMENTO DELL SVILUPPO

Qualsiasi pellicola sopporta l'indurimento durante lo sviluppo.

LABOR PARTNER consiglia di aggiungere LP-GELADUR alla soluzione d'uso di sviluppo seguendo la tabella sotto:

TABELLA DI DILUIZIONE PER 260 ml DI SOLUZIONE D'USO

1 + 7 (Standard)	32,5 ml di LP-SUPERGRAIN
	+ 138 ml di acqua
	+ 90 ml di LP-GELADUR
1 + 9	26 ml di LP-SUPERGRAIN
	+ 139 ml di acqua
	+ 95 ml di LP-GELADUR
1 + 12	20 ml di LP-SUPERGRAIN
	+ 144 ml di acqua
	+ 96 ml di LP-GELADUR
1 + 16	15 ml di LP-SUPERGRAIN
	+ 145 ml di acqua
	+ 100 ml di LP-GELADUR
1 + 19	13 ml di LP-SUPERGRAIN
	+ 147 ml di acqua
	+ 100 ml di LP-GELADUR

Le diluizioni 1 + 16 e 1 + 19 si utilizzino solo, dopo aver appurato la compatibilità della combinazione pellicola-sviluppo. Sono ideali le diluizioni, nelle quali la quantità di prodotto concentrato per ogni pellicola non sia al disotto dei 20 ml.

FRAMKALLER HERDING

En hver film tåler å bli herdet under framkallingen.

LABOR PARTNER tilrår å blande framkallerherderen LP-GELADUR i henhold til følgende tabell.

FORTYNNINGSTABELL FOR 260 ml FERDIG BLANDING

1 + 7 (Standard)	32,5 ml LP-SUPERGRAIN
	+ 138 ml vann
	+ 90 ml LP-GELADUR
1 + 9	26 ml LP-SUPERGRAIN
	+ 139 ml vann
	+ 95 ml LP-GELADUR
1 + 12	20 ml LP-SUPERGRAIN
	+ 144 ml vann
	+ 96 ml LP-GELADUR
1 + 16	15 ml LP-SUPERGRAIN
	+ 145 ml vann
	+ 100 ml LP-GELADUR
1 + 19	13 ml LP-SUPERGRAIN
	+ 147 ml vann
	+ 100 ml LP-GELADUR

Fortynningene 1 + 16 og 1 + 19 benyttes bare hvis en test har vist at filmen egner seg til denne kombinasjonen. Ideelt sett bør en ikke benytte mindre enn 20 ml konsentrat pr film.

TIDSKORREKTUR

Fortynning:	*Faktor:*
1+7	1
1+9	1,1
1+12	1,4
1+16	1,7*
1+19	2,0*

** må testes individuelt for hver filmtype*

DILUTION

The standard dilution is 1 + 7. For a standard tank with a contents of 260 ml, dilute as follows:

1 + 7 =	32.5 ml of LP-SUPERGRAIN concentrate
	+ 227.5 ml of water.

Quality will not improve with higher dilutions (aminophenol). Higher dilutions will, however, prolong development times and cut expenses for chemistry, which may be of interest to the private user.
We do advise against using higher concentrations for shorter development times; increasing temperature is certainly the better way to achieve this end.

DEVELOPER HARDENING

Any film can do with some additional hardening during development.
LABOR PARTNER recommends to add the developer hardener LP-GELADUR to the working solution of the developer as per the following chart.

DILUTION CHART FOR 260 ml OF WORKING SOLUTION

1 + 7 (Standard)	32,5 ml LP-SUPERGRAIN
	+ 138 ml of water
	+ 90 ml LP-GELADUR
1 + 9	26 ml LP-SUPERGRAIN
	+ 139 ml of water
	+ 95 ml LP-GELADUR
1 + 12	20 ml LP-SUPERGRAIN
	+ 144 ml of water
	+ 96 ml LP-GELADUR
1 + 16	15 ml LP-SUPERGRAIN
	+ 145 ml of water
	+ 100 ml LP-GELADUR
1 + 19	13 ml LP-SUPERGRAIN
	+ 147 ml of water
	+ 100 ml LP-GELADUR

Dilutions 1 + 16 and 1 +19 are only used if a test has shown the specific film/developer combination to work. Dilutions are ideal if the minimum quantity of concentrate is no less than 20 ml per film.

Ideal sind Verdünnungen, bei denen die Menge von 20 ml Konzentrat pro Film nicht unterschritten wird.

ZEIT-VERLÄNGERUNGSTABELLE

Verdünnung:	*Verlängerungsfaktor:*
1 + 7	1,0
1 + 9	1,1
1 + 12	1,4
1 + 16	1,7*
1 + 19	2,0*

Bei 1,7 und 2,0* ist die individuelle Eignung vorher zu testen.*

ÜBER- UND UNTERBELICHTUNG *(forcierte Entwicklung)*
In einem begrenzten Umfang ist der LP-SUPERGRAIN auch dafür einsetzbar. Die Qualität kann bei der Überbelichtung erheblich zunehmen, bei Unterbelichtung erheblich leiden. Dies ist vor allem abhängig von der Qualität des verwendeten Filmmaterials, weniger von dem vom Entwickler.
Es gelten Erfahrungswerte, die als Basis für eigene Versuche gelten können:

- Unterbelichtung um 1 Blende:
  Verlängerung der Entwicklung um 20-40 %.
- Unterbelichtung um 2 Blenden:
  Verlängerung der Entwicklung um 40-80 %.
- Überbelichtung um 1 Blende:
  Verkürzung der Entwicklung um 20-30%.

GRADATION
Die in der Entwicklungszeitentabelle angegeben Zeiten sollen ein mittleres Gamma von 0,65 erreichen.
Es kann jedoch sein, dass beim individuellen Vergrößern, andere Werte als optimaler angestrebt werden.
So erfordern Vergrößerungsgeräte mit einem Lichtmischschacht härtere Negative mit dem Gamma etwa 0,65 bis 0,7.
Geräte mit Doppelkondensoren weichere Negative mit dem Gamma 0,5 bis 0,55.
Der für den Laboranten mögliche Zeiten-Spielraum bewegt sich von 20% Zeiten-Verlängerung bis zu 20% Zeiten-Verkürzung.
Größere Abweichungen würden zwangsläufig Qualitätseinbußen bewirken.

ERGIEBIGKEIT BASIEREND AUF DER VERDÜNNUNG 1 + 7
In 1 Liter Gebrauchslösung können maximal 5 Kleinbild- oder Rollfilme oder 0,3 m² Planfilme verarbeitet werden.

TABELLA DELL'INCREMENTO DEI TEMPI

Diluizione:	*Fattore di prolunga:*
1 + 7	1,0
1 + 9	1,1
1 + 12	1,4
1 + 16	1,7*
1 + 19	2,0*

a 1,7 e 2,0* da testare secondo le esigenze individuali.*

SOPRA- E SOTTOESPOSIZIONE *(sviluppo spinto)*
LP-SUPERGRAIN è utilizzabile limitatamente anche in questo ambito.
La qualità può aumentare in modo ragguardevole in caso di sovraesposizione, e diminuire in caso di sottoesposizione. Ciò però dipende in maggior misura dalla qualità della pellicola utilizzata. Che dallo sviluppo stesso.
Valgono dei valori basati sull'esperienza, che possono valere quale base di partenza per prove individuali:

- Sottoesposizione di 1 diaframma:
  Aumento del tempo di sviluppo del 20-40 %
- Sottoesposizione di 2 diaframmi:
  Aumento del tempo di sviluppo del 40-80 %
- Sovraesposizione di 1 diaframma:
  Aumento del tempo di sviluppo del 20-30 %

GRADAZIONE
I tempi indicati sulla tabella di sviluppo dovrebbero portare ad un valore medi Gamma medio di 0,65. E' però possibile che per una stampa individuale si desiderino ottenere valori ottimali, differenti.
Ingranditori muniti di teste a luce diffusa necessitano di negativi più contrastati, con un Gamma di ca. 0,65 a 0,70.
Ingranditori invece con testa a condensatori necessitano di negativi più morbidi, con un Gamma di ca. 0,50 a 0,55.
La tolleranza a disposizione dello stampatore varia fra un 20 % di incremento e un 20 % di decremento del tempo .
Variazioni superiori implicano necessariamente un abbassamento della qualità.

RESA BASATA SU UNA DILUIZIONE DI 1 + 7
In 1 litro di soluzione d'uso possono essere trattate al massimo 5 pellicole di piccolo o medio formato, oppure 0,3 mq di pellicola piana.

OVER OG UNDEREKSPONERING *(pull og push framkalling)*
I et begrenset omfang kan LP-SUPERGRAIN også brukes til dette. Kvaliteten kan tilta betraktelig ved overeksponering, men også avta sterkt ved undereksponering.
Dette er framfor alt avhengig av filmen som benyttes, og ikke så mye av framkalleren.
Her noen erfaringsverdier som kan tjene som basis for egne forsøk:

- Undereksponering med 1 blender:
  økning av framkallertiden med 20-40 %
- Undereksponering med 2 blendere:
  økning av framkallertiden med 40-80 %
- Overeksponering med 1 blender
  minskning av framkallertiden med 20-30 %

GRADASJON
De oppgitte framkallingstidene gir en gjennomsnitts gamma på 0,65. Det kan være at din forstørrer krever en annen verdi for et optimalt resultat. Forstørrere med en blandingsjakt kan kreve gamma 0,65 til 0,7.
Dobbelkondensorer krever et mykere negativ med f.eks gamma 0,5 til 0,55. Dette oppnås ved å variere tiden med +/- 20 %. Større variasjoner vil medføre kvalitetstap.

UTNYTTELSESDRAD
Basert på en fortynning 1 + 7 vil 1 liter ferdig framakallerløsning maksimalt rekke til 5 filmer 35 mm eller rullfilm eller 0,3 m² planfilm.

AGGITASJON
Første 30 sek stadig og så hvert 30 sek 1 x.

ROTASJONSFRAMKALLING
ALLTID 1 + 13 (!).
Da gjelder tidene i henhold til filmtid tabellen.

JOBO ATL PROCESSOR
ALLTID 1+ 13 (!).
Forlengelsesfaktor ca 50 % i forhold til tabellen.
Framkallingstidene for 35 mm og rullfilm er lik.
Det blir gjordt oppmerksom på at en hver rotasjonsframkalling kan medføre minsket kvalitet pga kantskarphetens endring.

CHART SHOWING THE FACTOR BY WHICH TO PROLONG DEVELOPMENT WITH HIGHER DILUTION

1 + 7	1,0
1 + 9	1,1
1 + 12	1,4
1 + 16	1.7*
1 + 19	2.0*

For 1.7 and 2.0* tests of the specific combination prior to ›serious‹ use are mandatory.*

OVER- AND UNDEREXPOSURE *(push development)*

LP-SUPERGRAIN can be used to some extent for this kind of control.

Considerable gains in quality are achievable with overexposure; likewise, losses are possible with underexposure. This mainly depends on the quality of the film in question, less so on the developer.

The following empiric values can be used as a basis for your own experimentation:

- Underexposure by one f-stop:
  Prolong development by 20 to 40%.
- Underexposure by two f-stops:
  Prolong development by 40 to 80%.
- Overexposure by one f-stop:
  Curtail development by 20 to 30%.

GRADATION

The times given in the development chart are for an average gamma of 0.65. For individual printing habits, other target values may be optimal.

Enlargers with diffusor lighting systems, for example, require harder negatives, with a gamma of 0.65 to 0.7 while double-condensor enlargers require softer negatives, with a gamma of 0.5 to 0.55. The margin for development time modifications by the lab worker ranges from 20% extension to 20% curtailing. Deviating by a larger factor would definitely result in a loss in quality.

CAPACITY

based on a dilution of 1 + 7:

One litre of working solution can develop up to five 35-mm or medium format roll films or 0.3 m² of sheet film.

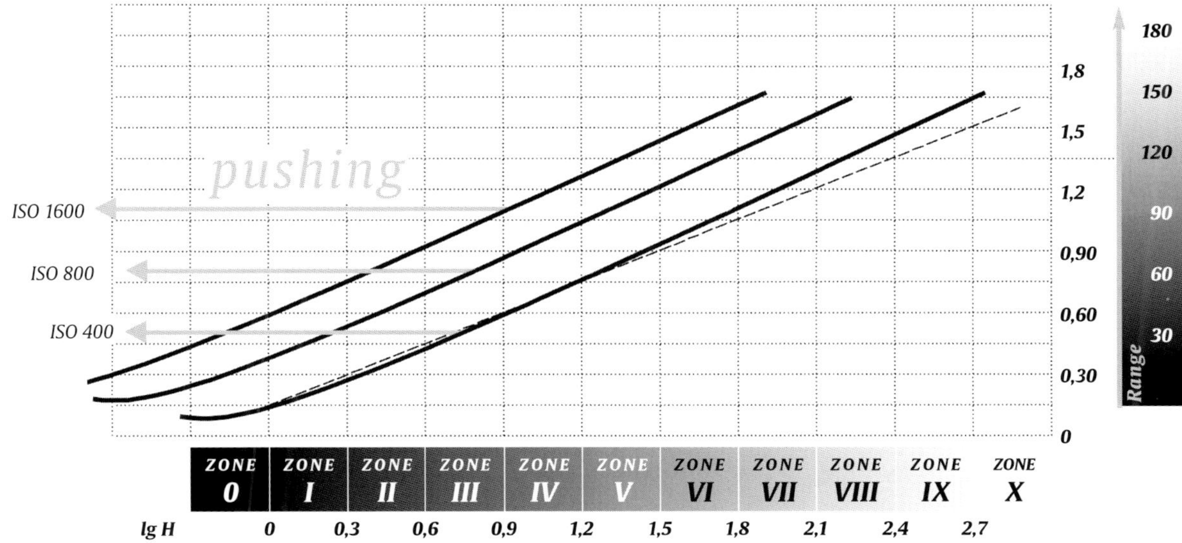

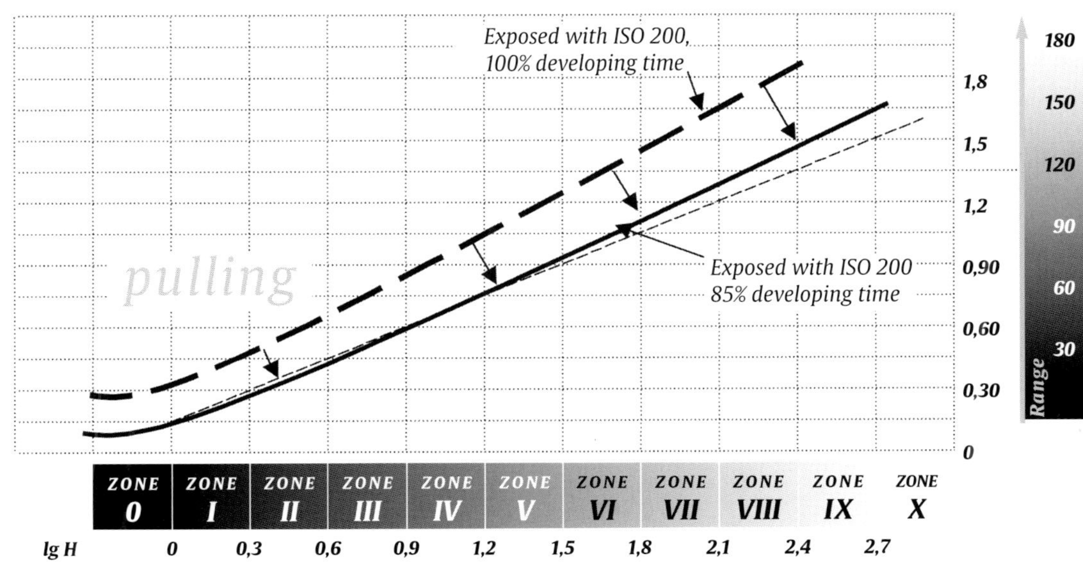

BEWEGUNG
In den ersten 30 Sekunden ist die Entwicklerdose ständig zu bewegen. Danach alle 30 Sekunden jeweils 1 x.

ROTATIONSENTWICKLUNG
Der Ansatz ist grundsätzlich 1 + 13 (!).
Dann gelten die Zeiten der Entwicklungszeitentabelle.

JOBO-ATL-PROCESSOR
Der Ansatz ist grundsätzlich 1 + 13 (!).
Die Entwicklungszeiten sind rund 50% gegenüber der Entwicklungszeitentabelle zu verlängern. Die Entwicklungszeiten sind für Rollfilme (120) und Kleinbildfilme (135-36) gleich.
Es sollte darauf hingewiesen werden, dass jede Rotationsentwicklung einen Qualitätsverzicht durch die Kantenschärfeüberhöhung bewirken kann.

HALTBARKEIT
Die original verschlossene, schwarze LABOR PARTNER ist etwa bis zu 2 Jahre nach dem Erwerb im Handel haltbar.
Die Farbe des Konzentrates darf sich nicht in Richtung Braun verfärbt haben. Sobald eine sichtbare Verfärbung vorliegt, ist die weitere Verwendung zu riskant.
Die angebrochene Flasche sollte nach der Entnahme des Konzentrates vor dem erneuten Verschließen so stark zusammengedrückt werden, dass sich keine Luft mehr in der Flasche befindet. Ist die Restmenge zu gering dafür, dann ist diese entweder in kleinere Flaschen umzufüllen oder der Inhalt der LP-Originalflasche mit Glaskugeln aufzufüllen.
Bei Beachtung dieser Hinweise gilt: *Anbrüche können etwa ein halbes Jahr aber auch erheblich länger aufbewahrt werden.*

MOVIMENTO / AGITAZIONE
La tank va agitata con continuità durante i primi 30 secondi. Successivamente 1 volta ogni 30 secondi

SVILUPPA A ROTAZIONE
Ad una diluizione di 1+13 (!).
In questo modo valgono gli stessi tempi di sviluppi indicati in tabella.

PROCESSORE TIPO JOBO-ATL
Ad una diluizione di 1+13 (!).
I tempi di sviluppo vanno incrementati di ca. il 50 % rispetto alla tabella dei tempi di sviluppo.
I tempi di sviluppo sono uguali per Rollfilm (120) e pellicole di piccolo formato (135/36).
Bisogna considerare che nello sviluppo in processore a rotazione bisogna accettare una riduzione della nitidezza dovuta all'incremento dell'effetto bordo.

CONSERVAZIONE
La bottiglia originale LABOR PARTNER, sigillata, Può durare fino a 2 anni dall'acquisto. Il colore del prodotto concentrato con deve colorarsi in direzione del marrone. Non appena si nota una accentuata colorazione del concentrato, l'uso diventa rischioso.
Dopo che la bottiglia è stata aperta ed asportato del concentrato, prima di richiuderla è consigliabile far uscire l'aria schiacciando la bottiglia finché il liquido appare dal beccuccio della bottiglia.
Quando la quantità si riduce ulteriormente, si consiglia di travasare il concentrato residuo in una bottiglia più piccola, o di riempire la bottiglia originale con biglie di vetro.
Seguendo tali consigli, *si può conservare il concentrato iniziato per mezz'anno o più.*

HOLDBARHET
I orginalembalasjen holdbar ca 2 år. Farven på konsentratet må ikke bli brun. Så snart en misfarging oppstår er videre bruk betenkelig.
Når konsentrat er fjernet fra flasken, bør denne presses sammen slik at det ikke er luft i denne. Er restmengden forliten til at dette er mulig kan konsentratet fylles i en minde flaske eller flasken kan fylles med glasskuler. Følges disse rådene *kan en åpnet flaske holde seg i mer enn 6 mnd.*

AGITATION
Agitate permanently for the first 30 s.
Then invert once every 30 s.

ROTATION DEVELOPMENT
Always use dilution 1+13(!).
Times are as given in the *development time chart.*

JOBO ATL PROCESSOR
Always use 1+13(!).
Prolong development times given in the chart by a factor of 50%.
Development times for medium format (120) and 35-mm roll films (135) are identical.
It should be noted that rotation development may result in a loss in quality due to excessive adjacency effects.

SHELF LIFE
An unopened black LABOR PARTNER bottle can be kept for up to 2 years after purchasing. The concentrate must not show any brownish discoloration. As soon as any discoloration is visible, use is too hazardous.
While in use, the bottle should be compressed to remove all air. If the remaining quantity is too small, it should be filled into smaller bottles, or the volume of the original LP bottle should be refilled with glass balls. When these recommendations are observed, *used bottles may be kept for half a year, or even considerably longer.*

Development chart **LP-SUPERGRAIN** | 1+7 / 1+15 20°C | 30 Seconds Agitation | Gamma 0,55

Columns: **Sensitivity** | **ISO** | **Development Time** (1+7, 1+15) | **ISO Standard** | **grainless Enlg.-Times** | **RMS Grain** | **Tonality** | **MFT Dissolving-Power**

AGFA APX 100

Panchromatic 400 - 650

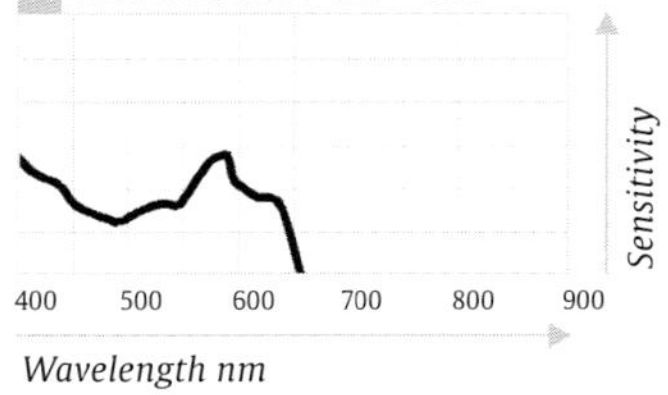

ISO	1+7	1+15
100		5
200	6,5	

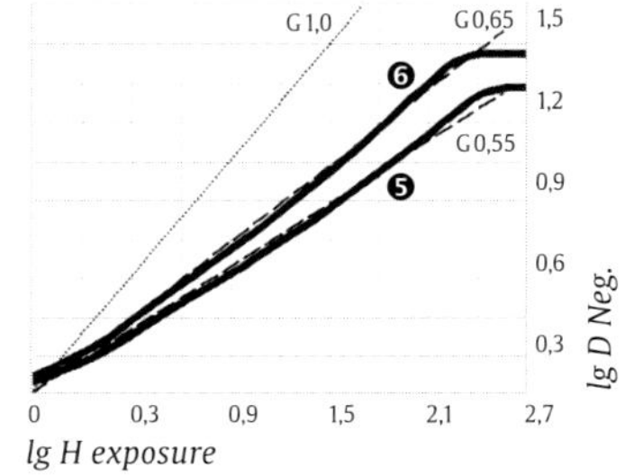

❻❺ = Development-Time in Minutes

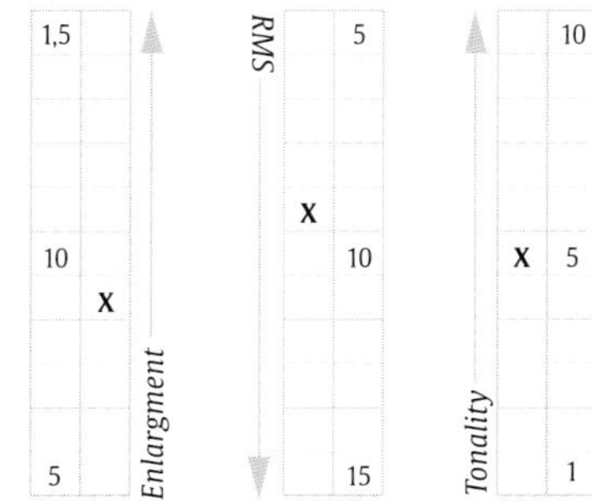

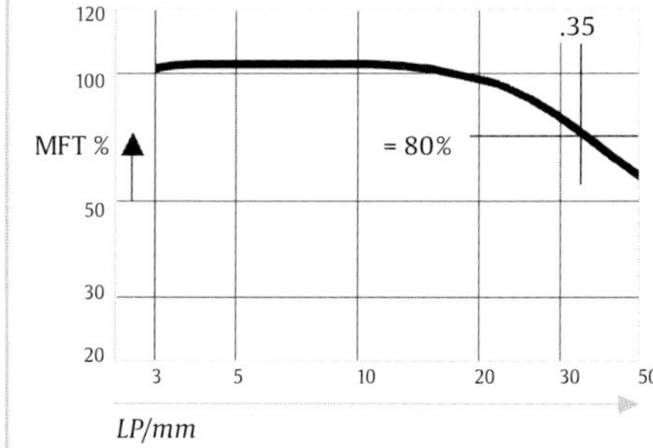

AGFA APX 200S

Panchromatic 400 - 650

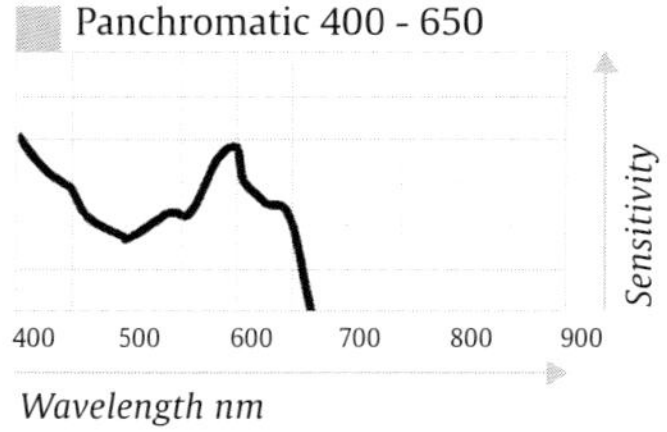

ISO	1+7	1+15
200	5	

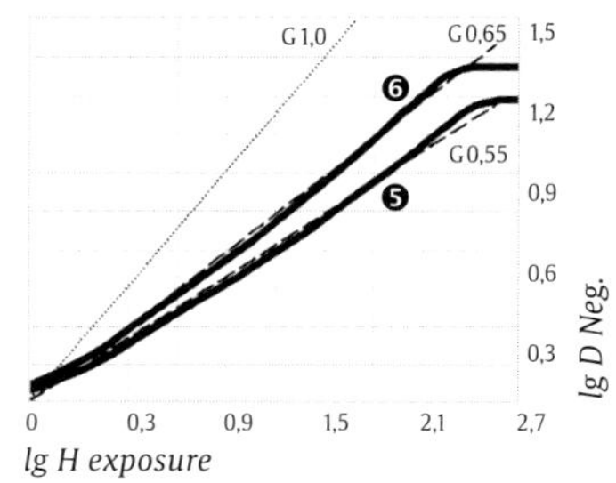

❻❺ = Development-Time in Minutes

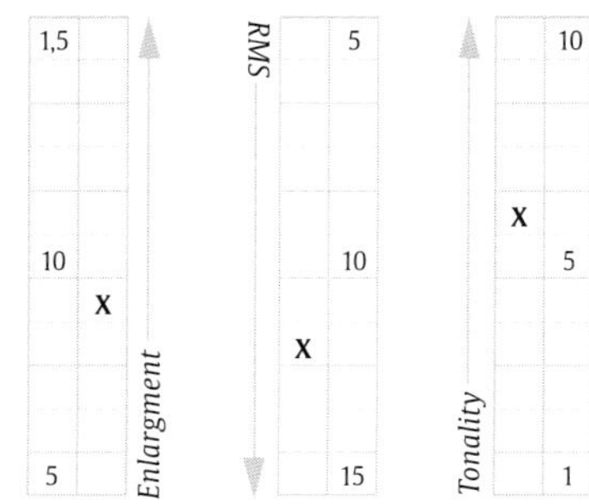

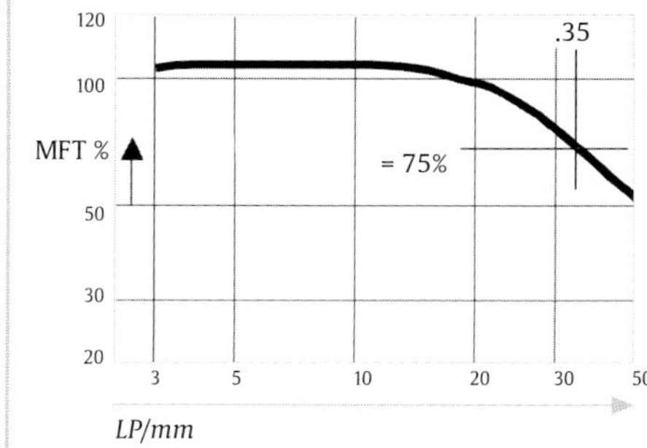

AGFA APX 400

Panchromatic 400 - 650

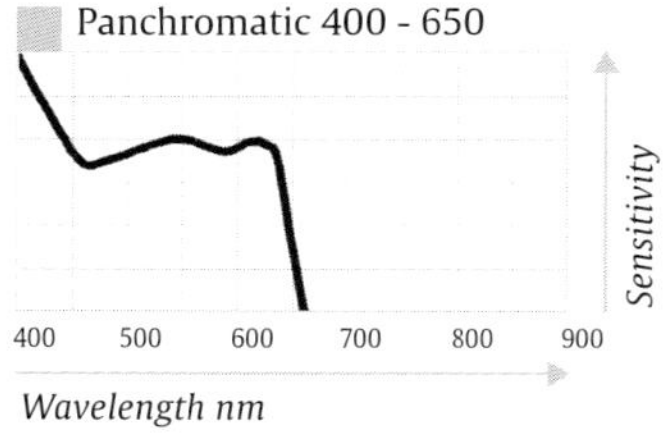

ISO	1+7	1+15
400		5
800		6,5

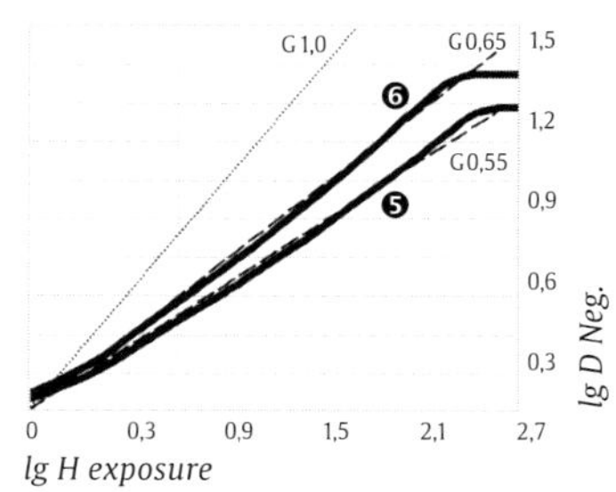

❻❺ = Development-Time in Minutes

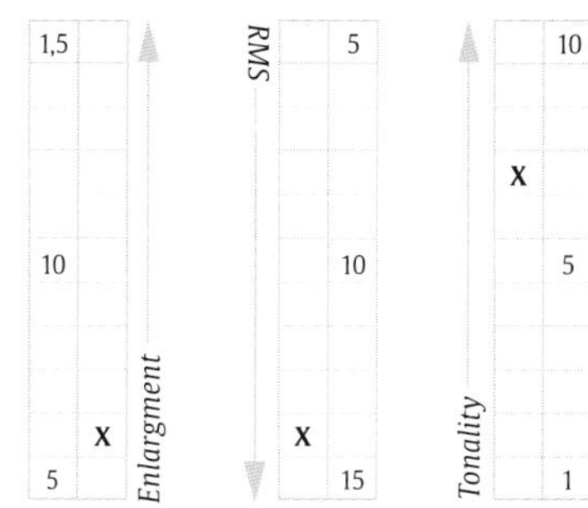

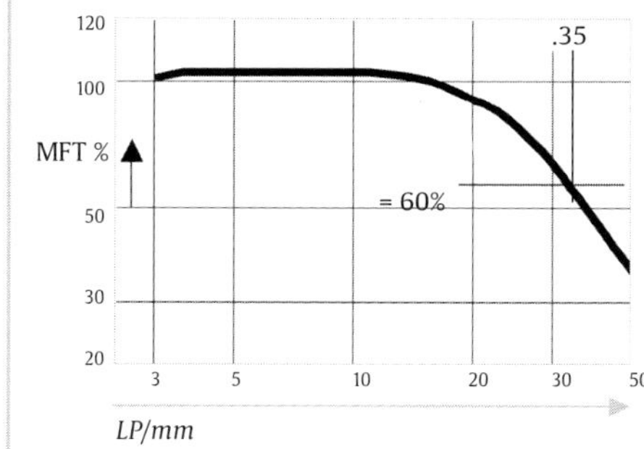

FUJI Neopan 100

Panchromatic 400 -700

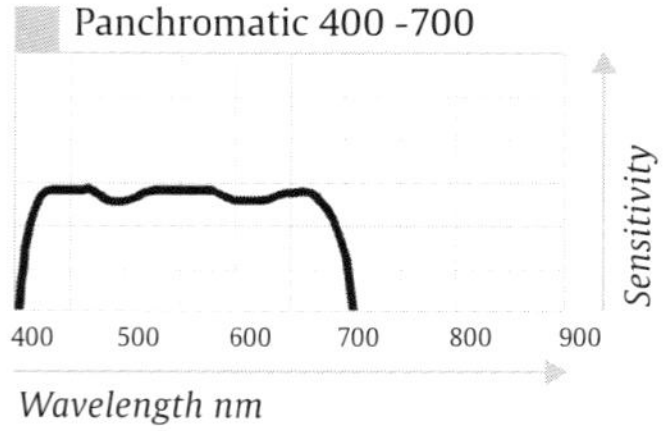

ISO	1+7	1+15
100		4
200		5,5

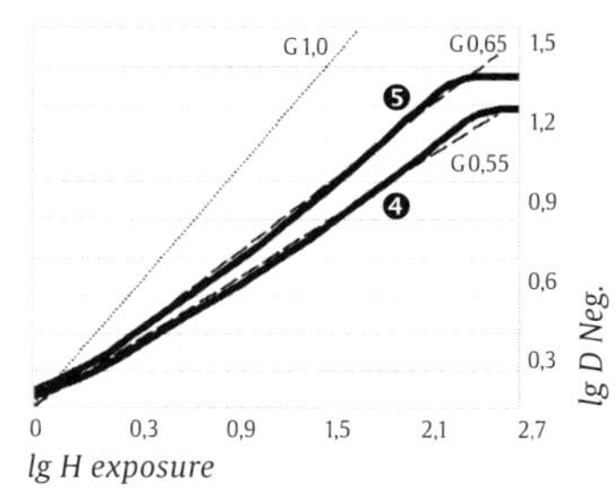

❻❺ = Development-Time in Minutes

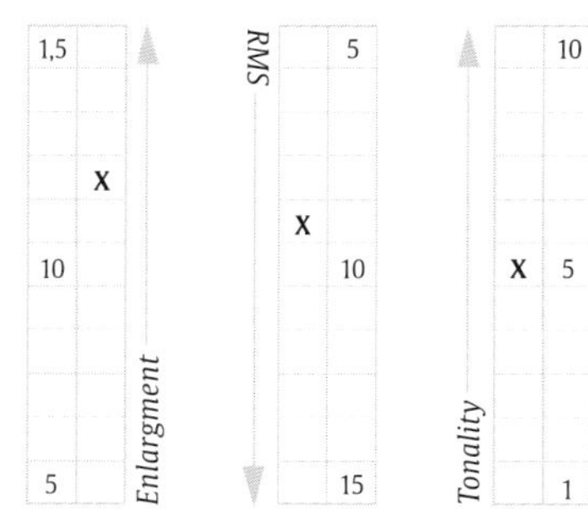

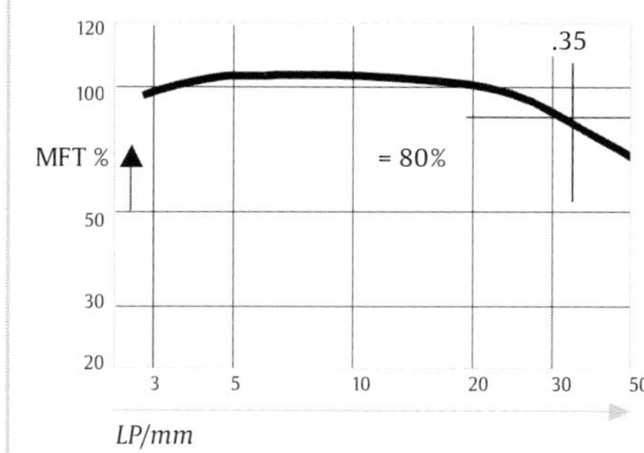

Development chart **LP-SUPERGRAIN** | 1+7 / 1+15 20°C | 30 Seconds Agitation | Gamma 0,55

Film	ISO	Development Time 1+7	Development Time 1+15
FUJI Neopan 400	400	6	
	800	7	
	1600	8	
FUJI Neopan 1600	1600	6	
	3200	7,5	
ILFORD Pan F	50	3	5
	100	3,5	5,5
ILFORD FP4	100	3	4,5
	200	4	
	400	5	

FUJI Neopan 400

Sensitivity: Panchromatic 400 - 700

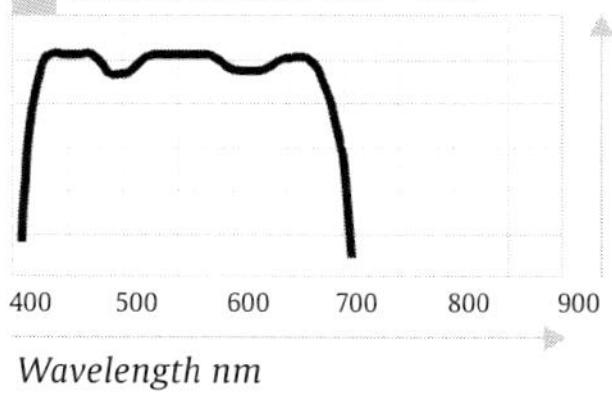

ISO Standard

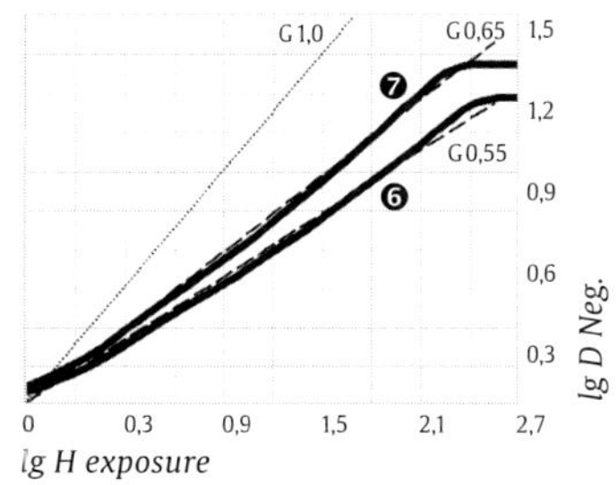

❻❺ = Development-Time in Minutes

grainless Enlg.-Times / RMS Grain / Tonality

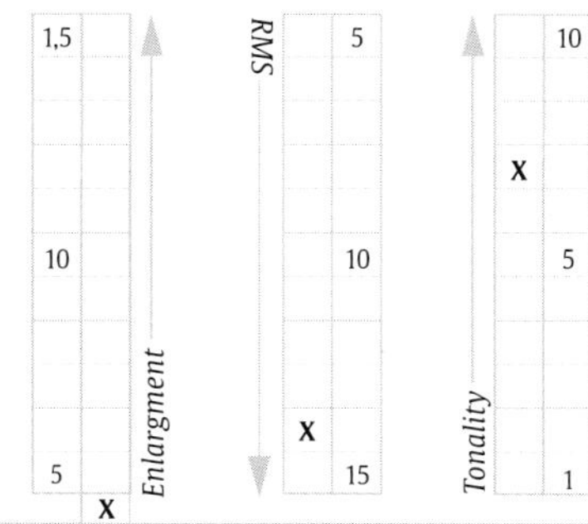

MFT Dissolving-Power

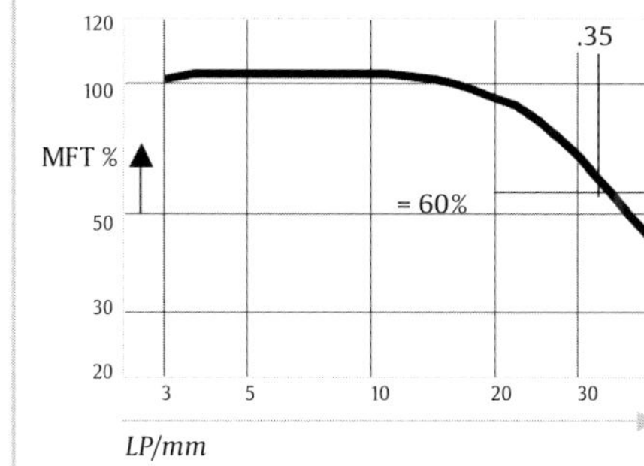

FUJI Neopan 1600

Sensitivity: Panchromatic 400 - 700

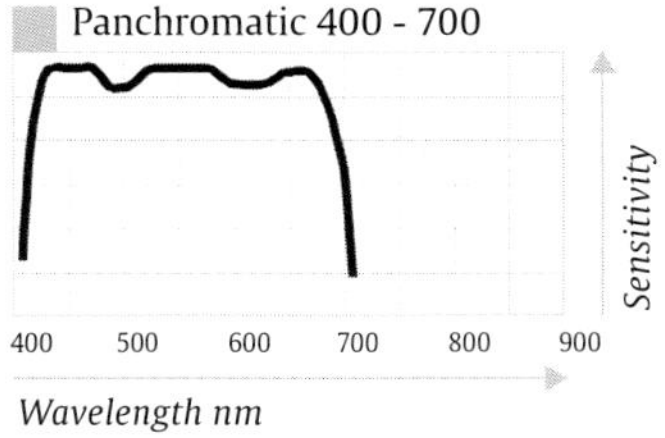

ISO Standard

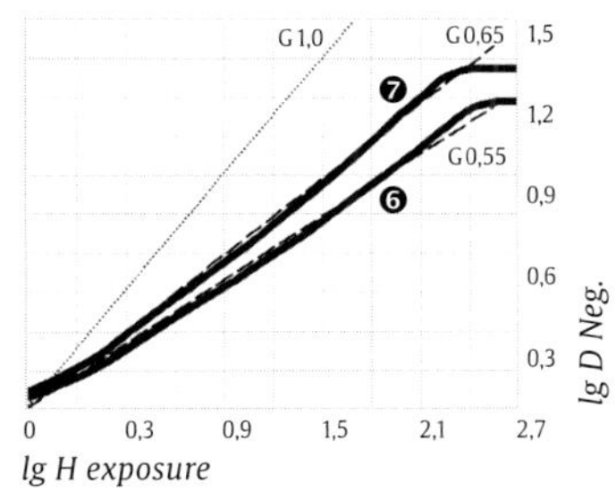

❻❺ = Development-Time in Minutes

grainless Enlg.-Times / RMS Grain / Tonality

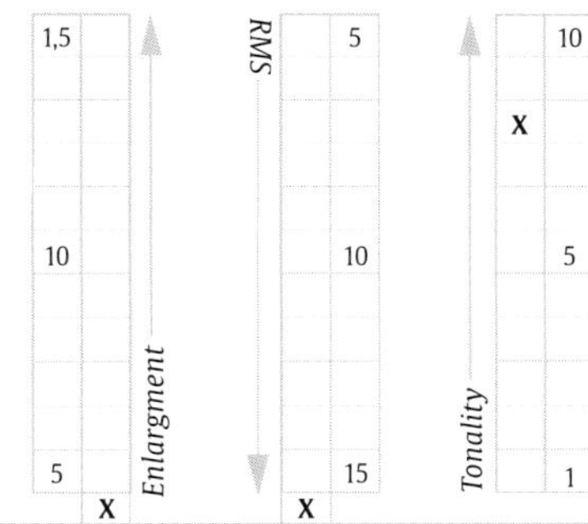

MFT Dissolving-Power

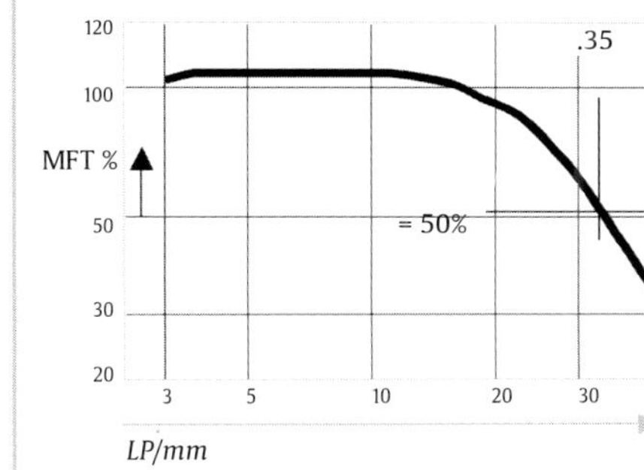

ILFORD Pan F

Sensitivity: Panchromatic 400 - 700

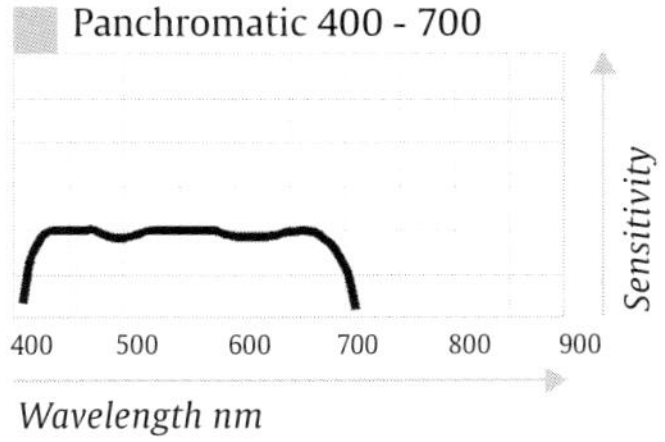

ISO Standard

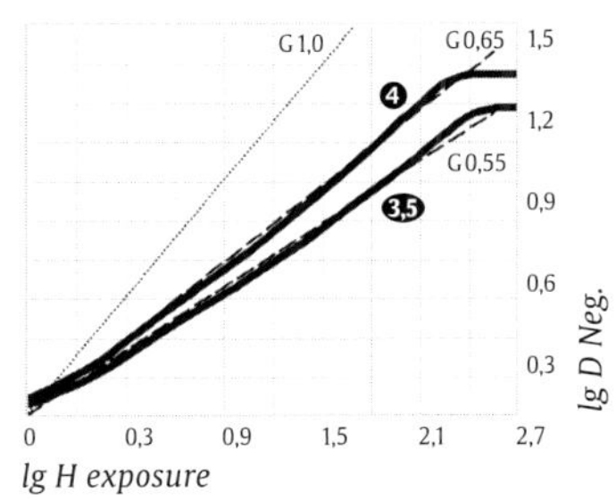

❻❺ = Development-Time in Minutes

grainless Enlg.-Times / RMS Grain / Tonality

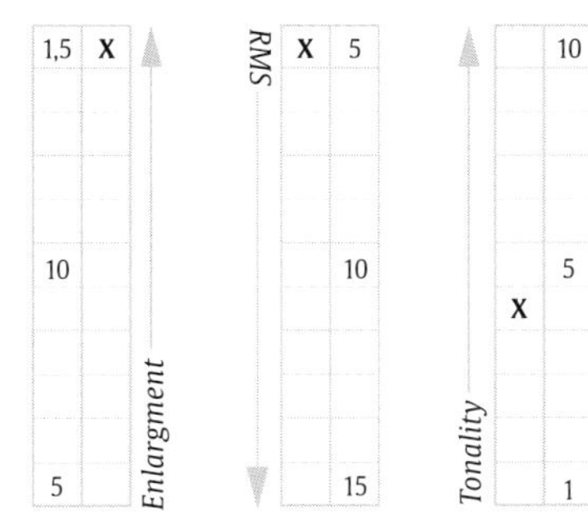

MFT Dissolving-Power

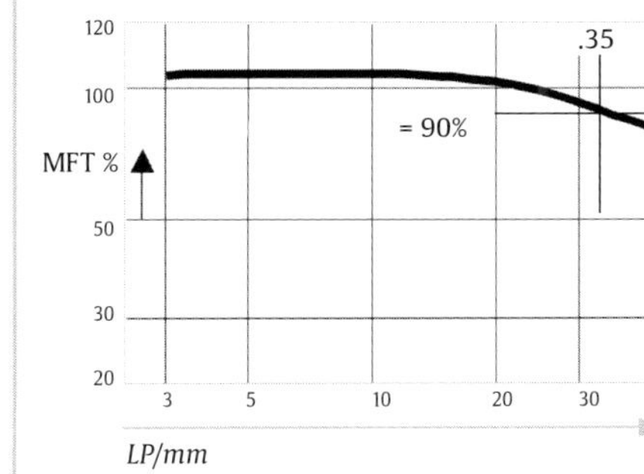

ILFORD FP4

Sensitivity: Panchromatic 400 -700

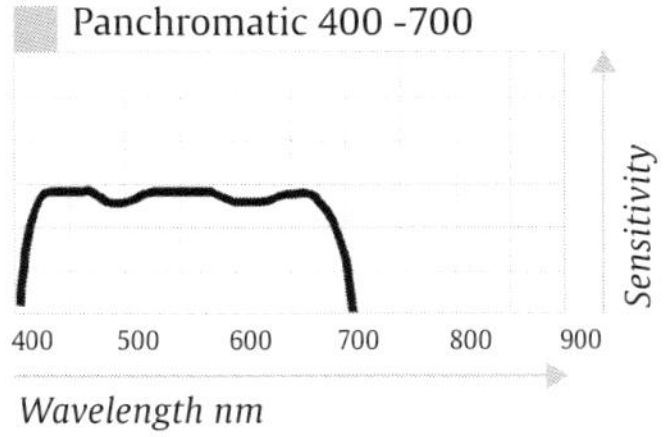

ISO Standard

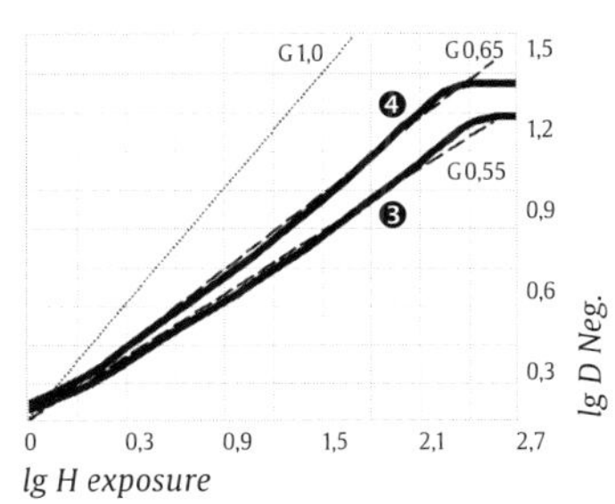

❻❺ = Development-Time in Minutes

grainless Enlg.-Times / RMS Grain / Tonality

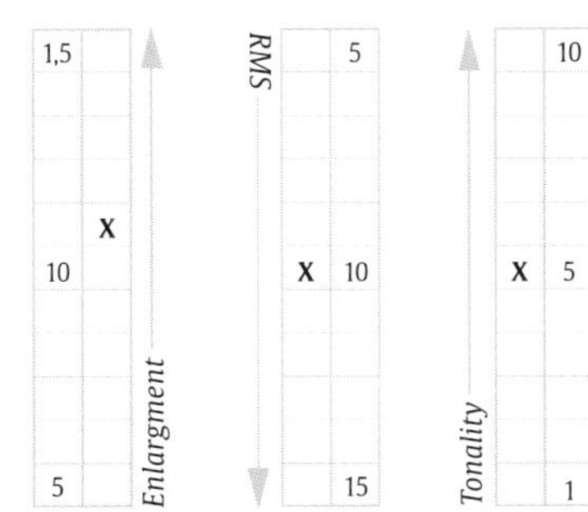

MFT Dissolving-Power

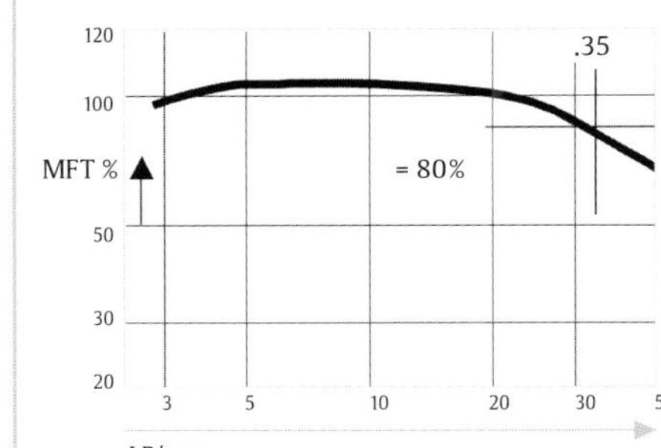

Development chart **LP-SUPERGRAIN** | 1+7 / 1+15 20°C | 30 Seconds Agitation | Gamma 0,55

Film	Sensitivity	ISO	Development Time 1+7	Development Time 1+15	ISO Standard	grainless Enlg.-Times / RMS Grain / Tonality	MFT Dissolving-Power
ILFORD HP5 plus	Panchromatic 400 - 700 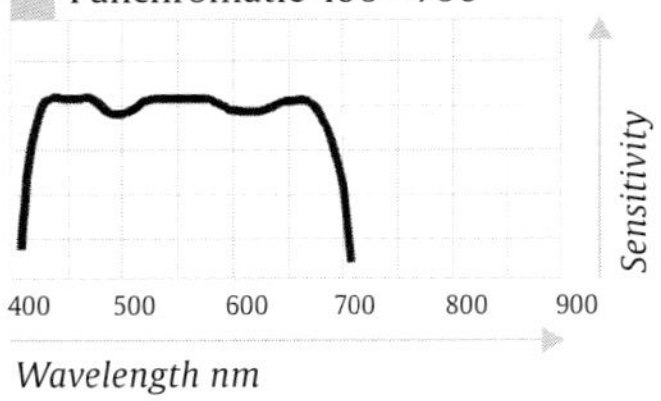	400 800	5 7		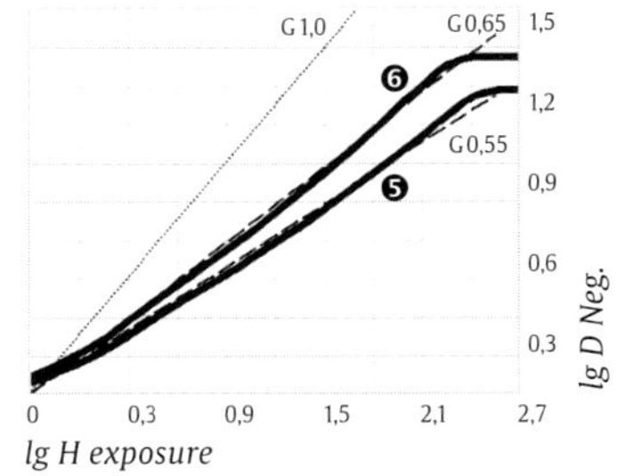 6 5 = Development-Time in Minutes	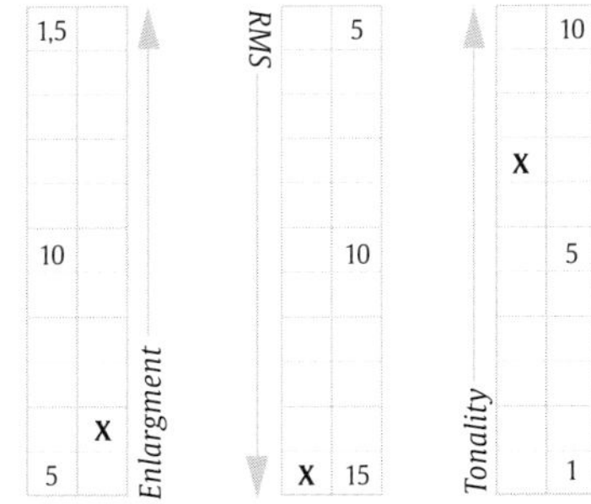	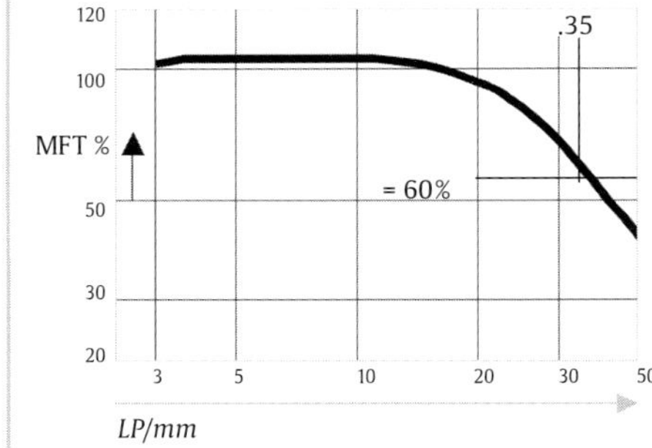
ILFORD SFX 200	Panchromatic 400 - 700 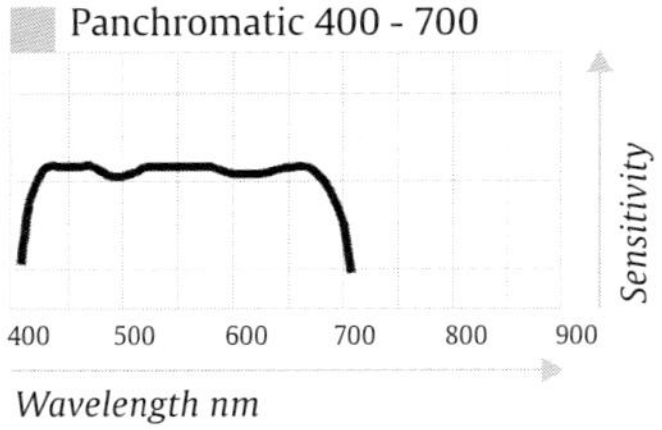	200	8		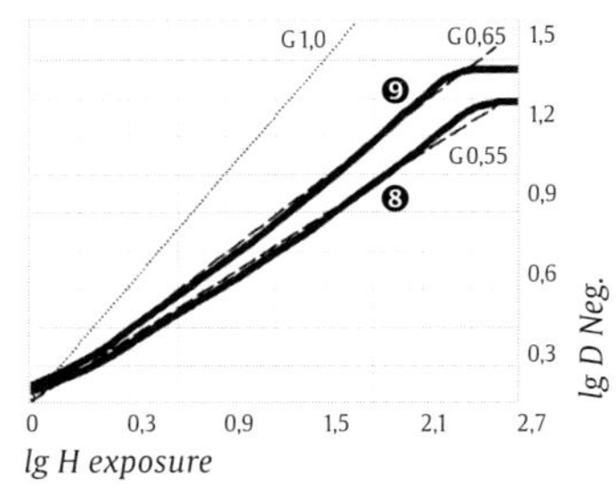 6 5 = Development-Time in Minutes	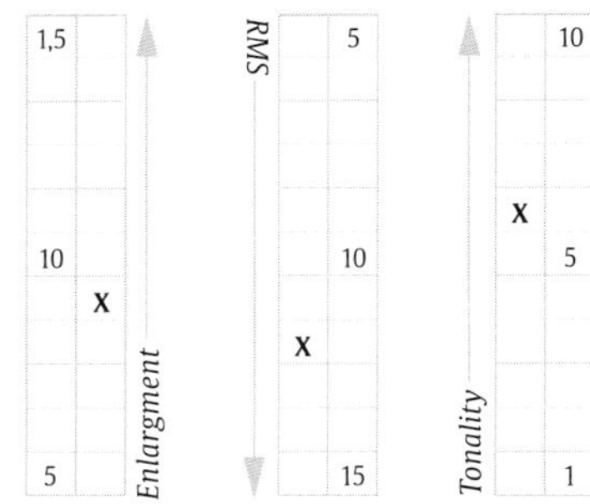	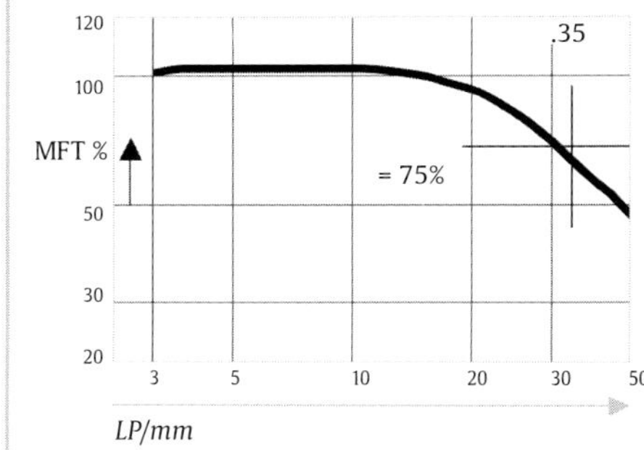
ILFORD DELTA 100	Panchromatic 400 - 700 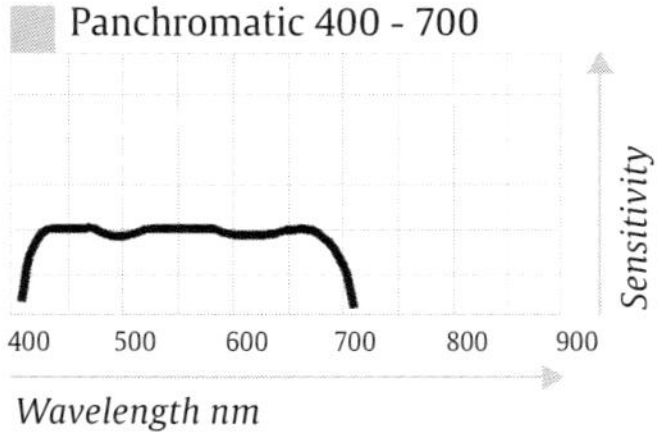	100 200	4 5	5,5	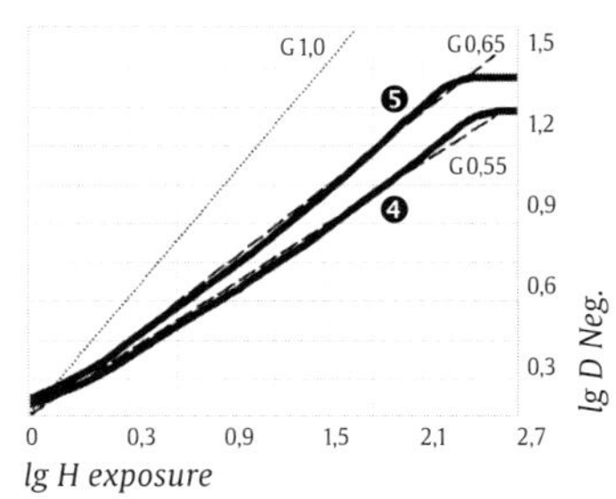 6 5 = Development-Time in Minutes	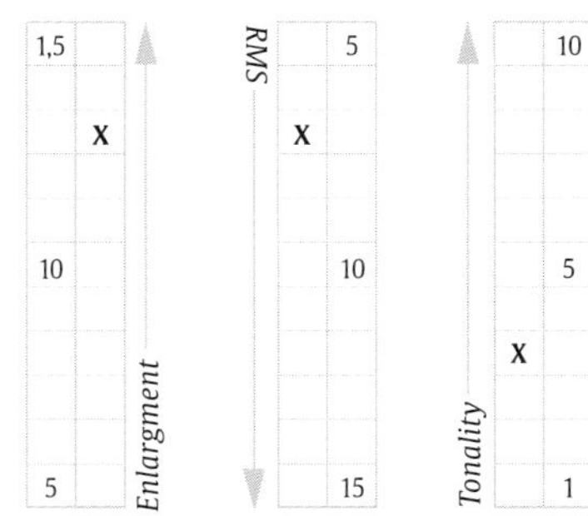	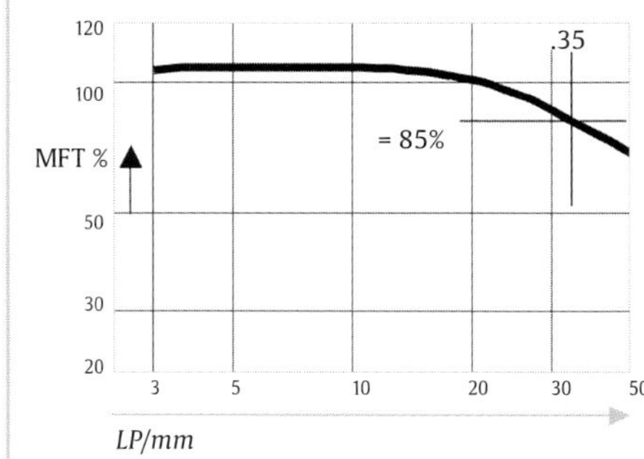
ILFORD DELTA 400	Panchromatic 400 -700 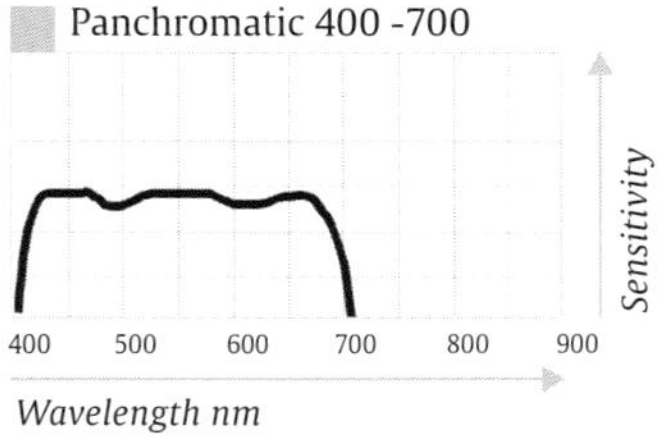	400 800	7,5 10		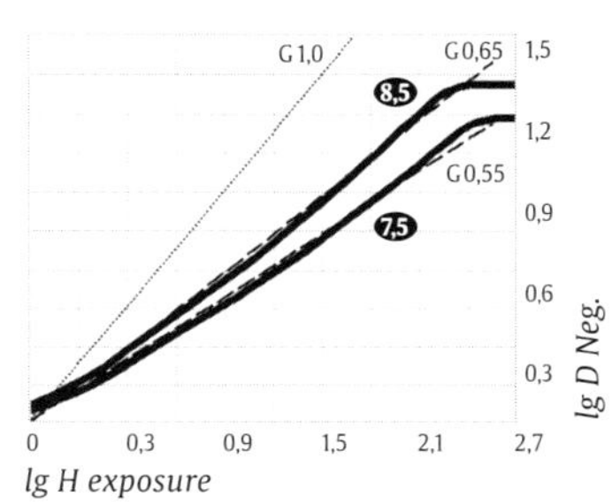 6 5 = Development-Time in Minutes	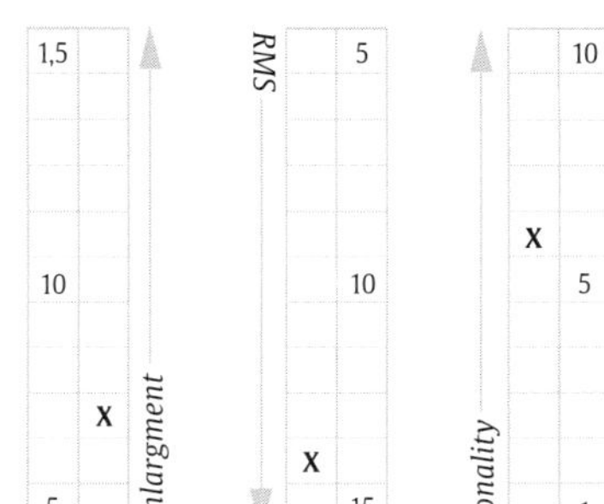	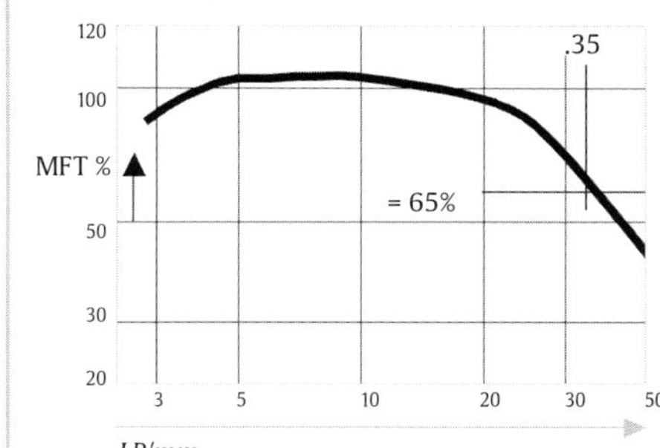

Development chart **LP-SUPERGRAIN** | 1+7 / 1+15 20°C | 30 Seconds Agitation | Gamma 0,55

Film	ISO	Development Time 1+7	Development Time 1+15
ILFORD DELTA 3200	3200	10,5	
	6400	13	
KODAK PLUS X	125	3,5	
	200	4,5	
KODAK TRI X	400	5	
KODAK HIE IR	200	5	
	400	7,5	

Columns: Sensitivity · ISO · Development Time · ISO Standard · grainless Enlg.-Times · RMS Grain · Tonality · MFT Dissolving-Power

ILFORD DELTA 3200

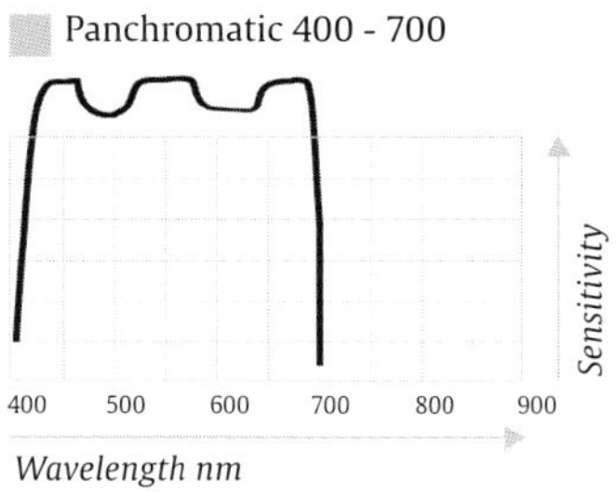

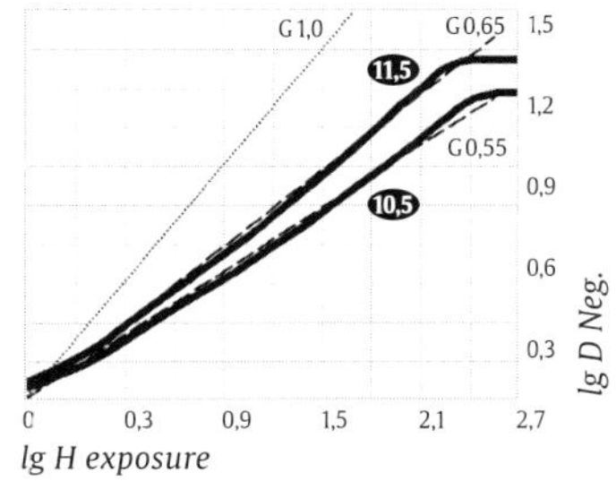

⑥⑤ = Development-Time in Minutes

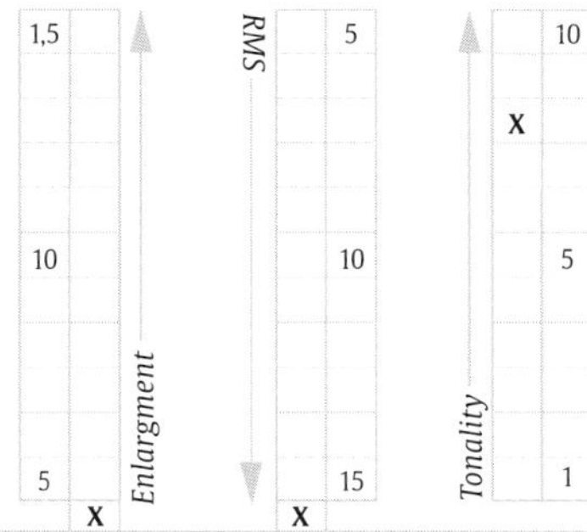

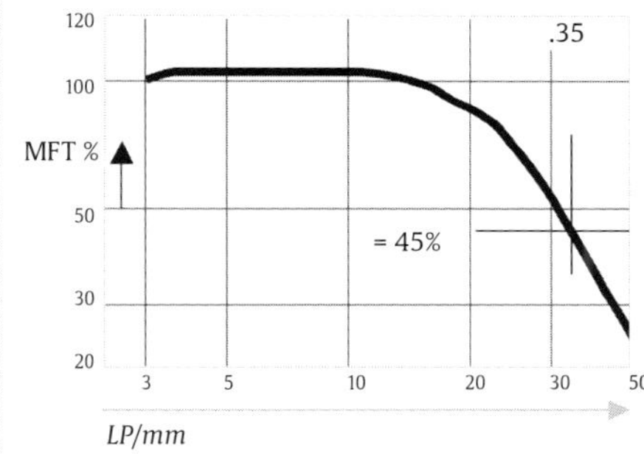

KODAK PLUS X

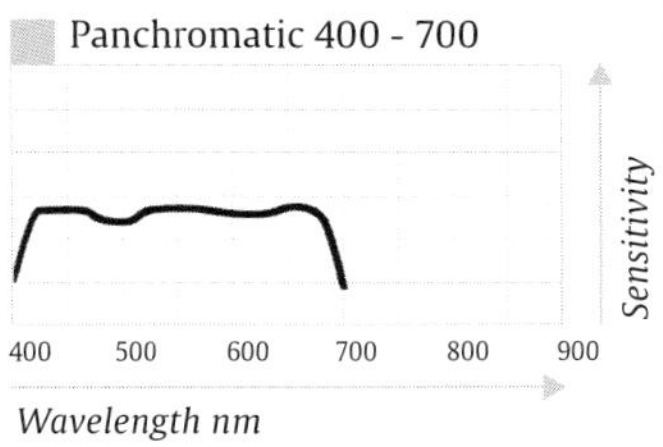

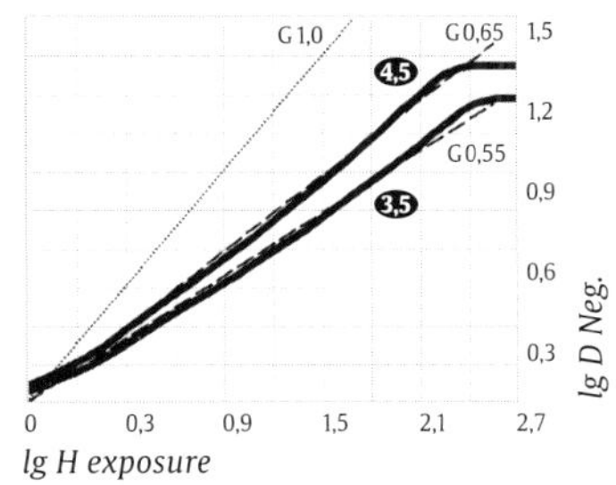

⑥⑤ = Development-Time in Minutes

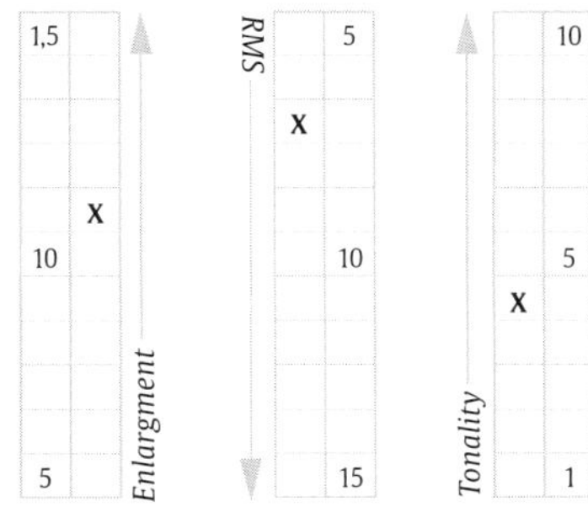

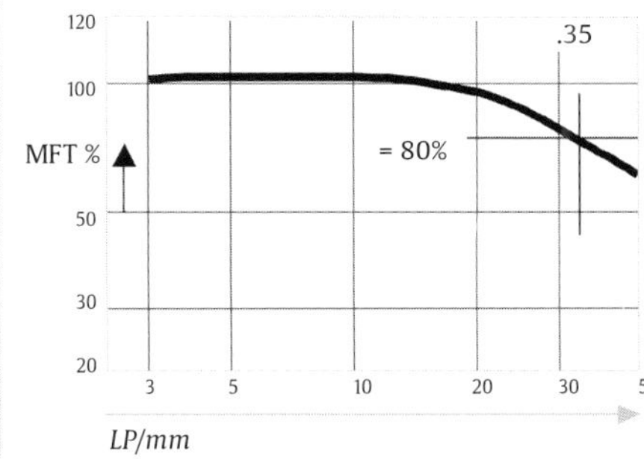

KODAK TRI X

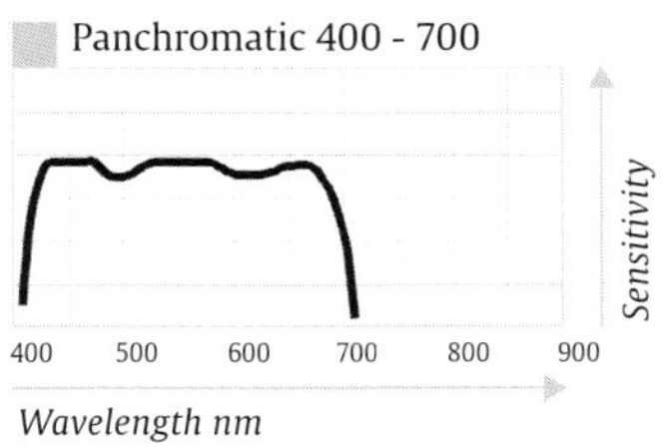

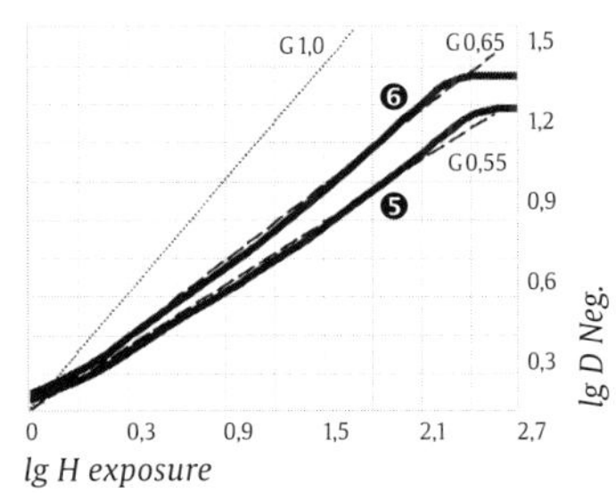

⑥⑤ = Development-Time in Minutes

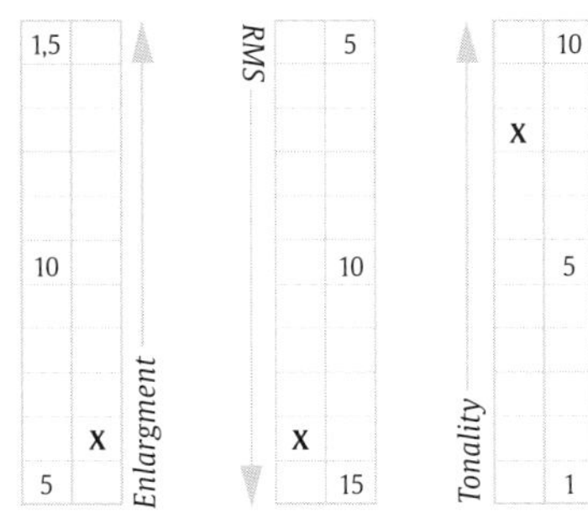

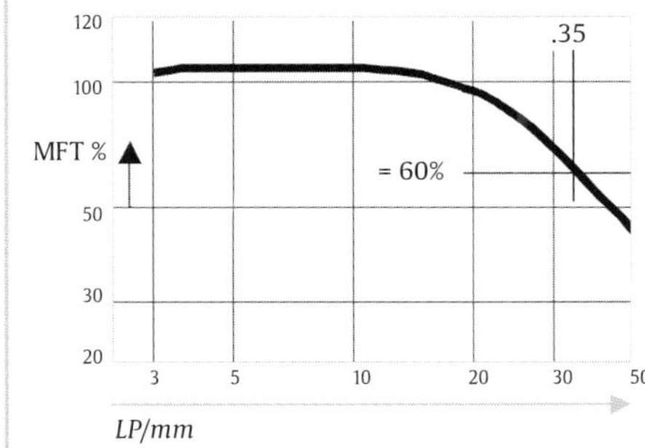

KODAK HIE IR

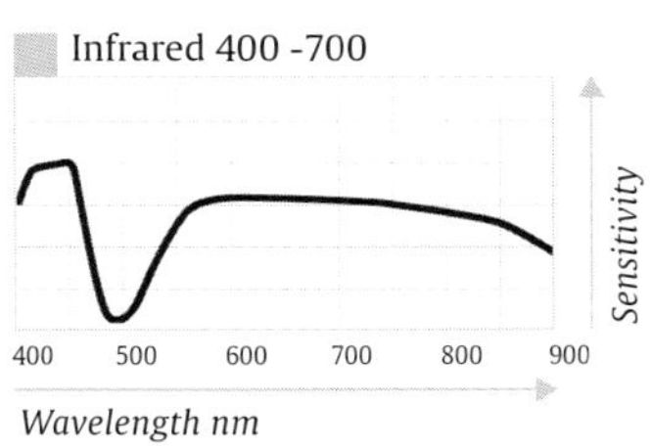

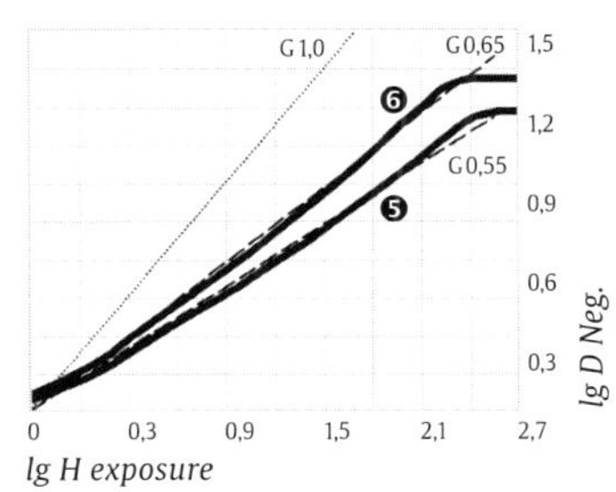

⑥⑤ = Development-Time in Minutes

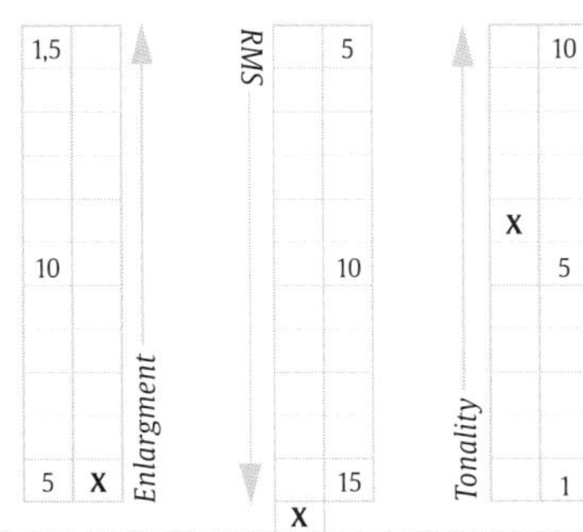

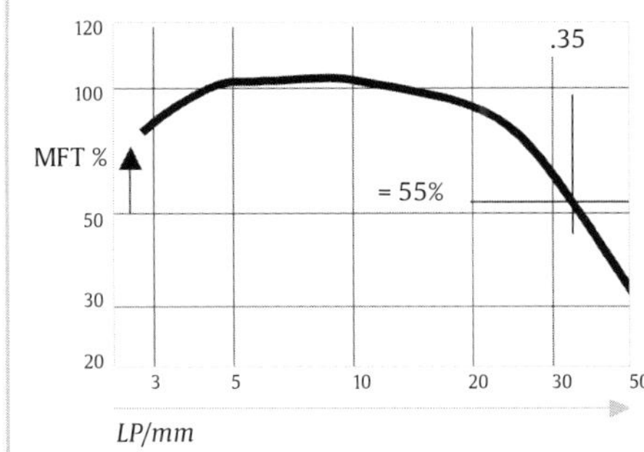

Development chart **LP-SUPERGRAIN** | 1+7 / 1+15 20°C | 30 Seconds Agitation | Gamma 0,55

Columns: Sensitivity · ISO · Development Time (1+7, 1+15) · ISO Standard · grainless Enlg.-Times · RMS Grain · Tonality · MFT Dissolving-Power

KODAK T-MAX 100

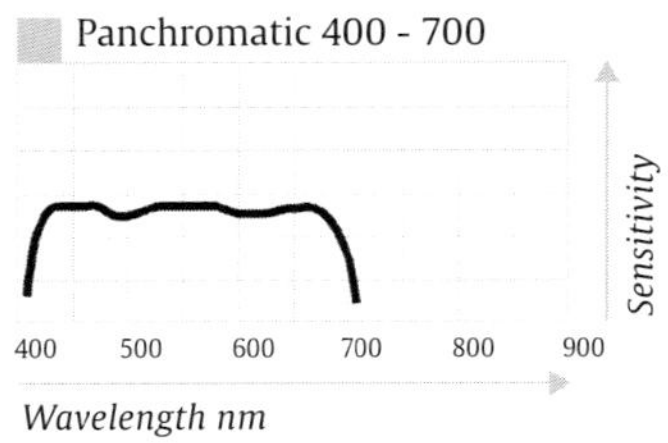

ISO	Development Time 1+7	Development Time 1+15
100	5	
200	6	

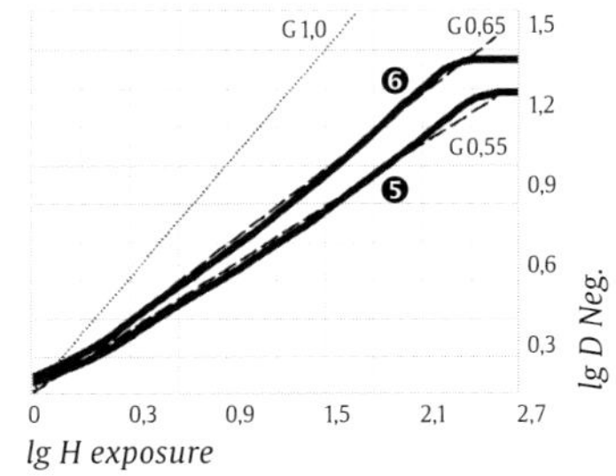

❻❺ = Development-Time in Minutes

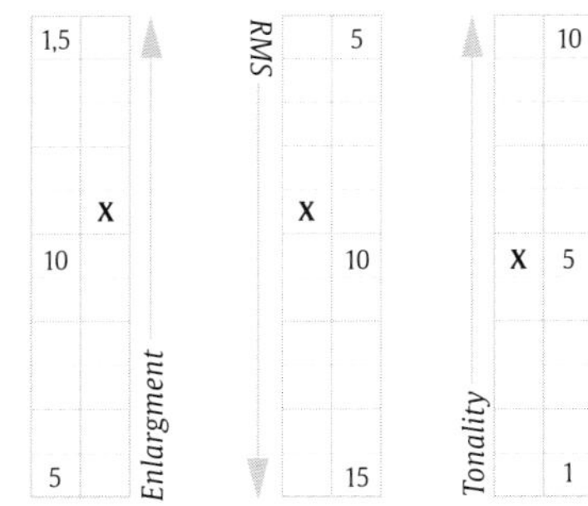

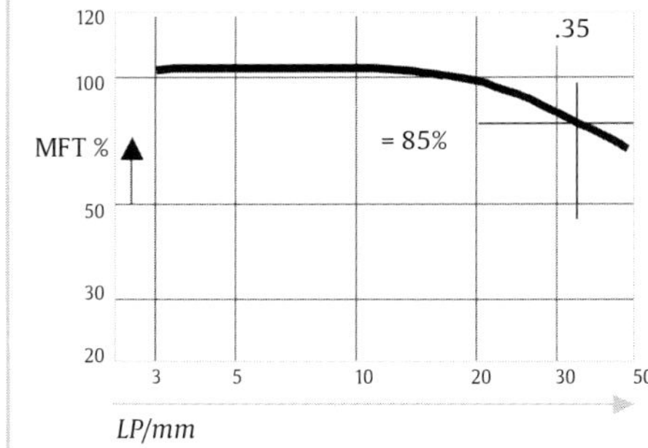

KODAK T-MAX 400

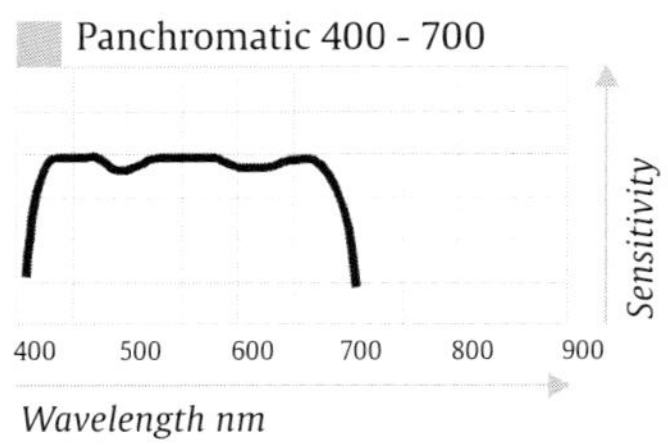

ISO	Development Time 1+7	Development Time 1+15
400	6	
800	6,5	
1600	7	

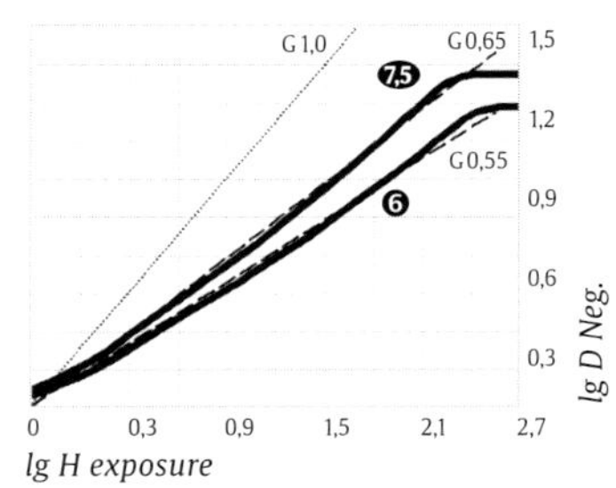

❻❺ = Development-Time in Minutes

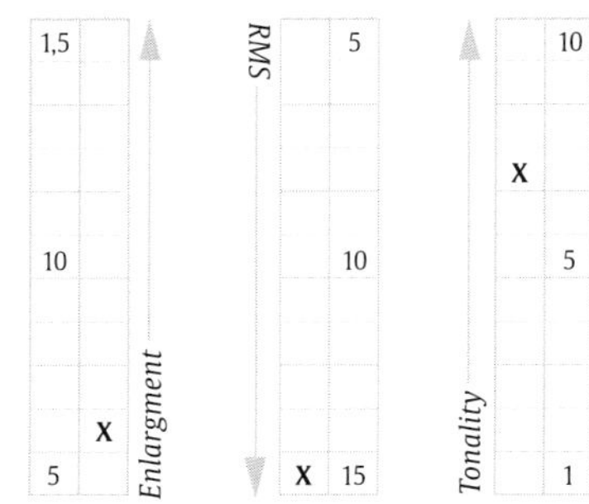

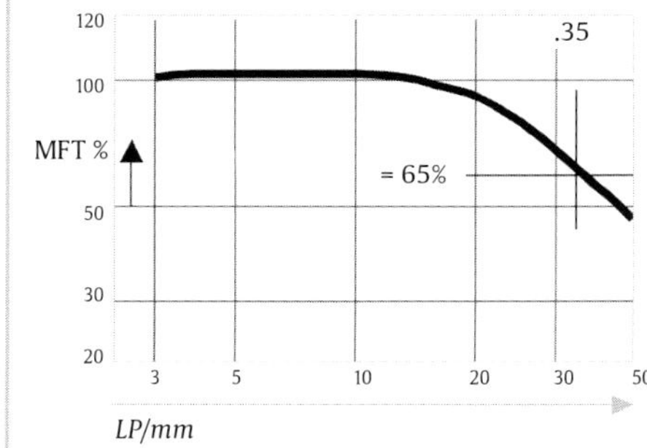

KODAK T-MAX 3200

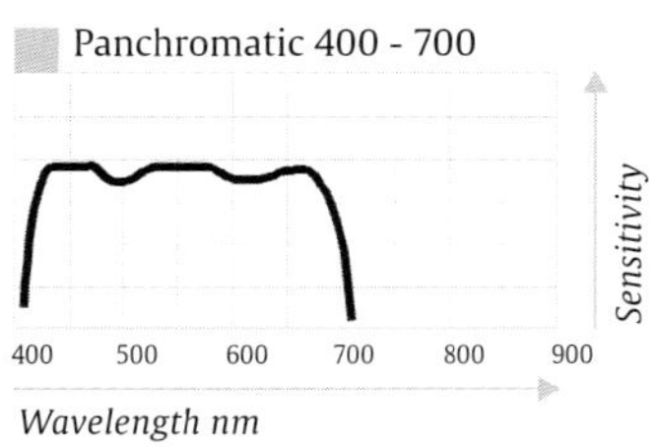

ISO	Development Time 1+7	Development Time 1+15
1600	5	
3200	6,5	
6400	8	

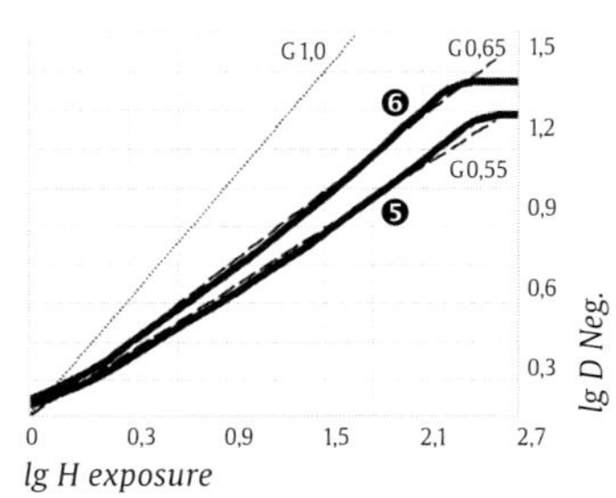

❻❺ = Development-Time in Minutes

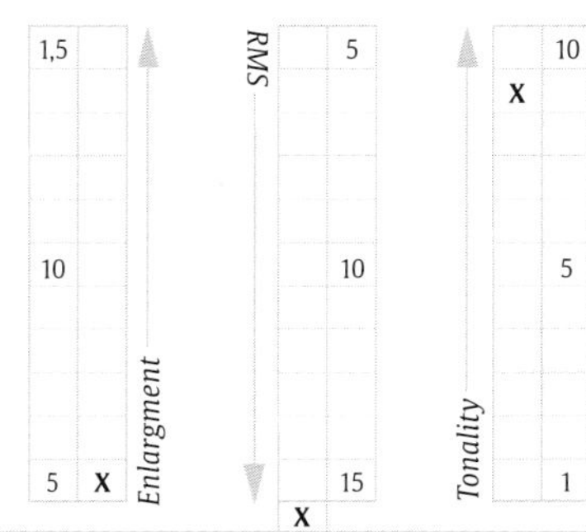

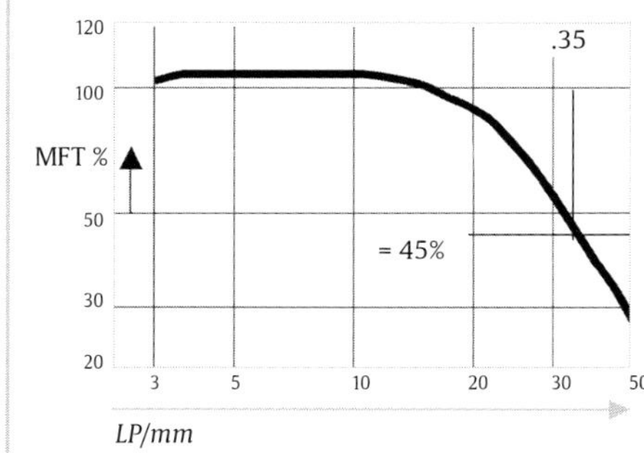

KONICA 200

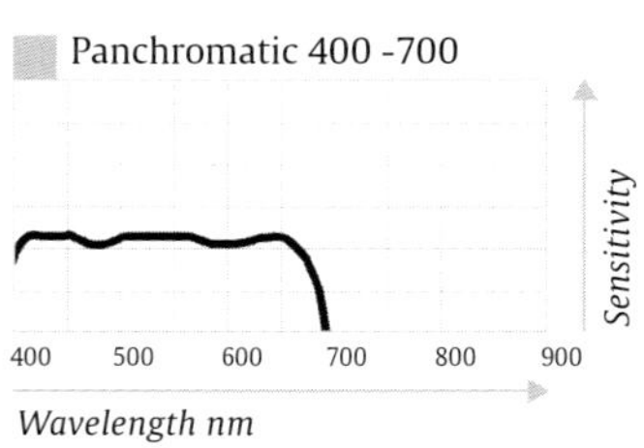

ISO	Development Time 1+7	Development Time 1+15
100	5	

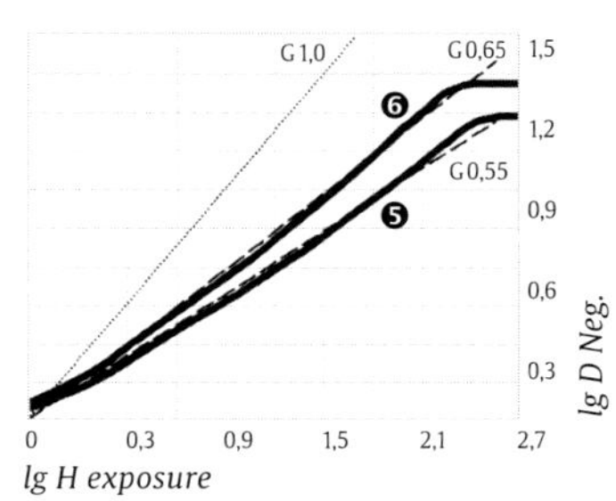

❻❺ = Development-Time in Minutes

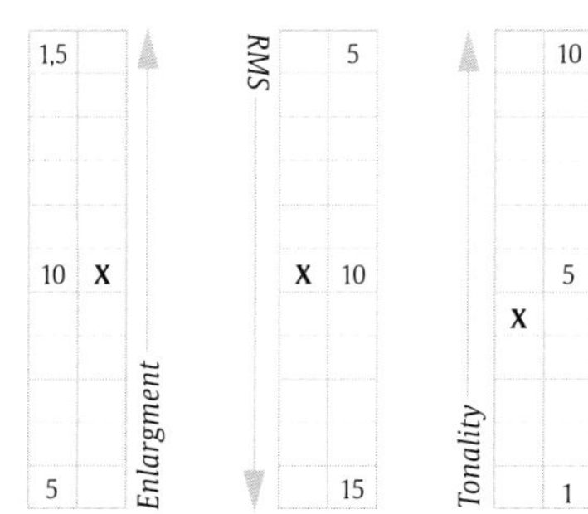

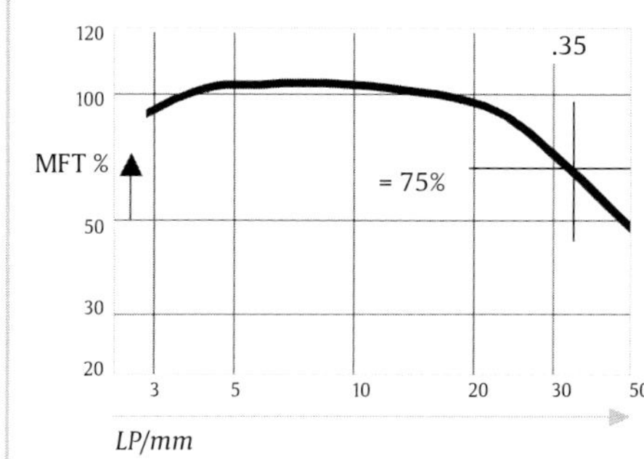

Development chart **LP-SUPERGRAIN** | 1+7 / 1+15 20°C | 30 Seconds Agitation | Gamma 0,55

Film	ISO	Development Time 1+7	Development Time 1+15
MACO UP 25plus	25	3	
	50	3,5	
MACO UP 64plus	50	3,5	
	100	4,5	
MACO UP 100plus	50		3,5
	100	3,5	5
	200		5
MACO UP 400plus	200	4	
	400	5	
	800	7	

Columns: Sensitivity | ISO | Development Time | ISO Standard | grainless Enlg.-Times | RMS Grain | Tonality | MFT Dissolving-Power

MACO UP 25plus

Panchromatic 400 - 700

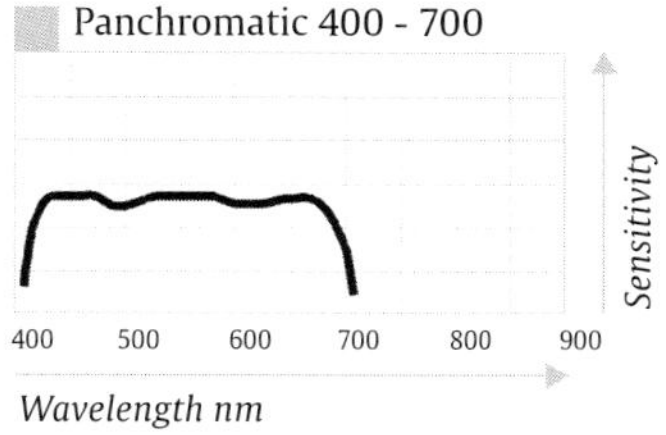

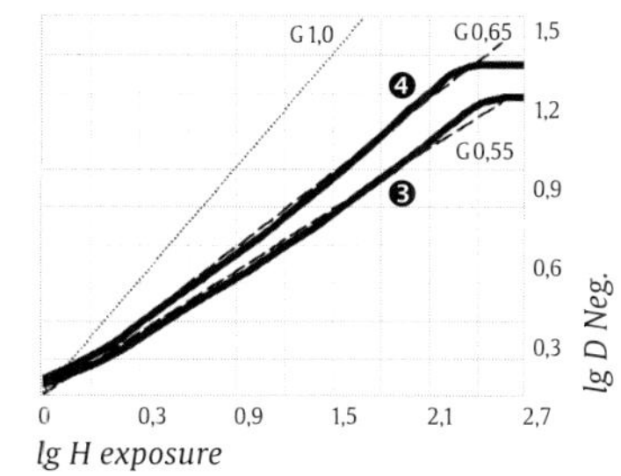

❻❺ = Development-Time in Minutes

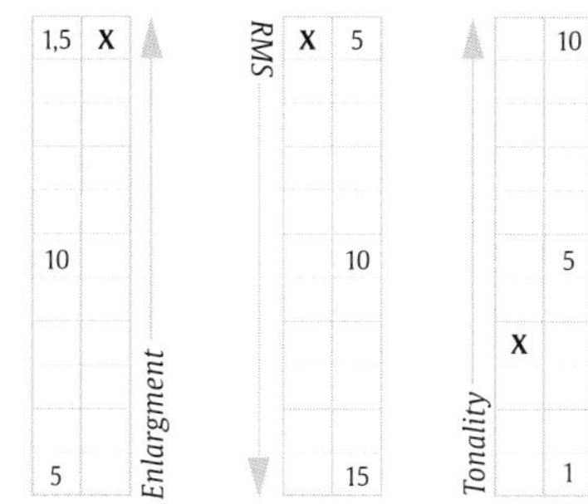

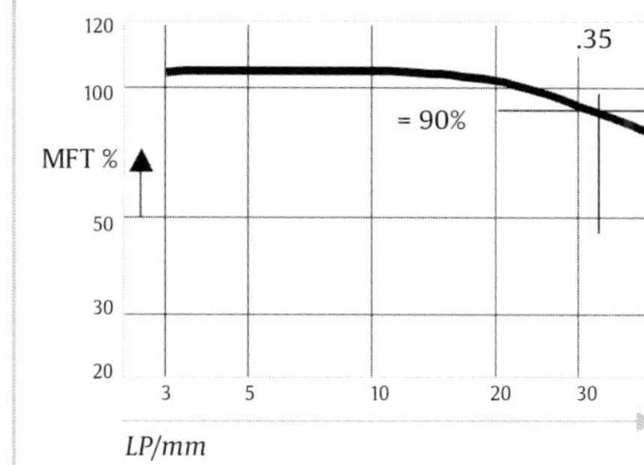

MACO UP 64plus

Panchromatic 400 - 700

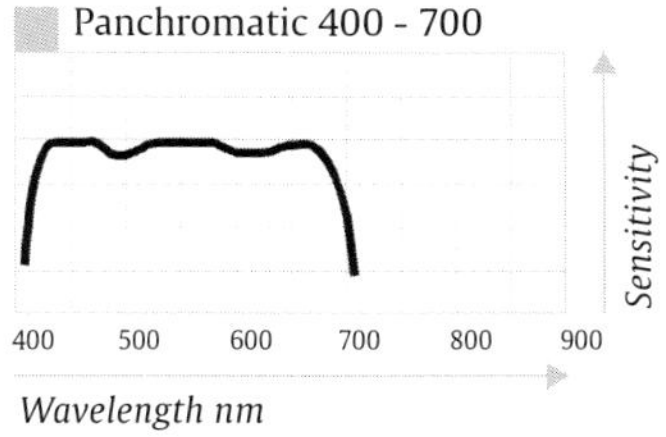

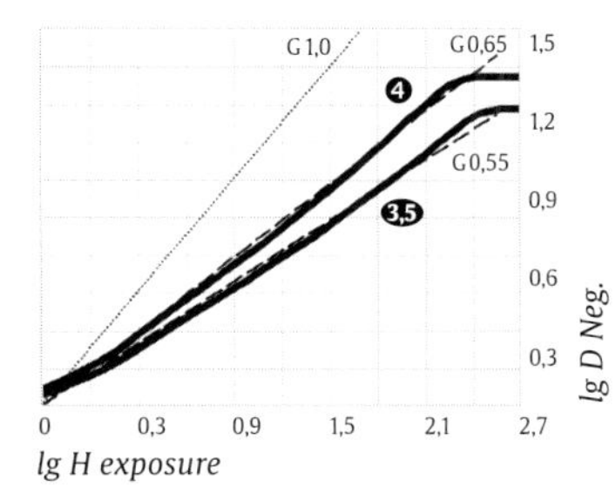

❻❺ = Development-Time in Minutes

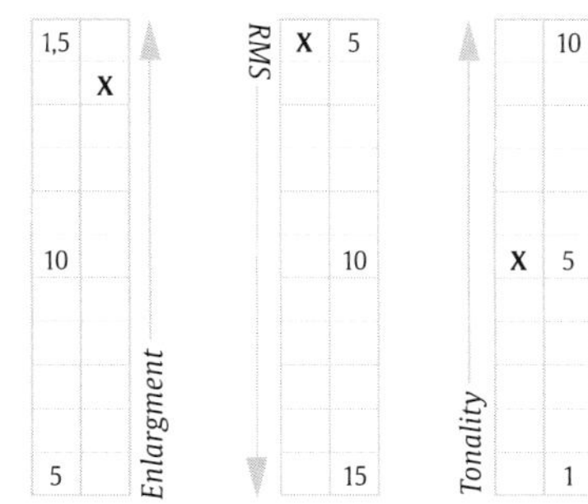

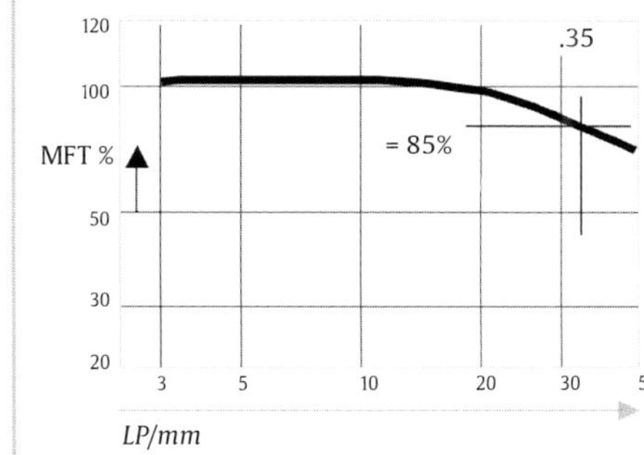

MACO UP 100plus

Panchromatic 400 - 700

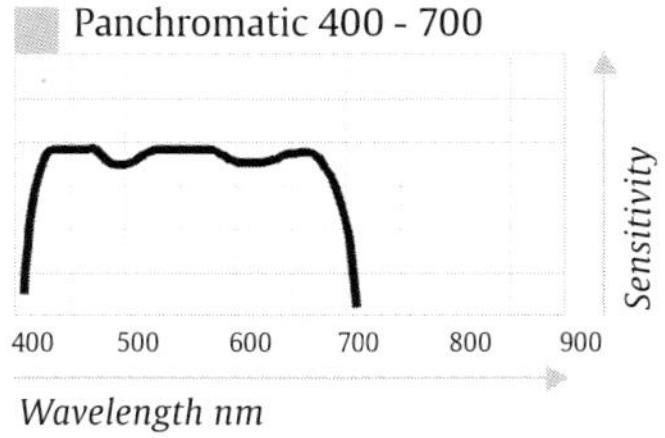

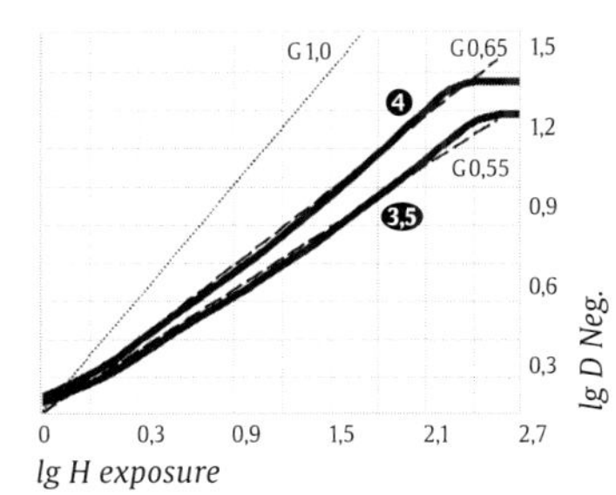

❻❺ = Development-Time in Minutes

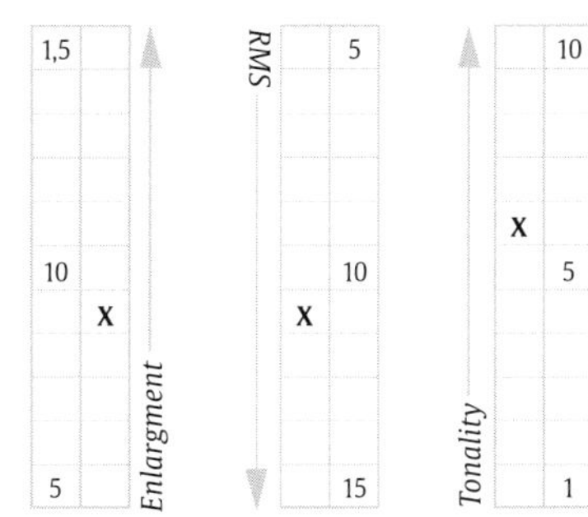

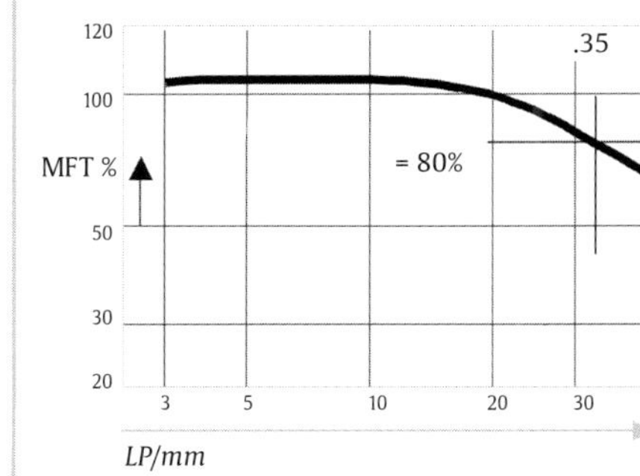

MACO UP 400plus

Panchromatic 400 -700

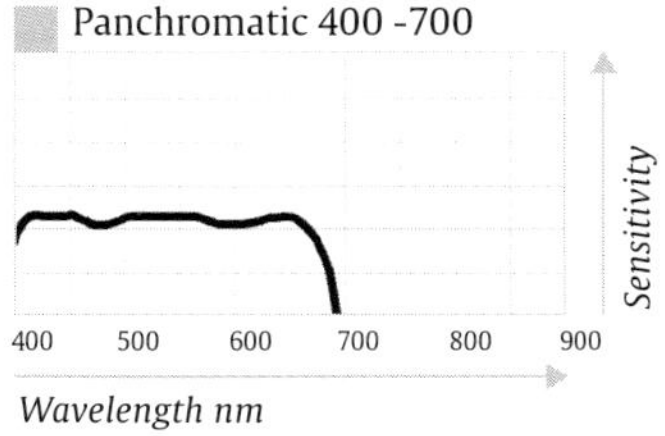

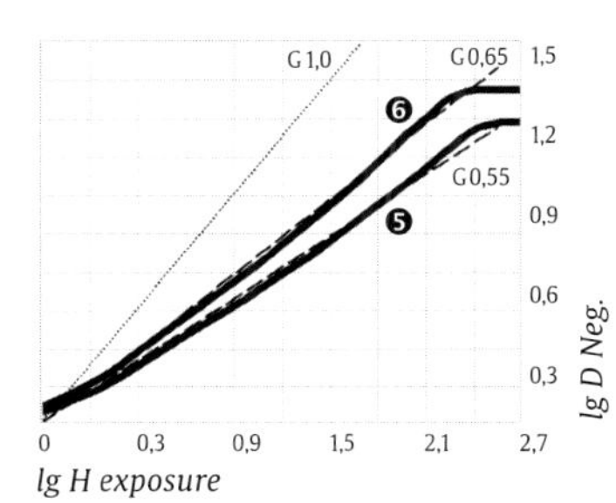

❻❺ = Development-Time in Minutes

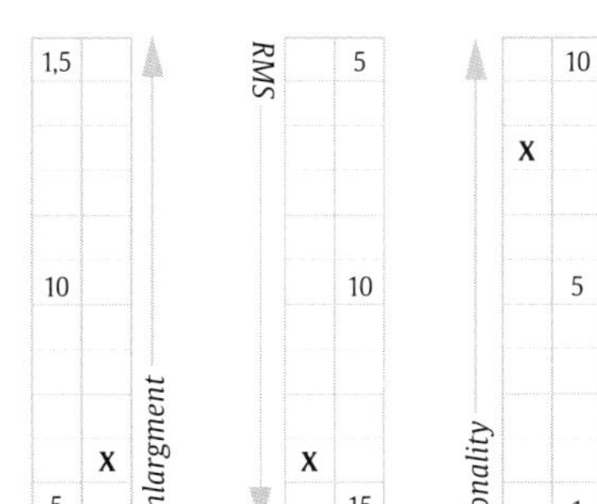

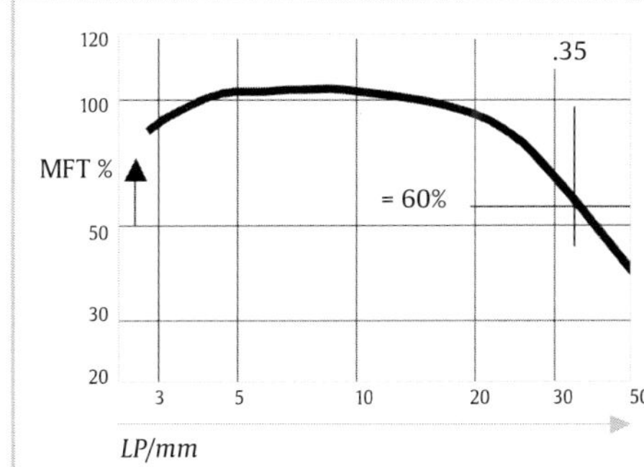

Development chart **LP-SUPERGRAIN**

1+7 / 1+15 20°C | 30 Seconds Agitation | Gamma 0,55

MACO IR 750 c

Sensitivity: Infrared 400 - 750

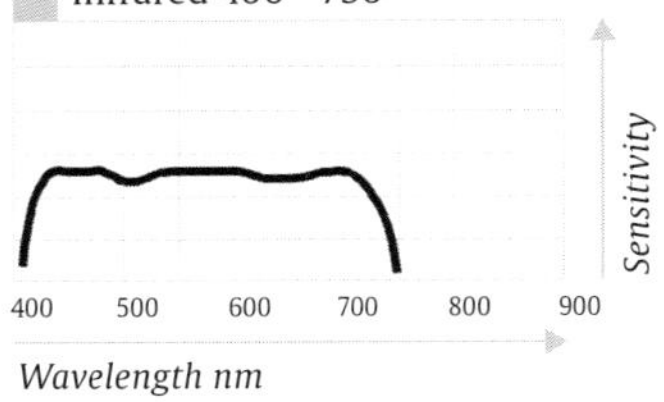

ISO	Development Time 1+7	Development Time 1+15
50		4
100		5,5
200	6	

ISO Standard

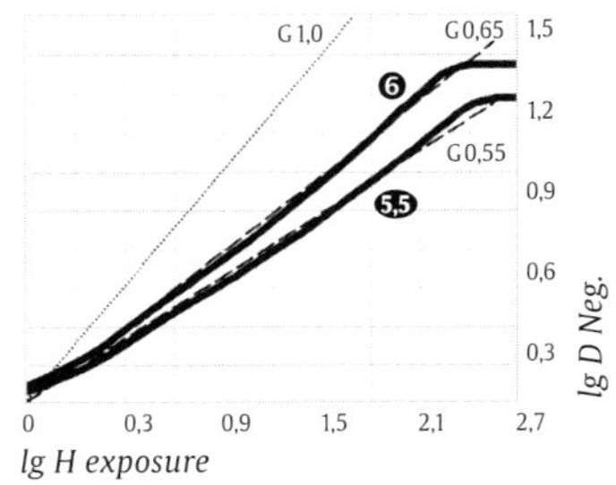

❻❺ = Development-Time in Minutes

grainless Enlg.-Times / RMS Grain / Tonality

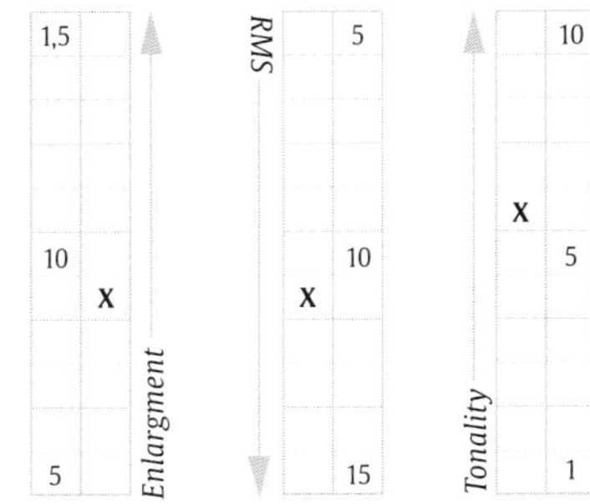

MFT Dissolving-Power

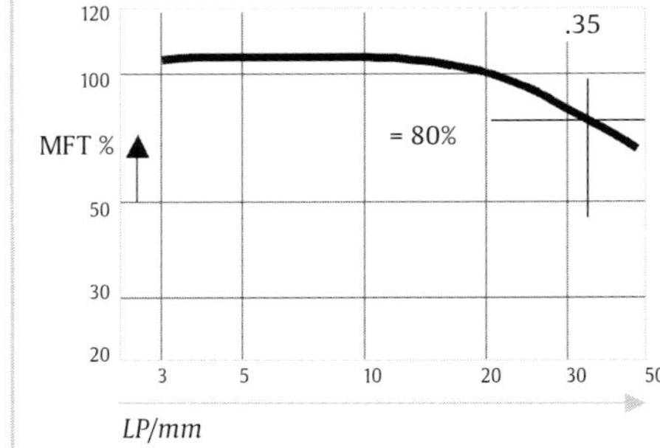

MACO IR 820 c

Sensitivity: Infrarot 400 - 820

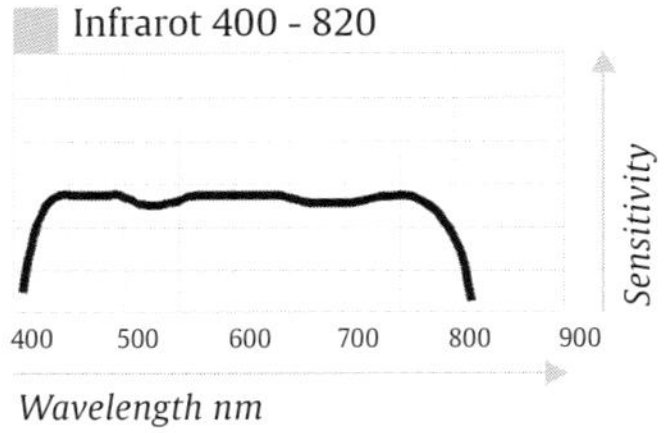

ISO	Development Time 1+7	Development Time 1+15
50		4
100		5,5
200	6	

ISO Standard

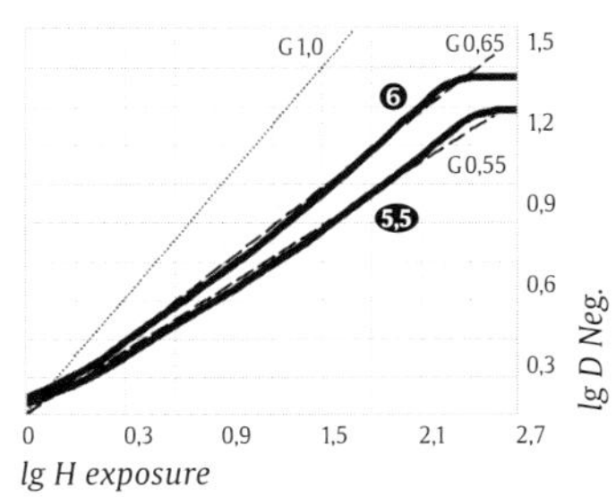

❻❺ = Development-Time in Minutes

grainless Enlg.-Times / RMS Grain / Tonality

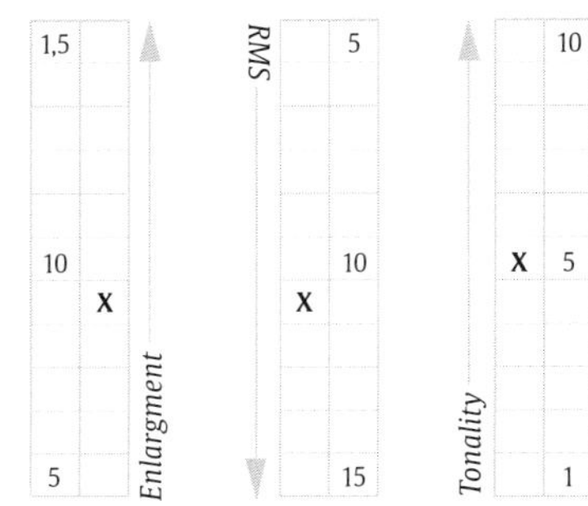

MFT Dissolving-Power

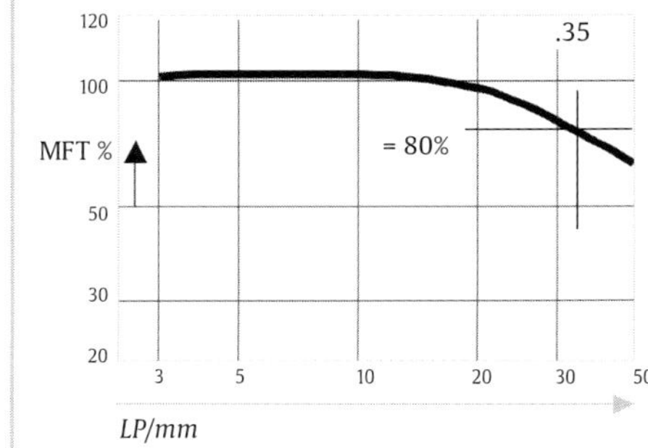

MACO CUBE 400 c

Sensitivity: Panchromatic - Infrared 400 - 750

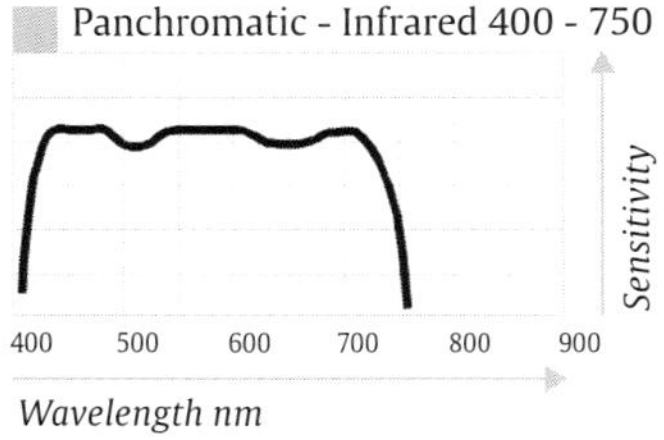

ISO	Development Time 1+7	Development Time 1+15
200	6	
400	8	
800	11	

ISO Standard

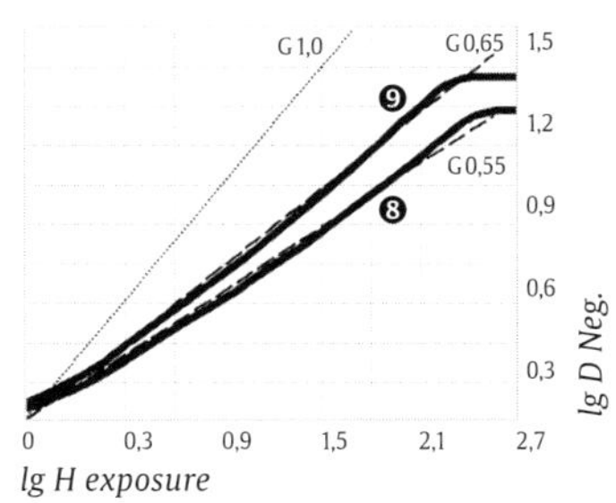

❻❺ = Development-Time in Minutes

grainless Enlg.-Times / RMS Grain / Tonality

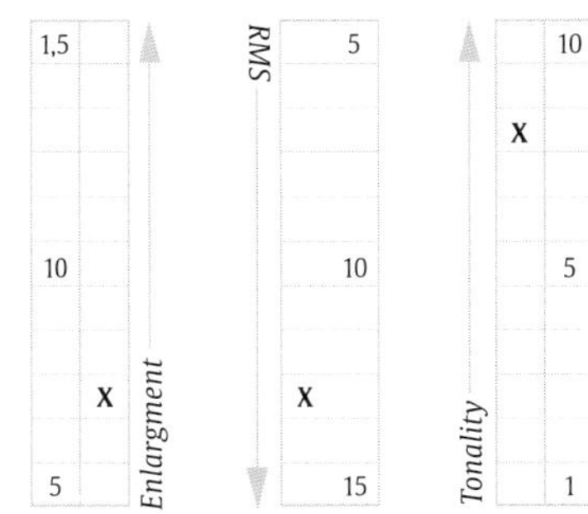

MFT Dissolving-Power

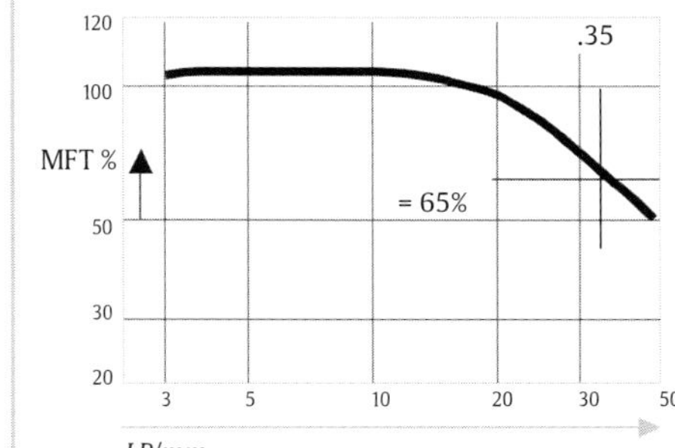

MACO PO 100 plus

Sensitivity: Orthopanchromatic 400 -620

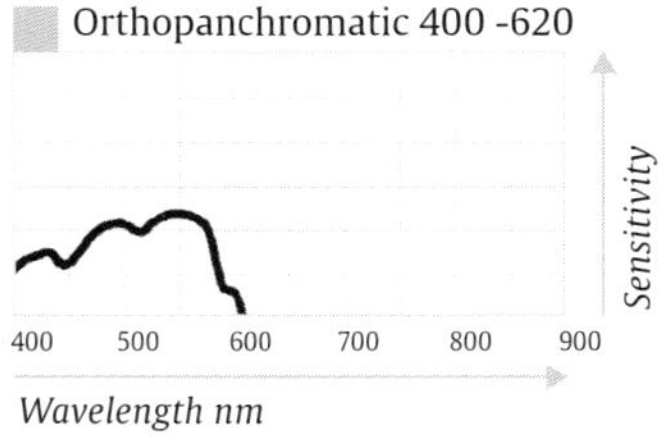

ISO	Development Time 1+7	Development Time 1+15
50		3,5
100	3,5	5
200		5

ISO Standard

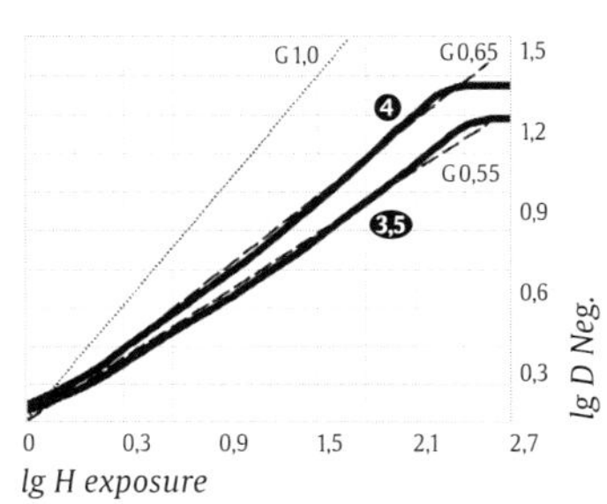

❻❺ = Development-Time in Minutes

grainless Enlg.-Times / RMS Grain / Tonality

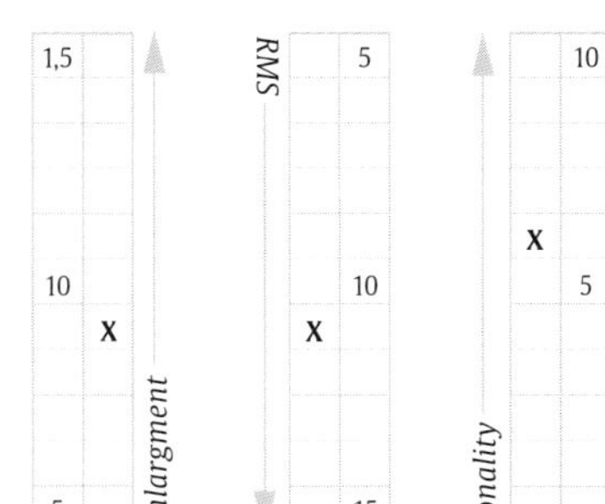

MFT Dissolving-Power

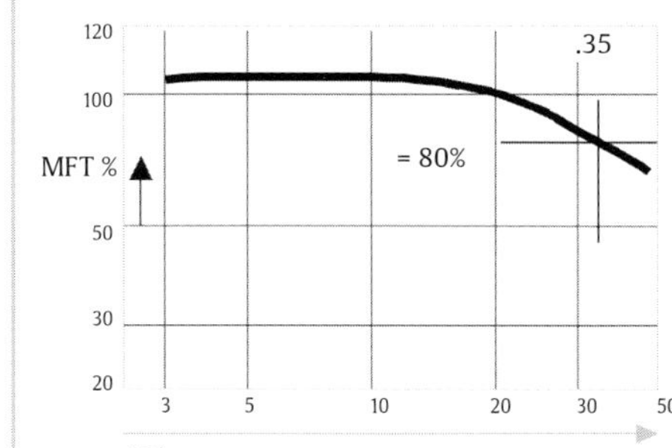

Development chart **LP-SUPERGRAIN** | 1+7 / 1+15 20°C | 30 Seconds Agitation | Gamma 0,55

Exposed ISO / ***time in minutes***

	25 1 + 7	25 1 + 15	50 1 + 7	50 1 + 15	100/125* 1 + 7	100/125* 1 + 15	200 1 + 7	400 1 + 7	800 1 + 7	1.600 1 + 7	3.200 1 + 7	6.400 1 + 7
AGFA APX 100	–	–	–	–	5	–	6,5	–	–	–	–	–
AGFA APX 200S	–	–	–	–	–	–	5	–	–	–	–	–
AGFA APX 400	–	–	–	–	–	–	–	5	6,5	–	–	–
EFKEpan 25	–	3	–	3,5	–	–	–	–	–	–	–	–
EFKEpan 50	–	–	3,5	–	4	–	–	–	–	–	–	–
EFKEpan 100	–	–	3,5	5	5	–	7	–	–	–	–	–
FOMApan 100	–	–	3,5	–	5	–	–	–	–	–	–	–
FOMApan 400	–	–	–	–	–	–	–	6	–	–	–	–
FUJI Neopan 100	–	–	–	–	4	–	5,5	–	–	–	–	–
FUJI Neopan 400	–	–	–	–	–	–	6	0	8	–	–	–
FUJI Neopan 1600	–	–	–	–	–	–	–	–	–	6	7,5	–
ILFORD Pan F	–	–	3	3,5	5	5,5	–	–	–	–	–	–
*ILFORD FP4**	–	–	3	–	4,5	–	5,5	–	–	–	–	–
ILFORD HP5	–	–	–	–	–	–	–	5	7	–	–	–
ILFORD SFX 200	–	–	–	–	–	–	8	–	–	–	–	–
ILFORD Delta 100	–	–	4	–	5,5	–	–	–	–	–	–	–
ILFORD Delta 400	–	–	–	–	–	–	–	7,5	10	–	–	–
ILFORD Delta 3200	–	–	–	–	–	–	–	–	–	–	10,5	13
*KODAK PLUS X**	–	–	3,5	5	4,5	–	–	–	–	–	–	–
KODAK TRI X	–	–	–	–	–	–	–	5	–	–	–	–
KODAK HIE	–	–	–	–	5	–	7,5	–	–	–	–	–
KODAK T-MAX 100	–	–	–	–	5	–	7,5	–	–	–	–	–
KODAK T-MAX 400	–	–	–	–	–	–	6	6,5	7	–	–	–
KODAK T-MAX 3200	–	–	–	–	–	–	–	–	–	5	6,5	8
KONICA IR 750	–	–	–	–	5	–	–	–	–	–	–	–
MACO UP 25plus	–	3	–	3,5	–	–	–	–	–	–	–	–
MACO UP 64clear	–	–	–	3,5	4,5	–	–	–	–	–	–	–
MACO UP 100plus	–	–	3,5	–	3,5	–	5	–	–	–	–	–
MACO IR 750clear	–	–	4	–	5,5	–	6	–	–	–	–	–
MACO IR 820clear	–	–	4	–	5,5	–	6	–	–	–	–	–
MACO UP 400plus	–	–	–	–	–	–	4	5	7	–	–	–
MACO CUBE 400clear	–	–	–	–	–	–	6	8	11	–	–	–

Filmentwickler
LP-CUBE XS

Dieser Entwickler ist ein moderner Schichttiefen-Feinkornentwickler. Bei geeigneten Filmen erlaubt dieser Entwickler eine ganz besondere Feinstkörnigkeit.
Die Besonderheit: Er reagiert besonders sensibel auf Bromide mit einer verhältnismäßig langen Induktionsperiode. Der LP-CUBE XS diffundiert durch die komplette Schichttiefe und erst nach längerer Einwirkzeit beginnt die Reduktion belichteter Silberhalogenide. Die Entwicklung erfolgt anfänglich an den stark belichteten Lichterpartien, praktisch gleichzeitig in der gesamten Schichttiefe. Die langsam verlaufende Entwicklung gestattet eine Substanzerneuerung und ein Ausschwemmen der gebildeten Bromide auch im Inneren der Schicht, so dass die dort befindlichen Kristalle nahezu gleichzeitig mit den stark belichteten Oberflächenkörnern entwickelt werden. Die Halbtöne werden um so langsamer entwickelt, je schwächer sie belichtet sind. Wird die Entwicklung so lange ausgedehnt, bis auch die Schattenpartien entsprechend reduziert sind, ist der Bildkontrast und somit die Gradation schon sehr hoch geworden.

Die Empfindlichkeitsausnutzung des LP-CUBE XS ist wie bei allen anderen Entwicklern der Gattung ›Schichttiefenentwickler‹ etwas geringer als auf der Filmschachtel angegeben. Dafür erhält man eine ausgezeichnete Lichterzeichnung bis in die Spitzlichtpartien.
LP-CUBE XS eignet sich vor allem für überbelichtete oder zumindest reichlich belichtete Negative. Die Bezeichnung CUBE für diesen Entwickler wurde in Anlehnung an den MACO CUBE 400clear Film gewählt. Die Kombination eines Filmes mit hoher Grundempfindlichkeit und eines die Empfindlichkeit senkenden Entwicklers (pullen) können bei Belichtungen auf 200 ISO zu einer merklich feineren Körnigkeit führen als bei Schichtoberflächenentwicklern (im Vergleich zu LP-SUPERGRAIN).
Im Gegensatz zu Oberflächenentwicklern zeigen die Gradationskurven der in LP-CUBE XS entwickelten Filme einen eigenen Empfindlichkeitspunkt. Dieser rückt mit zunehmender Entwicklungszeit immer weiter nach links.
Die Gattung der Schichttiefenentwickler war für lange Zeit kaum mit industriell gefertigten Produkten besetzt.
Seit einigen Jahren sind aufgrund neu erschlossener Grundsubstanzen, über die man noch vor einigen Jahren nicht

Sviluppo per pellicole
LP-CUBE XS

Questo sviluppo rappresenta un moderno sviluppo in profondità dello strato, a grana fine. Con pellicole adatte questo rivelatore consente una grana particolarmente fine.
La sua particolarità: Reagisce in modo particolarmente sensibile ai bromuri con un periodo di induzione relativamente lungo. Il LP-CUBE XS si diffonde attraverso tutta la profondità dello strato e solo dopo un tempo di azione inizia a ridurre gli alogenuri d'argento esposti. Lo sviluppo inizialmente lavora alle parti di luci molto esposte, in pratica contemporaneamente in tutta la profondità dello strato. La lenta azione dello sviluppo permette un rinnovamento della sostanza e un risciacquo dei bromuri formati anche all'interno dello strato, in modo tale da sviluppare quasi contemporaneamente i cristalli ivi presenti insieme ai granuli di superficie esposti. I mezzitoni vengono sviluppati più brevemente allorché meno esposti.
Se poi si prolunga l'azione dello sviluppo finché vengono ridotte anche le parti in ombra, il contrasto dell'immagine e pertanto la gradazione saranno di molto innalzate.

Lo sfruttamento della sensibilità del LP-CUBE XS, come del resto nel caso di tutti gli sviluppi cosiddetti ›Sviluppi di profondità nello strato‹, è leggermente più ridotto della sensibilità nominale dichiarata.
In compenso si ottiene una eccellente definizione delle luci fino alle parti estreme di luce. (alte luci).
LP-CUBE XS è particolarmente indicato per il trattamento di pellicole esposte abbondantemente o addirittura sovraesposte. Il nome CUBE è stato scelto per questo sviluppo in funzione alla pellicola MACO CUBE 400clear.
La combinazione fra una pellicola dalla alta sensibilità nominale e uno sviluppo che abbassa la sensibilità (pull), con esposizioni a 200 ISO consente di ottenere una grana più fine rispetto agi rivelatori di superficie dello strato.
(In confronto al LP-SUPERGRAIN).
Rispetto agli sviluppi di superficie, le pellicole sviluppate nel LP-CUBE XS mostrano delle curve di andamento della gradazione con un proprio punto di sensibilità. Questo si erge sempre più verso sinistra, più aumenta il tempo di sviluppo.

La specie degli sviluppi di profondità dello strato, per lungo tempo non veniva curata a livello di produzione industriale.

Filmframkaller
LP-CUBE XS

Dette er en moderne skikt- dybde finkorn framkaller. Ved passende filmer gir denne framkalleren ekstrem finkornethet.
Spesiellt er at den reagerer sensibelt på bromider med en forholdsvis lang induksjonsperiode.
LP-CUBE XS difunderer gjennom hele emulsjonsskiktet og først etter lengre tid begynner reduksjonen av sølvhalogenidene. Framkallingen starter i de mest eksponerte områdene, meni hele emulsjonens dybde. Det at framkallingen går langsom tillater at de frie bromidene kan vaskes ut samtidig med at ny framkaller kan nå fram til det indre skiktet slik at overflate og bund krystallene framkalles samtidig.
Halvtonene blir framkalt tilsvarende senere avhengig av eksponeringen.
Blir framkallingen forlenget slik at også skyggepartiene blir tilsvarende redusert da blir også kontrasten og dermed gradasjonen høy.

Følsomhetsutnyttelsen er som ved andre framkallerer av denne art, noe laverer enn det som er oppgitt på filmen.
Det som oppnås er gjennomtegning av høylysene.
LP-CUBE XS egner seg for alle overeksponerte eller i den minste rikelig eksponerte filmer .
Betegnelsen CUBE for denne framkalleren ble valgt i samsvar med MACO CUBE 400clear. Kombinasjonen av en film med høy grunnfølsomhet med en framkaller som senker følsomheten (pull-framkalling) gir med en EI 200 ISO et merkbart finkornigere reslutat en det en ville kunne oppnå f.eks med LP-SUPERGRAIN.
I motsetning til overflateframkallere viser gradasjonskurven ftil filmer framkallt i LP-CUBE XS et eget følsomhetspunkt. Dette beveger seg med tiltagene framkalling stadig mer mot venstre.

Denne type framkaller var i lengre tid knapest i produsjon.
I den senererd tid er det , ved hjelp av nye grundsubstanser, som ikke var kjent tidligere, blitt mulig å bringe skiktdybdeframkallere på markedet. LABOR PARTNER kan tilby denne som konsentrat.
De tidligere problemene med skyggetegning er blitt eliminert.

Negative Developer
LP-CUBE XS

This developer is a modern depth developer. Given suitable films, it allows extremely fine grain.
There is something special to consider: This developer responds very strongly to the presence of bromides by a relatively long induction period.
LP-CUBE XS diffuses through the entire thickness of the emulsion, and only after a prolonged time will the reduction of exposed silver halide begin. Development starts at the heavily exposed highlights, throughout the entire emulsion thickness. The slow process allows for diffusion to regenerate used developing agent and to remove bromide released, also deep in the emulsion, so that the crystals there as well as the heavily exposed surface crystals are developed practically simultaneously.
Halftones are developed the slower the weaker their exposure.
If development is extended to the point that the shadows are reduced as well, image contrast and gradation will be very high.

Like all depth developers, LP-CUBE XS will not make full use of the rated film speed. Highlight detail, in exchange, is excellent up to the extreme highlights.
LP-CUBE XS is particularly suited for overexposed, or at least generously exposed, negatives.
The name CUBE for this developer was chosen to be similar to MACO CUBE 400 clear film. The combination of a fast film with a speed-reducing developer (pulling) is capable of giving noticeably finer grain than emulsion surface developers *(See LP-SUPERGRAIN).*
Unlike emulsion surface developers, the characteristic curve of each film exhibits a speed point specific to the film in question. With increasing development time, this point is shifted progressively more to the left.
For quite a long time, hardly any depth developers were manufactured industrially. For a few years now, with the use of basic substances only recently made available, new depth developers have been introduced. LABOR PARTNER offers LP-CUBE XS as a liquid concentrate.
Former disadvantages with shadow detail were eliminated. Unfortunately, a gain in quality is still bought by a loss in speed, something one ought to be aware of when choosing a developer.

verfügte, wieder neue Schichttiefenentwickler auf dem Markt. LABOR PARTNER bietet den LP-CUBE XS als Flüssig-Konzentrat an. Die früheren Nachteile im Bereich der Schattenzeichnung wurden eliminiert. Leider geht die Qualität unverändert zu Lasten der Empfindlichkeitsausnutzung, das sollte man wissen, wenn man die Entscheidung der Entwicklerwahl treffen möchte.

VERPACKUNG
250 ml Glasflaschen

ANSATZ DER CHEMIE
Es wird Leitungs- oder demineralisiertes Wasser verwendet. Nach der Zugabe des LP-CUBE XS ist die Gebrauchslösung sofort gebrauchsfertig.

VERARBEITUNGSTEMPERATUR
Es sollte nicht unter 24°C entwickelt werden. Bei niedrigeren Temperaturen werden die Entwicklungszeiten zu lang.

EINMALENTWICKLER
LP-CUBE XS ist ein klassischer Einmalentwickler.

VERDÜNNUNG
Die Standardverdünnung ist 1+4. Bei einer Standard-Entwicklerdose von 260 ml Inhalt wird wie folgt verdünnt:

1 + 4 =	52 ml LP-CUBE XS-Konzentrat
	+ 208 ml Wasser

ENTWICKLERHÄRTUNG
Jeder Film verträgt es, während der Entwicklung zusätzlich gehärtet zu werden. LABOR PARTNER rät dazu, den Entwicklerhärter LP-GELADUR der Entwickler-Gebrauchslösung wie folgt zuzugeben:

VERDÜNNUNGSTABELLE FÜR 260 ml GEBRAUCHSLÖSUNG

1 + 4 (Standard)	52 ml LP-CUBE XS
	+128 ml Wasser
	+ 80 ml LP-GELADUR

ÜBER- UND UNTERBELICHTUNG
Am Beginn dieses Abschnittes haben wir Ihnen geschildert, dass der LP-CUBE XS nicht dafür gemacht ist, unterbelichtete Filme zu pushen.
Das ist nicht seine Aufgabe, also kann er es auch nicht.
Die unübertroffene Stärke dieses Entwicklertyps ist es, vor allem hochempfindliche Filme mit allerbesten Resultaten zu entwickeln, die bis zu einer Blende überbelichtet sind.

Da alcuni anni a questa parte, grazie all'acquisizione di nuove sostanze base, delle quali si era sprovvisti diversi anni fa, questi sviluppi di profondità sono apparsi nuovamente sul mercato. LABOR PARTNER propone il LP-CUBE XS sotto forma di concentrato liquido.
I passati svantaggi in campo di definizione nelle ombre sono stati eliminati.
Purtroppo la qualità continua a procedere a discapito dello sfruttamento della sensibilità, e questo bisogna saperlo, quando si deve prendere la decisione sulla scelta dello sviluppo.

CONFEZIONE
Bottiglia in vetro da 250 ml

PREPARAZIONE DELLO SVILUPPO
Si utilizza acqua di rubinetto oppure demineralizzata. Dopo aver aggiunto l'LP-CUBE XS la soluzione d'uso è pronta al trattamento.

TEMPERATURA DI TRATTAMENTO
Non si dovrebbe sviluppare sotto i 24°C. A temperature più basse i tempi si allungherebbero troppo.
SVILUPPO USA E GETTA:
LP-CUBE XS è un classico sviluppo monouso (›one-shot‹)

DILUIZIONE
La diluizione standard è di 1 + 4.
Con una tank standard di 260 ml di contenuto si diluisce come segue:

1 + 4 =	52 ml di concentrato LP-CUBE XS
	+ 208 ml di acqua

INDURIMENTO DELLO SVILUPPO
Ogni pellicola ben sopporta di essere indurita durante lo sviluppo.
LABOR PARTNER consiglia, di aggiungere alla soluzione d'uso l'induritore LP-GELADUR secondo la tabella seguente:

TABALLA DI DIUIZIONE PER 260 ml DI SOLUZIONE D'USO

1 + 4	52 ml di LP-CUBE XS
	+ 128 ml di acqua
	+ 80ml di LP-GELADUR

SOVRA E SOTTOESPOSIZIONE
All'inizio di questo capitolo abbiamo spiegato, che il LP-CUBE XS non è adatto a ›tirare‹ pellicole sottoesposte. Non è il suo compito, e del resto non ne è capace. Il suo inimita-

Dessverre går kvaliteten på bekostning av følsomhetsutnyttelsen, dette må en vite før en tar et valg av hvilken framkaller en velger.

FORPAKNING
Glassflasker 250 ml

BLANDING AV KJEMI
Det benyttes vann eller deminiralisert vann. Etter at LP CUBE XS er tilsatt vannet er løsningen klar for bruk.

BRUKSTEMPERATUR
Det kan ikke arbeides UNDER 24 0 C . Ved lavere temperaturer blir tidene forlange.
KUN engangsframkaller.

FORTYNNING
Standard fortynning er 1 + 4.
Ved en framkallingstank som trenger 260 ml gir dette

1 + 4 =	52 ml LP CUBE XS
	+ 208 ml vann

FRAMKALLER HERDING
En hver film tåler å bli herdet under framkallingen.
LABOR PARTNER tilrår å blande framkallerherderen LP-GELADUR i henhold til følgende tabell.

FORTYNNINGSTABELL FOR 260 ml FERDIG BLANDING

1 + 4	52 ml LP CUBE XS
	+ 128 ml vann
	+ 80 ml LP GELADUR

OVER OG UNDEREKSPONERING *(pull og push framkalling)*
I begynnelsen av avsnittet har vi beskrevet hvordan LP-CUBE XS virker og at den ikke er konsipert for å presse undereksponerte filmer. Den er ikke laget for dette formålet. Styrken ligger i å kunne få det allerbeste ut av , framforalt høyfølsomme, filmer, som i tillegg er overeksponert med 1 blender.
Skulle det, med en eller annen film være nødvendig å redusere farmkallingstiden, så vil det være et unntak. Bare ved overeksponering på mer enn 2 blendere kan en empirisk finne fram til en kortere framkallingstid.

PACKAGING
250 ml glass bottles

PREPARATION OF THE SOLUTION
Use tap water or demineralised water. The working solution is ready for use as soon as the LP-CUBE XS developer concentrate has been added.

PROCESSING TEMPERATURE
Do not develop below 24°C (75°F), or development times will be too long.

ONE-SHOT DEVELOPER
LP-CUBE XS is a classical one-shot developer.

DILUTION
The standard dilution is 1 + 4. For a standard tank with a contents of 260 ml, dilute as follows:

1 + 4 =	52 ml of LP-CUBE XS concentrate
	+ 208 ml of water

DEVELOPER HARDENING
Any film can do with some additional hardening during development.
LABOR PARTNER recommends to add the developer hardener LP-GELADUR to the working solution of the developer as per the following chart.

DILUTION CHART FOR 260 ml OF WORKING SOLUTION

1 + 4	52	ml LP-CUBE XS
	+ 128	ml of water
	+ 80	ml LP-GELADUR

OVER- AND UNDEREXPOSURE
At the beginning of this clause, we explained that LP-CUBE XS was not made for the pushing of underexposed films. It is not its task, and so it is not capable of it. The outstanding quality of this film mainly lies in developing fast films for best results when the films were overexposed by up to one f-stop.
A film really requiring curtailed development would actually be an exception. Normally, an overexposure of one f-stop (ISO 200 instead of ISO 400) does not require shorter development. Empirically determine any reduction in development time needed after a two-stop overexposure.
GRAPH:
The times given in the development chart are for an average gamma of 0.65. For individual printing habits, other

Falls bei dem einen oder anderen Film tatsächlich eine Reduzierung der Entwicklungszeit erforderlich sein sollte, wäre das eine Ausnahme. Normalerweise sind bei einer Blende Überbelichtung (200 ISO statt 400 ISO) keine kürzeren Zeiten erforderlich. Bei 2 Blenden Überbelichtung (100 ISO statt 400 ISO) sind etwaige Zeitverkürzung empirisch zu ermitteln.

DIAGRAMM
Die in der Entwicklungszeitentabelle angegeben Zeiten sollen ein mittleres Gamma von 0,65 erreichen. Es kann jedoch sein, dass beim individuellen Vergrößern, andere Werte als optimaler angestrebt werden. So erfordern Vergrößerungsgeräte mit einem Lichtmischschacht härtere Negative, Geräte mit Doppelkondensoren weichere Negative. Der für den Laboranten mögliche Spielraum bewegt sich von 20% Zeitenverlängerung bis zu 20% Zeitverkürzung. Größere Abweichungen würden zwangsläufig Qualitätseinbussen bewirken.

ERGIEBIGKEIT BASIEREND AUF DER VERDÜNNUNG 1 + 4
In 260 ml Gebrauchslösung kann ein Kleinbildfilm verarbeitet werden.

BEWEGUNG
In den ersten 30 Sekunden ist die Entwicklerdose ständig zu bewegen. Danach alle 30 Sekunden jeweils 1 x.

ROTATIONSENTWICKLUNG
Der Ansatz ist wie bei der Kippentwicklung 1 + 4.
Die Zeiten der Entwicklungszeitentabelle müssen um etwa 10 % reduziert werden.

JOBO-ATL-PROCESSOR
Der Ansatz ist 1 + 4. Die Entwicklungszeiten sind rund 50 % gegenüber der Entwicklungszeitentabelle zu verlängern. Die Entwicklungszeiten sind für Rollfilme (120) und Kleinbildfilme (135-36) gleich.

HALTBARKEIT
Die original verschlossene, braune LABOR PARTNER GLASFLASCHE ist etwa bis zu 2 Jahre nach dem Erwerb im Handel haltbar. Die Farbe des Konzentrates darf sich nicht in Richtung Braun verfärbt haben. Sobald eine sichtbare Verfärbung vorliegt, ist die weitere Verwendung zu riskant. Anbrüche können etwa ein halbes Jahr aber auch erheblich länger aufbewahrt werden.

bile punto di forza è rappresentato di sviluppare pellicole di alta sensibilità e/o sovraesposte di almeno 1 diaframma con risultati eccelsi. Qualora in casi particolari si dovesse ridurre il tempo di sviluppo, ciò rappresenterebbe l'eccezione!. Normalmente ad un diaframma di sovraesposizione (200 anziché 400 ISO) non è necessaria una riduzione del tempo di sviluppo. A 2 diaframmi di sovraesposizione (100 anziché 400 ISO) si determina il tempo di sviluppo in modo del tutto empirico.

DIAGRAMMA
I tempi indicati nella tabella dei tempi di sviluppo delle pellicole sono atti a far raggiungere un valore Gamma di 0,65. Ingranditori muniti di teste a luce diffusa necessitano di negativi più contrastati, con un Gamma di ca. 0,65 a 0,70.Ingranditori invece con testa a condensatori necessitano di negativi più morbidi, con un Gamma di ca. 0,50 a 0,55. La tolleranza a disposizione dello stampatore varia fra un 20 % di incremento e un 20 % di decremento del tempo. Variazioni superiori implicano necessariamente un abbassamento della qualità.

RESA BASANDOSI SU UNA DILUIZIONE DI 1 + 4
In 260 ml di soluzione d'uso si può trattare una pellicola di piccolo formato 135/36.

MOVIMENTO/AGITAZIONE
La tank va agitata con continuità durante i primi 30 secondi. Successivamente 1 volta ogni 30 secondi.

SVILUPPO A ROTAZIONE
La diluizione 1+4, come nel trattamento a capovolgimento. I tempi indicati in tabella vanno ridotti di ca. il 10 %.

PROCESSORE TIPO JOBO-ATL
Diluizione 1+4. I tempi di sviluppo sono da allungare di ca. il 50 % rispetto ai tempi indicati in tabella.
I tempi di sviluppo sono identici per le pellicole di piccolo (135/36 e medio formato (120).

CONSERVAZIONE
In bottiglia originale LABOR PARTNER in vetro marrone, la durata è di almeno 2 anni dalla data d'acquisto. Il colore del prodotto concentrato non deve colorarsi verso il marrone. Non appena avviene una colorazione visibile, l'uso diventa rischioso.
Bottiglie iniziate possono essere conservate per almeno 6 mesi o più.

DIAGRAM
De oppgitte framkallingstidene gir en gjennomsnitts gamma på 0,65. Det kan være at din forstørrer krever en annen verdi for et optimalt resultat.Forstørrere med en blandingsjakt kan kreve gamma 0,65 til 0,7.
Dobbelkondensorer krever et mykere negativ med f.eks gamma 0,5 til 0,55. Dette oppnås ved å variere tiden med +/- 20 %. Større variasjoner vil medføre kvalitetstap.

UTNYTTELSESGRAD
Basert på en fortynning 1+ 4 vil 260 ml ferdig framkaller rekke for 1 film 35 mm.

AGGITASJON
Første 30 sek stadig og så hvert 30 sek 1 x.

ROTASJONSFRAMKALLING
Ved fortynning 1 + 4 må tidene som er i tabellen reduseres med 10 %.

JOBO ATL PROCESSOR
1 + 4
Forlengelsesfaktor ca 50 % i forhold til tabellen
Framkallingstidene for 35 mm og rullfilm er lik.

HOLDBARHET
I orginalembalasjen holdbar ca 2 år.
Farven på konsentratet må ikke bli brun. Så snart en misfarging oppstår er videre bruk betenkelig.
Følges disse rådene kan en åpnet flaske holde seg i mer enn 6 mnd.

target values may be optimal. Enlargers with diffusor lighting systems, for example, require harder negatives, while double-condensor enlargers require softer negatives. The margin for development time modifications by the lab worker ranges from 20% extension to 20% curtailing. Deviating by a larger factor would definitely result in a loss in quality.

CAPACITY
based on a dilution of 1+4:
260 ml of working solution are required for one 35-mm roll film.

AGITATION
Agitate permanently for the first 30 s.
Then invert once every 30 s.

ROTATION DEVELOPMENT
Prepare the working solution 1+4 as for small tanks with manual inversion.
Reduce development times quoted in the chart by about 10%.

JOBO ATL PROCESSOR
Dilution is 1+4. Prolong development times given in the chart by a factor of 50%.
Development times for medium format (120) and 35-mm roll films (135) are identical.

SHELF LIFE
An unopened brown LABOR PARTNER GLASS BOTTLE can be kept for up to 2 years after purchasing. The concentrate must not show any brownish discoloration. As soon as any discoloration is visible, use is too hazardous.
Used bottles may be kept for half a year, or even considerably longer.

Development chart **LP-CUBE XS**

1 + 4 24°C 30 Seconds Agitation Gamma 0,55

	Exposed ISO / ***time in minutes***					
	50	100	100	200	400	1600
AGFA APX 100	***12***	–	***12***	–	–	–
AGFA APX 200S	–	–	***12***	–	–	–
AGFA APX 400	–	–	***12***	–	***14***	–
EFKEpan 25	***10***	–	–	–	–	–
EFKEpan 50	***12***	–	–	–	–	–
EFKEpan 100	***12***	***16***	–	–	–	–
FOMApan 100	–	–	***12***	–	–	–
FOMApan 400	–	–	–	***12***	***14***	–
FUJI Neopan 100	***12***	***16***	–	–	–	–
FUJI Neopan 400	–	–	***12***	***14***	***16***	–
FUJI Neopan 1600	–	–	–	***14***	***16***	***17***
ILFORD Pan F	***12***	–	–	–	–	–
ILFORD FP4*	***10***	***12***	–	–	–	–
ILFORD HP5	–	–	***12***	***13,5***	***15***	–
ILFORD SFX 200	–	–	–	***15***	–	–
ILFORD Delta 100	***10***	***12***	–	–	–	–
ILFORD Delta 400	–	–	***12***	***13***	***14***	–
ILFORD Delta 3200	–	–	–	–	***12***	***18***
KODAK PLUS X*	***10***	***12***	–	–	–	–
KODAK TRI X	–	–	***11***	***12***	–	–
KODAK HIE	–	–	***14***	–	–	–
KODAK T-MAX 100	***10***	***12***	–	–	–	–
KODAK T-MAX 400	–	–	***10***	***11***	***12***	–
KODAK T-MAX 3200	–	–	–	–	***13***	***15***
KONICA IR 750	–	–	–	***12***	–	–
MACO UP 25plus	***10***	–	–	–	–	–
MACO UP 64clear	***12***	***13***	–	–	–	–
MACO UP 100plus	***14***	***18***	–	–	–	–
MACO IR 750clear	–	***18***	–	–	–	–
MACO IR 820clear	–	***18***	–	–	–	–
MACO UP 400plus	–	–	***12***	***13,5***	***15***	–
MACO CUBE 400clear	–	–	***20***	***21***	***22,5***	–

Filmentwickler

LP-DOCUFINE LC

LP-DOCUFINE LC zeichnet sich durch eine *Besonderheit* aus: Je nach Entwicklungszeit ist dieser spezielle Entwickler in der Lage, die normalerweise sehr steile Gradation von technischen Filmen, wie KODAK TECHNICAL PAN, MACO TECHNICAL PAN TP 65clear und MAO ORT 25clear so zu beugen, dass diese Filme für die bildmässigebildmäßige Fotografie erschlossen werden können. Der LP-DOCUFINE LC besitzt die Fähigkeit, die GRADATION (den Kontrastumfang) des Filmes zu steuern. Dies erfolgt ganz einfach über eine Veränderung der Entwicklungsdauer.
Beim LP-DOCUFINE LC bleibt dabei der Grundschleier in einem sehr geringen Umfang nahezu unverändert. Dies ist eine Besonderheit bei Entwicklern dieser speziellen Gattung.
Bei perforierten Filmen besteht *nicht* die Gefahr von ›Wolkenbildung‹. Die Nennempfindlichkeit wird optimal ausgenutzt. Beim KODAK TP, sowie beim MACO ORT25clear erreicht man eine Empfindlichkeitsausnutzung von gut 25 ISO. Bei dem MACO TECHNICAL PAN TP 64clear gut das Doppelte.
Insbesondere bei diesen speziellen Filmen spielen die Aufnahmebedingungen, vor allem auch die Farbtemperatur eine entscheidende Rolle bei der real nutzbaren Empfindlichkeit. Daher sind entsprechende Rückschlüsse auf den Entwickler in diesem Zusammenhang nicht in jedem Fall zulässig.

■

Beim LP-DOCUFINE LC steht LC für Low Contrast.
Hierbei handelt es sich um einen *unechten* Feinkornentwickler. Von *echten* Feinkorn-Entwicklern spricht man, wenn die Entwicklersubstanz selbst, ohne zusätzliche Silberhalogenidlöser, neben der chemischen eine teilweise physikalische Entwicklung provoziert. *Unechte* Feinkornentwickler nutzen die Nominalempfindlichkeit beim Erreichen eines vernünftigen Kontrastes gut aus. Sie zeigen eine vergleichsweise feine Körnigkeit bei gleichzeitig guter Kantenschärfe und Auflösung.
Warum kaufen sich Fotografen die vergleichsweise teuren Spezialfilme und die teure Spezialchemie? Lange wurde dieses Wissen in Fachkreisen als ›Geheimtipp‹ gehandelt: Das Ergebnis dieser Film/Chemie-Kombination können 50 x 60 cm große Vergrößerungen sein, die praktisch kornfrei sind. Und das bei 35 mm Film. Auch die Tonalität ist beein-

Sviluppo per pellicole

LP-DOCUFINE LC

LP-DOKUFINE LC si caratterizza da:
Questo speciale sviluppo è in grado, a seconda del tempo di trattamento, di piegare la gradazione ripida di pellicole tecniche, quali KODAK TECHNICAL PAN, MACO TECHNICAL PAN TP 64clear, MACO ORT 25clear, in modo da poterle utilizzare anche nella fotografia tradizionale.
Il LP-DOKUFINE LC possiede la capacità di controllare la GRADAZIONE (perimetro di contrasto) della pellicola. Ciò avviene semplicemente modificando la durata del tempo di sviluppo. Con il LP-DOKUFINE LC, in questi casi non aumenta, se non in misura minima, ovvero rimane praticamente inalterato. Si tratta di una peculiarità di questa famiglia di sviluppi.
Con le pellicole a perforazione non sussiste il pericolo di formazione di ›nuvole‹. La sensibilità nominale viene sfruttata in modo ottimale. Nel caso della KODAK TP, come pure MACO ORT 25clear si raggiunge un grado di sensibilità di buoni 25 ISO. Nel caso della MACO TECHNICAL PAN TP64clear almeno il doppio. Specialmente nel caso di queste pellicole speciali le condizioni di ripresa, soprattutto la temperatura colore, sono determinanti per il reale sfruttamento della sensibilità. E' per questo motivo che le rispettive conclusioni da attribuire allo sviluppo non sono rilevanti in ogni caso specifico.

■

›LC‹ nella denominazione del LP-DOCUFINE LC sta per ›Low Contrast‹ (basso contrasto). Si tratta di uno sviluppo a grana fine cosiddetto ›IMPROPRIO‹. Si parla di un rivelatore finegranulante ›PROPRIO‹, quando la sostanza di sviluppo stessa, senza l'aggiunta di dissoluzione degli alogenuri d'argento, provoca uno sviluppo in parte fisico insieme a quello chimico. Sviluppi a grana fine ›IMPROPRI‹ a raggiungimento di un contrasto ragionevole, sfruttano in modo ottimale la sensibilità nominale. Allo stesso tempo mostrano in confronto ad una grana fine, una buona risoluzione e nitidezza. Ma perché i fotografi acquistano queste pellicole speciali e questa chimica speciale, di costo elevato?
Per lungo tempo nelle varie cerchie professionali si dibatteva di questo sapere quale ›chicca‹: Il risultato ottenuto con questa combinazione di pellicola/chimica sono ingrandimenti 50 x 60 cm, nitidi e praticamente privi di grana, e tutto ciò con pellicole 35 mm. Anche la resa tonale è sbalorditiva. Negativi di questa qualità impongono l'uso di

Filmframkaller

LP-DOCUFINE LC

LP- DOCUFINE LC har følgende egenheter:
Alt etter hvilken framkallingstid som blir valgt er dette framkalleren i stand til å påvirke den ellers svært steile gradasjonen til tekniske filmer som KODAK TECHNICAL PAN, MACO ORT 25clear og MACO TECHNICALPAN 64clear, slik at disse kan benyttes i billedmessig fotografi
LP-DOCUFINE LC har den egenskapen at den kan styre gradasjonen til filmen, dette skjer ganske enkelt ved å endre framkallingstiden.
Ved bruk av LP-DOCUFINE LC forblir grunnsløret nesten uforandret. Dette er det spesielle med denne type framkaller. Ved perforrerte filmer er det ikke fare for skydannelse rundt hullene.
Videre gir framkalleren en god utnyttelse av følsomheten. Både KODAK TP og MACO ORT 25clear oppnår 25 ISO. Ved MACO TECHNICALPAN TP 64clear opnår man mer enn det dobbelte.
Ved bruk av disse filmene spiller opptakssituasjonen en spesiell rolle, framfor alt er fargetemperaturen viktig for hvor stor den reelle følsomheten er. Derfor er det ikke riktig å dra forhastede sluttninger mellom framkaller og film uten først å ta alle hensyn.

■

Hos LP- DOCUFINE LC står LC for LOW CONTRAST.
Dette er en uekte finkornframkaller. Ekte finkornframkaller har en når framkallersubstansen selv, uten ekstra sølvhalogenidløser, framprovoserer en delvis fysikalsk framkalling i tillegg til den kjemiske.
UEKTE finkornframkallere utnytter den nominelle følsomheten ved en fornuftig kontrast. Den gir et forholdsvis fint korn samtidig som det oppnås høy kantskarphet og oppløsning.

Hvorfor kjøper en fotograf forholdsvis dyre spesialfilmer og tilsvarende kjemi? Det har vært kjent lenge som ›Stalltips‹ i fagkretser: Resultatet av en film/framkallerkobinasjon kunne gi forstørrelser 50 x 60 cm som nesten var kornløse, og det fra et 35 mm negativ. Også tonaliteten er fremragende. Disse negativene nærmest roper etter et ekstremt sølvholdig fotopapir som ORIENTAL for i det hele tatt å få til en passende omsetning til positiv.

Negative developer

LP-DOCUFINE LC

LP-DOCUFINE LC is special in a way:
Depending on the development time, this developer can tame the normally very steep gradation of technical films such as KODAK TECHNICAL PAN, MACO TECHNICAL PAN TP64clear, and MACO ORT 25clear in such as way as to open up the field of pictorial photography to these films.
LP-DOCUFINE LC is capable of controlling the gradation (contrast) of the film. This is achieved in a simple way by adapting the development time.
Fog density remains almost constant with LP-DOCUFINE LC, which is special for developers of this type. There is not the danger of ›clouding‹ with perforated film. Optimal use is made of the rated film speed. A speed of ISO 25 is easily obtained with KODAK TP and MACO ORT 25clear, twice this speed with MACO TECHNICAL PAN TP 64clear. Particularly with these specialised films, the exposure conditions, especially the colour temperature, play a decisive part for the actual useful speed. So speed losses are not always caused by the developer.

The ›LC‹ in LP-DOCUFINE LC stands for Low Contrast.
This developer is a solvent, or false fine-grain, developer.
TRUE fine grain developers are those where the developing agent itself, without any additional silver halide solvents, produces some degree of physical development in addition to chemical development.
FALSE fine grain developers make good use of the film's rated speed at reasonable contrast while producing relatively fine grain and good acutance and resolution.

Why do photographers buy the relatively expensive special films and expensive specialised chemistry?
For a long time this experience was handled as ›secret lore‹ in experts' circles: These film/developer combinations are capable of producing practically grainless 50 x 60 cm (20 x 24 in) enlargements – from 35-mm film! Tonality is impressive, too. These negatives seem to long for silver-rich ORIENTAL printing paper, which allows an appropriate rendering.

druckend. Diese Negative schreien geradezu nach extrem silberreichem Fotopapier von ORIENTAL, um eine adäquate Umsetzung ins Positiv zu realisieren.

VERPACKUNG: 250 ml Glasflaschen

ANSATZ DER CHEMIE
Es wird Leitungs- oder demineralisiertes Wasser verwendet. Nach der Zugabe des LP-CUBE XS ist die Gebrauchslösung sofort gebrauchsfertig.

VERARBEITUNGSTEMPERATUR
Es sollte nicht unter 20°C entwickelt werden.

EINMALENTWICKLER
LP-DOCUFINE LC ist ein klassischer Einmalentwickler.

VERDÜNNUNG
Die Standard-Verdünnung ist 1+4. Bei einer Standard-Entwicklerdose von 260 ml Inhalt wird wie folgt verdünnt:

1 + 4 =	52 ml LP-DOCUFINE LC-Konzentrat
	+ 208 ml Wasser

ENTWICKLERHÄRTUNG
Jeder Film verträgt es, während der Entwicklung zusätzlich gehärtet zu werden. LABOR PARTNER rät dazu, den Entwicklerhärter LP-GELADUR der Entwickler-Gebrauchslösung wie folgt zuzugeben:

VERDÜNNUNGSTABELLE FÜR 260 ML GEBRAUCHSLÖSUNG

1 + 4 =	52 ml LP-DOCUFINE LC
	+ 128 ml Wasser
	+ 80 ml LP-GELADUR

ÜBER- UND UNTERBELICHTUNG
Jeder Fotograf sollte sich seine eigenen Kenntnisse fundamental erarbeiten. Wir bewegen uns bei dieser Gattung auf einem sehr dünnen Eis, Vorschläge zur Entwicklung können nur annähernde Hinweise geben, sie dienen allenfalls als erste Zeiten, um dann im eigenen Labor das persönliche Optimum zu erarbeiten.
VORSCHLAG: Der Anwender sollte sich von allen drei in Frage kommenden Spezialfilmen jeweils eine kleine Menge kaufen und diese nach reproduzierbaren Kriterien sowohl unter Tages- als auch mit Blitzlicht mit verschiedenen ISO-Werten belichten. Diese erste Testreihe dann mit den Zeiten der LP-DOCUFINE LC Tabelle entwickeln. Der Film, der am meisten zusagt, der sollte dann noch erneut mit unter-

carte fotografiche ad alto contenuto d'argento, tipo ORIENTAL, per vedersi realizzati in modo adeguato una volta stampati.

CONFEZIONE: Bottiglia in vetro da 250 ml

PREPARAZIONE DELLO SVILUPPO
Si utilizza acqua di rubinetto oppure demineralizzata. Dopo aver aggiunto l'LP-DOCUFINE LC la soluzione d'uso è pronta al trattamento.

TEMPERATURA DI TRATTAMENTO
Non si dovrebbe sviluppare al disotto dei 20°C.

SVILUPPO MONOUSO
L'LP-DOCUFINE LC è un classico sviluppo mono-uso.

DILUIZIONE
La diluizione standard è di 1 + 4. Con una tank standard di 260 ml di contenuto si diluisce come segue:

1 + 4 =	52 ml di concentrato LP-DOCUFINE LC
	+ 208 ml di acqua.

INDURIMENTO DELLO SVILUPPO
Ogni pellicola ben sopporta di essere indurita durante lo sviluppo.
LABOR PARTNER consiglia, di aggiungere alla soluzione d'uso, l'induritore LP-GELADUR secondo la tabella seguente:

TABELLA DI DILUIZIONE PER 260 ML DI SOLUZIONE D'USO

1 + 4 =	52 ml di LP-DOCUFINE LC
	+ 128 ml di acqua
	+ 80 ml di LP-GELADUR

SOVRA E SOTTOESPSOSIZIONE
Ogni fotografo dovrebbe costruirsi le proprie conoscenze dalle radici. In questa famiglia ci muoviamo come su una lastra di ghiaccio molto sottile, proposte per il trattamento sono solamente indicativi, utilizzabili come base di partenza, che poi vanno man mano ottimizzati secondo le proprie esigenze. *PROPOSTA:* L'utilizzatore acquista pochi pezzi di tutte e tre le pellicole menzionate, le espone con criteri ripetibili sia in luce diurna che artificiale, a diverse regolazioni di sensibilità. Sviluppa poi la serie di pellicole di prova con LP-DOCUFINE LC seconde le indicazioni della tabella. La pellicola che più si addice alle aspettative deve ora essere riprovata e ritrattata nello stesso sviluppo, ma con diversi tempi di trattamento. Da considerare: Proprio

FORPAKNING
Glassflasker 250 ml

BLANDING AV KJEMI
Det benyttes vann eller deminiralisert vann. Etter at LP-DOCUFINE LC er tilsatt vannet er løsningen klar for bruk.

BRUKSTEMPERATUR
Det kan ikke arbeides UNDER 20°C . Ved lavere temperaturer blir tidene forlange.

ENGANGSFRAMKALLER
LP-DOCUFINE LC er en klassisk engangsframkaller.

FORTYNNING
Standard fortynning er 1 + 4.
Ved en framkallingstank som trenger 260 ml gir dette

1 + 4 =	52 ml LP- DOCUFINE LC
	+ 208 ml vann

FRAMKALLER HERDING
En hver film tåler å bli herdet under framkallingen.
LABOR PARTNER tilrår å blande framkallerherderen LP-GELADUR i henhold til følgende tabell.

FORTYNNINGSTABELL FOR 260 ML FERDIG BLANDING

1 + 4 =	52 ml LP- DOCUFINE LC
	+ 128 ml vann
	+ 80 ml LP GELADUR

OVER OG UNDEREKSPONERING *(pull og push framkalling)*
En hver fotograf må finne fram til sine egne erfaringer. Med denne sorten framkaller beveger vi oss på tynn is. Forslag til framkalling kan bare tilnærmelsesvis være rettesnorer , men alle må selv finne fram til det som er det optimale for sin egen person.
FORSLAG: Brukeren av en av de foreslåtte filmene kjøper et lite antall for så å eksponere dem etter reproduserbare kriterier, både i dagslys og med blitz og da med varianter i ISO verdi. Den første testrekken blir så framkallt i LP-DOCUFINE LC i hht tabellen. Den filmen som faller best i smak, bør så framkalles med variasjoner i framkallingstiden. Vær vennlig å merk følgende: Nettopp ved disse filmsortene vil filterbruk ha stor innflytelse på resultatet. Dette kan påvirke testresultatet i stor grad.
For den som gjerne eksprimenterer gir disse tre filmene med sin steile gradasjon i kombinasjon med LP-DOCUFINE LC uante muligheter.

PACKAGING
250 ml glass bottles.

PREPARATION OF THE SOLUTION
Use tap water or demineralised water. The working solution is ready for use as soon as the LP-DOCUFINE LC developer concentrate has been added.

PROCESSING TEMPERATURE
Do not develop below 20°C (68°F).

ONE-SHOT DEVELOPER
LP-DOCUFINE LC is a classical one-shot developer.

DILUTION
The standard dilution is 1+4. For a standard tank with a contents of 260 ml, dilute as follows:

1 + 4 =	52 ml of LP-SUPERGRAIN concentrate
	+ 208 ml of water.

DEVELOPER HARDENING
Any film can do with some additional hardening during development.
LABOR PARTNER recommends to add the developer hardener LP-GELADUR to the working solution of the developer as per the following chart.

DILUTION CHART FOR 260 ML OF WORKING SOLUTION

1 + 4 =	52 ml LP-CUBE XS
	+ 128 ml of water
	+ 80 ml LP-GELADUR

OVER- AND UNDEREXPOSURE
Each photographer should work in a fundamental way to obtain their experience. With this type of developer, we are treading on thin ice, meaning that any recommendations concerning development can only be approximate guidance. They are but first hints at the development time from which to start in order to find a personal optimum in your own lab.
SUGGESTION: The user should buy a small quantity of each one of the three specialised films, and should expose these according to reproducible criteria, under daylight as well as under flash light, rating the films at various ISO speeds. Develop this test series in LP-DOCUFINE LC using the times given in the development chart. Finally process the film you like best, using varying development times.
Remember: This type of film is particularly susceptible to

schiedlichen Entwicklungszeiten verarbeitet werden.
Bitte bedenken Sie: Gerade bei dieser Filmgattung sind erhebliche Einflussmöglichkeiten durch verschieden farbige Filter möglich. Diese können das Testergebnis massiv beeinflussen. Wer gerne experimentiert, für den bieten die drei steilen Filme in Kombination mit dem LP-DOCUFINE LC Entwickler fantastische Möglichkeiten.

GRADATION
Die in der Entwicklungstabelle angegeben Zeiten sollen ein mittleres Gamma von 0,65 erreichen. Es kannjedoch sein, dass beim individuellen Vergrößern, andere Werte als optimaler angestrebt werden. So erfordern Vergrößerungsgeräte mit einem Lichtmischschacht härtere Negative, Geräte mit Doppelkondensoren weichere Negative. Der für den Laboranten mögliche Zeiten-Spielraum bewegt sich von 20% Zeiten-Verlängerung bis zu 20% Zeiten-Verkürzung. Grössere Abweichungen würden zwangsläufig gerade bei diesem Entwicklertyp gravierende Gradationsveränderungen bewirken.

ERGIEBIGKEIT BASIEREND AUF DER VERDÜNNUNG 1 + 4
In 260 ml Gebrauchslösung kann ein Kleinbildfilm verarbeitet werden.

BEWEGUNG
In den ersten 30 Sekunden ist die Entwicklerdose ständig zu bewegen. Danach alle 30 Sekunden jeweils 1 x.

ROTATIONSENTWICKLUNG
Der Ansatz ist wie bei der Kippentwicklung 1+4. Die Zeiten der Entwicklungstabelle müssen um etwa 10 % reduziert werden.

JOBO-ATL-PROCESSOR
Der Ansatz ist 1 + 4.
Die Entwicklungszeiten sind rund 50 % gegenüber der Filmzeiten-Tabelle zu verlängern. Die Entwicklungszeiten sind für Rollfilme (120) und Kleinbildfilme (135-36) gleich.

HALTBARKEIT
Die original verschlossene, braune LABOR PARTNER GLASFLASCHE ist etwa bis zu 2 Jahre nach dem Erwerb im Handel haltbar. Die Farbe des Konzentrates darf sich nicht in Richtung Braun verfärbt haben. Sobald eine sichtbare Verfärbung vorliegt, ist die weitere Verwendung zu riskant. *Anbrüche können etwa ein halbes Jahr aber auch erheblich länger aufbewahrt werden.*

questa famiglia di pellicole possiede una enorme possibilità di influenza, generata dall'uso di diversi filtri durante la ripresa. Questi filtri possono influenzare massicciamente i risultati dei test. Chi di voi è uno sperimentatore accanito, queste pellicole ad andamento ripido in combinazione allo sviluppo LP-DOCUFINE LC rappresentano un mondo fantastico.

GRADAZIONE
I tempi indicati nella tabella dei tempi di sviluppo fanno raggiungere un Gamma medio di 0,65. E' possibile che a seconda del tipo di illuminazione dell'ingranditore debbano essere raggiunti valori ottimali, diversi. Ingranditori con illuminazione a condensatori implicano negativi più morbidi, al contrario di ingranditori con illuminazione diffusa, attraverso box di miscelazione, richiedono negativi più duri. Il campo di azione da parte dell'utilizzatore è limitato in un ambito di riduzione, ovvero incremento del tempo di sviluppo, di un più o meno 20 %. Maggiori sono le modifiche, più aumenta in modo incontrollabile la modifica del contrasto, proprio con questo tipo di sviluppo.

RESA SULLA BASE DI UNA DILUIZIONE DI 1 + 4
In 260 ml di soluzione d'uso si può trattare una pellicola di piccolo formato 135/36.

MOVIMENTO/AGITAZIONE
La tank va agitata con continuità durante i primi 30 secondi. Successivamente 1 volta ogni 30 secondi.

SVILUPPO A ROTAZIONE
La diluizione 1 + 4, come nel trattamento a capovolgimento. I tempi indicati in tabella vanno ridotti di ca. il 10 %.

PROCESSORE TIPO JOBO-ATL
Diluizione 1+4.
I tempi di sviluppo sono da allungare di ca. il 50 % rispetto ai tempi indicati in tabella.
I tempi di sviluppo sono identici per le pellicole di piccolo (135/36) e medio formato (120).

CONSERVAZIONE
In bottiglia originale LABOR PARTNER in vetro marrone, la durata è di almeno 2 anni dalla data di acquisto. Il colore del prodotto concentrato non deve colorarsi verso il marrone. Non appena avviene una colorazione visibile, l'uso diventa rischioso. *Bottiglie iniziate possono essere conservate per almeno 6 mesi o più.*

GRADASJON
De oppgitte framkallingstidene gir en gjennomsnitts gamma på 0,65. Det kan være at din forstørrer krever en annen verdi for et optimalt resultat. Forstørrere med en blandingsjakt kan kreve gamma 0,65 til 0,7.
Dobbelkondensorer krever et mykere negativ med f.eks gamma 0,5 til 0,55. Dette oppnås ved å variere tiden med +/- 20 %. Større variasjoner vil medføre kvalitetstap.

UTNYTTELSESGRAD
Basert på en fortynning 1 + 4 vil 260 ml ferdig framkaller rekke for 1 film 35 mm

AGGITASJON
Første 30 sek stadig og så hvert 30 sek 1 x.

ROTASJONSFRAMKALLING
Ved fortynning 1 + 4 må tidene som er i tabellen reduseres med 10 %.

JOBO ATL PROCESSOR
1+4
Forlengelsesfaktor ca 50 % i forhold til tabellen.
Framkallingstidene for 35 mm og rullfilm er lik.

HOLDBARHET
I orginalembalasjen holdbar ca 2 år. Farven på konsentratet må ikke bli brun. Så snart en misfarging oppstår er videre bruk betenkelig. *Følges disse rådene kan en åpnet flaske holde seg i mer enn 6 mnd.*

the effects of coloured filters, which may have considerable impact on the test results.

To those who like to experiment, the three contrasty films in combination with LP-DOCUFINE LC offer a fantastic potential.

GRADATION

The times given in the development chart are for an average gamma of 0.65. For individual printing habits, other target values may be optimal. Enlargers with diffusor lighting systems, for example, require harder negatives, while double-condensor enlargers require softer negatives. The margin for development time modifications by the lab worker ranges from 20% extension to 20% curtailing. Deviating by a larger factor would definitely result in a serious change in gradation, especially with this type of developer.

CAPACITY

based on a dilution of 1+4:

260 ml of working solution are required for one 35-mm roll film.

AGITATION

Agitate permanently for the first 30 s.

Then invert once every 30 s.

ROTATION DEVELOPMENT

Prepare the working solution 1+4 as for small tanks with manual inversion.

Reduce development times quoted in the chart by about 10%.

JOBO ATL PROCESSOR

Dilution is 1 + 4. Prolong development times given in the chart by a factor of 50%.

Development times for medium format (120) and 35-mm roll films (135) are identical.

SHELF LIFE

An unopened brown LABOR PARTNER GLASS BOTTLE can be kept for up to 2 years after purchasing. The concentrate must not show any brownish discoloration. As soon as any discoloration is visible, use is too hazardous.

Used bottles may be kept for half a year, or even considerably longer.

Development chart **LP-DOCUFINE LC**

1 + 4 20°C 30 Seconds Agitation Gamma 0,55

	Exposed ISO / ***time in minutes***				
	10	20	50	64	100
KODAK Technical Pan	***–***	***5-6***	***9-10***	***13-14***	***–***
MACO ORT 25clear	***4***	***6-7***	***10-11***	***–***	***–***
MACO TP 64clear	***–***	***8***	***12***	***14***	***18***
MACO IR 750clear	***–***	***–***	***–***	***–***	***7-8***
MACO IR 820clear	***–***	***–***	***–***	***–***	***7-8***

Dokumentenentwickler

LP-DOCUFINE HC

Die Besonderheit des LP-DOCUFINE HC ist die kräftige Schattenentwicklung, zuständig für einen auch mit dem bloßen Auge erkennbar höheren Kontrastumfang als mit einem normalen kräftig arbeitenden Papierentwickler.
Diese Fähigkeit hat dazu beigetragen, dass die klassischen Lith-Entwickler, die zur Verarbeitung von Strichfilmen (KODAK KODALITH, MACO ORT25clear und MACO GENIUS FILM) eingesetzt wurden, durch den LP-DOCUFINE HC erfolgreich ersetzt worden sind.
Die Anwendung ist erheblich einfacher, die Qualität meist besser, der Preis erheblich günstiger. Außerdem zeichnet sich der LP-DOCUFINE HC durch eine sehr hohe Ergiebigkeit und Haltbarkeit auch als Gebrauchslösung aus. Klassische 2-Part-Lith-Entwickler haben eine rechte kurze Haltbarkeit, eine recht geringe Ergiebigkeit, sind vergleichsweise teuer und sind nicht für jeden Filmtyp gleichermaßen geeignet. Der MACO ORT 25plus sollte daher bevorzugt im LP-DOCUFINE HC verarbeitet werden.

■

Hinweis: Falls Sie als Fotograf oder Laborant einmal Probleme mit der Kombination Dokumentenfilm und Lithchemie hatten, dann probieren Sie den LP-DOCUFINE HC aus. Sie werden überrascht sein, von der sehr hohen Maximalschärzung und dem Gradationsverlauf.

■

Beim LP-DOCUFINE HC steht das ›HC‹ für High Contrast.
Hierbei handelt es sich um einen Schichttiefenentwickler mit einer Induktionsperiode von etwa 30 Sekunden. Nach dieser Einwirkzeit erscheinen zuerst die stärker belichteten Schattenstellen und im weiteren Verlauf der Entwicklung nach und nach die schwächer belichteten Lichter. Nach der Induktionsperiode sind nach etwa 30 Sekunden die Lichter ausentwickelt. Danach nimmt die satte Schwärzung der tiefsten Schatten noch langsam zu, so dass der erzielbare Kontrast etwas anwächst und die Bildbrillanz steigt.

Sviluppo per documenti

LP-DOCUFINE HC

La particolarità del LP-DOCUFINE HC è rappresentato dalla forte azione di sviluppo in profondità, che si manifesta, anche ad occhio nudo, in un ambito di contrasto più alto rispetto ad uno sviluppo per carta ad azione vigorosa.
Queste sue capacità hanno contribuito a sostituire con successo i classici sviluppi lith, normalmente utilizzati per il trattamento delle pellicole al tratto tipo KODAK KODALITH, MACO ORT 25clear e MACO GENIUS FILM.
L'utilizzo è assai più semplice, la qualità spesso superiore ed il prezzo molto più competitivo. Il LP-DOCUFINE HC si distingue inoltre, da una alta resa e durata, anche sotto forma di soluzione d'uso.
I classici sviluppi lith a 2 parti hanno una durata assai ridotta una volta diluiti, la resa è ridotta, sono più costosi e non sono compatibili allo stesso modo con i vari tipi di pellicola. La MACO ORT 25clear dovrebbe essere trattata preferibilmente nel LP-DOKUFINE HC.

■

In qualità di fotografo o stampatore avrai forse avuto problemi in passato con la combinazione di pellicole tecniche e chimica lith, allora è il momento di provare e passare al LP-DOCUFINE HC. Rimarrai stupito dalla capacità all'annerimento massimo e all'andamento della gradazione.

■

Nel LP-DOKUFINE HC, ›HC‹ sta per High Contrast.
Si tratta di uno sviluppo di profondità nello strato con un periodo di induzione di ca. 30 secondi. Dopo questo lasso di tempo appaiono dapprima le zone di ombra maggiormente esposte, e man mano passa il tempo di sviluppo si arriva alle luci meno esposte.
A periodo di induzione terminato, dopo 30 sec. ca. sono sviluppate a fondo le alte luci, dopodiché si saturano i neri nelle ombre più profonde in modo tale da riuscire ad aumentare il contrasto ottenibile e ad accrescere la brillantezza dell'immagine.

Dokumentframkaller

LP-DOCUFINE HC

LP- DOCUFINE HC har følgende egenheter:
LP- DOCUFINE HC er en kraftig dybdeframkaller som øker kontrastomfanget på en måte som kan gjennkjennes med det blotte øyet og som er langt høyere enn en kraftig arbeidende papirframkaller.
Denne egenskapen bidrar til at LP- DOCUFINE HC kan erstatte klassiske lithframkallere når strekfilmer som KODAK KODALITH; MACO ORT 25 clear OG MACO GENIUS film skal framkalles.
Bruken er enklere og kvalitetet høyere og prisen er gunstigere. I tillegg har LP- DOCUFINE HC en høy utnyttelsesgrad og lang holdbarhet også når den er fortynnet. (Klassiske 2 part lithframkallere har kort levetid og lav utnyttelsesgrad, er dessuten relativt dyre og egner seg ikke for alle filmsorter. MACO ORT 25clear bør bare framkalles i LP- DOCUFINE HC)

■

Merk: Skulle du som fotograf eller laborant ha problemer med dokumentfilmer og lithframkallere bør du prøve LP-DOCUFINE HC. Du vil bli overrasket over gradasjonskurven og maksimalsværtningen.

■

LP- DOCUFINE HC ›HC‹ står for high contrast.
Dette er en dybdeframkaller med en induksjontid på 30 sek. Etter denne tiden kommer først de sterkere belyste skyggepartiene og så litt etter litt de svakere belyste høylysene.

Etter induksjonsperioden vil høylysene være ferdig framkalte etter ca 30 sek. Etter dette tiltar den dype sværntningen i de mørkeste skyggepartiene bare langsomt slik at den oppnåelige kontrasten øker og brilliansen stiger.

Document developer
LP-DOCUFINE HC

This developer is special in its development of rich shadows which are responsible for a visibly enhanced contrast range as compared to normal, highly active paper developers.
This capability of the film has contributed to make it a successful replacement for the classical lith developers used for the development of document films (KODAK KODALITH, MACO ORT 25clear, MACO GENIUS FILM).
Application is easier, quality mostly better, and the price is lower. Also, even the working solutions of LP-DOCUFINE HC have a high capacity and long life.
Classical lith developers don't live long, are relatively expensive, and are not equally suited for all types of films. MACO ORT 25 plus should, therefore, be preferably processed in LP-DOCUFINE HC.

■

Note: If you ever had problems with the combination of document film and lith chemistry, try LP-DOCUFINE LC, You will be surprised by the very high maximum density and its characteristic curve.

■

The ›HC‹ in LP-DOCUFINE HC stands for High Contrast.
This developer is a depth developer with an induction period of about 30 s. Following this time in the developer, the heavily exposed areas will emerge first, and the less heavily exposed areas will follow successively as development carries on.

Following the 30 s induction period, it takes another 30 s for the highlights to develop to completion while after this time, deepest shadows will continue to grow in density, enhancing the achievable contrast and the ›bite‹ of the image.

ANWENDUNG BEI 20°C
Der LP-DOCUFINE HC eingesetzt als Filmentwickler:

- AGFA, KODAK und MACO Strichfilme
  1 + 4 3-4 Minuten

- AGFA SCENTIA*, KODAK EM-Film*
  1 + 4 3-4 Minuten

- MACO EM-Film *
  1 + 5 4-5 Minuten
  **sind Filme für die Elektronenmikroskopie*

- KODALITH
  1 + 4 5-6 Minuten

- MACO ORT 25clear Kleinbild/Roll-und Planfilm
  1 + 5 4-5 Minuten

VERPACKUNG
- 1 Liter Polyethylenflaschen
- 5 Liter Kanister

ANSATZ DER CHEMIE
Es wird Leitungs- oder demineralisiertes Wasser verwendet. Nach der Zugabe des LP-DOCUFINE HC ist die Gebrauchslösung sofort gebrauchsfertig.

VERARBEITUNGSTEMPERATUR
Es sollte nicht unter 18°C entwickelt werden.

EINMALENTWICKLER
Normalerweise wird der LP-DOCUFINE HC *nicht* als Einmalentwickler eingesetzt. Er kann so verwendet werden, wie man es von den Papierentwicklern her kennt. Die Aufbewahrung der Gebrauchslösung sollte in hochgefüllten, gut verschlossenen Flaschen erfolgen.

VERDÜNNUNG
Die Standard-Verdünnungen sind 1 + 4 und 1 + 5. Es sind jedoch auch problemlos Verdünnungen von 1 + 7 und 1 + 9 möglich, dies richtet sich je nach Verwendungszweck.

VERDÜNNUNGSTABELLE FÜR 260 ml GEBRAUCHSLÖSUNG

1 + 4 =	52 ml LP-DOCUFINE HC
	+128 ml Wasser
	+ 80 ml LP-GELADUR

UTILIZZO A 20°C
LP-DOCUFINE HC utilizzato quale sviluppo per pellicole:

- Pellicole al tratto AGFA, KODAK e MACO
  1 + 4 3-4 minuti

- AGFA SCENTIA* , KODAK EM*
  1 + 4 3-4 minuti

- MACO EM*
  1 + 5 4-5 minuti
  ** pellicole per microscopio elettronico*

- KODALITH
  1 + 4 5-6 minuti

- MACO ORT 25clear piccolo, medio e grande formato
  1 + 5 4-5 minuti

CONFEZIONAMENTO
- Bottiglia in polietilene da 1 litro
- Fustino da 5 litri

PREPARAZIONE DELLA CHIMICA
Si utilizzi acqua di rubinetto o demineralizzata.
Dopo l'aggiunta del concentrato di LP-DOCUFINE HC la soluzione d'uso è pronta all'utilizzo immediato.

TEMPERATURA DI TRATTAMENTO
Si sconsiglia il trattamento al disotto dei 18°C.

SVILUPPO MONOUSO
Normalmente l'LP-DOCUFINE HC *non* viene utilizzato come monouso. Può essere utilizzato come nel caso di sviluppo per carta. La conservazione della soluzione d'uso dovrebbe avvenire in bottiglie ben colme e sigillate.

DILUIZIONE
La diluizione standard è di 1 + 4 e 1 + 5. Sono però possibili senza problemi anche diluizioni maggiori di p. es. 1 + 7 o 1 + 9, a seconda del campo di applicazione.

TABELLA DI DILUIZIONE PER 260 ml DI SOLUZIONE D'USO

1 + 4 =	52 ml di LP-DOCUFINE HC
	+128 ml si acqua
	+ 80 ml di LP-GELADUR

BRUK VED 20°C
LP- DOCUFINE HC som filmframkaller:

- AGFA, KODAK OG MACO strekfilmer
  1 + 4 3-4 min

- AGFA SCENTIA, KODAK EM film
  1 + 4 3-4 min

- MACO EM film
  1 + 5 4 -5 min

- KODALITH
  1 + 4 5-6 min

- MACO ORT 25clear rullfilm, 35 mm og planfilm
  1 + 5 4-5 min

FORPAKNING
- 1 l polythylenflasker
- 5 l kanne

BLANDING AV KJEMI
Det benyttes vann eller deminiralisert vann.
Etter at LP- DOCUFINE HC er tilsatt vannet er løsningen klar for bruk.

BRUKSTEMPERATUR
Det kan ikke arbeides UNDER 18°C.

ENGANGSFRAMKALLER
Vanligvis benyttes LP-DOCUFINE HC ikke som engangsframkaller. Den kan benyttes slik man er vant til fra papirframkallere. Ferdig bruksløsning må oppbevares lufttett.

FORTYNNING
Standard fortynning er 1 + 4 og 1 + 5.
Det er mulig å benytte 1 + 7 og 1 + 9, men det er avhengig av resultatet som ønskes.

FORTYNNINGSTABELL FOR 260 ml FERDIG BLANDING

1 + 4 =	52 ml LP- DOCUFINE LC
	+ 128 ml vann
	+ 80 ml LP GELADUR

APPLICATION AT 20°C (68°F)
LP-DOCUFINE used as negative developer:

- AGFA, KODAK, and MACO line films
  1 + 4 3-4 minutes

- AGFA SCIENTIA*, KODAK EM film*
  1 + 4 4-5 minutes

- MACO EM film*
  1 + 5 4-5 minutes
  ** These are films for electron microscopy*

- KODALITH
  1 + 4 5-6 minutes

- MACO ORT 25 clear 35-mm and medium format roll film and sheet film
  1 + 5 4-5 minutes

PACKAGING
- 1 l polyethylene bottles
- 5 l containers

PREPARATION OF THE SOLUTION
Use tap water or demineralised water. The working solution is ready for use as soon as the LP-DOCUFINE HC developer concentrate has been added.

PROCESSING TEMPERATURE
Do not develop below 18°C (64°F).

ONE-SHOT DEVELOPER
LP-DOCUFINE HC is not normally used as one-shot developer. It can thus be used like paper developer. Keep working solutions in full, well-sealed bottles.

DILUTION
The standard dilutions are 1 + 4 and 1 + 5.
1 + 7 and 1 + 9 can be used without problems, depending on the intended use.

FOR A STANDARD TANK, 260 ml – DILUTE AS FOLLOWS

1 + 4 =	52ml LP-DOCUFINE HC
	+ 128 ml of water
	+ 80 ml LP-GELADUR

GRADATION
Da die Verwendung des LP-DOCUFINE HC vor allem bei der Reproduktion bzw. Verarbeitung von Spezialfilmen für die Elektronenmikroskopie sind Angaben zur Gradation kaum sinnvoll. Gradationen von Gamma 1,8 sind leicht erreichbar. Gleichzeitig wird eine sehr hohe Maximalschwärzung erreicht, die leicht bis weit über 3 erreichen kann. Das ist abhängig vom jeweils verwendeten Film.

ERGIEBIGKEIT BASIEREND AUF DER VERDÜNNUNG 1 + 4
Bis zu 120 Blatt Planfilm pro Liter Gebrauchslösung. Bei Filmen hoher Silberpackungsdichte (MACO GENIUS FILM) können bis zu 60 Blatt erreicht werden.

HALTBARKEIT
Die original verschlossene, braune LABOR PARTNER PE-FLASCHE ist etwa bis zu 2 Jahre nach dem Erwerb im Handel haltbar. Die Farbe des Konzentrates darf sich nicht in Richtung Braun verfärbt haben. Sobald eine sichtbare Verfärbung vorliegt, ist die weitere Verwendung zu riskant. *Anbrüche können etwa ein halbes Jahr, aber auch erheblich länger aufbewahrt werden.*

GRADAZIONE
Dato che l'uso del LP-DOCUFINE HC è riservato alla lavorazione di pellicole per riproduzioni ovvero di pellicole speciali per microscopi elettronici, qualsiasi indicazione di gradazione risulta di scarso valore. Gradazioni con un Gamma di 1,8 sono ottenibili senza alcun problema. Massima densità dei neri che contemporaneamente riescono a raggiungere oltre 3,0 a dipendenza della pellicola utilizzata.

RESA IN BASE ALLA DILUIZIONE 1 + 4
Fino a 120 pellicole piane per litro di soluzione d'uso. Nel caso di trattamento di pellicole ad alto contenuto d'argento (MACO GENIUS FILM) si arriva a ca. 60 fogli.

CONSERVAZIONE
In bottiglia originale ben chiusa ha una durata di almeno 2 anni dalla data di acquisto presso il tuo distributore di fiducia. La colorazione del prodotto concentrato non deve spostarsi verso il color marrone. Non appena è visibile una colorazione l'uso diventa rischioso.
Il concentrato iniziato può durare almeno mezz'anno o addirittura più a lungo.

GRADASJON
Da LP- DOCUFINE HC framfor alt benyttes til reproduksjon og framkalling av spesialfilmer for elektromikroskoper er en gradasjonfastsettelse lite hensiktsmessig. Det er enkelt å oppnå en gamma på 1,8. Ved høy maksimalsværtning er også gamma 3,0 mulig å oppnå. Dette avhenger av den filmen som blir benyttet.

UTNYTTELSESGRAD
Basert på en fortynning 1 + 4 kan inntil 120 planfilmer framkalles pr liter ferdig framkaller. Ved filmer med høyt sølvinnhold (MACO GENIUS FILM) kan inntil 60 blad framalles.

HOLDBARHET
I orginalembalasjen holdbar ca 2 år. Farven på konsentratet må ikke bli brun. Så snart en misfarging oppstår er videre bruk betenkelig. *Følges disse rådene kan en åpnet flaske holde seg i mer enn 6 mnd.*

GRADATION
For repography and the processing of special films, the main application for LP-DOCUFINE HC, gradation is hardly a meaningful concept. A gamma of 1,8 is easily achieved, the maximum density being very high, values in excess of 3 are easily attained, depending on the film in use.

CAPACITY BASED ON A DILUTION OF 1 + 4
One litre of working solution will last for up to 120 sheets of film. Up to 60 sheets of silver-rich films (like MACO GENIUS FILM) can be processed.

SHELF LIFE
An unopened brown LABOR PARTNER GLASS BOTTLE can be kept for up to 2 years after purchasing. The concentrate must not show any brownish discoloration. As soon as any discoloration is visible, use is too hazardous. *Used bottles may be kept for half a year, or even considerably longer.*

Stoppbad
LP-CITRIN

Citrin steht für Zitronensäure mit Indikator. Zitronensäure anstatt Essigsäure vermeidet weitestgehend störende und atemwegsbelastende Emissionen. Zudem ist Zitronensäure weniger gefährlich. Bei Essigsäure können bereits Konzentrationen von nur 10% zu starken Hautverbrennungen und nicht selten zur Ausbildung einer Essigsäureallergie führen. Dämpfe von konzentriertem Essig dürfen wegen Verätzungsgefahr der Bronchien nicht eingeatmet werden.
Im Fotohandel sind weitestgehend industriell gefertigte Produkte mit ca. 60% Konzentration vertreten.

■

Zwischen Entwicklung und Fixierung wird ein saures Unterbrecherbad geschaltet, um einerseits das in der Fotoemulsion aufgenommene Alkali zu neutralisieren und damit die Entwicklung zuverlässig zu unterbrechen, andererseits aber auch, um den pH-Wert des Fixierbades nicht zu erhöhen und damit dessen Haltbarkeit zu verlängern.
Vorsicht beim Ansatz von Stoppbädern. Eine zu hoch konzentriert angesetzte Stoppbad-Gebrauchslösung würde das Fixierbad zersetzen. ZITRONENSÄURE hat zwar nicht die hohe Aziditätsreserve wie Essigsäure, allerdings handelt es sich beim Stoppbad um ein Folgebad, das normalerweise nach dem Gebrauch verworfen wird.
Von einer Aufbewahrung und erneuter Nutzung gebrauchter Stoppbäder wird abgeraten.

■

Die Vorteile von Zitronensäure als wirksame Substanz haben LABOR PARTNER überzeugt. Das erste Produkt von LABOR PARTNER war im Jahr 1984 LP-CITRIN. Die Qualität von damals wurde zwischenzeitlich mehrfach modernisiert, die Grundrezeptur basiert jedoch unverändert auf Zitronensäure.
Optimal ist ein Unterbrecherbad mit einem pH-Wert um 4. Das Bad sollte spätestens dann ersetzt werden, wenn ein pH-Wert von 6 erreicht ist. Bei diesem Wert reagiert auch der dem LP-CITRIN-Konzentrat beigegebene Indikatorfarbstoff mit einem Farbumschlag nach Rot.
Wer an Allergien leidet oder sich durch die Emissionen gestört fühlt (frisches Stoppbad sprudelt wie Champagner, wenn das Alkali des Entwicklers eingebracht wird), ist gut beraten, zwischen dem Entwickler und dem Unterbrecherbad die Filme/Papiere kurz mit klarem Wasser abzuspülen. Dies minimiert die Schadstoffemission, verbessert die

Bagno d'arresto
LP-CITRIN

Citrin sta per acido citrico con indicatore. L'acido citrico al posto di acido acetico evita emissioni rilevanti e dannose alle vie respiratorie. Fra sviluppo e fissaggio si inserisce un bagno d'arresto acido, d'un canto per neutralizzare gli alcali assunti dall'emulsione fotografica e interrompere l'azione dello sviluppo in modo affidabile, d'altro canto anche per non aumentare il valore pH del fissaggio e allungarne la conservazione.
Attenzione nella preparazione di bagni d'arresto. Una soluzione d'uso di bagno d'arresto troppo concentrata decompone il bagno di fissaggio(!).

■

ATTENZIONE all'utilizzo di acido acetico. Concentrazioni già a partire dal 10 % possono provocare forti bruciature della pelle e lo scoppio di un'allergia all'acido acetico. I vapori acetici non possono essere inalati in quanto determinano un pericolo di corrosione dei bronchi. Sono disponibili sul mercato prodotti industriali con una concentrazione del 60 %. Nella letteratura specializzata si fa spesso riferimento all'allergia all'acido acetico.
L'ACIDO CITRICO non contiene una così grande riserva di acidità come d'acido acetico, però nel caso dei bagni d'arresto si tratta di un bagno sequenziale, che normalmente viene neutralizzato dopo il suo utilizzo.
Si sconsiglia la conservazione e il riutilizzo di bagno d'arresto.

■

I vantaggi dati dall'acido citrico quale agente attivo hanno convinto LABOR PARTNER. Il primo prodotto di LABOR PARTNER nell'anno 1984 era l'LP-CITRIN. La qualità di allora è stata migliorata più volte nel frattempo, ma la ricetta originaria è sempre basata sull'acido citrico.

Un bagno d'arresto ottimale possiede un valore pH di 4. La soluzione deve essere sostituita al più tardi quando viene raggiunto un valore pH di 6. A raggiungimento di questo valore reagisce anche l'indicatore di colore
LP-CITRIN, con un mutamento di colore verso il rosso.

Chi soffre di allergie o a chi danno fastidio le emissioni (un bagno d'arresto fresco, frizza come champagne, quando si introduce alcali provenienti dallo sviluppo), si consiglia di anteporre al passaggio dallo sviluppo al bagno d'arresto, un rapido risciacquo in acqua pura. Ciò minimizza le emissioni

Stoppebad
LP-CITRIN

Citrin står for sitronsyre med indikator. Sitronsyre i stedet for eddiksyre gjør at en unngår emmisjoner som er forstyrrende og som belaster luftveiene.

Mellom framkalleren og fikserbadet benyttes et surt stoppebad, på den ene siden for å nøytralisere alkaliene som er tatt opp i fotoemulsjonen for derved å stoppe framkallingen effektivt, på den annen side for ikke å øke pH verdien på fikserbadet og derved minske holdbarheten til dette badet. OBS. ved blanding av stoppebad. Et forsterkt stoppebad vil kunne få fikserbadet til å spalte seg (!).

■

OBS ved bruk ac eddiksyre. Konsentrasjoner over 10 % kan føre til sterke hudforbrenninger og også til at en får eddiksyreallergi. Damp fra eddiksyre kan føre til skade på bronkiene hvis den blir pustet inn, alså unngå denne belastningen. I fotohandelen finnes for det meste konsentrat med 60 %. I litteraturen blir det ofte vist til eddiksyreallergi.
SITRONSYRE har riktignok ikke den samme høye aziditetsreserven som eddiksyre, men stoppebadet er et følgebad som vanligvis kastes etter bruk.
Oppbevaring og gjennbruk av stoppebad frarådes på det sterkeste.

■

Fordelene med å benytte sitronsyre har overbevist LABOR PARTNER. LABOR PARTNER første produkt i 1984 var nettopp LP CITRIN. Produktet og kvaliteten er blitt videreutviklet og modifisert, men grunnlaget er fortsatt sitronsyre.

Et optimalt stoppebad har en pH på 4. Badet må skiftes når det har pH 6. Ved denne verdien reagerer også LP-CITRIN ved at fargeindikatoren slår ut med rødfarge.

Den som lider av allergier eller som forstyrres av emisjoner (friskt stoppebad bruser som champange når det kommer i kontakt med alkaliet fra framkalleren) bør følge rådet om å spyle film/papir kort i vann før det kommer i stoppebadet. Dette minsker ytterligere emisjonene, bedrer luften i mørkerommet og øker levetiden til LP-CITRIN. Framfor alt er luftkvaliteteten et av de viktigste argumentene for å bruke LP- CITRIN. Ved bruk av mellom spyling oppnår en et tilnærmet ›luktfritt‹ mørkerom.

Stop bath

LP-CITRIN

Citrin stands for citric acid plus indicator. Using citric acid instead of acetic acid allows to avoid fumes which are annoying and irritating to the respiratory tract to the largest possible degree. Also, citric acid is much less hazardous than acetic acid. Of the latter, concentrations as low as 10% can result in skin burns and the (not so seldom) formation of an allergy against acetic acid. Concentrated-acetic-acid fumes must not be inhaled because of the danger of acid burns of the bronchii. Photographic supply stores largely offer industrial products with a concentration of about 60%.

An acid stop bath is used between development and fixation for two ends: first, to neutralise any alkali absorbed in the emulsion, reliably stopping development, and second, to avoid raising the pH value of the fixing bath, prolonging its life.

Caution when preparing stop baths. Excessive stop bath concentrations will result in degradation of the fixing bath. The neutralising capacity of CITRIC ACID may not be as high as that of acetic acid, but the stop bath is for one-shot use, and normally disposed of after use.

We advise against keeping and re-using stop bath.

LABOR PARTNER is convinced of the advantages of citric acid as the effective agent. LABOR PARTNER's first product, back in 1984,was LP-CITRIN. The quality of 1984 has been updated several times in the meantime, but the formulation is still based on citric acid.

The optimal pH for a stop bath lies around 4. The bath should be replaced when the pH is 6, at the very latest. The indicator dye added to the LP-CITRIN concentrate changes to red at this pH.

It is good advice to those suffering from allergies, and those feeling disturbed by the emissions (Fresh stop bath forms gas bubbles like champagne when the developer alkali is added.) to briefly rinse films/prints with clear water prior to putting them into the stop bath. This minimises pollutant emissions, improves the air you breathe, and prolongs the life of LP-CITRIN. Better air in the lab is the argument in favour of LP-CITRIN, up to ›odourless processing‹ in the lab, when an intermediate rinse is used.

Atemluft und verlängert die Lebenserwartung des LP-CITRIN. Vor allem die angenehme Atemluft, bis hin zum ›geruchlosen Arbeiten‹ im Labor bei einem vorgeschalteten Wasserbad, ist das Argument für LP-CITRIN.

VERPACKUNG

- 1 Liter Polyethylenflaschen
- 5 Liter Kanister

ANSATZ DER CHEMIE

Es wird Leitungswasser verwendet. Nach der Zugabe des LP-CITRIN Stoppbadkonzentrates ist die Gebrauchslösung sofort gebrauchsfertig.

VERARBEITUNGSTEMPERATUR

Es sollte nicht unter 18°C gearbeitet werden.

VERDÜNNUNGSTABELLE FÜR 260 ml GEBRAUCHSLÖSUNG

1 + 19 =	13 ml LP-CITRIN
	+ 247 ml Wasser

VERARBEITUNGSZEIT / BEWEGUNG

Filme werden 30 Sekunden unter regelmäßigem Kippen der Filmdose bearbeitet. Diese Zeit ist möglichst genau einzuhalten.

ERGIEBIGKEIT

In 1 Liter Gebrauchslösung können maximal 10 m² Film- oder Fotopapieremulsion bearbeitet werden. Das sind theoretisch über 150 Kleinbildfilme oder 200 Blatt Papier im Format 20 x 25 cm.
Es wird empfohlen, nur die Gebrauchslösung anzusetzen, die für die täglich benötigte Arbeit
vorgesehen ist. Die gebrauchte LP-CITRIN-Lösung sollte täglich entsorgt werden. Es darf niemals eine Gebrauchslösung, die bereits zur Verarbeitung im Positivprozess verwendet worden ist, für die Filmverarbeitung verwendet werden, denn es wird sich feinster Papierfaserstaub darin befinden. Dieser wird sich als mikrofeine Flecken bei der Vergrößerung zeigen.

HALTBARKEIT

LP-CITRIN ist in der original verschlossenen, schwarzen LABOR PARTNER Flasche etwa bis zu 2 Jahre nach dem Erwerb im Handel haltbar.

dannose, migliora l'aria da respirare ed allunga la vira del bagno di LP-CITRIN. La gradevole aria respirata è proprio l'argomento scritto in maiuscolo del LP-CITRIN, fino ad un ›trattamento privo di cattivi odori‹ nella camera oscura anteponendo un bagno d'acqua.

CONFEZIONAMENTO

- Bottiglia in polietilene da 1 litro
- Fustino da 5 litri

PREPARAZIONE DELLA CHIMICA

Si utilizzi acqua di rubinetto. Dopo l'aggiunta di concentrato di bagno d'arresto LP-CITRIN, la soluzione è pronta all'uso.

TEMPERATURA DI TRATTAMENTO

Non bisogna lavorare al disotto dei 18°C.

TABELLA DI DILUIZIONE

1 + 19 =	13 ml di LP-CITRIN
	+ 247 ml di acqua

TEMPO DI LAVORAZIONE / AGITAZIONE

Le pellicole vengono trattate durante 30 secondi a capovolgimento regolare della tank.
Il tempo è da rispettare rigorosamente.

RESA

1 litro di soluzione d'uso è sufficiente per trattare al massimo 10 m² di emulsione di pellicole, ciò che corrisponde a ca. 150 pellicole di piccolo formato.
Si consiglia di preparare soluzione d'uso sufficiente da soddisfare le esigenze giornaliere di trattamento delle pellicole. Le soluzioni d'uso di LP-CITRIN esauste dovrebbero essere smaltite giornalmente. Non bisogna mai utilizzare soluzioni già utilizzate per carta anche per pellicole, in quanto vi è contenuto il finissimo pulviscolo di fibra della carta. Ciò provocherebbe delle macchioline microscopiche visibili sugli ingrandimenti.

CONSERVAZIONE

In bottiglia sigillata, originale nera LABOR PARTNER, si mantiene per almeno 2 anni dalla data di acquisto presso il tuo fornitore di fiducia.

FORPAKNING

- 1 l polythylenflasker
- 5 l kanne

BLANDING AV KJEMI

Det benyttes vann eller deminiralisert vann. Etter at LP-CITRIN er tilsatt vannet er løsningen klar for bruk.

BRUKSTEMPERATUR

Det kan ikke arbeides UNDER 18°C .

FORTYNNING
Standard fortynning er 1 + 19

FORTYNNINGSTABELL FOR 260 ml FERDIG BLANDING

1 + 19 =	13 ml LP- CITRINC
	+ 247 ml vann

AGGITASJON

Filmer aggiteres i 30 sek. Ikke overskrid tiden.

UTNYTTELSESGRAD

I 1 l bruksløsning kan 10 m² filmemulsjon bli behandlet. Det er teoretisk ca 150 35 mm filmer.
Det blir anbefalt å bare blande den mengde stoppebad som er nødvendig for daglig bruk. Den brukte LP-CITRIN oppløsningen bør destrueres daglig. Aldri benytt stoppe bad fra papirprosessen til film. Det kan være papirpartikler i denne som vil skade filmen. Dette fører til mikrofine prikker i forstørrelsene.

HOLDBARHET

I orginalembalasjen holdbar ca 2 år.

PACKAGING

- 1 l polyethylene bottles
- 5 l containers

PREPARATION OF THE SOLUTION

Use tap water. The working solution is ready for use as soon as the LP-CITRIN stop bath concentrate has been added.

PROCESSING TEMPERATURE

Do not process below 18°C (64°F).

DILUTION CHART FOR 260 ml OF WORKING SOLUTION

1+19 =	13 ml LP-CITRIN
	+ 247 ml of water

PROCESSING TIME/AGITATION

Films are treated for 30 s with regular inversions of the tank. Keep this time as precisely as possible.

CAPACITY

One litre of working solution has a maximum capacity of 10m2 of photographic film or paper emulsion. Theoretically, this equals more than 150 35-mm roll films or 200 sheets of paper in 20 x 25 cm (8 x 10 in) format.
We recommend that you prepare but the quantity of working solution needed for your daily processing.
Used LP-CITRIN solution should be disposed of each day.
Never use any working solution previously used for print processing for film as it will contain suspended fine paper fibres which you will find as fine spots in your prints.

SHELF LIFE

LP-CITRIN in unopened black LABOR PARTNER bottle can be kept for up to two years after purchase.

Härtendes Stoppbad
LP-CITRODUR

›Citro‹ steht für Zitronensäure mit Indikator, ›dur‹ für das Härtevermögen.
Zitronensäure anstatt Essigsäure vermeidet weitestgehend störende und atemwegsbelastende Emissionen.
LP-CITRODUR neigt aufgrund seiner Rezeptur dazu, einen Eigengeruch in Richtung ›Metallverarbeitung‹ zu verbreiten. Das ist nicht schädlich, vielleicht auch nicht einmal unangenehm. Das liegt an der Zugabe eines modernen Härtezusatzes zur LP-CITRIN- Grundrezeptur.

■

Die Filmemulsion, die nicht bereits im Entwickler durch LP-GELADUR Zugabe gehärtet wurde, sollte spätestens im Unterbrecherbad gehärtet werden. Dafür wurde die LP-CITRIN Formulierung um ein Härtezusatz erweitert. Seit vielen Jahren wird diese Stoppbad-Version vor allem dort eingesetzt, wo hoher Wert auf den exzellenten Zustand von Filmen gelegt wird. Daher gehören Museen, Bildarchive im gewerblichen Bereich und Fotografen zu den Verwendern, die einen ganz besonderen Wert auf den Zustand ihrer Filme legen müssen. Das Härtevermögen von LP-CITRODUR erhöht die Widerstandsfähigkeit von fotografischen Emulsionen. Die Empfindlichkeit gegenüber Kratzern bei der weiteren Behandlung des Filmmaterials, sei es bei der Archivierung oder dem Ziehen durch die Buchbildbühne, wird erheblich verbessert. Zwischen der Entwicklung und Fixierung wird ein saures Unterbrecherbad geschaltet, um einerseits das in der Fotoemulsion aufgenommene Alkali zu neutralisieren und damit die Entwicklung zuverlässig zu unterbrechen, andererseits aber auch, um den pH-Wert des Fixierbades nicht zu erhöhen und damit dessen Haltbarkeit zu verlängern.
Zwingend erforderlich sind Unterbrecherbäder nur dann, wenn die Filmentwicklung 4 und mehr Minuten andauerte, bzw. Entwickler mit hoher Alkalität Einsatz finden.

■

Vorsicht beim Ansatz von Stoppbädern. Eine zu hoch konzentriert angesetzte Stoppbad-Gebrauchslösung würde das Fixierbad zersetzen.

■

Vorsicht beim Gebrauch von Essigsäure. Konzentrationen von bereits 10% können zu starken Haut-Verbrennungen und der Bildung einer Essigsäure-Allergie führen. Dämpfe von konzentriertem Essig dürfen wegen Verätzungsgefahr

Bagno d'arresto induritore
LP-CITRODUR

›Citro‹ sta per acido citrico con indicatore, ›dur‹ per potere indurente.
Acido citrico al posto di acido acetico evita in pratica emissioni di disturbo e a carico dell'apparato respiratorio.
LP-CITRODUR a causa della sua formulazione tende ad una propria emissione di odore in direzione ›lavorazione del metallo‹. Questa emissione non è dannosa, e per la maggior parte degli utilizzatori neppure sgradevole. Responsabile di questa emissione è l'aggiunta di una moderna sostanza di indurimento alla ricetta di base del LP-CITRIN.

■

L'emulsione della pellicola, che non è già stata indurita durante lo sviluppo con LP-GELADUR, dovrebbe esserlo al più tardi nel bagno d'arresto. A questo scopo la formulazione dell'LP-CITRIN è stata integrata da una sostanza di indurimento. Da parecchi anni si utilizza questa combinazione di bagno d'arresto e induritore dove si da la massima importanza all'eccellente condizione delle pellicole. Musei, archivi di immagini sia in ambito commerciale che dei fotografi professionisti, sono gli utilizzatori più sensibili alla perfetta conservazione delle proprie pellicole.
Il potere indurente del LP-CITRADUR aumenta la resistenza fisica delle emulsioni fotografiche. La sensibilità ai graffi nell'uso successivo del materiale in pellicola, sia durante l'archiviazione o l'inserimento del porta-pellicole durante la stampa, viene minimizzata notevolmente.

Fra sviluppo e fissaggio viene inserito un bagno d'arresto acido, d'un canto per neutralizzare gli alcali raccolti dall'emulsione fotografica e per interrompere l'azione dello sviluppo in modo affidabile, d'altro canto anche, per non incrementare il valore pH del bagno di fissaggio aumentando così la sua durata ed efficacia.
I bagni di arresto sono assolutamente indispensabili nei casi un cui la durata dello sviluppo delle pellicole è di 4 minuti e oltre, oppure se questi sviluppo sono di alcalinità elevata.

■

Attenzione durante la preparazione dei bagni d'arresto. Una bagno d'arresto troppo concentrato deteriora il bagno di fissaggio (!).

■

Attenzione all'utilizzo di acido acetico. Concentrazioni già a partire dal 10 % possono provocare forti bruciature della

Herdende Stoppebad
LP-CITRODUR

›Citro‹ står for sitronsyre med indikator, ›dur‹ står for herdeevnen

Sitronsyre i stedet for eddiksyre gjør at en unngår emmisjoner som er forstyrrende og som belaster luftveiene. LP-CITRODUR har en tendens pga av oppskriften til å ha en ›egenlukt‹ som ligner på ›metallarbeid‹ Denne er ikke skadelig, ikke engang ubehagelig. Dette pga av herdertilsettingen som er tilføyd til LP-CITRIN.

■

Filmemulsjonen som ikke er blitt herdet av LP GELADUR i framkalleren, bør senest i stoppebadet herdes. Derfor ble LP-CITRIN tilsatt en herder. I mange år er LP- CITRODUR blitt benyttet av museer, billedarkiver etc og av fotografer når det gjaldt å oppnå en ekselent tilstand for filmene.

Herde evnen til LP- CITRODUR øker motstandskraften til fotografiske emulsjoner. Følsomheten overfor mekanisk påvirknink blir betydelig senket og dermed forbedret, det være seg under arkivering eller ved kopiering.

Mellom framkalleren og fikserbadet benyttes et surt stoppebad, på den ene siden for å nøytralisere alkaliene som er tatt opp i fotoemulsjonen for derved å stoppe framkallingen effektivt, på den annen side for ikke å øke pH verdien på fikserbadet og derved minske holdbarheten til dette badet. Stoppebad er bare tvingende nødvendig når filmframkallingen er lengre enn 4 min eller det benyttes frakallere med høy allkali andel.

■

OBS. ved blanding av stoppebad. Et forsterkt stoppebad vil kunne få fikserbadet til å spalte seg (!).

■

OBS. ved bruk ac eddiksyre. Konsentrasjoner over 10 % kan føre til sterke hudforbrenninger og også til at en får eddiksyreallergi. Damp fra eddiksyre kan føre til skade på bronkiene hvis den blir pustet inn, alså unngå denne belastningen. I fotohandelen finnes for det meste konsentrat med 60%. I litteraturen blir det ofte vist til eddiksyreallergi.

SITRONSYRE har riktignok ikke den samme høye aziditetsreserven som eddiksyre, men stoppebadet er et følgebad som vanligvis kastes etter bruk.

Hardening stop bath

LP-CITRODUR

›Citro‹ stands for citric acid with indicator, and ›dur‹ for its hardening capacity.

Using citric acid instead of acetic acid allows to avoid fumes which are annoying and irritating to the respiratory tract to the largest possible degree. As a consequence of its formulation, LP-CITRODUR tends to emit a smell like when you are processing metal. This odour is not harmful, maybe not even unpleasant. It is caused by the addition of a modern hardening agent to the basic LP-CITRIN formulation.

Any film emulsion not previously hardened in the developer by a LP-GELADUR treatment should be hardened in the stop bath at the latest. To this end, a hardening agent was added to the basic LP-CITRIN formulation. For years, this version of our stop bath has been used primarily where films must be in excellent condition. So museums, commercial photographic archives, and photographers, who all have to give particular consideration to the condition of their films, use LP-GELADUR.
The hardening capacity of LP-GELADUR enhances the resistance of photographic emulsions. The susceptibility to scratches inflicted in the further course of processing, be it during storage or when pulling the negatives through the film holder of your enlarger, is reduced considerably.

An acid stop bath is used between development and fixation for two ends first, to neutralise any alkali absorbed in the emulsion, reliably stopping development, and second, to avoid raising the pH value of the fixing bath, prolonging its life. Stop baths are only mandatory when film development took 4 minutes or more, or when strongly alkaline developer was used.

Caution when preparing stop baths. Excessive stop bath concentrations will result in degradation of the fixing bath.

The buffering capacity of CITRIC ACID may not be as high as that of acetic acid, but the stop bath is for one-shot use, and normally disposed of after use. We advise against keeping and re-using stop bath.

der Bronchien nicht eingeatmet werden. Im Fotohandel sind weitestgehend industriell gefertigte Produkte mit ca. 60% Konzentration im Handel vertreten. Fahrlässiger Umgang mit Essig kann zu Essigsäure-Allergien führen.

ZITRONENSÄURE hat zwar nicht die hohe Aziditätsreserve wie Essigsäure, allerdings handelt es sich beim Stoppbad um ein Folgebad, das normalerweise nach dem Gebrauch verworfen wird. Von einer Aufbewahrung und erneuter Nutzung gebrauchter Stoppbäder wird abgeraten. Optimal ist ein Unterbrecherbad mit einem pH-Wert um 4.
Das Bad sollte spätestens dann ersetzt werden, wenn ein pH-Wert von 6 erreicht ist. Bei diesem Wert reagiert auch der dem LP-CITRODUR-Konzentrat beigegebene Indikatorfarbstoff mit einem Farbumschlag nach Rot.
Wer an Allergien leidet oder wen die Emissionen stören (frisches Stoppbad sprudelt wie Champagner, wenn das Alkali des Entwicklers eingebracht wird), ist gut beraten, zwischen dem Entwickler und dem Unterbrecherbad die Filme/Papiere kurz mit klarem Wasser abzuspülen. Dies minimiert die Schadstoffemission, verbessert die Atemluft und verlängert die Lebenserwartung des LP-CITRODUR.

pelle e lo scoppio di un'allergia all'acido acetico. I vapori acetici non possono essere inalati in quanto determinano un pericolo di corrosione dei bronchi.
Sono disponibili sul mercato prodotti industriali con una concentrazione del 60%. Nella letteratura specializzata si fa spesso riferimento all'allergia all'acido acetico.

L'ACIDO CITRICO non contiene una così grande riserva di acidità come d'acido acetico, però nel caso dei bagni d'arresto si tratta di un bagno sequenziale, che normalmente viene neutralizzato dopo il suo utilizzo. Si sconsiglia la conservazione e il riutilizzo di bagno d'arresto.

Un bagno d'arresto ottimale possiede un valore pH di 4. La soluzione deve essere sostituita al più tardi quando viene raggiunto un valore pH di 6. A raggiungimento di questo valore reagisce anche l'indicatore di colore LP-CITRODUR, con un mutamento di colore verso il rosso.

Chi soffre di allergie o a chi danno fastidio le emissioni (un bagno d'arresto fresco, frizza come champagne, quando si introduce alcali provenienti dallo sviluppo), si consiglia di anteporre al passaggio dallo sviluppo al bagno d'arresto, un rapido risciacquo in acqua pura. Ciò minimizza le emissioni dannose, migliora l'aria da respirare ed allunga la vira del bagno di LP-CITRODUR.

Oppbevaring og gjennbruk av stoppebad frarådes på det sterkeste. Et optimalt stoppebad har en pH på 4. Badet må skiftes når det har pH 6. Ved denne verdien reagerer også LP- CITRODUR ved at fargeindikatoren slår ut med rødfarge.

Den som lider av allergier eller som forstyrres av emisjoner (friskt stoppebad bruser som champange når det kommer i kontakt med alkaliet fra framkalleren) bør følge rådet om å spyle film/papir kort i vann før det kommer i stoppebadet. Dette minsker ytterligere emisjonene, bedrer luften i mørkerommet og øker levetiden til LP-CITRODUR.

The optimal pH for a stop bath lies around 4. The bath should be replaced when the pH is 6, at the very latest. The indicator dye added to the LP-CITRODUR concentrate changes to red at this pH.

It is good advice to those suffering from allergies, and those feeling disturbed by the emissions (Fresh stop bath forms bubbles like champagne when the developer alkali is added.) to briefly rinse films/prints with clear water prior to putting them into the stop bath. This minimises pollutant emissions, improves the air you breathe, and prolongs the life of LP-CITRODUR.

VERPACKUNG
- 1 Liter Polyethylenflaschen
- 5 Liter Kanister

ANSATZ DER CHEMIE
Es wird Leitungswasser verwendet.
Nach der Zugabe des LP-CITRODUR Stoppbadkonzentrates ist die Gebrauchslösung sofort gebrauchsfertig.

VERARBEITUNGSTEMPERATUR
Es sollte nicht unter 18°C gearbeitet werden.

VERDÜNNUNGSTABELLE FÜR 260 ml GEBRAUCHSLÖSUNG

1 + 16 =	15 ml LP-CITRODUR
	+ 244 ml Wasser

VERARBEITUNGSZEIT / BEWEGUNG
Filme werden 30 Sekunden unter regelmäßigem Kippen der Filmdose bearbeitet. Diese Zeit ist möglichst genau einzuhalten.

ERGIEBIGKEIT
In 1 Liter Gebrauchslösung können maximal 10 m^2 Film- oder Fotopapieremulsion bearbeitet werden. Das sind theoretisch über 150 Kleinbildfilme oder 200 Blatt Papier im Format 20 x 25 cm.
Es wird empfohlen, nur die Gebrauchslösung anzusetzen, die für die täglich benötigte Film-Verarbeitung vorgesehen ist. Die gebrauchte LP-CITRODUR Lösung sollte jeweils täglich entsorgt werden. Es darf niemals eine Gebrauchslösung, die bereits zur Verarbeitung im Positiv-Prozess verwendet worden ist, für die Filmverarbeitung verwendet werden, denn es wird sich feinster Papierfaserstaub darin befinden. Dieser wird sich als mikrofeine Flecken bei der Vergrößerung zeigen.

HALTBARKEIT
LP-CITRODUR ist in der original verschlossenen, schwarzen LABOR PARTNER Flasche etwa bis zu 2 Jahre nach dem Erwerb im Handel haltbar.

CONFEZIONAMENTO
- Bottiglia in polietilene da 1 litro
- Fustino da 5 litri

PREPARAZIONE DELLA CHIMICA
Si utilizzi acqua di rubinetto. Dopo l'aggiunta di concentrato di bagno d'arresto LP-CITRODUR, la soluzione è pronta all'uso.

TEMPERATURA DI TRATTAMENTO
Non bisogna lavorare al disotto dei 18°C.

TABELLA DI DILUIZIONE

1 + 16 =	15 ml di LP-CITRIN
	+ 244 ml di acqua

TEMPO DI LAVORAZIONE / AGITAZIONE
Le pellicole vengono trattate durante 30 secondi a capovolgimento regolare della tank.
Il tempo è da rispettare rigorosamente.

RESA
1 litro di soluzione d'uso è sufficiente per trattare al massimo 10 m2 di emulsione di pellicole, ciò che corrisponde a ca. 150 pellicole di piccolo formato.
Si consiglia di preparare soluzione d'uso sufficiente da soddisfare le esigenze giornaliere di trattamento delle pellicole. Le soluzioni d'uso di LP-CITRODUR esauste dovrebbero essere smaltite giornalmente. Non bisogna mai utilizzare soluzioni già utilizzate per carta anche per pellicole, in quanto vi è contenuto il finissimo pulviscolo di fibra della carta. Ciò provocherebbe delle macchioline microscopiche visibili sugli ingrandimenti.

CONSERVAZIONE
In bottiglia sigillata, originale nera LABOR PARTNER, si mantiene per almeno 2 anni dalla data di acquisto presso il tuo fornitore di fiducia.

FORPAKNING
- 1 l polythylenflasker
- 5 l kanne

BLANDING AV KJEMI
Det benyttes vann eller deminiralisert vann. Etter at LP-CITRODUR er tilsatt vannet er løsningen klar for bruk.

BRUKSTEMPERATUR
Det kan ikke arbeides UNDER 18 0 C .

FORTYNNINGSTABELL FOR 260 ml FERDIG BLANDING

1 + 16 =	135 ml LP-CITRODUR
	+ 245 ml vann

AGGITASJON
Filmer aggiteres i 30 sek. Ikke overskrid tiden.

UTNYTTELSESGRAD
I 1 l bruksløsning kan 10 m2 filmemulsjon bli behandlet. Det er teoretisk ca 150 35 mm filmer.
Det blir anbefalt å bare blande den mengde stoppebad som er nødvendig for daglig bruk. Den brukte LP- CITRODUR oppløsningen bør destrueres daglig. Aldri benytt stoppe bad fra papirprosessen til film. Det kan være papirpartikler i denne som vil skade filmen. Dette fører til mikrofine prikker i forstørrelsene.

HOLDBARHET
I orginalembalasjen holdbar ca 2 år.

PACKAGING

- 1 l polyethylene bottles
- 5 l containers

PREPARATION OF THE SOLUTION

Use tap water. The working solution is ready for use as soon as the LP-CITRIN stop bath concentrate has been added.

PROCESSING TEMPERATURE

Do not process below 18°C (64°F).

DILUTION CHART FOR 260 ml OF WORKING SOLUTION

1 + 16 =	15 ml LP-CITRODUR
	+ 244 ml of water

PROCESSING TIME / AGITATION

Films are treated for 30 s with regular inversions of the tank. Keep this time as precisely as possible.

CAPACITY

One litre of working solution has a maximum capacity of 10m2 of photographic film or paper emulsion. Theoretically, this equals more than 150 35-mm roll films or 200 sheets of paper in 20 x 25 cm (8 x 10 in) format.

We recommend that you prepare but the quantity of working solution needed for your daily processing.
Used LP-CITRODUR solution should be disposed of each day. Never use any working solution previously used for print processing for film as it will contain suspended fine paper fibres which you will find as fine spots in your prints.

SHELF LIFE

The unopened black LABOR PARTNER bottle can be kept for up to two years after purchase.

Fixierbad
LP-FIX SUPRA

Die außerordentliche Qualität vom LP-FIX SUPRA lässt nicht nur eine Verwendung als Fixierer bei der Kippentwicklung oder Tankentwicklung zu, sondern schliesst-schließt auch eine Anwendung als Maschinen-Fixierer ein. So arbeiten heute weltweit sehr viele maschinelle Negativ- und Positiv-Maschinen mit dem Hochleistungsfixierbad LP-FIX SUPRA.
In diesem Hochleistungsfixierbad stecken mehrere Jahrzehnte Erfahrung im Umgang mit Filmemulsionen. Nicht nur mit klassischen kubischen Filmemulsionen sowie T-Kristall-Emulsionen, sondern auch Erfahrungen mit Filmen sehr hoher Silberpackungsdichte, wie sie im Repro- und vor allem im Röntgen-Bereich vorliegen.

Die ›normalen‹ Fixierkonzentrate, die bevorzugt im Fotohandel vermarktet werden, sind meist völlig ausreichend, um klassische kubische Filmemulsionen zu fixieren. Wenn es jedoch darum geht, T-Kristall-Filme und Planfilme zu fixieren, dann stoßen diese recht preiswerten Rezepturen an ihre vorgegebenen Grenzen. Auch LABOR PARTNER produziert derartige, gut gepufferten und preiswerten Fixierbäder im Auftrage von Großkunden, jedoch nicht zum Verkauf unter dem eigenen Namen an die sehr anspruchsvollen Fotografen und Laboranten, die von der Marke LABOR PARTNER ausschließlich sehr hohe Qualität erwarten.
Das nach der Entwicklung in der Emulsionsschicht verbliebene, nicht belichtete und daher nicht entwickelte Silberhalogenid ist noch lichtempfindlich und muss daher aus der Schicht entfernt werden.
Silberhalogenid ist jedoch nicht ohne weiteres löslich und muss daher im Fixierprozess in einem relativ komplizierten Stufenprozess in ein leichtlösliches Komplexsalz umgewandelt werden, das zum größten Teil bereits während dem Fixiervorgang in Lösung gehen muss.

Bagno di fissaggio
LP-FIX SUPRA

L'eccezionale qualità di LP-FIX SUPRA oltre all'utilizzo del fissaggio nel trattamento a capovolgimento, in tank, non esclude anche l'uso come bagno di fissaggio in sviluppatrice. In tutto il mondo numerosi operatori utilizzano l'LP-FIX SUPRA in sviluppatrici automatiche sia per pellicole che per carta.

In questo fissaggio ad alte prestazioni è contenuta l'esperienza di decenni nell'utilizzo di emulsioni fotografiche.
L'esperienza acquisita non solo con emulsioni di pellicole cubiche o a cristalli piatti T-Grain, ma anche con emulsioni ad altissimo contenuto d'argento, come nel campo repro e radiografico.

I fissaggi ›normali‹ proposti maggiormente sul mercato fotografico, sono spesso assolutamente sufficienti per fissare le classiche emulsioni cubiche delle pellicole. Nei casi in cui si deve invece fissare pellicole con emulsioni a cristalli piatti T-Grain e pellicole piane, ci si imbatte nelle limitazioni intrinseche di queste ricette sicuramente più a basso costo. Anche LABOR PARTNER produce questa specie di fissaggio economico, ben tamponato soprattutto per grandi consumatori. Ciò però non avviene sotto il proprio marchio LABOR PARTNER, nel quale fotografi esigenti e laboratori professionali ripongono fiducia e si aspettano solo una qualità eccellente.
Gli alogenuri d'argento non esposti e di conseguenza non sviluppati, che permangono nello strato di emulsione dopo lo sviluppo sono ancora sensibili alla luce e devono essere pertanto eliminati dallo strato fotosensibile.
Gli alogenuri d'argento non sono però così facilmente solubili e bisogna pertanto trasformarli in un sale complesso facilmente solubile nel processo di fissaggio in un procedimento a gradini relativamente complicato, che nella maggior parte deve essere assolto appunto dal procedimento di fissaggio.

Fikserbad
LP-FIX SUPRA

Den spesielle kvaliteten til LP-FIX SUPRA gjør at den ikke bare benyttes ved tankframkalling, men også i framkallingsmaskiner. Derfor benyttes LP-FIX SUPRA i dag over hele verden i negativ og positiv framkallingsmaskiner.

I dette høyytelse fikserbadet inngår flere tiårs erfaring med omgang med filmemulsjoner. Ikke bare klassike kubiske emulsjoner og T-krystall emulsjoner , men også filmer med ekstremt høyt sølvinnhold som repro og røngten filmer.
›Normale‹ fikserkonsentrater som finnes i handelen er somregel tilfredsstillende for klassiske kubiske filmemulsjoner. Når det gjelder T-krystall-emulsjoner og planfilmer møter disse ofte gunstige fikserene sine grenser.
Også LABOR PARTNER produserer slike, med bufferer, fiksere i oppdrag for storkunder. Vi selger disse ikke med vårt eget navn, da fotografer og laboranter bare forventer det ypperste fra LABOR PARTNER.

De, etter framkallingen, gjenværende ubelyste og derfor uframkallte, sølvhalogenidene er fortsatt lysfølsomme og må derfor fjernes fra skiktet.
Sølvhalogenider er ikke utenvidere vannløslige og derfor må de i fikseringsprosessen gjennomgå en relativt komplisert flertrinns omvandling til et lettløslig komplekst salt. Noe som for en stor del løser seg allrede i fikserbadet.

Fixing bath

LP-FIX SUPRA

The extraordinary quality of LP-FIX SUPRA makes it suitable not only for inversion and tank development, but also for machine processing. So many negative- and print-processing machines today work with the high-performance fixing bath LP-FIX SUPRA.

Several decades of experience with film emulsions, not only classical, cubic-crystal emulsions, but also T-grain emulsions, and films with a high silver density as those used in reprography and x-ray photography, have gone into this high-performance fixer.

Conventional fixing bath concentrates like those primarily sold mostly suffice for the fixing of classical cubic-crystal film emulsions. However, where T-grain emulsions and sheet films are to be fixed, these inexpensive formulations will come to their built-in limits. LABOR PARTNER also manufactures such well-buffered and inexpensive fixing baths for customers who buy large quantities, but not for sale under the LABOR PARTNER label to the very demanding photographers and lab workers who expect only the highest quality when buying this brand.

The unexposed and thus undeveloped silver halides still present in the emulsion after development are still sensitive to light and must therefore be removed.
Silver halides, however, are not easily dissolved, so they must be converted to soluble complexes in a relatively complex process. Most of these complexes must already be dissolved during fixing.

Als Fixiermittel wird durch LABOR PARTNER kein Natriumthiosulfat eingesetzt. Dieses Fixiermittel wurde komplett ersetzt durch Ammoniumthiosulfat. Daher handelt es sich beim LP-FIX SUPRA um ein klassisches SCHNELLFIXIERBAD. Die bei der Anwendung von Ammoniumthiosulfat entstehenden SILBER-AMMONIUM-DOPPELSALZE sind wesentlich leichter löslich und auswaschbar.

Nachteil:

- *Fixierbäder auf Basis Ammoniumthiosulfat sind teurer als die auf Natriumthiosulfat. Bei zu langer Verweildauer der fotografischen Emulsion wird es zum ›Ausfressen‹ der Lichter kommen.*

Vorteil:

- *Erheblich kürzere Wässerungszeiten.*
- *Erheblich kürzere Fixierzeiten.*
- *Optimiert für T-Kristall-Filme (KODAK T-MAX, ILFORD DELTA).*
- *Optimal für MIKRO- und RÖNTGEN-Filme.*
- *Geeignet auch für maschinelle Hochtemperaturverarbeitung*

Verfügbar in 2 Versionen: LP-FIX SUPRA und LP-FIX NEUTRAL. Das pH-neutrale Fixierbad ist optimiert für die Barytverarbeitung.

FIXIERZEIT

Die optimale Fixierzeit ist abhängig von unterschiedlichen Faktoren. Daher weichen die Angaben auf den Flaschenetiketten oft von denen ab, die sich in ausführlicheren, technischen Informationen finden. Dies ist kein Fehler, sondern hat damit zu tun, dass feinkörnige Filme schneller ausfixiert sind als grobkörnige. Silberchlorid wird rascher fixiert als Silberbromid. Daher sind die Fixierzeiten für moderne Chlorsilberpapiere auf PE-Basis (RC=resin coated; RP=resin protected; PE= polyethylen beschichtet) oft kürzer, als für Filme.

Auch ist die Fixiergeschwindigkeit auch von der Temperatur der Gebrauchslösung abhängig. Bei ca. 10°C arbeitet ein Bad dreimal langsamer als bei 20°C. Die Bewegung des Filmmaterials während der Fixage hat einen entscheidenden Einfluss auf die Fixier-Geschwindigkeit.

Einige Filmhersteller raten sogar dazu, während der Fixage die Entwicklungsdose unentwegt zu kippen, wie sonst nur beim Unterbrecherbad. Wenn eine Filmemulsion senkrecht in der Dose steht, dann ist die Fixierzeit kürzer, als wenn - wie bei Schalenverarbeitung - die Emulsion nach unten zeigt.

LABOR PARTNER non utilizza tiosolfato di sodio come agente di fissaggio. Questo agente di fissaggio è stato completamente sostituito con il tiosolfato di ammonio. Per questo motivo nel caso del LP-FIX SUPRA si tratta di un BAGNO DI FISSAGGIO RAPIDO. Con l'utilizzo di tiosolfato di ammonio i doppi sali di argento-ammonio sono chiaramente più facilmente solubili e lavabili.

Svantaggio:

- *I bagni di fissaggio a base di tiosolfato di ammonio sono più costosi dei loro omonimi a base di tiosolfato di sodio. Se si lascia il materiale sensibile da fissare per troppo tempo in questo bagno, questi ›mordenza‹ le alte luci.*

Vantaggio:

- *Tempi di lavaggio assai più brevi.*
- *Tempi di fissaggio assai più brevi.*
- *Ottimizzato per pellicole T-Grain (KODAK T-MAX, ILFORD DELTA).*
- *Ottimale per pellicole microfilm e radiografiche.*
- *Adatto alla lavorazione ad alta temperatura in sviluppatrici automatiche.*

Disponibile in due versioni: LP-FIX SUPRA e LP-FIX NEUTRAL. Il bagno di fissaggio pH-neutro è particolarmente stato ottimizzato per il trattamento di carte baritate.

TEMPO DI FISSAGGIO

Il tempo di fissaggio ottimale dipende da diversi fattori. E' per questo motivo che spesso le indicazioni riportate sulle etichette delle bottiglie divergono dalle indicazioni riportate dalle schede tecniche, più dettagliate. Non si tratta di errori, bensì ha a che fare con il fatto che pellicole a grana fine sono fissate a fondo prima di pellicole a grana più grossa. Il cloruro d'argento è fissato più rapidamente del bromuro d'argento. E' per questo motivo che i tempi di fissaggio sono spesso più brevi nel caso di carte fotografiche moderne al cloruro d'argento su base PE (RC=resin coated, RP=resin protected, PE=stratificate con olietilene), piuttosto che delle pellicole.

La velocità di fissaggio è pure determinata dalla temperatura della soluzione d'uso. A 10°C un bagno lavora tre volte più lentamente che a 20°C.

L'agitazione della pellicola fotosensibile durante il fissaggio ad agitazione a capovolgimento ha un'influenza determinante nella rapidità del tempo necessario al fissaggio. Alcuni produttori di pellicole consigliano addirittura di agitare in continuazione la tank durante il fissaggio, come

Som fiksermiddel benytter LABOR PARTNER ikke natriumthiosulfat. Dette er blitt ersattet av ammoniumthiosulfat. Derfor er LP-FIX SUPRA en klassisk HURTIG FIKSERER Ved å benytte ammoniumthiosulfat oppstår SØLV- AMMONIUM- DOBBELSALT som er vesentlig letter løselig og derfor lette å vaske ut.

Ulemper:

- *Fikserbad med ammoniumthiosulfat er dyrere enn bad med natriumthiosulfat. Ved for lang tid i badet vil fotografiske skikt, framfor alt i høylysene bli ›spist opp‹.*

Fordeler:

- *Betydelig kortere spyletider.*
- *Betydelig kortere fiksertider.*
- *Optimert for T-krystall filmer (KODAK T-MAX og ILFORD DELTA).*
- *Optimert for MIKRO OG RØNTGEN FILMER.*
- *Egnet for maskinframkalling også ved høye temperaturer.*

Finnes i 2 versjoner LP- FIX SUPRA og LP- FIX NEUTRAL. Det pH nøytrale fikserbadet er optimert for barytt papir.

FIKSERINGSTID

Den optimale fikseringstiden er avhengig av forskjellige faktorer. Derfor skiller opplysningene fra pakningen seg ofte fra utførlige tekniske informasjoner. Dette er ingen feil.men har heller med det å gjøre at finkornete filmer blir fortere fiksert enn grovkornete filmer. Sølvklorid fikserer raskere enn sølvbromid. Derfor er ofte fikseringstidene for moderne klorsølv fotopapir på PE / RC basis ofte kortere enn for filmer. Fikserhastigfheten er avhengig av temperaturen. Ved 10°C arbeider badet tre ganger langsommere enn ved 20°C.

Aggitasjonen av filmmaterialet under fikseringen er avgjørende for hastigheten. Noen filmprodusenter anbefaller en kontinuerlig aggitasjon, noe som eller bare gjelder stoppebadet.

Hvis en film står loddret i en tank er tiden kortere enn hvis, ved planfilmer eller fotopapir, emulsjonen er vendt nedover.

TIPS FOR Å FINNE FRAM TIL OPTIMAL FIKSERINGSTID

I praksis bedømmer en fikseringstiden ut fra den til det tar til filmen er klar/ gjennomsiktig.

Dette tilsvarer temmlig nøyaktig halvparten av fikseringstiden. Er denne tiden lengre enn 5 min. så må fikserbadet skiftes.

LABOR PARTNER does not use sodium thiosulphate as fixing agent. This chemical was superseded by ammonium thiosulphate. So LP-FIX SUPRA is a classical RAPID FIXER. The SILVER-AMMONIUM DOUBLE SALTS are much more soluble and can be washed out more easily.

Disadvantage:

- *Ammonium thiosulphate fixers are more expensive than sodium thiosulphate fixers. Excessive fixing will lead to ›highlight bleaching‹.*

Advantage:

- *Washing times are considerably shorter.*
- *Fixing times are considerably shorter.*
- *LP-FIX SUPRA was optimised for T-grain emulsions (KODAK T-MAX, ILFORD DELTA).*
- *It is optimal for microfilms and x-ray films.*
- *It can be used for machine processing.*

Two versions are available: LP-FIX SUPRA and LP-FIX NEUTRAL. The neutral-pH fixer has been optimised for the processing of FB paper.

FIXING TIME

The optimum fixing time depends on a couple of different factors. This is the reason for deviations between the data given on the labels of bottles and data given in more comprehensive technical documents. This is not a mistake, but the consequence of the fact that fine-grained films fix faster than coarse-grained ones. Silver chloride fixes faster than silver bromide. So fixing times for modern silver chloride RC (resin-coated, aka RP for resin-protected, or PE for polyethylene-coated) papers are often shorter than times for films.

Also, fixing speed depends on the temperature of the working solution. When fixing at 10°C (50°F), the fixer works at one-third of its rate at 20°C (68°F).

Agitation during fixing in an inversion tank is a decisive factor for fixing speed. Some film manufacturers even recommend permanent agitation during fixing, as is commonly recommended for the stop bath only.

For a vertical film plane, fixing is faster than for a horizontal arrangement with the emulsion side down (as is the case with tray processing).

HINWEIS ZUR ERMITTLUNG DER OPTIMALEN FIXIERZEIT
In der Praxis wird die Fixierzeit für Filme bestimmt, indem man feststellt, wie nach welcher Einwirkzeit der Film transparent erscheint (Klärzeit).
Dies entspricht bei Filmen mit kubischer Kristaltechnologie recht genau der halben Gesamtfixierzeit, bei T-Kristallfilmen einem Drittel. Bei Klärzeiten von über 5 Minuten sollte die Fixier-Gebrauchslösung nicht mehr verwendet werden.
Um die Klärzeit festzustellen, benutzt man den Anfang vom Film, der normalerweise aus der Metallpatrone herausschauen wird. Dann nimmt man eine kleine Menge der Fixierbadgebrauchslösung und steckt das kurze Filmstück in die Lösung. Es ist zu ermitteln, wie lange das Filmstück benötigt, um klar zu werden. Die Fixierzeit ist dann die Klärzeit mal zwei bzw. drei.

ERGIEBIGKEIT
Ein Film-Fixierbad kann so lange benutzt werden, bis es maximal 5 Gramm Silber pro Liter Gebrauchslösung enthält (bei Papieren 3 Gramm).

QUALITÄT DER FIXAGE
Diese steht in einem ursächlichen Zusammenhang mit der Wässerung des Filmmaterials. Ein fix und fertig gewässert Film darf auf gar keinen Fall mehr 'nach Chemie' riechen. Dabei ist es wichtig, mit der richtigen Zeit zu fixieren. Über- oder Unterfixierung werden Qualitätseinbussen nach sich ziehen. Daher sollte bei einem Wechsel auf eine andere Filmsorte (auch vom gleichen Hersteller) in jedem Fall die Klärzeit / optimierte Fixierzeit ermittelt werden. Bei einem großen Filmdurchsatz wird empfohlen, das Fixierbad zu regenerieren.

DIE WÄSSERUNG
Saure Fixierbäder lassen sich schwieriger auswässern als pH-neutrale. Die beim Fixieren entstandenen Silberammoniumthiosulfat-Komplexsalze und die restlichen Chemikalien müssen aus der Filmemulsion entfernt werden. Von der mehr oder weniger vollständigen Entfernung dieser Salze hängt die Haltbarkeit der Filme ab. Das Wässern beruht auf DIFFUSION und OSMOSE. Durch Eindringen und Ausbreiten von frischem Wasser innerhalb der Fotoemulsion entsteht eine ständige Konzentratverdünnung der auszuwaschenden Salze. Die Geschwindigkeit des Diffusionsprozesses hängt vor allem vom Gefälle der Thiosulfatkonzentration zwischen Gelatine und Waschwasser, von der Temperatur

ciò avviene normalmente solo durante il bagno d'arresto.
Quando l'emulsione della pellicola è posta verticalmente nella tank, il tempo di fissaggio necessario è più breve, rispetto al caso in cui l'emulsione delle pellicole piane o carta fotografica, sono rivolte orizzontalmente verso il basso della bacinella.

CONSIGLI SULLA DETERMINAZIONE DEL TEMPO DI FISSAGGIO OTTIMALE
Nella pratica si determina il tempo di fissaggio delle pellicole, in modo da constatare quanto tempo ci vuole finché la pellicola risulta trasparente (tempo di chiarificazione).
Ciò corrisponde quasi esattamente alla *metà del tempo totale di fissaggio.* Con tempi di chiarificazione di oltre 5 minuti non bisognerebbe più utilizzare la soluzione d'uso di fissaggio.

Per determinare il tempo di chiarificazione si utilizza l'inizio della pellicola, che normalmente affiora dal caricatore. Si preleva una piccola quantità di soluzione d'uso di fissaggio e si immerge lo spezzone. Si determini ora quanto tempo necessita lo spezzone di pellicola per diventare trasparente. Il tempo di fissaggio rappresenta poi il tempo di chiarificazione moltiplicato per due.

RESA
Il bagno di fissaggio per pellicole può essere utilizzato finché questi contiene al *massimo* 5 grammi d'argento per litro di soluzione d'uso (nel caso delle carte il limite è a 3 grammi).

QUALITA' DELL'AZIONE DEL FISSAGGIO
Questa è in stretto rapporto con il lavaggio della pellicola fotosensibile. Una pellicola fissata e lavata a fondo non deve assolutamente più odorare di ›chimica‹. A tale scopo è importante, fissare per il giusto tempo. Sovra o sotto-fissaggio determineranno deterioramenti nella qualità. Bagni di fissaggio acidi si lasciano lavare più difficilmente di bagni pH-neutri.
A questo proposito è importante che ad ogni cambiamento del tipo di pellicola (anche dello stesso fabbricante) segua una nuova determinazione del tempo ottimale di chiarificazione/fissaggio.
Nel caso di un grande apporto di pellicole da trattare è consigliabile rigenerare il bagno di fissaggio.

IL LAVAGGIO
I sali complessi di tiosolfato d'ammonio argenteo emersi

For å kunne finne den rette tiden, benytter en begynnelsen på filmen, som jo oftest klippes bort. I en liten mengde fikser blir det så testet hvor lang tid det tar før denne biten er blitt klar. Den tiden du da finner blir fordoblet og du har rett fikseringstid for denne filmen.

UTNYTTELSESGRAD
En filmfikserer kan benyttes inntil den har maksimalt 5 g sølv pr liter bruksløsning (Papir fiks max 3 g).

FIKSÉRKVALITET
Dette står i direkte sammenheng med spylingen av filmen. En helt ferdig spylt film må under ingen omstendigheter lukte av kjemi. Det er derfor viktig å benytte den rette tiden for fikseringen. Over eller under fiksering medfører nedsatt kvalitet.
Sure fikserbad er vanskeligere å spyle en pH nøytrale.
Derfor er det viktig å finne fram til rett tid ved filmbytte, også om produsenten er den samme.
Ved stort gjennomløp av film anbefaler vi at du regenererer fikseren.

SPYLINGEN
De komplekse sølvammoniumthiosulfatene som oppstår i fikseren og de øvrige kjemikalierestene må fjernes fra filmemulsjonen. Hvorvidt dette lykkes er avgjørende for holdbarheten til filmen.
Spylingen bygger på DIFFUSJON og OSMOSE. Ved å trenge inn og ved å fortrenge kjemi vil konsentrasjonen av salter stadig minske. Hastigheten til diffusjonsprosessen er framfor alt avhengig av forholdet mellom thiosulfatene på den ene siden og gelantine og vann på den annen side, noe som igjen er avhengig av temperatureen på spylevanne, pH verdien til vannet samt sammensetningen av fikseren og fikseringstiden.
Ved utilstrekkelig spyling blir det rester av kompleksssalter og thiosulfater i emulsjonen som igjen danner brun sølvsulfid under påvirkning av lys, luft og fuktighet. Sølvsulfid vil med tiden blekne.

FLYTENDE VANN
er ikke det optimale slikt det ofte blir framstillt. En udiskutable måte å spyle på er å skifte vann i tanken 8 ganger. Ved den mengden som er valgt i denne boken (260 ml tank) er dette i tillegg en generøs mengde.
Gjennomsnitts tid for hver gjennomgang er for lavføl-

GUIDANCE ON DETERMINING THE OPTIMAL FIXING TIME

Practically, the fixing time of films is determined by measuring the time it takes for the film to become clear (clearing time).

This time is with sufficient accuracy half the total fixing time for cubic-crystal films, and one third of it for T-grain films. Do not use any fixer where the clearing time exceeds 5 min.

For determining the clearing time, use the film end of 35-mm roll film, or an equivalent piece of film for medium-format roll film or cut sheet film. Dunk this piece of film into a small quantity of fixer and measure the time it takes the piece of film to become entirely clear. The fixing time is twice, or three times, this time, respectively.

CAPACITY

Film fixer can be used up to a silver content of 5 g of silver per litre of working solution. (Up to 3 g/l are permissible for papers.)

FIXING QUALITY

There is an intimate relationship between the quality of fixing and the washing of the film. A completely fixed and washed film must not "smell like chemicals". So using the right fixing time is mandatory. Both overfixation and insufficient fixation will degrade quality!

Therefore, when changing from one type of film to a different one, even if it comes from the same manufacturer, determine the clearing time/optimal fixing time.

If your throughput is large, we recommend that you replenish your fixing bath.

WASHING

Acid fixing baths are harder to wash out than neutral-pH ones.

The ammonium-argento-thiosulphates generated during fixing and other residual chemicals must be removed from the emulsion. It is the more or less complete removal of these salts that determines the permanence of the film.

Washing is based on DIFFUSION and OSMOSIS. The penetration and spreading of fresh water in the emulsion result in a continuous dilution of the salts to be washed out. The speed of the diffusion process is primarily a function of the gradient of the thiosulphate concentration between the gelatine and the water, of the temperature and pH of the water, and of the composition and duration of the fixing bath.

und dem pH-Wert des Waschwassers sowie der Zusammensetzung und der Dauer des vorangegangenen Fixierbades ab. Bei ungenügender Wässerung verbleiben in der Filmemulsion Komplexsalze, Thiosulfate, die unter Einwirkung von Luft, Licht, Wäre und Feuchtigkeit bräunliches Silbersulfid bilden. Silbersulfid ist aber nicht beständig und bleicht mit der Zeit aus.
Fliessendes Wasser ist für die Schlusswässerung nicht so optimal, wie es oft dargestellt wird. Eine einwandfreie Auswässerung ist vor allem dann gewährleistet, wenn der Inhalt der Filmdose 8 mal nach ausreichender Einwirkzeit ausgewechselt wird. Bei den in diesem Buch gewählten Beispielen, basierend auf 260 ml Doseninhalt, ist diese Angabe sehr großzügig bemessen. Die jeweilige Verweildauer pro Durchgang kann bei niedrigempfindlichen Filmen 2-3 Minuten betragen. Bei hochempfindlichen, vor allem T-Kristall-Filmen und dem MACO CUBE 400clear bis zu 3-4 Minuten. Bei der Wässerung bleibt die Dose stehen und wird nicht bewegt. Nur so ist eine optimale Wässerung gewährleistet. Eine ständige Bewegung würde die Osmose stören.

AUSWÄSSERUNGSBESCHLEUNIGER

Unter Beachtung der obigen Hinweise und Regeln ist es bei der Film-Entwicklung eigentlich nicht erforderlich, einen zusätzlichen Arbeitsgang in Form einer Auswässerungsbeschleunigung durchzuführen. Wenn ein Laborant unbedingt etwas in dieser Richtung unternehmen möchte, dann hilft ggfs. eine Neutralisation. Dazu setzt man eine 1%ige Sodalösung an (10 Gramm Natriumcarbonat auf einen Liter Wasser). Der Film wird wie oben beschrieben fixiert. Danach kurz mit Wasser abgespült. Dann für etwa eine Minute in der Sodalösung behandelt. Die folgende Wässerungsdauer kann dann um rund 50 % reduziert werden.

VERPACKUNG

- 1 Liter Polyethylenflaschen
- 5 Liter Kanister

ANSATZ DER CHEMIE

Es wird Leitungswasser verwendet. Nach der Zugabe des LP-FIX SUPRA Fixierbad-Konzentrates ist die Gebrauchslösung sofort gebrauchsfertig.

VERARBEITUNGSTEMPERATUR

Es sollte nicht unter 18°C gearbeitet werden.

durante il fissaggio ed i rimanenti agenti chimici, devono essere asportati dall'emulsione della pellicola. La durata delle pellicole dipende proprio dall'eliminazione più o meno totale di questi sali.
Il lavaggio si basa sulla DIFFUSIONE e OSMOSI. Previo induzione e diffusione di acqua fresca all'interno dell'emulsione fotografica si costituisce una continua diluizione del concentrato dei sali da lavare a fondo. La velocità del processo di diffusione dipende soprattutto dalla precipitazione della concentrazione di tiosolfato fra gelatina ed acqua di lavaggio, dalla temperatura e dal valore pH dell'acqua di lavaggio, come pure dalla composizione e la durata del bagno di fissaggio appena proceduto.
Ad un lavaggio insufficiente nell'emulsione delle pellicola permangono sali complessi, tiosolfati, che sotto l'azione di aria, luce, calore ed umidità, formano del solfito d'argento marroncino. Solfito d'argento non è però costante, bensì con il passare del tempo si sbianca.

L'ACQUA CORRENTE non è poi così ottimale per il lavaggio finale, come spesse declamato (!).
Un lavaggio può essere considerato ottimale soprattutto quando il contenuto della tank viene sostituito per 8 volte. Negli esempi scelti in questo libro, sulla base di un contenuto di tank di 260 ml, questa indicazione viene misurata molto ampliamente. La rispettiva durata per ogni ciclo, nel caso di pellicole di bassa sensibilità, può ammontare anche a 2-3 minuti. Nel caso di pellicole ad alta sensibilità, soprattutto nel caso di pellicole T-Grain e MACO CUBE 400clear addirittura a 3-4 minuti.
Durante il lavaggio la tank rimane ferma e non viene agitata (!). Solo in questo modo si garantisce un lavaggio ottimale. Un'agitazione o movimento continuo disturberebbe l'osmosi.

ACCELERATORE DI LAVAGGIO FINALE

Seguendo le indicazioni e regole di sui sopra nel trattamento delle pellicole non è necessario sottoporre la pellicola ad un trattamento supplementare, sotto forma di acceleratore di lavaggio. Qualora l'utilizzatore volesse fare qualcosa in quella direzione, eventualmente aiuta una cosiddetta neutralizzazione. A questo scopo si prepari una soluzione di soda all'1% (10 grammi di carbonato di sodio su 1 litro di acqua). La pellicola viene fissata come sopra descritto. Poi brevemente sciacquata in acqua. Poi trattata per 1 minuto ca. nella soluzione di soda. La durata successiva del lavaggio può essere così ridotta di ca. il 50 %.

somme filmer 2-3 min. Ved høyfølsomme filmer, framfor alt T-krystall filmer og MACO CUBE 400 clear trenges 3-4 min pr gjennomgang. Ved denne form for spyling blir tanken stående i ro og ikke bevegt. Bare slik er en optimal spyling mulig. Bevegelse vil forstyrre osmosen.

SPYLINGSHJELPEMIDDLER

Ved å benytte den metoden som vi har beskrevet er det egentlig ikke nødvendig med slike hjelpemiddler. Dette medfører egentlig bare et ekstra arbeidstrinn. Hvis laboranten insisterer på et slikt trinn så kan en nøytralisering hjelpe.
Det benyttes da en 1 % sodaoppløsning (10 g natriumcarbonat på 1 liter vann).
Filmen fikseres vanlig.
Spyles så kort.
Ett minutt i sodaløsningen
Dedn etterfølgende spylingen kan reduseres med 50 %.

FORPAKNING

- 1 l polyethylenflasker
- 5 l kanne

BLANDING AV KJEMI

Det benyttes vann eller deminiralisert vann. Etter at LP- FIX SUPRA er tilsatt vannet er løsningen klar for bruk.

BRUKSTEMPERATUR

Det kan ikke arbeides UNDER 18°C .

FORTYNNINGSTABELL FOR 260 ml FERDIG BLANDING

1 + 7 =	32,5 ml LP-FIX SUPRA
	+ 247 ml vann

AGGITASJON

Fikserers noen minutt, Fikseringstid = 2 x klaringstiden.

UTNYTTELSESGRAD

I 1 l bruksløsning:Det er teoretisk mulig å fiksere ca 150 135/36 bilder eller 120 filmer i en liter fikser.
Det blir anbefalt å bare blande den mengde fikserbad som er nødvendig for daglig bruk. Den brukte LP- FIX SUPRA oppløsningen bør destrueres daglig ved mindre mengder. Aldri benytt fikserbad fra papirprosessen til film. Det kan være papirpartikler i denne som vil skade filmen. Dette fører til mikrofine prikker i forstørrelsene.

Insufficient washing leaves complex salts in the emulsion. These are thiosulphates which, under the action of air, light, heat, and humidity, form brownish silver sulphides which lead to discolorations.

FLOWING WATER is not as optimal as often claimed. Proper washing is primarily ensured by changing the washing water in the tank 8 times, leaving it in the tank for a sufficient time during each cycle. For the examples chosen in this book, based on a tank volume of 260 ml, this recommendation is on the safe side.
A cycle time of 2 to 3 minutes is appropriate for slow films, 3 to 4 minutes are recommended for fast films, and especially for T-crystal films and MACO CUBE 400 clear. Do not agitate during washing, as this would reduce washing efficiency by interfering with osmosis.

HYPO CLEARING AGENTS
When the above recommendations are observed, no additional hypo clearing treatment is needed for films. Where a lab worker insists on taking steps in this direction, neutralisation may be helpful.
To this end, prepare a 1% soda solution (10 g of sodium carbonate in 1 l of water).
Fix films as described above.
Rinse briefly.
Then apply the soda solution for about one minute.
Subsequent washing can then be reduced by 50%.

PACKAGING
- 1 l polythylene bottles
- 5 l containers

PREPARATION OF THE SOLUTION
Use tap water. The solution is ready for use as soon as the LP-FIX SUPRA concentrate has been added.

PROCESSING TEMPERATURE
Working below 18°C (64°F) is not recommended.

DILUTION CHART FOR 260 ml OF WORKING SOLUTION

1 + 7 =	32,5 ml LP-FIX SUPRA
	+ 247 ml of water

PROCESSING TIME / AGITATION
Fix for the time determined according to the above procedure (fixing time = twice the clearing time).

VERDÜNNUNGSTABELLE FÜR 260 ml GEBRAUCHSLÖSUNG

1 + 7 =	32,5 ml LP-FIX SUPRA
	+ 247 ml Wasser

VERARBEITUNGSZEIT / BEWEGUNG

Filme werden einige Minuten (Fixierzeit = doppelte bis dreifache Klärzeit) fixiert.

ERGIEBIGKEIT

In 1 Liter Gebrauchslösung könnten maximal 150 Kleinbild-Filme 135-36 bzw. Rollffilme 120 fixiert werden.
Es wird empfohlen, nur die Gebrauchslösung anzusetzen, die für die täglich benötigte Filmverarbeitung vorgesehen ist. Die gebrauchte LP-FIX SUPRA Lösung sollte bei kleineren Mengen jeweils täglich entsorgt werden. Es darf niemals eine Gebrauchslösung, die bereits zur Verarbeitung im Positivprozess verwendet worden ist, für die Filmverarbeitung verwendet werden, denn es wird sich feinster Papierfaserstaub darin befinden. Dieser wird sich als mikrofeine Flecken bei der Vergrößerungen zeigen.
Im Gegensatz zum Unterbrecherbad kann es sich schon lohnen, die Fixierbad-Gebrauchslösung aufzubewahren, bzw. nach dem Gebrauch als Filmfixierer, danach als PE-Papier-Fixierer aufzubrauchen. Nicht für Barytpapiere, dafür werden pH-neutrale Fixierbäder empfohlen.

HALTBARKEIT

Die original verschlossene, schwarze LABOR PARTNER Flasche ist etwa bis zu 2 Jahre nach dem Erwerb im Handel haltbar.

CONFEZIONAMENTO

- Bottiglia in polietilene da 1 litro
- Fustino da 5 litri

PREPARAZIONE DELLA CHIMICA

Si utilizzi acqua di rubinetto. Dopo l'aggiunta di concentrato di bagno d'arresto LP-FIX SUPRA, la soluzione è pronta all'uso.

TEMPERATURA DI TRATTAMENTO

Non bisogna lavorare al disotto dei 18°C.

TABELLA DI DILUIZIONE PER 260 ml DI SOLUZIONE D'USO

1 + 7 =	32,5 ml di LP-FIX SUPRA
	+ 247 ml di acqua

TEMPO DI LAVORAZIONE / AGITAZIONE

Le pellicole vengono fissate per alcuni minuti (tempo di fissaggio = doppio tempo di chiarificazione).

RESA

1 litro di soluzione d'uso è sufficiente per trattare al massimo 150 pellicole di piccolo formato o 120 rollfilm.
Si consiglia di preparare soluzione d'uso sufficiente da soddisfare le esigenze giornaliere di trattamento delle pellicole. Le soluzioni d'uso di LP-FIX SUPRA esauste dovrebbero essere smaltite giornalmente. Non bisogna mai utilizzare soluzioni già utilizzate per carta anche per pellicole, in quanto vi è contenuto il finissimo pulviscolo di fibra della carta. Ciò provocherebbe delle macchioline microscopiche visibili sugli ingrandimenti. A differenza con i bagni d'arresto può essere vantaggioso conservare le soluzioni d'uso di fissaggio e magari riutilizzarle per il trattamento della carta fotografica politenata. Non per le carte baritate, per le quali si consigliano i bagni di fissaggio pH-neutri.

CONSERVAZIONE

In bottiglia sigillata, originale nera LABOR PARTNER, si mantiene per almeno 2 anni dalla data di acquisto presso il tuo fornitore di fiducia.

I motsettning til stoppebadet kan det lønne seg å oppbevare fikseren for å bruke den til PE/RC papir. Den egner seg ikke for baryttpapi, benytt da et nøytral fikserbad.

HOLDBARHET

I orginalembalasjen holdbar ca 2 år.

CAPACITY

One litre of working solution could fix up to 150 135-36 films or 120 roll films.

We recommend that you prepare but the quantity of working solution you need for one working day. Used LP-FIX SUPRA solution should be disposed of each day. Never use any working solution previously used for print processing for film as it will contain suspended fine paper fibres which you will find as fine spots in your prints. In contrast to stop baths, keeping fixing-bath working solutions may prove worthwhile, not for use with FB papers, but for use with RC papers. For FB papers, neutral fixers are recommended.

SHELF LIFE

The unopened black LABOR PARTNER bottle can be kept for up to two years after purchase.

Entwicklerhärter

LP-GELADUR

Die Härtung der Emulsion durch einen Entwicklerhärter. Für viele Fotografen/Laboranten mag das vielleicht neu sein, jedoch ist diese Methode ist seit Jahrzehnten bewährt unter dem Begriff *Tropenentwicklung*. Vor allem den Maschinenentwicklern wurde traditionell ein
entsprechender Zusatz beigefügt. Oft realisiert man nicht, dass es sich um einen Härtezusatz handelte, es war einfach ein Part unter vielen.
LP-GELADUR ist keine innovative Neuentwicklung von LABOR PARTNER, sondern der Rückgriff auf Bewährtes.
LP-GELADUR ist ein härtender Film-Entwicklerzusatz. Ein identisches Produkt wird auch unter der Bezeichnung LP-BLACK MAGIC Härte-Additiv angeboten.
In südlichen Ländern liegt die normale Arbeitstemperatur naturgemässnaturgemäß auf einem höheren Niveauhöher als z.B. in Nordeuropa. Wenn die meisten Verarbeitungsangaben auf 20°C beruhen, sind diese Werte in der Praxis oft nicht zu bewerkstelligen. Um auch bei höheren Verarbeitungstemperaturen eine Beschädigung der Filmschichten zu umgehen, benutzt man *Tropenentwickler*. Früher setzte man dazu einfach etwas Natriumsulfat der Entwickler-Gebrauchslösung zu um das zu starke Quellen der Gelatine zu unterbinden. Dieses Verfahren unterliegt jedoch gravierenden Einschränkungen. Einerseits sind dabei die
Verarbeitungszeiten erheblich zu verlängern, andererseits verbraucht sich dieser Härtezusatz schneller als der Entwickler selbst. Auch ist es nicht ausgeschlossen, dass in den Folgebädern die härtende Wirkung teilweise abgebaut wird.
Die Unsicherheiten, die sich aus diesem Verfahren ergeben können, treten bei der Verwendung von LP-GELADUR nicht auf.

EIGENSCHAFTEN
LP-GELADUR härtet Filmemulsionen gleich während des Entwicklungsvorganges. Das hat keine Auswirkungen auf die Entwicklungszeiten. Die mit LP-GELADUR gehärteten Filme weisen eine erhöhte Widerstandsfähigkeit gegenüber mechanischer Beanspruchung auf. Die Filme trocknen schneller, neigen weniger zu statischer Aufladung (Staub ist ein grosser Feind des Laboranten) und verbessern die Planlage.
Besonders die Marktpräsenz der Polyester-Film-Unterlagen

Induritore di sviluppo

LP-GELADUR

L'indurimento dell'emulsione fotografica previo un induritore nello sviluppo.
Per molti fotografi e stampatori ciò potrà sembrare una novità, ma questo metodo è acquisito nei decenni con la definizione: *sviluppo tropicale*. Un simile additivo viene spesso aggiunto agli sviluppi per sviluppatrice automatica. Spesso non si faceva caso, che si trattava di un additivo indurente, bensì una semplice parte come tante altre.
LP-GELADUR non è una innovazione di LABOR PARTNER, ma la riedizione di una vecchia conoscenza.
LP-GELADUR è un additivo indurente per sviluppi di pellicole. Un prodotto identico viene pure offerto con la denominazione LP-BLACK MAGIC Additivo.
Nei paesi del sud la normale temperatura di lavoro è naturalmente su un livello più elevato rispetto p. es. ai paesi del Nord-Europa. Se la maggior parte delle indicazioni sul trattamento si basano sui 20°C, nella pratica spesso questi valori non sono proponibili. Per prevenire lo strato delle pellicole da danneggiamenti anche durante il trattamento a temperature alte si utilizza appunto uno *sviluppo tropicale.*
In passato si aggiungeva semplicemente del solfato di sodio alla soluzione d'uso di sviluppo per evitare l'eccessivo rigonfiamento della gelatina. Questa azione determina però gravose limitazioni. D'un canto i tempi di sviluppo devono essere allungati in modo rilevante, d'altro canto l'additivo si deteriora più velocemente rispetto allo sviluppo.
Non è inoltre escluso, che nei bagni seguenti, l'azione indurente venga in parte vanificata.
Le insicurezze determinate da questo procedimento non appaiono con l'uso di LP-GELADUR.

CARATTERISTICHE
LP-GELADUR indurisce le emulsioni delle pellicole direttamente durante l'azione dello sviluppo.
Questa azione n o n provoca alcuna conseguenza sui tempi di sviluppo-
Nelle pellicole indurite con LP-GELADUR si determina una maggiore resistenza alla sollecitazione meccanica.
Le pellicole si asciugano più rapidamente, tendono a caricarsi meno elettrostaticamente (la polvere è il tuo peggiore nemico) e migliora la planearità.
Soprattutto la presenza sul mercato di pellicole su base in

Framkallerherder

LP-GELADUR

Herding av emulsjonen ved hjelp av en framkallerherder. For mange fotografer og laboranter er dette kansje en ny måte å herde på, men denne metoden har vært kjent i årtider som *tropeframkaller*. Framfor alt i framkallermaskiner ble det tradisjonelt benyttet tilsvarende hjelpemiddel. Ofte viste man ikke at det var en herder da det bare var en av mange deler som ble blandet sammen.
LP-GELADUR er ikke noe nytt som LABOR PARTNER har utviklet, men gjennopptakelsen av noe som er kjent.

LP-GELADUR er en herdene filmframkaller tilsetning som også selges undernavnet LP-BLACK MAGIC HERDER ADDITIV.

I mer sydlige land ligger den normale arbeidstemperaturen naturligvis betraktelig høyere enn det den gjør i nordeuropa. Selv om de fleste prosesser er lagt rundt 200C så vil det ikke være gjennomførbart i varmere strøk. For ikke å skade filmemulsjonen benytter en derfor en tropeframkaller.
Tidligere tilsatte en litt natriumsulfat til framkalleren for å hindre at gelantinen svulmet for mye opp. Denne metoden har sterke begrensninger. På den ene side ble framkallingstiden merkbart lengre, på den annen side ble herderen fortere oppbrukt enn framkalleren. Videre ville vfirkningen avta etter hvert som filmen kom i de neste badene.
Usikkerheten som følger denne gamle metoden er ukjent for LP-GELADUR.

EGENSKAPER
LP-GELADUR herder filmen under framkallingen. Dette har ingen innvirkning på framkallingstiden.
Filmer som er herdet med LP-GELADUR har større motstandskraft mot mekanisk påvirkning.
Filmene tørker fortere, blir ikke like statisk ladet og har bedre planhet, (filmen krøller seg ikke sammen)
Spesiellt filmer på polyesterbase krever en bedre planhet, da disse filmene har en tendens til å krølle seg i større grad enn det som er kjent fra acetatfilmer.
LP-GELADUR kan sammen med et stoppebad LP-CITRADUR og vetemiddelet LP- MASTERPROOF bidra til å få kontroll med forstyrrende elementer ved filmer på polyesterbase.

Developer hardener

LP-GELADUR

Hardening of the emulsion by means of a hardener added to the developer
This may be news to quite a number of photographers/lab workers, but the method has been known under the heading *tropical developer* for a long time. An additive was mainly used for machine development, although it was not realised that it was a hardener, because it was just one part in many.
So LP-GELADUR is not a new development by LABOR PARTNER, but learning from history.
LP-GELADUR is a hardening developer additive. An identical product is offered as LP-BLACK MAGIC hardening additive.

In the Southern hemisphere, the normal working temperature is naturally higher than, e.g., in Northern Europe. If most of the processing information refers to 20°C (68°F), these values are often impractical. In order to avoid damage to the emulsion at higher temperatures, "tropical developers" are used.
Sodium sulphate was formerly added to the developer working solution to suppress any excessive swelling of the gelatine. However, this method is subject to serious limitations. On the one hand, processing times must be prolonged considerably. On the other hand, the hardening additive is consumed faster than the developer proper. Also, a degradation of the hardening effect in subsequent baths cannot be ruled out.
The uncertainties of that method are not encountered with LP-GELADUR.

CHARACTERISTICS
LP-GELADUR hardens the film emulsion during development.
Processing times are not affected.
Films hardened using LP-GELADUR are less susceptible to mechanical damage.
Films dry faster, are less prone to static charge (dust is the great enemy of the lab worker), and improve flatness.
Particularly polyester-based films call for improvements of film flatness as polyester-based films tend to curl stronger than acetate-based ones, and to stay curled. LP-GELADUR, together with other measures (hardening stop bath LP-

fordert eine Verbesserung der Planlage-Eigenschaften, den Polyesterfilme neigen grundsätzlich dazu, sich mehr als Acetatfilme zu krümmen, störrisch zu sein. LP-GELADUR kann dazu beitragen, im Verbund mit anderen Maßnahmen (härtendes Stoppbad LP-GELADUR und Netzmittel LP-MASTERPROOF) diese etwas störenden Eigenschaften der Polyester-Filmbasis in der Griff zu bekommen. LP-GELADUR kann zu einer Verfärbung der Filmemulsion führen. Diese Färbung hat jedoch keinen negativen Einfluss auf die fotografischen Eigenschaften des Films. LP-GELADUR kann allen handelsüblichen, industriell gefertigten Entwicklern zugegeben werden. Zum Zeitpunkt der Drucklegung ist dem Verfasserteam kein industriell gefertigter Entwickler von AGFA, ILFORD, KODAK und TETENAL bekannt, der sich nicht eignen würde. Die Entwicklerhärterzugabe beschränkt sich dabei nicht auf Entwickler-Flüssigkonzentrate, sondern ist gleich gut auch für Entwickler auf Pulver-Bbasis geeignet. Auch dort wird die Wassermenge reduziert und durch die Zugabe von Härter-Konzentrat ausgeglichen.

VERPACKUNG

- 1 Liter Polyethylenflaschen
- 5 Liter Kanister

ANSATZ DER CHEMIE

LP-GELADUR wird direkt der Entwickler-Gebrauchslösung anstatt Wasser zugesetzt. Die ursprüngliche Wassermenge wird um die Menge LP-GELADUR reduziert. Es ist daher kein Zusatz, sondern ein Wasser- Ersatz.
LP-GELADUR hat als Konzentrat einen sehr niedrigen pH-Werte. Daher ist unter allen Umständen ein Zusammenbringen von Entwickler-Konzentrat und LP-GELADUR-Konzentrat zu vermeiden. Dies könnte zu Verätzungen führen. Zuerst sollten die genau abgemessenen Mengen an Wasser, Filmentwicklerkonzentrat und Härte-Konzentrat bereitgestellt werden.

- ***Schritt 1:*** In einen Messbecher wird zuerst das Entwickler-Kkonzentrat gegeben.
- ***Schritt 2:*** Dann wird langsam und ohne Luftblasenbildung das Wasser dazu gegeben, die Lösung wird dabei automatisch gut durchmischt.
- ***Schritt 3:*** Danach erst wird das LP-GELADUR-Konzentrat langsam, ebenfalls ohne Luftblasenbildung eingerührt.

Diese zwingend vorgeschriebene Reihenfolge ist aus Sicherheitsgründen unbedingt einzuhalten. Die Ansatzmengen entnehmen Sie bitte den jeweiligen Filmtabellen.

poliestere richiede caratteristiche di planearità migliori, in quanto le pellicole in poliestere tendono alla curvatura, più delle pellicole in acetato. LP-GELADUR può contribuire, insieme ad altri accorgimenti (bagno d'arresto induritore LP-CITRODUR + imbibente LP-MASTERPROOF) a tenere sotto controllo la planearità delle pellicole sulla base di poliestere, piuttosto ostiche.
LP-GELADUR può provocare una colorazione dell'emulsione della pellicola. Questa colorazione non ha però influenze negative sulle caratteristiche fotografiche delle pellicole.
LP-GELADUR può essere aggiunto a tutti gli sviluppi normalmente reperibili sul mercato. Al momento di questa pubblicazione non è a conoscenza del team di autori alcuno sviluppo prodotto a livello industriale da AGFA, ILFORD, KODAK e TETENAL, che non sia adatto. L'additivo di indurimento dello sviluppo non si limita ai soli concentrati di sviluppo liquidi, ma è adatto anche agli sviluppi in polvere. Anche in quel caso si riduce la quantità di acqua e si compensa con l'aggiunta di concentrato di indurimento.

CONFEZIONAMENTO

- Bottiglia in polietilene da 1 litro
- Fustino da 5 litri

PREPARAZIONE DELLA CHIMICA

LP-GELADUR viene aggiunto direttamente alla soluzione d'uso di sviluppo, a n z i c h è all'acqua. La quantità d'acqua originaria viene ridotta della quantità di LP-GELADUR.
Non si tratta pertanto di un aggiunta, bensì di una *sostitu zione d'acqua.*
LP-GELADUR come concentrato ha un valore pH molto basso. Per questo motivo bisogna assolutamente evitare il congiungimento di concentrato di sviluppo e LP-GELADUR (!). Ciò potrebbe provocare corrosioni.
Dapprima si preparino le esatte quantità in acqua, concentrato di sviluppo e concentrato di induritore.

- ***Passo 1:*** Si immette dapprima il concentrato di sviluppo nel misurino.
- ***Passo 2:*** Aggiungere lentamente l'acqua senza provocare la formazione di bollicine d'acqua, mescolando bene la soluzione
- ***Passo 3:*** Aggiungere poi lentamente il concentrato di LP-GELADUR, mescolando senza provocare la formazione di bollicine d'aria.

Questa sequenza obbligata è prescritta ed è da rispettare a *ssolutamente.* Rileva le quantità di preparazione dalle rispettive tabelle di trattamento delle pellicole.

LP-GELADUR kan føre til misfarging av filmemulsjonen.. Dette har imidlertid ingen invirkning på de fotografiske egenskapene til filmen.
LP-GELADUR kan brukes sammen med alle framkallere som er i handel. Det er oss ikke kjent at noen av framkallerne til AGFA, ILFORD, KODAK eller TETENAL ikke kan benyttes sammen med LP-GELADUR. Dette gjelder både for konsentrat og pulver. Begge steder blir vannmengden redusert og kompensert med LP-GELADUR.

FORPAKNING

- 1 l polyethylenflasker
- 5 l kanne

BLANDING AV KJEMI

LP-GELADUR erstatter en mengde vann ved balnding av framkallerkonsentrat. Det er derfor ikke en tilsettning, men en vannerstatning.
Da LP-GELADUR konsentratet har en meget lav pH verdi er det viktig å blande framkaller konsentrat med vann før LP-GELADUR tilsettes. Hvis dette ikke gjøres kan det oppstå forbrenninger.
Først må en måle opp de rette mengdene vann, framkallerkonsentrat og LP-GELADUR.

- ***Steg 1:*** Hell framkallerkonsentratet i et passe stort målebeger.
- ***Steg 2:*** Vann blir tilsatt uten at det røres luft inn.
- ***Steg 3:*** Så blandes LP-GELADUR langsomt inn også uten at det blir dannet luftbobbler.

Denne rekkefølgen er påkrevet av sikkerhetsmessige hensyn. Rett mengde kan avleses fra tabellen til hver film.

GELADUR + wetting agent LP-MASTERPROOF) can contribute to control these drawbacks of the polyester film base.

LP-GELADUR can cause discolorations of the film emulsion, but the colour does not affect the photographic characteristics of the film in any negative way.
LP-GELADUR can be added to any commercially available, industrial-manufacture developer. At the time of writing, the authors are not aware of any industrial-manufacture developer made by AGFA, ILFORD, KODAK, or TETENAL, where the additive is not suitable. The hardener additive is not limited to liquid developer concentrates, powder developers are equally suitable. Reduce the quantity of water and replace by hardener concentrate.

PACKAGING

- 1 l polyester bottles
- 5 l containers

PREARATION OF THE SULUTION:

LP-GELADUR is added directly to the developer working solution. The quantity of water used for the developer working solution is reduced by the quantity of LP-GELADUR. So LP-GELADUR is not so much an additive, as a water substitute.
The pH of LP-GELADUR concentrate is very low. Mixing developer concentrate and LP-GELADUR concentrate must therefore be avoided, as this might lead to corrosion.
First, prepare exactly the required quantities of water, negative developer concentrate, and hardener concentrate.

- ***STEP 1:*** Pour developer concentrate into a graduated beaker.
- ***STEP 2:*** Slowly add the water, without forming bubbles. The solution will be mixed well automatically.
- ***STEP 3:*** Then add LP-GELADUR concentrate, also slowly, without forming bubbles.

This prescribed sequence shall be observed at any rate for safety reasons. For the quantities needed, please refer to the

VERDÜNNUNGSTABELLE FÜR ENTWICKLER
Die jeweiligen Ansätze entnehmen Sie bitte den Entwicklungszeitentabellen in diesem Buch.

VERDÜNNUNGSTABELLE, ALLGEMEIN, FÜR JEWEILS EINEN LITER GEBRAUCHSLÖSUNG

Temp	*Entwicklerkonzentrat*	*Wasser*	*LP-GELADUR*
20°C	125ml	775ml	100ml
25°C	125ml	675ml	200ml
30°C	125ml	625ml	250ml
35°C	125ml	575ml	300ml

VERARBEITUNGSZEIT / BEWEGUNG
Richten sich nach den Vorgaben, die für die Filmentwickle angegeben sind. Keine Zeitverlängerung durch Zugabe des Entwickler-Härters notwendig.

ERGIEBIGKEIT
Es gelten die Vorgaben für die Entwickler. Die Zugabe von LP-GELADUR schränkt die Entwickler-Leistungsfähigkeit nicht ein.

HALTBARKEIT
Die original verschlossene, schwarze LABOR PARTNER Flasche ist etwa bis zu 2 Jahre nach dem Erwerb im Handel haltbar.

TABELLA DI DILUIZIONE PER SVILUPPO
Rileva le rispettive preparazioni dalle rispettive tabelle di trattamento delle pellicole riportate in questo libro.

TABELLA DI DILUIZIONE, GENERALE, PER RISPETTIVAMENTE 1 LITRO DI SOLUZIONE D'USO

Temperatura	*Concentrato di sviluppo*	*Acqua*	*LP-GELADUR*
20°C	125 ml	775 ml	100 ml
25°C	125 ml	675 ml	200 ml
30°C	125 ml	625 ml	250 ml
35°C	125 ml	575 ml	300 ml

TEMPO DI LAVORAZIONE / AGITAZIONE
Basati sulle indicazioni date per gli sviluppi delle pellicole. Non sono necessari incrementi del tempo di sviluppo per l'aggiunta dell'induritore dello sviluppo.

RESA
Valgono le indicazioni dello sviluppo. L'aggiunta di LP-GELADUR allo sviluppo non limita le prestazioni dello sviluppo stesso.

CONSERVAZIONE
In bottiglia sigillata, originale nera LABOR PARTNER, si mantiene per almeno 2 anni dalla data di acquisto presso il tuo fornitore di fiducia.

FORTYNNINGSTABELL
se hver enkelt LABOR PARTNER filmframkaller.

FORTYNNINGSTABELL, GENERELT, FOR 1 LITER BRUKSLØSNING

Temp	*Framkaller kons*	*Vann*	*LP-GELADUR*
20°C	125 ml	775 ml	100 ml
25°C	125 ml	675 ml	200 ml
30°C	125 ml	625 ml	250 ml
35°C	125 ml	575 ml	300 ml

AGGITASJON
Tilpasse det som gjelder for framkalleren

UTNYTTELSESGRAD
Det samme som for framkalleren. LP- GELADUR endrer ikke framkallerens ytelse

HOLDBARHET
I orginalembalasjen holdbar ca 2 år.

film charts.

DILUTION CHART, FOR LABOR PARTNER DEVELOPERS
Please refer to the developing time charts in this book.

DILUTION CHART, GENERAL, FOR ONE LITRE OF WORKING SOLUTION

Temp.	*Dev. conc.*	*Water*	*LP-GELADUR*
20°C (68°F)	125ml	775ml	100ml
25°C (77°F)	125ml	675ml	200ml
30°C (86°F)	125ml	625ml	250ml
35°C (95°F)	125ml	575ml	300ml

PROCESSING TIME / AGITATION
Observe the recommendations for the developer in question. The hardening additive does not require an extension of the development time.

CAPACITY
As mentioned for the developer in question. LP-GELADUR does not reduce developer capacity.

SHELF LIFE
The unopened black LABOR PARTNER bottle can be kept for up to two years after purchase.

Netzmittel-Schutzbad

LP-MASTERPROOF

LP-MASTERPOOF ist eine exklusive Besonderheit unter den in der Branche verfügbaren Netzmitteln, bzw. Schutzbädern. LABOR PARTNER produziert seit 1986 hervorragende fotografische Netzmittel. Die Rezeptur wurde immer wieder entscheidend verbessert.

War zu Beginn die Hauptsache die biologische Abbaubarkeit und der Umweltschutz (nachwachsende Rohstoffe, biologische Tenside), ist heute die Summe aller Eigenschaften nahezu einzigartig für ein fotografisches Netzmittel. Nicht ohne Grund wurde daher bereits in der Einleitung zu diesem Buch auf das LP-MASTERPROOF hingewiesen. Es erfüllt uns mit großer Freude, dass mit dem Produkt aus unserem Hause viele Millionen Schwarzweiß Filme (theoretischer Wert, Rückschluss auf die Kapazität des bisher in alle Welt verkauften LP-MASTERPROOF) in exzellenter Qualität getrocknet worden sind.
Das diese Filme geschützt sind gegen Bakterienbefall, gegen Pilzbefall, die antistatische Wirksamkeit den Staubbefall minimierte und die partielle Schichthärtung für weniger Kratzer auf den Film verantwortlich zeichnet. Auch wenn Sie als interessierter Leser (hätten Sie sonst das Geld für unser Buch ausgegeben ?) vielleicht denken, wir sollten einem Netzmittel nicht so viel Aufmerksamkeit schenken - Jeder
Fotograf, jeder Laborant, der nur einmal mit einem zerkratzen, verstaubten oder fleckigen Filmstreifen
zu kämpfen hatte, wird unsere Ansicht zu diesem Thema mit vollem Engagement unterstützen.
Ja, auch wir wissen, dass es unendlich viele und auch sehr gute Netzmittel in der Fotoszene gibt. Daher prüfen Sie für sich, ob die Produkte, die Sie vielleicht bisher sogar selbst verwendet haben, die folgenden Eigenschaften erfüllen:

- Verdünnung 1 + 100 (10 ml Konzentrat auf 990 ml dest. Wasser). Dieser Ansatz wurde gewählt, weil diese Menge ist recht einfach auch mit groben Labormensuren abzumessen ist.
- Transparente Filme, ohne Ablaufstreifen.
- Keine Trockenflecken. Dies ist sehr, sehr wichtig. Beim LP-MASTERPROOF läuft das Wasser gleichmäßig ab, je gleichmäßiger die Gelatineschicht trocknet, desto weniger krümmt sich der Film. Dies ist besonders wichtig bei Polye-

Bagno imbibente-protettivo

LP-MASTERPROOF

L'LP MASTERPROOF di LABOR PARTNER rappresenta una particolarità esclusiva in ambito di bagni imbibenti, ovvero di protezione disponibili nel settore. LABOR PARTNER produce dal 1986 ottimi prodotti imbibenti ad uso fotografico. La ricetta è stata man mano migliorata in modo significativo.

Se in passato la cosa più importante era la bio-degrabilità e il rispetto ambientale (sostanze base reintegrabili, agenti tensioattivi biologici), oggi la somma di tutte le caratteristiche è pressoché unica nel suo genere per una sostanza imbibente ad uso fotografico.
Non senza motivi già nell'introduzione di questo libro si è voluto riferirsi al LP-MASTERPROOF. Ci fa enorme piacere, che con questo prodotto di nostra produzione diversi milioni di pellicole sono state asciugate con una eccellente qualità finale (valore teorico, basato sulla capacità di LP-MASTERPROOF venduto in tutto il mondo).
Le pellicole sono protette contro l'attacco di batteri, contro l'attacco di funghi, con una protezione antistatica che minimizza l'attacco di polvere e si caratterizza pure per un parziale indurimento dell'emulsione per garantire meno graffi sulla pellicola.
Anche se in qualità di lettore interessato di questo libro, (avresti altrimenti speso dei soldi per il nostro libro?) potresti pensare che abbiamo dato troppa importanza ad un bagno ausiliario -
Ogni fotografo, ogni stampatore, che ha dovuto combattere con una striscia di pellicola graffiata, impolverata o macchiata, sosterrà ad armi tratte il nostro parere in merito a questo tema. Sì, sappiamo benissimo che sono disponibili sul mercato numerosi prodotti imbibenti di ottima qualità. E' per questo motivo che ti consigliamo di provare se il prodotto, che hai attualmente in uso, rispondono alle seguenti caratteristiche:
- Diluizione 1+100 (10 ml di concentrato in 990 ml di acqua distillata). Questa diluizione è stata scelta, perché questa quantità è facilmente misurabile in classiche provette da laboratorio fotografico.
- Pellicole trasparenti senza striature di colature. Nessuna macchia di asciugatura. Ciò è molto, molto importante.
- Con LP-MASTERPROOF l'acqua cola lentamente, più lentamente lo strato di gelatina si asciuga, meno la pellicola

Vetemiddel og Beskyttelbad

LP-MASTERPROOF

LP-MASTERPOOF er en eksklusiv spesialitet bland vete og beskyttelses bad. LABOR PARTNER produserer siden 1986 fremragende vetemidler. Oppskriften er gjennstand for stadige forbedringer som har bidratt til en høy ytelse.

Selv om det i begynnelsen var målet å finne fram til et middel som var biologisk nedbrytbart og gynstig for miljøet (regenererbare råstoff, biologiske tensider), så har det i dag, som summen av sine egenskaper blitt et enestående fotografisk vetemiddel.
Ikke uten grunn ble det i begynnelsen av denne boken vist til LP-MASTERPROOF. Det fyller oss med stor glede at dette produktet har ført til at millioner av sort/hvitt filmer (teoretisk ut i fra mengden som er solgt) er blitt tørket på en ekselent måte.
Disse filmene er beskyttet mot bakterieangrep, mot soppangrep, og de er antistatiske overfor støv og i tillegg har de også fått en partiell skiktherding som minsker muligheten for striper.
Selv om du som en oppmerksom leser tenker at vi ikke burde bruke så mye tid og plass på et vetemiddel:
En hver fotograf og laborant som bare en eneste gang har stridt med oppskrapte, støvete eller flekkete negativer, forstår vår interesse for dette temaet.
Vi vet også at det finnes en mengde , også svært gode, vetemiddler på markedet. Se derfor om ditt valg har de egenskapene som LP-MASTERPROOF har:

- Fortynning 1+100 (10 ml på 990 ml vann)
Denne konsentrasjonen ble valgt fordi den er enkel å få til selv med grove målebeger.
- Transparente filmer, uten tørkestriper eller flekker.
- Dette er svært viktig. Ved å bruke LP-MASTERPROOF renner vannet så langsomt av at gelantinen tørker langsomt og gjevnt.. Dette fører til mindre krumming av filmen. Dette er spesiellt viktig ved polyesterbase. Men også filmer med acetatbase har en positiv effekt av dette og ligger bedre i glasløse filmholdere.
- Forkortet tørketid. Etter 10 min i romtemperatur kan det ettertørkes med føn. Etter dette kan en forstørre med en gang.
- Filmene blir antistatiske og trekker derfor til seg mindre støv.

Protective wetting agent

LP-MASTERPROOF

LP-MASTERPROOF is unique among the wetting agents and protective baths available in this field.
LABOR PARTNER has been producing excellent wetting agents since 1986. The formulation has repeatedly undergone considerable improvements.

In the beginning, biological degradability and environmental protection (regenerative raw materials, biological surfactants) were the principal concepts. Nowadays, however, the total of all its characteristics is almost unrivalled in any photographic wetting agent.

This is why LP-MASTERPROOF deserved some space already in the introduction to this book. We are delighted by the fact that this product has helped to dry, in excellent quality, many millions of b&w films (This is a theoretical value, estimated on the basis of the capacity of our LP-MASTERPROOF sales figures.) all over the world.
These films are protected against bacteria and fungi, the antistatic effect minimised dust collection, and the partial hardening of the emulsion reduces scratches on the films.

Even you as an interested reader (Or why did you spend the money on this book?) might still think that a wetting agent does not deserve this kind of attention.
But any photographer or lab worker who ever had to work with scratched or dusty negatives, or negatives marked by fungi or bacteria, will whole-heartedly support our view on this.

Yes, we know there is an infinite number of excellent wetting agents available for film. So check for yourself if any of these (including the one you are using) gives you all of the following characteristics:

- 1+100 dilution (10ml of concentrate, water to make 1 l)
This dilution was chosen as it is easily measured even with imprecise graduated beakers.

- Clear films, no drying marks.
This is very very important. The water will run off the film surface very uniformly. The more uniformly it runs off, the more uniformly the gelatine dries, and the less the film will

ster-Filmen. Aber auch Azetat-Filme reagieren darauf und lassen sich so besser in glaslosen Buchbildbühnen vergrößern.

■ Verkürzte Trockenzeit. Nach 10 Minuten an der Raumluft, kann mit einem Haartrockner nachgeholfen werden. Danach kann sofort vergrößert werden.

■ Die Filme werden durch die Behandlung antistatisch und ziehen dadurch weniger Staub an. Sie werden fungizid, d.h. widerstandsfähig gegenüber Pilzbefall. Dies ist vor allem für Azetat-Filme sehr, sehr wichtig, wie die Archivare Ihnen sicher bestätigen werden.

■ Die heute immer mehr verbreiteten Filme auf Polyester-Basis sind kaum glatt zu bekommen. Neben dem LP-GELADUR bereits im Film-Entwickler und dem LP-CITRODUR hilft auch die zusätzliche Behandlung im LP-MASTERPROOF. Die so behandelten Filme werden immer noch nicht so plan liegen, wie man es von Azetat gewohnt (verwöhnt) war, aber sicher besser, als ganz ohne Maßnahmen.

■ Der Preis ist sehr günstig in Relation zu der hohen Kapazitätsausnutzung und der sparsamen Verdünnung. Für Fachverbraucher stellt LABOR PARTNER ein LP-MASTERPROOF SUPERKONZENTRAT her, Verdünnung 1+1.000.

Die Summe dieser Eigenschaften macht das LABOR PARTNER Produkt zu einer Besonderheit in der Fotoszene.
Viele, sehr viele Laboranten haben bereits vor Jahren den Weg zu LABOR PARTNER Produkten über den Einstieg mit dem LP-MASTERPROOF gefunden.

■

Sobald die Filme ausgewässert sind, müssen sie zum Trocknen aufgehängt werden. Damit das überschüssige Wasser abläuft, sollte man nach der Schlusswässerung während einer Minute das Netzmittelbad LP-MASTERPROOF einschalten. Das Netzmittel verhindert eine zu große Oberflächenspannung und begünstigt ein gleichmäßiges Abfließen des Wassers. Die Kalkablagerungen, die sich bei fehlender Netzmittelbehandlung vor allem auf der Filmrückseite bilden, werden so vermieden.
Nach dem Netzmittelbad nimmt man den Film vorsichtig aus der Spirale oder Schale. Spiralen werden dazu geöffnet. Sofern man spezielle Filmaufhängeklammern besitzt, klammert man den Filmanfang an. So vorbereitet geht man an einen staubfreien Ort und hängt den Film zum Trocknen auf. Damit er sich beim Trocknen nicht zusammenrollen kann, beschwert man das Filmende mit einer Gewichtsklammer.

■ ***Niemals*** den Film abstreifen. *Niemals.* Auch wenn die einschlägige Industrie auf den ersten Blick überzeugende

si curva (!). E' particolarmente nel caso di pellicole in poliestere. Anche le pellicole su base di acetato reagiscono positivamente e si lasciano stampare meglio anche in portanegativi senza vetrini.

■ Tempo di asciugatura abbreviato. Dopo 10 minuti a temperatura ambiente si può aiutarsi con un asciugacapelli, dopodiché si può passare direttamente alla stampa.

■ Grazie al trattamento antistatico le pellicole attirano meno polvere. L'azione fungicida le protegge contro l'attacco di funghi o muffe. Nel caso di pellicole su base di acetato, ciò è molto, molto importante, come gli archivi certamente ti confermeranno.

■ Le pellicole su base in poliestere, sempre più diffuse, difficilmente sono da tenere piane. Accanto al LP-GELADUR nello sviluppo e al LP-CITRODUR anche il trattamento supplementare in LP-MASTERPROOF aiuta. Anche le pellicole così trattate non rimarranno mai così piane come eravamo abituati (viziati), con le pellicole in acetato, ma certamente meglio, che senza alcun trattamento.

■ Il costo è assai competitivo in relazione all'alto sfruttamento e alla parca diluizione. (Per in grossi consumatori LABOR PARTNER mette a disposizione un LP-MASTERPROOF SUPERCONCENTRATO, diluizione 1+1000).

La somma di queste caratteristiche rende questo prodotto di LABOR PARTNER unico nella scena fotografica.
Numerosi utilizzatori si sono avvicinati diversi anni fa ai prodotti LABOR PARTNER proprio con il LP-MASTERPROOF.

■

Non appena le pellicole sono lavate a fondo, devono essere appese stese per l'asciugatura. Per fare scivolare via l'acqua eccedente, dopo il lavaggio finale bisogna immergere la pellicola per un minuto nel prodotto imbibente LP-MASTERPROOF. L'imbibente evita una tensione troppo grossa della superficie e agevola un deflusso omogeneo dell'acqua. I depositi di calcare, che si formano soprattutto sul retro della pellicole in assenza di imbibente, vengono evitati.
Dopo il bagno imbibente nel caso di trattamento in tank si asporta la spirale dalla tank, la si apre, qualora si tratti di spirali sintetiche regolabili. La pellicola si trova su una metà della spirale e può ora essere prelevata con attenzione.
Se si possiedono le apposite pinze appendi-pellicole si procede ad appenderle dal lato d'inizio della pellicola. Per evitare l'arrotolamento durante l'essiccamento, si munisce la fine della pellicola con un'apposita pinza con peso.

■ De blir i seg selv soppdrepende og er derfor motstandsdyktige mot soppangrep.
Dette er spesiellt viktig ved acetat filmer, noe en hver arkivar kan bevidtne.

■ De stadig mer populære polyesterfilmene er det vanskelig å få plane. Ved bruk av LP- GELADUR i framkalleren, LP-CITRADUR i stoppebadet og LP - MASTERPROOF i slutt badet vil en komme nærmere målet ; plan film. De vil forstatt ikke være så plane som acetat filmer, men i alle fall mye bedre en de blir uten behandling.

■ Prisen er gunstig i forhold til kapasiteten og den store fortynningen. (for storforbrukere finnes et LP - MASTERPROOF SUPERKONSENTRAT, som fortynnes 1 + 1000)

Summen av disse egenskapene gjør at LABOR PARTNERs produkt har en særstilling i fotoscenen. Svært mange laboranter brukte LP - MASTERPROOF som det første fra LABOR PARTNER og har slikt funnet veien til resten av våre produkter.

■

Straks filmen er spylt ferdig, må den henges til tørk. For at overflatevannet skal renne lett av bør filmen behandles 1 min i LP - MASTERPROOF. Vetemiddelet hindrer en for stor overflatespenning og fører til at vannet renner gjevnt av. Eventuelle kalkavleiringer, som kan dannes når en ikke benytter vetemiddel blir dermed unngått.
Etter behandling i vetemiddelet åpner en spolen, når dette er mulig. Filmen ligger da på den ene spiralhalvdelen og kan tas forsiktig ut.
Har en spesielle filmklyper benyttes disse og filmen henges på et trekk og støvfritt sted. En bår benytte en filmklype med lodd i nedre ende av filmen slik at den ikke krøller seg.

■ ***Aldri*** tørk av filmen. *Aldri.* Selv om det finnes mange tenger og andre innrettninger for dette på markedet. Gjør det aldri. Filmtørking kan naturligvis også gjøres i tørkeskap. Max temperatur er da 40°C. Bedre er det å tørke med romtemperatur. Husk at det er støvfritt. Dette er det optimale for filmemulsjonen og gir filmer som er plane.

be prone to curling. This is of particular importance with polyester-based films, but acetate-based film responds, too, allowing better printing in glassless negative carriers.

▪ Reduced drying time. A hairdryer may be used to speed up drying after 10 min at room temperature. Immediate printing is possible.

▪ The treatment makes films antistatic, they attract less dust.
▪ The fungicide makes them resistant to fungi. Conservationists will tell you that this is of particular importance for acetate films.

▪ Polyester-based films, which conquer more and more of the market, are hard to get flat. In addition to LP-GELADUR already in the negative developer and LP-CITRODUR, the additional LP-MASTERPROOF treatment will help, too. The films may still not be as flat as you are used to from acetate films (These are extremely good-natured in this respect.), but they will lie much flatter.

▪ When seen in relation to the high capacity and the high dilution, the price is very affordable. (For expert users, LABOR PARTNER manufactures LP-MASTERPROOF super concentrate which is to be diluted 1+1,000.

It is the total of these characteristics that makes LP-MASTERPROOF stand out in the phtographic world. Many, very many, lab workers have found their way to LABOR PARTNER products by starting with LP-MASTER-PROOF.

▪

As soon as the films are washed out, they must be hung to dry. For surface water to run off, it is recommended to insert a one-minute bath in LP-MASTERPROOF as the final treatment. The wetting agent reduces the surface tension, allowing the water to run off uniformly. Deposits caused by water hardness, which mainly form on the back of the film, are thus avoided.
Following the wetting-agent treatment the film is diligently removed from the reels or tray. To remove the film from reels, remove one reel of the pair.
Attach a hanging clip to the beginning of roll films only. Then go to a dust-free place to hang the film for drying. To avoid curling up during drying, attach a weighted clip to the bottom end.

Filmabstreifzangen bereit hält. Die Filmtrocknung erfolgt auch in entsprechenden Trockenschränken. Dabei sollte eine Temperatur von 40°C nicht überschritten werden. Bei der Verwendung von LP-MASTERPROOF ist von dem Einschalten der Heizeinrichtung abzuraten. Im Trockenschrank (staubfrei) ohne Heizstufe. Das ist optimal für die Emulsion und die verbessert die Planlage.

VERPACKUNG

- 2 x 250 ml Polyethylenflaschen, Einweg
- 1 Liter Polyethylenflaschen

ANSATZ DER CHEMIE

Es wird kein Leitungswasser verwendet. Es wird ausschließlich demineralisiertes Wasser (Batteriewasser) oder Aqua dest. verwendet.
Nach der Zugabe des LP-MASTERPROOF ist die Gebrauchslösung sofort gebrauchsfertig.

VERARBEITUNGSTEMPERATUR

Es sollte nicht unter 18°C gearbeitet werden.

VERDÜNNUNGSTABELLE FÜR 260 ml GEBRAUCHSLÖSUNG

1 + 100 =	2,5 ml LP-MASTERPROOF
	+ 257,5 ml Wasser

VERARBEITUNGSZEIT / BEWEGUNG

Filme werden 30 Sekunden unter regelmäßigem und sehr langsamen Kippen der Filmdose bearbeitet. Bläschenbildung ist zu vermeiden.

ERGIEBIGKEIT

1 Liter Gebrauchslösung reicht theoretisch für 300 Kleinbildfilme. Es wird empfohlen, nur die Gebrauchslösung anzusetzen, die für die täglich benötigte Film-Verarbeitung vorgesehen ist. Die gebrauchte LP-MASTERPROOF Lösung sollte jeweils täglich entsorgt werden. Es darf niemals eine Gebrauchslösung, die bereits zur Verarbeitung im Positiv-Prozess verwendet worden ist, für die Filmverarbeitung verwendet werden, denn es wird sich feinster Papierfaserstaub darin befinden. Dieser wird sich als mikrofeine Flecken bei der Vergrößerung zeigen.

HALTBARKEIT

Die original verschlossene, schwarze LABOR PARTNER Flasche ist etwa bis zu 3 Jahre nach dem Erwerb im Handel haltbar.

- ***Non*** tergere *mai* la pellicola, anche se l'industria decanta pinze tergi-film che a prima vista sembrano anche efficaci.

L'essiccamento delle pellicole può avvenire anche in un apposito armadio essiccatore. In tal caso però la temperatura non dovrebbe mai superare i 40°C. Dopo l'uso del LP-MASTERPROOF si sconsiglia l'inserimento del riscaldamento (!). Nell'armadio essiccatore (privo di polvere) senza regolazione del riscaldamento. Ciò è ottimale per l'emulsione e migliora le caratteristiche di planearità.

CONFEZIONAMENTO

- 2 x 2 bottiglie da 250 ml in polietilene, monouso
- Bottiglia da 1 litro in polietilene

PREPARAZIONE DELLA CHIMICA

Non si utilizza acqua di rubinetto.
Si usa esclusivamente acqua demineralizzata (liquido per batterie) o acqua distillata.
Dopo l'aggiunta di LP-MASTERPOROOF la soluzione d'uso è pronta all'utilizzo.

TABELLA DI DILUIZIONE PER 260 ml DI SOLUZIONE D'USO

1 + 100 =	2,5 ml LP-MASTERPROOF
	+ 257,5 ml di acqua

TEMPO DI TRATTAMENTO / AGITAZIONE

Si trattano le pellicole per 30 secondi ad una agitazione a capovolgimento della tank regolare e molto lenta.

RESA

1 litro di soluzione d'uso è sufficiente per teoriche 300 pellicole di piccolo formato.
Si consiglia di preparare solo la soluzione d'uso necessaria al trattamento giornaliero delle pellicole.
Le soluzioni di LP-MASTERPROOF esauste dovrebbero essere smaltite giornalmente. Non bisogna mai utilizzare soluzioni già utilizzate per carta anche per pellicole, in quanto vi è contenuto il finissimo pulviscolo di fibra della carta. Ciò provocherebbe delle macchioline microscopiche visibili sugli ingrandimenti.

CONSERVAZIONE

In bottiglia sigillata, originale nera LABOR PARTNER, si mantiene per almeno 3 anni dalla data di acquisto presso il tuo fornitore di fiducia.

FORPAKNING

- 2 x 250 ml polyethylenflasker (Engansflasker)
- 1 l polyethylenflasker

BLANDING AV KJEMI

Bruk aldri vann fra springen, men bare deminiralisert vann (batterivann) eller Aqua dest.
Etter blanding er LP - MASTERPROOF klar til bruk.

BRUKSTEMPERATUR.

Må ikke ligge under 18°C.

FORTYNNING

1 + 100=	2,5 ml LP - MASTERPROOF
	+ 257,5 ml vann

AGGITASJON

Filmer blir aggiter helt gjevnt og langsomt i 30 sek. Det er viktig å unngå bobbler.

UTNYTTELSESGRAD

1 liter ferdig blanding holder i teorien til 300 135/ 36.
Det anbefales bare å lage så mye som trenges for filmframkallingen. Brukt LP-MASTERPROOF må destrueres daglig. En blanding som er blitt benyttet til papir må aldri benyttes videre i filmframkalling pga av mulig papirstøv i vesken. Disse vil kunne føre til flekker på filmen.

HOLDBARHET

I orginalembalasjen holdbar ca 3 år.

- ***Don't*** squeegee your films. *Never ever*. Distributors offer a multitude of convincing-looking squeegees and tongs.

Films can also be dried in drying cabinets. A temperature of 40°C (104°F) should not be exceeded in this case. We advise against using the heating when LP-MASTERPROOF is used. Dry your film in the (dust-free) drying cabinet but don't use the heating. This is optimal for the emulsion and improves flatness.

PACKAGING

- Two 250 ml polyethylene bottles, for single use
- 1 l polyethylene bottles

PREPARATION OF THE SOLUTION

Do not use tap water.
Use only demineralised water (car battery water) or Aqua dest. The solution is ready for use as soon as the LP-MASTERPROOF concentrate has been added.

PROCESSING TEMPERATURE

Working below 18°C (64°F) is not recommended.

DILUTION CHART FOR 260 ml OF WORKING SOLUTION

1 + 100 =	2,5ml LP-MASTERPROOF
	+ 257,5ml of water

PROCESSING TIME / AGITATION

Films are given a one-minute treatment with uniform and very gentle inversions of the film tank. Avoid the formation of foam.

CAPACITY

Theoretically, one litre of working solution is sufficient for 300 35-mm films.
We recommend that you prepare but the quantity of working solution you need for one working day. Used LP-MASTERPROOF solution should be disposed of each day. Never use any working solution previously used for print processing for film as it will contain suspended fine paper fibres which you will find as fine spots in your prints.

SHELF LIFE

The unopened black LABOR PARTNER bottle can be kept for up to three years after purchase.

INFRAROT FOTOGRAFIE

E inige persönliche Worte vom Autor:

Die Schwarzweiß Infrarot (IR) Fotografie ist ein Gebiet innerhalb der Fotografie, das einen sehr hohen Stellenwert einnimmt. Persönlich hatte ich zwar immer Zugang zu den verfügbaren Produkten, vor allem zum HIE von KODAK, allerdings fehlte mir leider der Mut, es damit konsequent selbst zu versuchen. Daher findet man in älteren LABOR PARTNER Informationen auch kein Wort dazu.
Den ›Durchbruch‹ brachte das Internet. Die dort verfügbaren fantastischen Bilder, basierend auf der IR-Technik, faszinierten und begeisterten mich. Mich erstaunte, dass die weitaus meisten Bilder aus dem englischsprachigen Raum stammten. Aus Europa, vor allem auch aus Deutschland, waren vergleichsweise wenig Aktivitäten zu erkennen. Der Durchbruch erfolgte 1998, als sich ein traditionsreicher Film-Hersteller an LABOR PARTNER wandte, um die LABOR PARTNER Fotochemie für seine neuen IR-Filme zu perfektionieren. Da faszinierte mich der Gedanke an das enorme Potenzial an Ausdrucksfähigkeit dieser besonderen Sorte von Filmen. Es hatte mich ›erwischt‹. In der Folge optimierte ich die LABOR PARTNER Entwickler entsprechend.
Wenn die LABOR PARTNER Fotochemie ihren Teil zur Verbreitung dieser interessanten Technik beitragen kann, dann erfüllt mich das mit Genugtuung. Mein persönliches und besonderes Augenmerk habe ich auf Nachtaufnahmen mit IR-Blitz gerichtet. Dazu wird das Blitzgerät mit einer Filterfolie (B&W) versehen. Das kann auch heißen, dass mit dem Blitz im Theater oder bei Künstlern fotografische Arbeiten möglich sind, bei denen Blitzaufnahmen ansonsten nicht gestattet sind. Auch Presse-Reporter gehören zu den Anwendern diese ›Fotografieren im Dunkeln‹.

DIE ANWENDUNGSGEBIETE: Diese sind ausserordentlich reichhaltig und vielseitig. Sie reichen von Tieraufnahmen im Dunkeln bis zur Mikrofotogafie. Von kriminalistischen Schriftprüfungen, von Textil- und Gemäldeuntersuchungen bis zur Feststellung von Wasserverschmutzung. Von Luftbildaufnahmen für Wissenschaft, Militär und Technik bis zur Pflanzenpathologie. Im letzten Fall macht man sich den Wood- oder Chlorophyll-Effekt zunutze, da gesundes und krankes Gewebe von IR-Material verschieden wiedergegeben werden kann.

FOTOGRAFIA INFRAROSSO

Alcune parole personali dell'autore:

La fotografia infrarosso (IR) in bianco/nero è degna di un'alta considerazione nel campo della fotografia. Personalmente ho sempre avuto accesso ai prodotti disponibili sul mercato, soprattutto alla HIE di KODAK, ma mi è sempre mancato il coraggio di sperimentare in modo coerente. E' per questo motivo che in pubblicazioni passate di LABOR PARTNER non ce n'è alcun cenno.
La ›breccia‹ me l'ha data Internet. Le immagini affascinanti basate sulla tecnica IR, che ho potuto vedere, mi affascinano e mi entusiasmano allo stesso tempo. Ero meravigliato, che la maggior parte delle immagini provenivano dalle zone anglosassoni. Dall'Europa continentale, Germania compresa, in confronto si poteva riconoscere una scarsa attività. La breccia avvenne nel 1998, quando un produttore di pellicole convenzionali si rivolgeva a LABOR PARTNER, per ottimizzare la chimica fotografica di LABOR PARTNER alle proprie pellicole IR di nuova concezione. A questo punto rimanevo affascinato dalla prospettiva sull'enorme potenziale espressivo che queste nuove pellicole IR potevano suscitare. Sono stato ›contaminato‹. La conseguenza fu che LABOR PARTNER ottimizzava i propri sviluppi ad hoc. Ogni volta che LABOR PARTNER riesce a contribuire nella divulgazione di una tecnica interessante, mi ritengo soddisfatto.
Ho rivolto il mio sguardo personale e particolare alle riprese notturne, per le quali il flash viene munito di un filtro in foglio (p. es. B+W). Riprese notturne possono significare l'uso del flash in teatro o durante attività fotografiche artistiche anche quando normalmente il flash non viene auspicato. Anche i fotoreporter appartengono alla categoria di utilizzatori di questa ›Fotografia al buio‹ in ambito IR.

I CAMPI DI APPLICAZIONE: Questi sono particolarmente vasti e variegati. Spaziano dalla fotografia di animali al buio alla microfotografia; dal controllo calligrafico in ambito investigativo, dalle perizie sui tessili o su quadri fino all'indagine sull'inquinamento atmosferico e delle risorse idriche; dalla ripresa aerea a scopi scientifici. Militari e tecnici, fino ad arrivare alla patologia delle risorse naturali. Nell'ultimo caso ci si avvale dell'effetto di wood o clorofilla, inquanto il materiale IR è in grado di riprodurre in modo diverso un tessuto sano e uno ammalato.

INFRARØD FOTOGRAFERING

Noen personlige anmerkninger fra forfatteren:

Sort/hvitt infrarød (IR) fotografi er et område som har en høy stjerne inne fotografien. Personlig har jeg riktignok alltid hat tilgang til alle akktuelle produkter framfor alt HIE fra KODAK, men jeg manglet mot til å gjøre konsekvente forsøk på egenhånd. Derfor finner en ikke i eldre LABOR PARTNER litteratur informasjoner om kring dette.

Gjennombruddet kom fra internett. Bildene som var der, som baserte på IR teknikk fasinerte og begeistret meg. Jeg undret meg over hvorfor de fleszte bildene var fra det enelskspråklige området. Fra europa og framfor alt Tyskland, var det sparsomt med aktivitet. Gjennombruddet ko i 1998, da en tradisjonell filmprodusent henvendte seg til LABOR PARTNER for å be om at vi kunne tilpasse kjemi til deres nye IR filmer. Jeg ble mektig fasinert av tanken på det enorme potensiale som lå i uttrykksmulighetene til denne spesielle sorten film. Jeg ble ›hekta‹ og som følge av det optimerte jeg framkallerne fra LABOR PARTNER til disse filmene. Hvis LABOR PARTNER med vår kjemi, kan bidra til utbredelsen av denne interessante teknikken, så er det en tilfredsstillelse for meg.

Min personlige interesse gjelder nattopptak, hvor en blitz med IR filterfolie (B&W) blir benyttet som lyskilde. Nattopptak kan også bety opptak under en teaterforestilling med blitz som ingen ser, eller kunstneriske opptak hvor det ikke ertillatt med blitz. Også pressefotografer tilhører gruppen av brukere som ›fotograferer i mørket‹, dvs IR fotografi.

BRUKSOMRÅDER:
Disse er utrolig mangfoldige og variable. De rekker fra dyreopptak om natten til mikrofotografi. Kriminalistiske skriftprøver, tekstil og maleri undersøkelser, og til undersøkelser av vannforurensning. Flyfoto for forskning, militær og tekniske opptak og plantepathologi. I den siste gjør en seg nyte av Wood eller Chlorofyll effekten, da friskt vev og sykt vev blir gjenngitt forskjellig på IR film. Spesielt interessant for oss er den uvanlige gjenngivingen som kan oppnås med IR fotografering som kunstig månebelysning på sort/hvitt opptak

INFRARED PHOTOGRAPHY

Some personal observations by one of the authors:

Black-and-white infrared (IR) photography is a very important branch of photography. To me, personally, the available products, mainly KODAK HIE, were always available, but I lacked the courage to consequently try them out. This is why you will not find a word on it in older LABOR PARTNER publications.
For me, the ›breakthrough‹ came via the Internet. The fantastic IR images I saw there fascinated me and stimulated me. I was surprised to see that most of the images were made by photographers in English-speaking countries. Europe, particularly Germany, showed little activity in this field. I got off the ground in 1998 when a film manufacturer with a long tradition approached LABOR PARTNER aiming at perfecting LABOR PARTNER photo chemicals for their IR films. It was then that I was taken with the enormous expressive potential of this special type of films. I was hooked, and I optimised LABOR PARTNER developers accordingly.
Where LABOR PARTNER chemistry can make a contribution to spreading this interesting technique, this is an element of satisfaction to me.

Personally, I am focused on night photography. Here, the flash is fitted with a gel filter (B&W). Night photography of this kind includes using the flash in a theatre or when watching artists, where the use of flash is otherwise prohibited. Journalists are also potential users of this kind of ›stealth photography‹.

APPLICATIONS:
There is a host of applications, ranging from wildlife shots in the dark to microphotography, criminological investigations of writings, examinations of textiles and paintings, even up to the determination of water pollution, aerial photography for scientific, military, and technical purposes, as well as plant pathology. In the latter case, use is made of Wood and chlorophyll effects, as sick and healthy plants can be represented differently by IR material. But we take particular interest in the extraordinary pictorial effects of IR photography, like an artificial moonlight effect in b&w images.

MACO IR 750clear with filter Heliopan 715
Caribbean

© Marcus Schwier

Besonders interessant sind aber für uns die aussergewöhnlichen Bildeffekte der IR-Fotografie wie künstliche Mondscheinstimmungen bei Schwarzweiß-Aufnahmen.

ZITAT:
In dem englischsprachigen IR-Buch ›Infra-Red Photography, a complete workshop guide‹ von Hugh Milsom, (ISBN 0863433731) erschienen Ende 2001, führt der Verfasser in seiner Einleitung sinngemäss aus:
Worin liegt also das Geheimnisvolle der IR-Fotografie?
„Wir müssen die Wirkungen verschiedener Filter auf die Filmempfindlichkeit und den Bildeindruck verstehen lernen. Infrarotfotografie wird oft als unvorhersagbar betrachtet. Wenn Sie den Anleitungen in diesem Buch folgen, werden Sie als Leser verstehen, wie Infrarotfotografie funktioniert, und Sie werden in die Lage versetzt, das ›Unvorhersagbare vorherzusagen‹. Wenn die Technik erst einmal zur zweiten Natur geworden ist, öffnet sie Ihnen den Weg zu kreativen und interessanten Bildern."

TECHNISCHE GRUNDLAGEN:
IR-Strahlen sind Wärmestrahlen. Ihre Frequenzen liegen unterhalb der Frequenzen des für das menschliche Auge sichtbaren Lichts. Will man mit ihnen fotografieren, so benötigt man dazu ein infrarot empfindliches Aufnahmematerial. Im Moment der Drucklegung stehen folgende IR-Filme zur Verfügung:

- ILFORD SFX
- KODAK HIE
- KONICA IR 750
- MACO IR 750clear
- MACO IR 820clear
- MACO CUBE 400clear

Kreative Fotografen sind auf der Suche nach interessanter Abwechslung.
IR-Filme bietet dabei ein großes Betätigungsfeld.

AUFNAHMEN IM DUNKELN:
Ein entscheidender Vorteil des IR-Materials ist, dass man mit ihm Aufnahmen im Dunkeln machen kann. Man benötigt dazu nur einen ›Infrarotblitz‹. Diesen macht man sich einfach selbst, wenn dem Blitz eine IR-Filter-Folie vorgeklebt wird. Dann, wenn ein Blitz nicht stören oder auffallen soll, kann man den ›Infrarotblitz‹ verwenden.
Hinweis: Ein billiger IR-Filter für den Blitz kann aus einem Stück unbelichtetem, entwickeltem Dia-Rollfilm bestehen, weil die Dia-Farbstoffe IR-transparent sind. Blitzfilter gehen wegen der enormen Energie, die sie absorbieren müssen, oft recht schnell kaputt. Bei dem improvisierten Filter aus Film macht das nichts.

Per noi sono però più interessanti i suggestivi effetti ottenuti dalle pellicole IR nella fotografia in bianco/nero, come per esempio l'effetto ›chiaro di luna‹.

CITZIONE:
In un libro su IR di lingua inglese ›Infra-Red Photography, a complete workshop guide‹ di Hugh Milson‹ (ISBN 086343 3731) apparso fine del 2001, l'autore si esprime così nella sua introduzione:
Quali sono i motivi del mistero IR?
„Per riconoscere gli effetti-IR dobbiamo capire gli effetti dei diversi filtri, le diverse sensibilità delle pellicole ed il carattere delle immagini finite. La fotografia infrarossa viene spesso osservata come se non fosse influenzabile o determinabile in anticipo. ›Calcola l'incomputabile‹. La tecnica è sì in secondo piano, ma essa spiana la strada alla creatività ed a immagini interessanti."

BASI TECNICHE:
I raggi IR sono raggi di calore. Le loro frequenze sono poste al disotto delle frequenze della luce visibile dall'occhio umano. Se si vuole fotografare con esse bisogna utilizzare materiale da ripresa sensibile all'infrarosso.
Al momento della pubblicazione sono a disposizione le seguenti pellicole IR in bianco/nero:

- ILFORD SFX
- KODAK HIE
- KONICA IR 750
- MACO IR 750clear
- MACO IR 820clear
- MACO CUBE 400clear

Fotografi creativi sono alla costante ricerca di varianti interessanti. Le pellicole IR offrono un grande campo di azione.

RIPRESE AL BUIO:
Uno dei vantaggi determinanti del materiale IR è rappresentato dalla possibilità di fare riprese al buio. Si necessita di un cosiddetto ›flash infrarosso‹.
Lo si auto-costruisce semplicemente applicando un filtro IR in foglio ad un normale flash. Poi nel caso il flash non deve né disturbale né farsi notare, basta usare questo ›flash infrarosso‹.

SITAT:
I den engelske IR boken ›Infra-Red photography, a comple workshop guide‹ by Hugh Milsom (ISBN 0863433731) som ble utgitt i 2001 sier forfatteren i sin innledning:
Hva er grunnene for IR-mysteriet?
„For å kunne forstå IR-effekten må vi kjenne til hvordan forskjellige filter og forskjellige følsomhet ho de enkelte filmene, påvirker det endelige resultatet og karrakteren til bildet.
IR-fotografi blir ofte settpå som noe som ikke kan beregnes eller påvirkes. ›Kontroler det ukontrolerbare‹. Teknikken kommer på annen plass, men den åpner likevel veien til kreativitet og interessante bilder."

TEKNISK GRUNNLAG
IR-stråler er varmestråler. Frekvensen ligger utenfor det som det mennesklige øye kan oppfatte. Ønsker en å bruke det til å ta bilder med, må man ha et opptaksmeteriell som er følsomt for infrarød lys. Vi kjenner til følgende IR-filmer:

- ILFORD SFX
- KODAK HIE
- KONICA IR 750
- MACO IR 750clear
- MACO IR 820clear
- MACO CUBE 400clear

Kreative fotografer er alltid på utkikk etter interessant avveksling. IR filmer er et stort område med mange muligheter.

OPPTAK I MØRKE:
En fordel med IR-materiell er at det er mulig å ta bilder i mørke. Det en trenger er en infrarød blitz.
En slik kan en lage selv ved å plassere et IR filterfolie foran blitz (pass på strølys!). Da kan man bruke blitz uten å bli oppdaget og uten at den forstyrrer.

QUOTATION:
The English book ›Infra-Red Photography, A Complete Workshop Guide‹ by Hugh Milsom, (ISBN 0 86343 3731) published 2001, the author writes:
So what are the reasons for this mystique?
“We need to understand the effects of different filters on the speed of the film and the characteristics of the image. Infrared photography is often regarded as unpredictable. By following the guidelines laid out in this book, the reader will gain an understanding of infrared photography and be able to ›predict the unpredictable‹. Once technique is second nature, it opens the way to some creative and interesting images.”

TECHNICALITIES:
IR radiation is heat radiation. Its frequency band lies below the frequencies of the light the human eye can see. To record it in photographic material, you need a film that ›sees‹ infrared radiation. At the time of publication, the following IR films are available:

- ILFORD SFX
- KODAK HIE
- KONICA IR 750
- MACO IR 750clear
- MACO IR 820clear
- MACO CUBE 400clear

Creative photographers are always looking for something new to try for a change. Here, IR films offer a wide variety.

PHOTOGRAPHY IN THE DARK:
It is one great advantage of IR material that you can shoot in the dark. All you need for this is a so-called ›infrared flash‹.
This is an easy-to-build DIY item: just mount an IR-transmitting (and visually opaque) filter in front of your flash. Then use the ›infrared flash‹ where you need or desire its unobtrusiveness.

Spectral sensitivity of infrared films

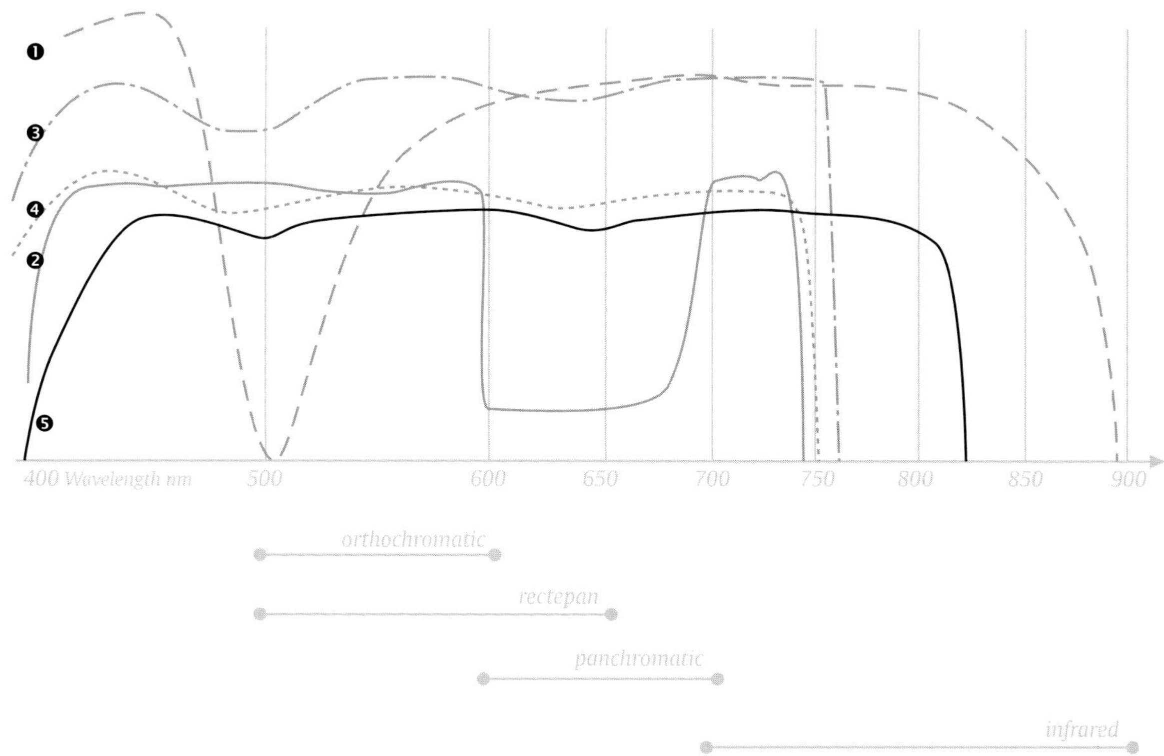

❶ KODAK HIE

❷ KONICA

❸ MACO CUBE 400clear

❹ MACO IR 750clear

❺ MACO 820clear

AUFNAHMEN BEI NEBEL ODER DUNST, BZW. VERFREMDUNGEN: Will man tagsüber Aufnahmen durch Nebel oder Dunst hindurch machen, so muss man dem Objektiv einen IR-Filter vorschalten. Zur Aufnahme mit IR-Material kann jede normale Kamera benutzt werden. Allerdings sind Lederbalgen, auch wenn sie optisch dicht sind, für IR-Strahlen häufig durchlässig, was zu Verschleierungen führen würde. IR-Material wird nur für den sich unmittelbar an das sichtbare Rot anschließenden Bereich von etwa 700 bis 1.100 nm sensibilisiert, während das gesamte Infrarotgebiet von 700 bis 400.000 nm reicht. Um ein bestimmtes IR-Material richtig verwenden zu können, muss man dessen Sensibilisierungsmaximum kennen, denn dieses variiert bei den einzelnen Fabrikaten erheblich.
Obwohl IR-Filme interessante Einsatzgebiete erschließen, sollte man keine Wunder erwarten. Auch der ›beste‹ Film registriert IR nur bis zu einer Wellenlänge von maximal 900 nm. Die Körperwärme, die ein Mensch abgibt, liegt bei etwa entspricht maximaler IR-Abstrahlung bei 1.450 nm. Es ist daher nicht möglich, mit IR-Filmen Menschen oder Tiere ohne eine zusätzliche IR-Bestrahlung abzubilden. Dazu siehe unsere Ausführungen zum IR-Blitz. Auch lassen sich keine Wärmeunterschiede an Fahrzeugen oder Häusern mit Schwarzweiß-IR-Filmen dokumentieren, weil auch diese in anderen Wellenlängenbereichen liegen.

VERLÄNGERUNGS-FAKTOREN UND IR-FILTER: Weiterhin muss man wissen, dass IR-Material auch für den sichtbaren roten und blau-violetten Spektralbereich lichtempfindlich ist. Die Belichtung mit sichtbarem Licht ist bei Aufnahmen unter Tageslichtbedingungen so stark, dass der IR-Effekt völlig überdeckt wird. Daher müssen zum Ausschalten dieses Bereiches INFRAROT-FILTER benutzt werden. IR-Filter sind von schwarzer bis roter Einfärbung, je nachdem ob mit reinen IR-Stahlen oder mit einer Kombination von IR-Strahlen und sichtbarem roten Licht gearbeitet werden soll. IR-Filter und IR-Filme müssen aufeinander abgestimmt sein. Das Filter muss den Wellenbereich durchlassen, für den der IR-Film sensibilisiert ist.
Der Verlängerungsfaktor des Filters ist zum Teil beachtlich. Er beträgt je nach Filterdichte und Lichtempfindlichkeit des Aufnahmematerials 2 bis 25 für die Belichtungszeit bzw. 1 bis 4 1/2 Blendenstufen bei Tageslichtaufnahmen. Demzufolge ist es auch schwer, durchschnittliche Belichtungszeiten anzugeben. Auch die Aufnahmebedingungen können bereits innerhalb einer Aufnahmeserie sehr stark schwanken. Die Lichtempfindlichkeit des IR-Materials kann nicht mit den üblichen Mitteln bestimmt und auch nicht in ISO

RIPRESE IN PRESENZA DI NEBBIA O FOSCHIA, OVVERO EFFETTI SPECIALI: Nel caso in cui si desideri fotografare di giorno attraverso la nebbia o foschia, basta applicare davanti all'obiettivo un filtro IR.
Per le riprese con materiale IR possono essere utilizzati normali apparecchi fotografici. Attenzione però ai soffietti, che anche nei casi in cui risultino a tenuta di luce per riprese tradizionali, spesso non lo sono ai raggi IR, ciò che provoca inevitabili velature.
I materiali IR sensibilizzati a partire dal rosso ancora visibile verso un campo compreso fra 700 e 1100 nm, quando l'intero campo dell'infrarosso spazia fra 700 e 400 000 nm. Per utilizzare iin modo corretto un determinato materiale sensibili all'infrarosso, bisogna conoscere il suo massimo picco si sensibilizzazione, che varia in modo sostanziale fra i diversi prodotti.
Le pellicole IR pur comprendo campi si applicazioni assai interessanti, non bisigna però aspettarsi dei miracoli. Anche la ›migliore‹ pellicola IR reagisce al massimo fino a 900 nm. Il calore corporale, che un'essere umano emana, è posto a ca. 1450 nm. Non è pertanto possibile riprendere persone o animali senza una radiazione ir supplementare. A questo proposito vedi il capitolo dedicato al flash IR.
D'altra parte non è neppure possibile documentare le differenze di calore a veicoli o costruzioni con le pellicole IR in bianco/nero.

FILTRI IR + FATTORI DI PROLUNGAMENTO: Bisogna inoltre sapere, che i materiali IR sono sensibile anche alla luce visibile nel campo spettrale del rosso e blu-violetto. Per questo motivo per escludere questo campo bisogna utilizzare un FILTRO INFRAROSSO. I filtri IR hanno una colorazione dal nero al rosso, a seconda se bisogna lavorare con i puri raggi IR, o in combinazione fra raggi IR e luce visibile rossa. I filtri IR e le pellicole IR devono essere calibrati fra loro. Il filtro deve pertanto far passare il medesimo campo d'onde, per il quale è sensibilizzata la pellicola IR.
Il fattore di prolungamento del tempo di esposizione è in parte massiccio. Ammonta a 2 fino 25 volte per riprese alla luce del giorno a seconda dellla densità del filtro e della sensibilità alla luce del materiale sensibile. Di conseguenza è estremamente difficile indicare dei tempi di esposizione medi. Anche le condizioni di ripresa possono oscillare perfino entro la medesima serie di riprese. La sensibilità alla luce dei materiali IR non può essere determinata con i mezzi comuni e non può essere nemmeno espressa in valori ISO. Ogni fotografo deve determinare in propri valori in modo empirico con prove su prove.

OPPTAK I TÅKE OG DIS ELLER KUNSTNERISKE EKSPRIMENTER. Vil en om dagen ta bilder gjennom tåke og dis, må en benytte et IR-filter.
For å fotografere med IR-film kan ethvert normat kamera benyttes. Har kameraet en belg av skinn, så kan denne, selv om den er optisk lystet ofte slippe igjennom IR-stråler som da vil kunne sløre filmen. IR-materialer blir bare sensibilisert for den delen av IR-spekteret som følger etter rødt dvs fra ca 700nm til 1100 nm, mens hele det IR-spekteret går fra ca 700nm til 400 000 nm. For å kunne bruke IR-film på en riktig måte. må man kjenne til max senibiliseringen for filmen en benytter. Dette varierer fra film til film.
Selv om IR-filmer åpner for nye interessante bruksområder, så kan man ikke vente seg mirakler. Selv ›den beste‹ filmen registrerer bare stråling inntil ca 900 nm.
Kropsvarmen som mannesker gir fra seg er ca 1450 nm. Det er derfor ikke mulig å fotografere mennesker og dyr uten en ekstra IR-lyskilde. Se avsnittet om IR-blitz.
Det er heller ikke mulig å registrere varmeforskjeller i kjøretøy eller hus ved hjelp av sort/hvitt IR-filmer.

IR-FILTER + FORLENGELSESFAKTORER: Videre er det viktig å vite at IR-filmer er følsomme for den synlige delen av det røde og det blåfiolette spekteret. Derfor må en benytte et IR-filter for å utelukke denne delen av lyset. IR-filter er svarte til røde på farge, alt etter som hvor mye av det synlige spekteret som en ønsker å benytte ved opptaket. Det er viktig at IR-filter og IR film passer sammen dvs at filteret slipper igjennom stråler som filmen er sensibilisert for.

Forlengelsesfaktoren for eksponeringen er delvis ekstrem stor. Avhengig av filtertetthet og følsomheten til filmen kan den , i dagslys varire mellom faktor 2 og 25. Derfor er det vanskelig å oppgi en gjennomsnits eksponeringstid. Opptaksforholdene kan også varierre sterkt i en og samme opptaksserie. Følsomheten til en IR-film kan ikke bli bestemt på samme måte som for andre filmer og det kan derfor heller ikke bestemmes en ISO-verdi. En hver fotograf må derfor ved egne forsøk arbeide seg fram til et resultat.

HOLDBARHET / OPPBEVARING: En IR-films holdbarhet er selv i kjøleskap og uten lufttilgang begrenset.
Selv om mange produsenter oppgir relativ lang lagringstid, så mener de tiden IR-filmen kan benyttes som ›normal‹ film. Den effektive IR-effekten er sterkt begrenset, mellom 4 til 12 måneder. Etter denne tiden synker følsomheten i IR-

SHOOTING IN MISTY OR FOGGY CONDITIONS, ABSTRACTIONS: If you want to penetrate fog or mist during daylight hours, an IR-transmitting filter must be mounted on the lens.
Any conventional camera can be used for IR photography. Only leather bellows, albeit visually opaque, are often transparent in the IR region, which results in fogging.
IR material is only sensitised for the region immediately adjacent to the red region of the spectrum, i.e. for the range between 700 and 1,100nm. The entire IR region, however, stretches from 700 to approximately 400,000nm. In order to be able to properly use an IR-sensitive material, one must know its maximum sensitivity which varies significantly from one brand to the next.
Although IR films open up interesting applications, one should not expect miracles. Even the ›best‹ film will only record infrared radiation with wavelengths up to 900 nm. The body heat of humans is such that the radiation is centred around 1,450nm. So it is not possible to photograph human beings or animals using IR films without an additional source of IR radiation. In this context, see explanations concerning the IR flash.
Also, temperature differences in houses or vehicles cannot be recorded using b&w IR film, as the spectral range is a different one, too.

IR-TRANSMITTING FILTERS AND FILTER FACTORS
You must be aware of the fact that IR-sensitive material can also be exposed by light in the visible, red, and blue/violet range of the spectrum. Under daylight, the exposure by visible light is so strong as to completely cover the IR effect. So in order to block this part of the spectrum, you need an IR-TRANSMITTING FILTER. IR-transmitting filters have a red to black colour, depending on whether you wish to use IR radiation only, or a mixture of IR and visible red light. IR films and filters must be matched. The filter must allow that region of the spectrum to pass, which the film can record.
The filter factor is sometimes huge. Depending on filter density and the speed of the recording material, it may range from 2 to 25 to be applied to the exposure time, or one to four and a half f-stops, for daylight exposures. Accordingly, it is difficult to quote average exposure times. The conditions of exposure, too, may vary within one series of exposures. The speed of IR films cannot be determined using the usual methods, and it is, logically, not given in terms of an ISO speed. Every photographer must rely on their own tests to derive empirical values.

MACO IR 750clear with filter Heliopan 715
Caribbean

© Marcus Schwier

angegeben werden. Jeder Fotograf ist darauf angewiesen, seine eigenen Werte empirisch durch Versuche zu ermitteln.

HALTBARKEIT / AUFBEWAHRUNG:
Die Haltbarkeit der IR-Filme ist selbst im Kühlschrank und unter Luftabschluss begrenzt. Auch wenn manche Film-Hersteller recht lange Ablaufzeiten auf ihren Filmsorten angeben, so meint dies doch immer nur die Fähigkeit, diese Filme als ›normales‹ Aufnahmematerial verwenden zu können. Die effektive Nutzbarkeit der IR-Fähigkeit ist sehr stark begrenzt. Sie beträgt 4 bis 12 Monate. Danach sinkt die Empfindlichkeit für Infrarot ab, was durch längere Belichtungszeit auszugleichen ist. Gleichzeitig steigt jedoch die Schleierbildung. Es ist zu beachten, das IR-Filme nach der Entnahme aus dem Kühlschrank erst auf die Temperatur unter Aufnahmebedingungen gebracht werden muss. Keinesfalls darf das Erwärmen unter Zuhilfenahme heißer Geräte geschehen.

ENTWICKLUNG VON IR-FILMEN:
In der Entwicklung besteht kein großer Unterschied zu sonstigen Schwarzweiß-Filmen. Es ist jedoch darauf zu achten, dass der benutzte Entwickler kontrastreich arbeitet und die Entwicklungszeiten nicht zu kurz sind. In der Praxis bestehen einige Fotografen darauf, unbedingt ihre sonst bewährte Entwicklungschemie auch für IR-Filme anwenden zu wollen. Dies kann zu nicht optimalen Resultaten führen, die dann oft und zu Unrecht dem Filmmaterial angelastet werden. Der LP-SUPERGRAIN wurde 1998 speziell für die Entwicklung von IR-Filmen neu formuliert und ist daher entsprechend optimiert.

KÖRNIGKEIT:
Die mittlere Korngröße von IR-Material beträgt etwa 1 bis 2 Nanometer (im Durchmesser), das Auflösungsvermögen 40 bis 60 Linienpaaren je Millimeter.

SCHARF STELLEN:
Unschärfen in den Aufnahmen entstehen vor allem durch Fokusdifferenz, da die Lichtstrahlen für gelb-grünes Licht (auf das das menschliche Auge am besten anspricht) von Linsen anders gebrochen werden als für das IR-Licht. Die Fokusdifferenz beträgt für das fotografisch genutzte Infrarot etwa 1/300 der Brennweite. Einige Kamerahersteller haben ihren Objektiven IR-Marken mitgegeben, die somit eine optimale Anwendung sehr erleichtern können.

DURATA / CONSERVAZIONE:
La durata di pellicole IR vergini è limitata anche in frigorifero e a tenuta d'aria. Anche se diversi fabbricanti indicano delle date di scadenza assai lunghe sulle proprie confezioni di pellicole, si intende sempre la loro prestazione in ambito di riprese ›normali‹. L'effettiva capacità IR è assai circoscritta. Essa ammonta a 4 fino 12 mesi, dopodiché la sensibilità all'infrarosso cade, ciò che può essere compensato, aumentando il tempo di posa.
Contemporaneamente aumenta la formazione del velo.
Bisogna osservare di portare la pellicola IR in condizioni di temperatura di ripresa dopo averla tolta dal frigorifero. Non bisogna mai riscaldarla in prossimità di apparecchiature calde.

SVILUPPO DELLE PELLICOLE IR:
Il trattamenti non rappresenta grosse difficoltà rispetto al normale trattamento delle pellicole in bianco/nero. Bisogna però fare attenzione, che lo sviluppo utilizzato lavori in modo ricco di contrasto e che i tempi di trattamento non siano troppo brevi. Nella pratica molti fotografi esigono di utilizzare a tutti i costi solo sviluppi normalmente in uso anche per le pellicole IR. Spesso però questa ostinazione non porta a risultati ottimali, che poi vengono spesso attribuiti, a torto, alla pellicola. Il LP-SUPERGRAIN è stato riformulato nel 1998 specialmente per lo sviluppo delle pellicole IR e di conseguenza è stato ottimizzato.

GRANULOSITA':
La grandezza media del granulo del materiale IR ammonta a ca. 1 a 2 nanometri (di diametro), il potere risolvente di 40 a 60 linee al millimetro.

MESSA A FUOCO:
La sfocatura nelle riprese si produce soprattutto per la differenza del fuoco, in quanto i raggi luminosi per la luce giallo/verde (che viene percepita al meglio dall'occhio umano) vengono spartiti dalle lenti in modo diverso rispetto a quelli per la luce IR. La differenza del fuoco rappresenta per l'infrarosso, usato fotograficamente, ca. 1/300 della focale. Alcuni produttori di obiettivi li muniscono di indicatori IR, che ne semplificano l'uso ottimale.

området, noe som kan kompenseres ved lengre eksponering. Samtidig øker dessverre grunnsløret.
Det er viktig å temperere IR-filmene etter at de er tatt ut av kjøleskapet. Bruk aldri varme til å få dette til, ta tiden til hjelp.

IR-FILM FRAMKALLING:
Denne skiller seg ikke særlig fra andre sort/hvitt filmer. Man skal merke seg at framkalleren arbeider med høy kontrast og at framkallingstiden ikke er for kort.
I praksis insisterer noen fotografer på å benytte samme kjemi som den de ellers benytter også til IR-filmene. Dette kan ikke føre til optimale resultater, noe som da ofte filmen får skylden for. Oppskriften til LP-SUPERGRAIN ble i 1998 tilpasset IR-filmer og er derfor optimert også for disse filmene.

KORN:
Gjennomsnittlig kornstørrelse for IR-filmer er ca 1 til 2nm i diameter, oppløsningen er ca 40 til 60 linjepar pr mm.

DET Å STILLE SKARPT:
Uskarphet i opptaket oppstår i all hovedsak gjennom fokusdifferansen som oppstår da gulgrønnt lys (som er det øyet ser best) har en annen brytning enn IR-lys. Denne forskjellen utgjør ca 1/300 av brennvidden. Noen objektiver har en egen IR- indikator for innstilling av avstanden, dette gjør det enklere å få til optimale resultater.

SHELF LIFE / STORAGE:
Even in a refrigerator and when air is excluded, the life of IR films is limited. Even where some manufacturers do quote pretty long best-before dates, these always refer to the capacity of the film to be used as ›normal‹ recording material. Effective use of the IR capabilities of the material extends over a period of 4 to 12 months. After that, the IR speed falls off, which has to be compensated by prolonged exposure times.
At the same time, however, the fog density increases.
IR films which were stored in a refrigerator must first be acclimatised to the environmental conditions. Never use heating equipment to warm them up.

IR FILM DEVELOPMENT:
Development is much the same as for other b&w films. However, use a contrasty developer, and development times should not be too short. In practice, some photographers insist on using their proven chemistry on the IR films, too, which may not lead to optimum results. These are often falsely attributed to the film material. In 1998, LP-SUPERGRAIN was re-formulated specifically for IR films, so this developer is optimised for this application.

GRAININESS:
The average grain size in IR films is 1 to 2 nm (in diameter), the resolution lies around 40 to 60 line pairs per millimetre.

FOCUSING:
A lack of sharpness in IR exposures is mainly due to the focus difference which arises from the fact that IR radiation is refracted less by lenses than yellow-green radiation for which the human eye is sensitive. For the photographically relevant IR range, the focus difference amounts to about 1/300 of the focal length. Some lens manufacturers provide an IR mark on their lenses, which may greatly facilitate optimal focusing.

MACO IR 750clear with filter Heliopan 715
Gran Canaria

© Marcus Schwier

VERFÜGBARES FILM-SORTIMENT: Die IR-Filme, die im Jahr 2002 dem Fotografen zur Verfügung stehen:

ILFORD SFX: Der Ilford SFX entspricht weitestgehend dem ILFORD HP5, wurde jedoch modifiziert um eine längere spektrale Empfindlichkeit im nahen IR-Bereich zu erhalten. Er verhält sich wie ein 200 ISO panchromatischer Film. Der Film kann bei gedämpftem Licht in die Kamera eingelegt werden. Aufgrund der geringen IR-Sensibilisierung kann er auch bei Kameras Verwendung finden, die über IR-Sensoren verfügen.

- *Vorteil:* hohe Empfindlichkeit, unkritische Handhabung, mittlerer Filmpreis
- *Nachteil:* starkes Korn, niedrige IR-Empfindlichkeit

KONICA IR 750: Im Gegensatz zu allen anderen IR-Filmen weist der KONICA eine Besonderheit auf: Es ist praktisch ein orthochromatischer Film mit einem IR-Anschluss. Diese Eigenschaft ist zuständig für den ausgeprägten IR-Effekt auch schon bei der Verwendung von Rotfiltern. Der Film sollte in absoluter Dunkelheit eingelegt werden.

- *Vorteil:* starker Wood-Effekt, Feinkörnig, scharf, sehr hoher Kontrast
- *Nachteil:* geringe Empfindlichkeit, nur begrenzt lieferbar, hoher Filmpreis

KODAK HIE: Die ›Mutter aller IR-Filme‹. Etwas betagt, aber immer noch eine sehr interessante Alternative, wenn man kräftige IR-Effekte, verbunden mit einer hohen Empfindlichkeit und der Fähigkeit zur Überstrahlung wegen der fehlenden Lichthofschutzschicht mag. Der Film muss in absoluter Dunkelheit eingelegt werden.

- *Vorteil:* starker Wood-Effekt, hohe Empfindlichkeit, Tiefenschärfereserve
- *Nachteil:* grobes Korn, Schärfe stark eingeschränkt, schwierige Lagerung, kurze Haltbarkeit, nur als Kleinbildfilm erhältlich, sehr hoher Filmpreis

MACO IR 750clear: Basiert auf der Emulsionstechnologie des MACO UP 100plus. Der UP 100plus hört bei 690 nm auf, der IR 750clear erst bei 750 nm. Das ist der gravierende Unterschied. Er steht nur als recht preiswerter Kleinbildfilm zur Verfügung. Der Film kann bei gedämpften Licht in die Kamera eingelegt werden.

- *Vorteil:* sehr feines Korn, mittlere IR-Empfindlichkeit, sehr gute Schärfe, mittlere ISO-Empfindlichkeit, sehr preiswert
- *Nachteil:* nur als Kleinbildfilm erhältlich

ASSORTIMENTO DI PELLICOLE DISPONIBILI: Le pellicole IR disponibili per i fotografi nell'anno 2002:

ILFORD SFX: La Ilford SFX corrisponde all'origine alla Ilford HP5 modificata però, ricevendo una sensibilità spettrale più allungata, entrando nel campo IR ravvicinato. Si comporta in tutto per tutto come una pellicola pancromatica 200 ISO. Si carica nell'apparecchio a luce attenuata. Per via della sua scarsa sensibilizzazione IR può essere utilizzata anche con apparecchi muniti di sensori IR.

- *Vantaggi:* Alta sensibilità, Manipolazione non critica
- *Svantaggi:* Grana accentuata, Bassa sensibilità IR, Prezzo un po' alto

KONICA IR 750: Rispetto a tutte le altre pellicole IR la KONICA mostra una particolarità: E' in pratica una pellicola ortocromatica con un'appendice IR. Questa peculiarità rende il suo effetto IR già a partire dell'utilizzo di filtri rossi. Questa pellicola dovrebbe essere caricata al buio completo.

- *Vantaggi:* Effetto di wood accentuato, Grana fine, Buona nitidezza
- *Svantaggi:* Sensibilità ridotta, Contrasto molto alto, Difficile reperibilità, Prezzo relativamente alto

KODAK HIE: E' ›la madre di tutte le pellicole IR‹. Un po' appannata, ma rappresenta sempre un'alternativa assai interessante, quando si cercano accentuati effetti IR, insieme ad una sensibilità relativamente alta e una spiccata capacità di sovraradiazione causata dalla mancanza dello strato antialone. La pellicola deve essere manipolata al buio completo. Al momento attuale come pellicola standard è disponibile solamente ancora nel piccolo formato.

- *Vantaggi:* Effetto di wood accentuato, Alta sensibilità, Riserva di profondità di campo
- *Svantaggi:* Grana grossa, Nitidezza molto limitata, Immagazzinamento difficoltoso

MACO IR 750clear: E' basata sulla tecnologia della MACO UP 100plus. La UP 100plus si ferma a 690 nm, la IR 750clear appena a 750 nm. Questa è la differenza essenziale. E' disponibile solo in versione 135 dal costo assai interessante. La pellicola può essere caricata a luce attenuata.

- *Vantaggi:* Grana molto fine, Ottima nitidezza, Molto competitiva nel prezzo
- *Svantaggi:* Sensibilità media all'IR, Media sensibilità nominale, Disponibile solo in 35 mm

FILM SORTEMENT:
Disse filmene står i 2002 til rådighet.

ILFORD SFX: Denne filmen tilsvarer i det vesentlige IFORD HP5, men er modifisert med en følsomhet inn i det IR-området. Den forholder seg som en 200 ISO pankromatisk film. Filmen kan settes i kamera ved dempet belysning. Da IR-følsomheten er liten kan den også benyttes i kamera med IR-sensorer (f,eks CANON EOS).

- *Fordeler:* høy følsomhet, ukritisk håndtering
- *Ulemper:* kornete, lav IR følsomhet, middels pris

KONICA IR 750: I motsetning til alle andre IR-filmer er denne filmen fra KONICA spesiell i og med at den praktisk er en ortokromatisk film med IR-følsomhet. Denne egenskapen er grunnen til den gode IR-effekten også ved bruk av rødfilter. Filmen bør sette i kamera i absolutt mørke.

- *Fordeler:* sterk Woodeffekt, finkornet og skarp
- *Ulemper:* lavfølsomhet, svært høy kontrast, begrennset tilgjenngelighet, kostbar

KODAK HIE: Dette er ›moren til alle IR-filmer‹. Den er litt eldre, men ikke mindre et svært interessant alternativ, fram for alt, når en ønsker sterke IR-effekter, koblet opp mot høy følsomhet og evnen til overståling da den ikke har antihalogenasjonskikt. Filmen bør sette i kamera i absolutt mørke. Finnes for tiden bare i 135/36.

- *Fordeler:* sterk Woodeffekt, høy følsomhet, Dybdeskarphetsreserve
- *Ulemper:* grovt korn, innskrenket skarphet, vanskelig lagring, kort holdbarhet, finnes bare 135, svært kostbar

MACO IR 750clear: Denne filmen bygger på MACO UP 100plus. UP 100 plus går til 690 nm, mens IR 750clear har en følsomhet inntil 750 nm. Dette er en stor forskjell. Med denne filmen står en relativ gunstig film til rådighet i 135/36, Filmen kan settes i kamera ved dempet lys.

- *Fordeler:* svært fint korn, svært god skarphet, gunstig pris
- *Ulemper:* middels IR følsomhet, middels følsomhet, finnes bare i 135

FILMS AVAILABLE: In 2002, the following IR films are available to photographers:

ILFORD SFX: This film is pretty similar to Ilford HP5 except in its spectral sensitisation which has been extended into the IR region. It behaves pretty much like an ISO 200 panchromatic film. It can be loaded into the camera in subdued light. Due to its low sensitivity to IR light, it can also be used with cameras which use IR LEDs to count frames.

- *Strenghts:* High speed, easy handling
- *Weaknesses:* Coarse grain, low IR sensitivity, average price

KONICA IR 750: This film is different from all other IR films in that it is actually an orthochromatic film with an IR extension. This is what causes the strong IR effects already with red filters. The film should be loaded into the camera in complete darkness.

- *Strenghts:* Strong Wood effect, fine grain, sharp, very high contrast,
- *Weaknesses:* Low speed, limited availability, high price

KODAK HIE: The ›mother of all IR films‹. Not a modern film, but still a very interesting alternative if you like strong IR effects at high film speed, and the tendency to halation which owes to the omission an anti-halation backing. This film must be loaded in complete darkness. Currently, only 35-mm roll films are commonly available.

- *Strenghts:* Strong Wood effect, high speed, great depth of field
- *Weaknesses:* Coarse grain, reduced sharpness, difficult storage

MACO IR 750clear: This film relies on the emulsion technology of MACO UP100plus. The UP100plus stops at 690nm, 750clear carries on to 750nm.
This is the important difference. This film is only available as affordable 35-mm roll film. It can be loaded into the camera in subdued light.

- *Strenghts:* Very fine grain, very good sharpness, very low price
- *Weaknesses:* Medium IR sensitivity, medium speed, only available as 35-mm film

MACO IR 750clear with filter Heliopan 715
Gran Canaria

© Marcus Schwier

MACO IR 820clear: Basiert ebenfalls auf der Emulsionstechnologie des MACO UP 100plus. Der IR-Bereich reicht bin 820 nm. Es handelt sich um eine echte Alternative zum KODAK HIE Film. Die Preise sind erheblich günstiger als beim Kodak Film. Es steht neben dem Kleinbild, auch ein Rollfilm sowie Planfilme von 4 x 5"; 5 x 7" und 8 x 10" zur Verfügung. Die Kleinbildpatrone muss wie der Kodak in vollkommener Dunkelheit eingelegt und entnommen werden. Der Rollfilm kann bei gedämpftem Licht eingelegt werden.

- *Vorteil:* feines Korn, gute Schärfe, hohe IR-Empfindlichkeit, starker Wood-Effekt, umfassendes Sortiment
- *Nachteil:*schwierige Lagerung, hoher Filmpreis

MACO CUBE 400clear: Dieser Film ist völlig anders aufgebaut als die obigen Vergleichsfilme. Auch schon der Kleinbildfilm, wie auch der Rollfilm sind auf leicht blau gefärbtem Polyester gegossen. Die Lichthofschutzschicht befindet sich direkt unter der Emulsion auf der Filmbasis. Die Empfindlichkeit ist vergleichbar der vom Kodak HIE-Film. Die Schärfe ist aufgrund der Lichthofschutzschicht auf einem nicht vergleichbaren hohen Qualitätsstand. Die Körnigkeit ist nicht vergleichbar. Auch bei empfindlichkeitssteigernden Entwicklern neigt der CUBE 400clear nicht zur Grobkörnigkeit. Die Tonwertabstufung ist erstklassig und ermöglicht sehr grosse Vergrößerungen, wie sie eigentlich in der IR-Fotografie bisher so nicht möglich waren. Sobald das Blitzgerät mit einem entsprechenden IR-Filter ausgestattet ist, eignet sich insbesondere der CUBE 400clear aufgrund seiner hohen Empfindlichkeit, der Schärfe und der Tonalität exzellent für Nachtaufnahmen. Insbesondere diese Art der Fotografie ist leider völlig in den Hintergrund getreten, das sollte sich jetzt wieder ändern. Der CUBE 400clear bietet dafür die besten Voraussetzungen.

- *Vorteil:* sehr feines Korn, mittlere IR-Empfindlichkeit, hohe ISO-Empfindlichkeit, mittlerer Preis, Allroundfilm, Polyesterfilmbasis, auch bei Kleinbild

MACO IR 820clear: Anche questa pellicola si basa sulla tecnologia di emulsionamento della UP 100plus. La fascia IR arriva fino a 820 nm. Si tratta dell'unica vera alternativa alla Kodak HIE. I prezzi sono assai più competitivi e la gamma assai più vasta. Rientrano infatti, oltre alla pellicola di piccolo formato, anche i rollfilm e le pellicole piane 4 x 5" e 8 x10". Come nel caso della Kodak il caricatore 35 mm deve essere caricato al buio completo, il rollfilm, invece, a luce attenuata, sufficiente per intravede le indicazioni di inizio pellicola nell'apposita finestrella dell'apparecchio.

- *Vantaggi:* Grana molto fine, Ottima nitidezza, Effetto di wood accentuato, Vasta gamma di formati offerti
- *Svantaggi:* Immagazzinamento critico, Prezzo relativamente alto

MACO CUBE 400clear: Questa pellicola è costruita in modo completamente diverso rispetto alle pellicola sopra descritte. Sia la versione di piccolo formato, che il rollfilm viene stesa su un supporto in poliestere con una leggera colorazione di base azzurrognola. Lo strato antialone si trova direttamente sotto l'emulsione *sulla* base della pellicola. La sensibilità è simile a quella della Kodak HIE. La nitidezza è su un altissimo livello qualitativo difficilmente confrontabile, grazie al suo sistema di stratificazione antihalo. La struttura della grana non è confrontabile. Anche trattandola con sviluppi che incrementano la sensibilità la pellicola CUBE 400clear non tende ad aumentare la granulosità. La graduazione tonale è eccellente e consente a forti rapporti d'ingrandimento, ciò che fino ad ora non era verosimile nella fotografia IR. Non appena il flash elettronico è munito di filtro IR, la CUBE 400clear grazie alla sua alta sensibilità si presta particolarmente alla fotografia notturna sia con qualità in ambito di nitidezza che di resa tonale. Proprio questo ambito della fotografia era stata relegata in secondo piano, ma oggi la situazione dovrebbe nuovamente mutare. La CUBE 400clear offre le migliori prerogative.

- *Vantaggi:* Grana molto fine, Alta sensibilità, Pellicola multiuso, Base in poliestere, Media sensibilità all'IR, Prezzo un po' alto

MACO IR 820clear: Denne filmer bygger også på MACO UP 100plus. IR-følsomheten gårr til 820 nm. Dette er et ekte alternativ til KODAK HIE. Prisen er gunstigere. Den finnes i 135/36, 120 og planfilm 4 x 5", 5 x 7" og 8 x 10".
135/36 filmen må settes i kamera i absolutt mørke som hos KODAK, rullfilmen kan settes inn i dempet lys.

- *Fordeler:* Svært finkornet, god skarphet, sterk Wood effekt, stort utvalg
- *Ulemper:* Vanskelig å lagre, middels pris

MACO CUBE 400clear: Denne filmer har en helt annen oppbygning en det de andre filmene har. Både 35mm filmen og rullfilmen er støpt på en lett blåtonet polyesterbase. Antihalogenasjonsskiktet er rett under emulsjonen dvs på samme side av filmbasen. Følsomheten tilsvarer KODAK HIE. Skarpheten er på et nivå som ike har vært mulig tidligere pga av antihalogenasjonskiktets plassering. En kan ikke sammenlikne kornet. Selv ved pressing blir ikke MACO CUBE 400clear grovkornet. Gråtonegjenngivelsen er førsteklasses og muliggjør store forstørrelser, noe som ike var mulig før med IR-filmer. Hvis blitzen er utstyrt med IR-filter blir det mulig å benytte MACO CUBE 400clear, til nattopptak, spesiellt takket være den høye følsomheten, skarpheten og gråtonegjenngivelsen som alle bidrar til ekselente bilder. Denne formen for IR-fotografi har nærmest gått i glemmeboke, noe alle kan være med på å endre. MACO CUBE 400clear oppfyller alle krav for å gjøre dette mulig.

- *Fordeler:* svært fint korn, høy følsomhet, Allround film, Polyesterbase
- *Ulemper:* middels IR-følsomhet, middels pris

MACO IR 820clear: This film also relies on the emulsion technology of MACO UP100plus. Its IR sensitisation extends up to 820nm. This film is a real alternative to KODAK HIE. The prices are considerably lower, and in addition to 35-mm, medium format roll films and 4 x 5in, 5 x 7in and 8 x 10in sheet film is also available. As with KODAK HIE, the 35-mm cartridge must be loaded into the camera in complete darkness. The roll film can be loaded in subdued light.

- *Strenghts:* Fine grain, good sharpness, strong Wood effect, available in all formats
- *Weaknesses:* Difficult storage, high price

MACO CUBE400clear: This film has a structure that is completely different those from the aforementioned IR films. 35-mm and medium format roll films are coated onto a slightly blue polyester base. The anti-halation layer lies under the emulsion, right on the film base. Thanks to its presence, the sharpness of this film is unrivalled. Its grain is beyond comparison. Even when processed in speed-increasing developers, MACO CUBE 400clear will not appear grainy. Tonality is first-class and allows for big enlargements beyond what used to be possible in IR photography. When an IR flash is available, the high speed of this film make it particularly suitable for night photography. Unfortunately, this particular sort of photography has faded into oblivion, which should change now. MACO CUBE 400clear offers the right basis for it.

- *Strenghts:* Very fine grain, high speed, multi-purpose film, polyester base
- *Weaknesses:* Medium IR sensitivity, average price

MACO IR 750clear with filter Heliopan 715
Little Curacao

© Marcus Schwier

ZUSAMMENFASSENDER ÜBERBLICK
über die Eigenschaften der verfügbaren IR-Filme:

	Nanometer	*ISO*	*Korn*	*Filmladen*	*Sortiment*	*Grundschleier*
KODAK HIE	350-920	800	grob	Dunkel	135-36	klar
KONICA IR	350-750	50	fein	Gedämpft	135-24/120	grau
ILFORD SFX	350-740	200	mittel	Gedämpft	135-36	grau
MACO IR 750	350-750	100	fein	Gedämpft	135-36	transparent
MACO IR 820	350-820	100	fein	Dunkel	135-36/120/Plan	transparent
MACO CUBE	390-750	400	fein	Gedämpft	135-36/120	transparent

HINWEISE ZUM KAUF VON IR-FILMEN:
Der Fotograf sollte vom Kauf von Billigangeboten und Sonderangeboten Abstand nehmen. In diesem Fall werden die Filme oft entweder überlagert oder falsch gelagert sein. Gerade bei IR-Filmen ist es sehr wichtig, ja geradezu Voraussetzung, dass die Filme auch beim Fotohändler im Kühlschrank gelagert werden. Kaufen Sie nie IR-Filme, die bei Raumtemperatur gelagert worden sind.

HINWEISE FÜR DIEJENIGEN, DIE ERSTMALIG MIT IR-FILMEN ARBEITEN: Beginnen Sie mit manuellen oder automatischen Sucher-Kleinbildkameras. Sie erkennen durch den Sucher Ihr Motiv. Es muss eine manuelle Korrektur (oder die Bracketing-Funktion) der evtl. automatisch eingestellten Filmempfindlichkeit (DX-Kodierung) vorgenommen werden. Bei der Belichtungsmessung ohne externem Belichtungsmesser muss bei der Einstellung der Filmempfindlichkeit beachtet werden, ob die Belichtungsmessung durch das Objektiv oder über eine extra Messzelle erfolgt. Praktisch ist es, mit einem Handbelichtungsmesser die Werte zu ermitteln und manuell an der Kamera einzustellen. Bei Spiegelreflex-Kameras ist ebenfalls eine externe Messung sinnvoll, da sonst vor jeder Messung der Filter abzuschrauben wäre. Neuere Autofocus-Kameras mit IR-Abtastung, wie die CANON EOS 500, sind für die IR-Fotografie leider nicht geeignet. Die IR-Diode darf nicht abgeklebt werden.

BELICHTUNGS-HINWEISE:
Jede Belichtung, gleich ob auf ›normalen‹ oder IR-Filmen erfordert Akkuratesse. Befürchten Sie nicht, dass das Thema Belichtung bei IR-Filmen kompliziert ist. Nein, das ist es nicht. Nur muss man sich mit dem Thema vertraut gemacht haben und Kenntnisse besitzen, wie die, die Sie sich ja jetzt anlesen; sollte dieses Thema Neuland für Sie sein. Sie wissen, dass Sie aufgrund der Filter länger zu belichten haben. Wie viel genau, ist sowieso erst einmal empirisch durch Versuchsreihen zu ermitteln.

TABELLA RIASSUNTIVA
di descrizione delle pellicole:

	Nanometri	*ISO*	*Grana*	*Caricamento*	*Assortimento*	*Velo base*
KODAK HIE	350-920	800	grossa	al buio	135-36	chiaro
KONICA IR	350-750	50	fine	a luce attenuata	135-24/120	grigio
ILFORD SFX	350-740	200	media	a luce attenuata	135-36	grigio
MACO IR 750	350-750	100	fine	a luce attenuata	135-36	trasparente
MACO IR 820	350-820	100	fine	al buio	135-36/120/Plan	trasparente
MACO CUBE	390-750	400	fine	a luce attenuata	135-36/120	trasparente

CONSIGLI PER L'ACQUISTO DI PELLICOLE IR:
Il fotografo dovrebbe desistere dall'acquisto di offerte a buon mercato. Spesso in questi casi le pellicole risultano mal o iperconservate. Proprio nel caso delle pellicole IR è molto importante, addirittura imperativo, che le pellicole vengano conservate in frigorifero anche dal fotonegoziante. Non acquistate mai pellicole conservate a temperatura ambiente.

CONSIGLI PER TUTTI I NEOfiTI NELL'USO DI PELLICOLE IR: Cominciate con fotocamere manuali o automatiche a telemetro. Il soggetto da fotografare viene inquadrato attraverso il mirino. E' necessario provvedere ad una correzione manuale (chiamata anche funzione di bracketing) della sensibilità eventualmente regolata automaticamente. Nella misurazione dell'esposizione senza esposimetro esterno bisogna osservare nella impostazione della sensibilità della pellicola se la misurazione esposimetrica avviene attraverso l'obiettivo oppure attraverso una cellula applicata.
In pratica è più consigliabile di inserire i dati manualmente, da una misurazione effettuata con un esposimetro esterno. Nel caso di apparecchi reflex una misurazione esterna è consigliabile, in quanto in caso contrario è comunque necessario svitare tutte le volte il filtro di ripresa, applicato all'obiettivo. Non sono adatte alla fotografia IR, le reflex autofocus di concezione attuale, con scansione IR, come p. es. Canon EOS 500.

INDICAZIONI SULL'ESPOSIZIONE:
Qualsiasi esposizione, di pellicole ›normali‹ come IR richiede la massima accuratezza. Non c'è da spaventarsi perché il tema ›esposizione‹ non è complicato con le pellicole IR. No, non lo è: Bisogna solo abituarsi a questo tema e curare le conoscenze, che stai acquisendo leggendo queste righe, e questo argomento non sarà più una chimera. E' risaputo che utilizzando i filtri bisogna incrementare l'espsoizione. Di quanto esattamente, bisogna comunque determi-

TABELL:
Film beskrivelse i kortform

	Nanometer	*ISO*	*Korn*	*Filmlading*	*Sortement*	*Grunnslør*
KODAK HIE	350-920	800	grob	Grovt i mørke	135-36	klar
KONICA IR	350-750	50	fint	dempet lys	135-24/120	grått
ILFORD SFX	350-740	200	mittel	dempet lys	135-36	grått
MACO IR 750	350-750	100	fein	dempet lys	135-36	transparent
MACO IR 820	350-820	100	fein	Grovt i mørke	135-36/120/Plan	transparent
MACO CUBE	390-750	400	fein	dempet lys	135-36/120	transparent

TIPS TIL KJØP AV IR-FILM:
Ikke kjøp restposter eller ›kjempe tilbud‹. Filmene er da ofte enten lagret feil eller for lenge. Spessielt ved IR-filmer er det viktig, ja egentlig avgjørende at filmen er blitt lagret i kjøleskap. Kjøp aldri filmer som er lagret i rommtemperatur.

TIPS FOR NYBEGYNNERE I IR-FOTOGRAFERING:
Begynn gjerne med et manuelt eller automatisk søkerkamera. Du vil da kunne se motivet i søkeren. Du må benytte manuell korrektur eller bracketing control av en eventuelt automatisk innstilling av filmfølsomheten. Ved intern lysmåling må det tas hennsyn til om det måles gjennom objektivet eller ivia en ekstern målecelle.
Det er praktisk å benytte en håndlysmåler for så å overføre verdiene til kamera. Ved bruk av speilreflkskamera er denne metoden også mest hensiktsmessig, da du ellers vil måtte fjerne filteret før lysmåling. Noen nyere autofokus kamera som f.eks CANON EOS serien benytter en intern IR-måling for filmframtrekk. Dette gjør det umulig å benytte disse til IR-fotografering. Det går ikke an å koble ut IR-dioden.

EKSPONERING:
En hver lysmålin, for ›normal‹ film eller IR-film krever nøyaktighet. Du må ikke tro at lysmåling med IR-filmer er spesiellt komplisert. Det er det ikke. Du må bare sette deg inn i hvordan og ha kjennskap til dette emne. Det er derfor du leser dette nå, ike sant?
Du vet at du må eksponere lengre pga filteret. For å finne ut nøyaktig hvor mye må en foreta en test rekke. Benyttes LP-SUPERGRAIN så er den utgjevnende egenskapen til framkalleren stor, slik at du ikke kan se forskjellen mellom for små forandringer.

OVERVIEW
of films:

	Sensitisation	ISO	Grain	Loading	Available in	Base
KODAK HIE	350-920nm	800	coarse	dark	135-36	clear
KONICA IR	350-750nm	50	fine	subdued	135-24/120	grey
ILFORD SFX	350-740nm	200	medium	subdued	135-36	grey
MACO IR 750	350-750nm	100	fine	subdued	135-36	transparent
MACO IR 820	350-820nm	100	fine	dark	135-36/120/sheet	transparent
MACO CUBE	390-750nm	400	fine	subdued	135-36/120	transparent

GUIDANCE ON BUYING IR FILMS:
Don't be tricked by cheap offers. In many cases, the films have either been stored excessively long, or improperly. Particularly with IR films, it is important, even vital, that the films are stored in a refrigerator at the distributor's. Never buy IR film that has been stored at room temperature.

GUIDANCE FOR FIRST-TIME USERS:
Start with 35-mm rangefinder cameras, either automatic or manual. You can compose your frame using viewfinder. A manual correction (or a bracketing feature) must be available to adapt any automatic speed settings (DX coding). When using an in-camera light meter, check whether metering is through the lens or by a separate sensor. It is convenient to meter with a hand-held meter and manually set the values at the camera.
Separate meters are also convenient with SLR cameras as using the TTL meter would require the filter to be removed every time you wish to meter.
Some modern autofocus cameras with IR film counters, such as CANON EOS 500, are not suitable for IR photography. The IR LED must not be masked.

GUIDANCE ON EXPOSURE:
Any exposure, regardless of the film used, requires precision. No need to fear that IR exposure is a complicated matter. It isn't. But if this is a new area to you, you need to familiarise yourself with it, acquiring some knowledge as you are currently doing by reading this text.
You know that the filters require more exposure. Exactly how much more must be determined by your own tests. When using LP-SUPERGRAIN developer, the compensating effect of the developer is so pronounced that small variations in exposure may easily go unnoticed.

MACO IR 750clear with filter Heliopan 715
Gran Canaria

© Marcus Schwier

Bei der Verwendung des LP-SUPERGRAIN-Entwicklers ist das Ausgleichsvermögen so gut, dass kleine Belichtungs-Veränderungen kaum auffallen können. Am Beispiel des MACO IR 750clear, dem robustesten IR-Film, haben wir selbst Anfänger-Schritte durchgeführt und sind zu folgenden Resultaten gekommen:

MACO IR 750clear	*Belichtungsmessung mit der Kamera*	*Belichtungsmessung Handbelichtungsmesser*
Filter Dunkelrot	ISO 100	ISO 25
Kunstlicht	minus 1 Blende	
Sonne mittags	*macht kaum Sinn, ausser in der Karibik*	
Sonne morgens/abends	minus 1 Blende	ISO 50
Bewölkt	plus 1 Blende	ISO 25
Grün – Laub/Gras	minus 1 Blende	ISO 50

Sehr wichtiger Hinweis: Machen Sie grundsätzlich die erste Aufnahme ohne Filter und stellen Sie dabei die Belichtungsmessung auf die Nennempfindlichkeit des IR-Filmes ein. So bekommen Sie in jedem Fall Gewissheit, ob der Film nicht verschleiert war, ob die Entwicklung funktionierte, ob alle anderen für Sie wichtigen Beurteilungsparameter realisiert werden konnten. Erst dann werden Filter aufgeschraubt und die Belichtungsreihen realisiert. Wer sich nicht an diesen Vorschlag hält, muss vom schwarzen Filmanfang und ggfs. der Filmsignierung Rückschlüsse auf die Qualität ziehen.

EMPFINDLICHKEITSTABELLE KODAK HIE — MACO IR 820clear

	HIE / ISO	IR 820c / ISO
Tageslicht ohne Filter	80	64
Tageslicht mit Filter 25, 29, 70, 89B	50	25
Tageslicht mit Filter 87, 88A	25	15
Tageslicht mit Filter 87c	10	6
Kunstlicht ohne Filter	200	125
Kunstlicht mit Filter 25, 29, 70, 89B	125	64
Kunstlicht mit Filter 87, 88A	64	32
Kunstlicht mit Filter 87c	25	10

AUSWIRKUNGEN AUF DAS BILDRESULTAT UNTER VERWENDUNG VON IR-TAUGLICHEN FILTERN:

- Frisches Blätter und Gras — *wirken sehr hell*
- Stille Gewässer — *wirken sehr dunkel*
- Stark bewegtes Wasser — *wirkt sehr hell*
- Strahlend blauer Himmel — *wirkt sehr dunkel*
- Bewölkter Himmel — *wirkt dramatisch*

narlo facendo delle sequenze test in modo empirico. Utilizzando per lo sviluppo l'LP-SUPERGRAIN, grazie al suo alto potere coompensativo, le piccole differenze di posa saranno appena visibili.
Con ad esempio l'uso della MACO IR 750clear, la pellicola IR più tollerante, abbiamo voluto eseguire i primi passi, tipici del principiante, con i risultati seguenti:

MACO IR 750clear	*Misurazione esposimetrica attraverso l'apparecchio*	*Misurazione esposimetrica con esposimetro esterno*
Filtro rosso scuro	ISO 100	ISO 25
Luce artificiale	- 1 diaframma	
Sole di mezzogiorno	*non ha praticamente senso, a parte ai Caraibi*	
Sole di mattina/sera	- 1 diaframma	ISO 50
Nuvoloso	+ 1 diaframma	ISO 25
Verde di fogliame/erba	- 1 diaframma	ISO 50

CONSIGLIO:
Fai la prima ripresa senza filtro e regola l'esposimetro sulla sensibilità nominale della pellicola IR. In questo modo hai modo di appurare con certezza che la pellicola non sia velata, che lo sviluppo funzioni e che tutti i parametri di giudizio siano stati realizzati. Ora si può applicare il filtro e si realizza la sequenza di esposizioni. Chi intende seguire questa proposta, deve trarre le conclusioni sulla qualità n base allo spezzone nero d'inizio pellicola o della numerazione della pellicola.

TABELLA DI SENSIBILITA' KODAK HIE — MACO IR 820clear

	HIE / ISO	IR 820c / ISO
Luce diurna senza filtro	80	64
Luce diurna con filtro 25, 29, 70, 89B	50	25
Luce diurna con filtro 87, 88A	25	15
Luce diurna con filtro 87c	10	6
Luce artificiale senza filtro	200	125
Luce artificiale con filtro 25, 29, 70, 89B	125	64
Luce artificiale con filtro 87, 88A	64	32
Luce artificiale con filtro 87c	25	10

EFFETTO SUL RISULTATO DELL'IMMAGINE IN BASE ALL'UTILIZZO DI fiLTRI IR-COMPATIBILI:

- Fogliame e erba fresca — *effetto molto chiaro*
- Acque tranquille — *effetto molto scuro*
- Acque molto mosse — *effetto molto chiaro*
- Cielo azzurro intenso — *effetto molto scuro*
- Cielo nuvoloso — *effetto drammatico*

Vi har fortatt en test med MACO IR750clear, da dette er en spesiellt robust film. Første tester kan se slik ut.

MACO IR 750clear	*Lysmåling i kamera*	*Lysmåling med løs lymåler*
Filter Mørkerødt	ISO 100	ISO 25
Kunstlys	- 1 blender	
Sol ved middag	*har liten hensikt uten om i Karibien*	
Sol morgen/kveld	- 1 blender	ISO 50
Overskyet	+ 1 blender	ISO 25
Grønnt / løv	- 1 blender	ISO 50

TIPS: Ta alltid først et bilde uten filter og benytt den oppgitte ISO verdien til filmen. Slik får du sikkerhet i om filmen er blitt sløret eller ikke, om framkallingen var OK og om du har hatt kontroll over alle andre parameter. Da først tar du testrekken MED filter. Uten denne framgangsmåten må en trekke sine slutninger ut i fra eventuelle filmsignetter og begynnelsen av filmen som jo vil bli svar.

FILMFØLSOMHETSTABBEL KODAK HIE — MACO IR 820clear

	HIE / ISO	IR 820c / ISO
Dagslys uten filter	80	64
Dagslys med filter 25, 29, 70, 89B	50	25
Dagslys med filter 87, 88A	25	15
Dagslys med filter 87c	10	6
Kunstlys uten filter	200	125
Kunstlys med filter 25, 29, 70, 89B	125	64
Kunstlys med filter 87, 88A	64	32
Kunstlys med filter 87c	25	10

PÅVIRKNING AV RESULTATET VED BRUK AV IR-FILTER

- Friske grønne blader og gress — *blir svært lyst*
- Stille vann — *blir svært mørkt*
- Vann i sterk bevegelse — *blir svært lyst*
- Strålende blå himmel — *blir svært mørk*
- Himmel med skyer — *blir svært dramatisk*

We have retraced the beginner's steps using MACO IR 750clear, the most robust film, as an example. Here's what we came up with:

MACO IR 750clear	*In-camera meter*	*Hand-held meter*
Dark red filter	adjust to ISO 100	adjust to ISO 25
Tungsten light	- 1 f-stop	
Sun at noon	*hardly makes sense, except in the Caribbean*	
Morning/evening sun	- 1 f-stop	ISO 50
Cloudy sky	+ 1 f-stop	ISO 25
Foliage/grass	- 1 f-stop	ISO 50

SUGGESTION: Always take the first shot without any filter, and set the meter to the rated speed of the film in use. This will make you sure that the film was not fogged, that development and that all other parameters were in order. Then mount the filter and shoot brackets. If you don't do it this way, you may have to rely on the film leader and the frame numbering to draw conclusions on the quality.

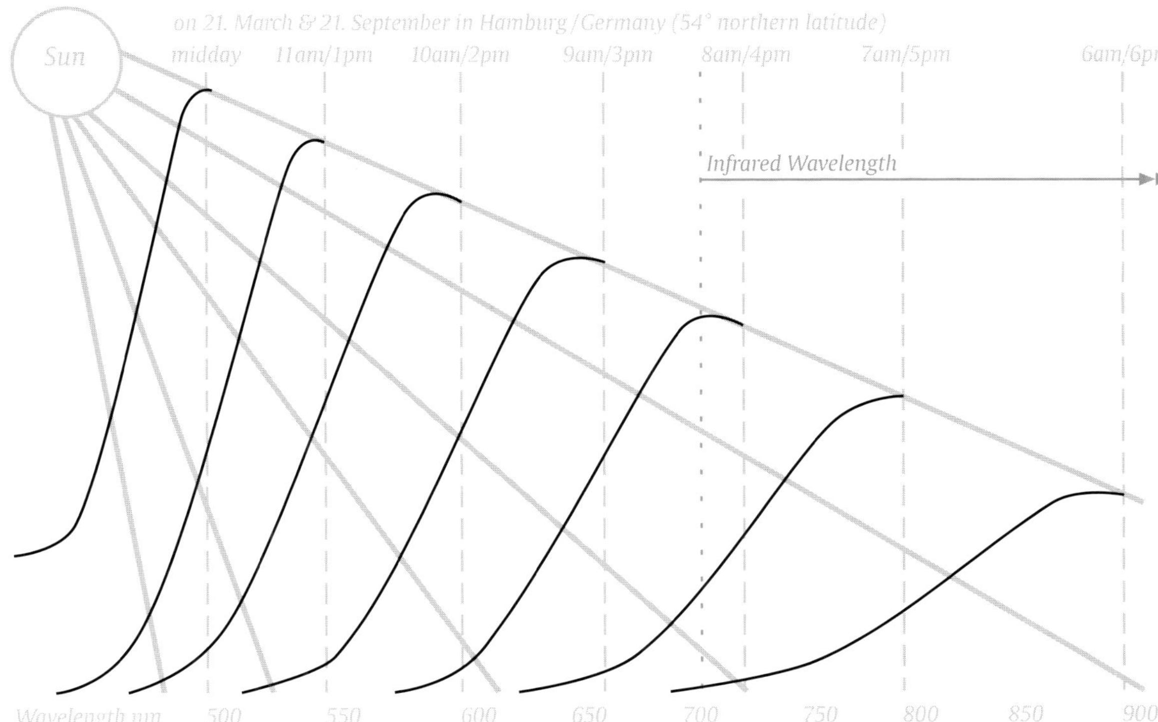

COMPARATIVE SPEEDS OF KODAK HIE — MACO IR 820clear

	HIE / ISO	IR 820c / ISO
Daylight, no filter	80	64
Daylight, w/ filter 25, 29, 70, 89B	50	25
Daylight, w/ filter 87,88A	25	15
Daylight, w/ filter 87c	10	6
Artificial light, no filter	200	125
Artificial light, w/ filter 25, 29, 70, 89B	125	64
Daylight, w/ filter 87, 88A	64	32
Daylight, w/ filter 87c	25	10

EFFECTS OF IR-TRANSMITTING fILTERS ON THE PICTORIAL EFFECT:

- fresh foliage, grass — *very bright*
- calm water — *very dark*
- turbulent water — *very bright*
- clear blue sky — *very dark*
- cloudy sky — *very dramatic*

LADEN DER KAMERAS BZW. DER FILMSPIRALEN: Die Kleinbildfilme des KODAK HIE und des MACO IR 820clear müssen bei vollkommener Dunkelheit eingelegt werden. Das Licht würde sonst durch den Filmschlitz über das Filmbasismaterial auch den Film innerhalb der Metallkassette fallen und verschleiern. Falls es aus Gründen, die zwingend sein können nicht anders geht, als einen dieser Filme bei gedämpften Tageslicht einlegen zu müssen, dann ist damit zu rechnen, dass die ersten bis zu 15 Aufnahmen mehr oder weniger verschleiert sein werden. Es ist daher zu empfehlen, sich einen lichtdichten Wechselsack anzuschaffen, der nicht zu klein sein sollte.

KAUF VON IR-FILMEN AUßERHALB DER HEIMAT: Meistens ist es kein Problem, bei bekannten und guten Fotohändlern oder speziellen Versandhändlern IR-Filme preisgünstig und frisch zu erhalten. Der Fotograf befürchtet jedoch, im Ausland nicht so optimal betreut zu werden. Sei es er bangt um die Frische oder befürchtet hohe Preise. Hier verweisen wir auf den Text ganz zu Beginn dieses Abschnitts. Gerade in Ländern wie Australien, Neuseeland, Großbritannien, in ganz Skandinavien, den USA und Kanada wird man auch MACO IR-Filme relativ problemlos erhalten können. Im Zweifel fragt man vor Reiseantritt bei den entsprechenden Filmhersteller-Hotlines nach, um die Details zu klären. Es kann schon schwieriger werden, unsere LABOR PARTNER Fotochemie in all diesen Ländern zu bekommen. Fotochemie ist schwer und verursacht erhebliche Transportkosten, im Gegensatz zu den leichten Filmen. Wir arbeiten daran, dass Sie auch die LABOR PARTNER Fotochemie bald in allen Ländern bekommen können.

CARICAMENTO DELL'APPARECCHIO OVVERO SPIRALE DI SVILUPPO:
Le pellicole di piccolo formato KODAK HIE e MACO IR 820clear devono essere caricate al buio assoluto. La luce filtrerebbe altrimenti attraverso la feritoia del caricatore direttamente sulla base della pellicola e provocherebbe velature. Qualora proprio non fosse possibile caricare le pellicole al buio, bensì in luce diurna attenuata, bisogna rassegnarsi che i primi 15 fotogrammi saranno più o meno velati. In queste condizioni è bene munirsi di un manicotto di caricamento, dalle dimensioni generose.

APPROVVIGIONAMENTO DI PELLICOLE IR AL DI FUORI DEL PROPRIO PAESE:
Nella maggior parte dei casi non rappresenta alcun problema ricevere le pellicole IR ad un prezzo adeguato e fresche da parte di fotonegozianti o grossisti specializzati, abituali. I fotografi temono però di non essere seguiti in modo ottimale all'estero, sia per i costi che per la freschezza delle pellicole. Ricordiamo quanto detto in un capito all'inizio di questo testo. In paesi europei, compresa Inghilterra e Scandinavia, come pure USA, Canada, Australia e Nuova Zelanda, pure le pellicole MACO IR saranno relativamente facili da reperire. In caso di dubbi consigliamo di chiedere dettagli sulla reperibilità al produttore stesso, prima di intraprendere il viaggio. Può invece rappresentare un problema trovare i chimici LABOR PARTNER in alcuni di questi paesi. I chimici fotografici sono pesanti e provocano alti costi di trasporto al contrario delle ›leggere‹ pellicole, ecco il motivo. Stiamo lavorando affinché anche in tali paesi la chimica di LABOR PARTNER sia reperibile a breve termine.

DET Å SETTE FILM I KAMERA HHV I FILMSPOLEN: 35mm kassettene fra KODAK HIE og MACO IR 820clear må settes i kamera i fullkomment mørke. Filmen kan ellers bli sløret gjennom den delen av filmen som stikker ut av patronen. Hvis det ikke er mulig på annen måte en å benytte dempet lys, bør de første 15 eksponeringene ikke benyttes, da de kan være sløret. Det anbefalles derfor å ha en lystett vekslesekk (transportabelt mørkerom) til å bytte film i. All framkalling naturligvis i mørket

KJØP AV IR-FILM: For det meste er det ikke et problem å kjøpe IR-filmer fra fotobutikken eller fra internettbutikker. Hvis en er på reise er en kanskje redd for ikke å få topp service og faglig veiledning. Det kan være andre priser og dårlig lagring. Vi viser til innledningen, i Europa, Ny Zealand, Australa, Storbritania, Skandinavia, USA og Kanada bør det være uproblematisk å skaffe seg bl.a MACO IR-filmer. En kan alltid ta kontakt med sin lokale leverandør på forhånd for å få vite hvor man kan skaffe seg produktet under reisen. Det kan være vanskeligere å få tak i LABOR PARTNERs fotokjemi over alt. Foto kjemi er tungt og medfører betraktelige transportkostnadder, i motsettning til filmer som jo er lette. Vi arbeider med å gjøre vår kjemi tilgjengelig over hele verden.

LOADING OF CAMERA AND REELS:
KODAK HIE and MACO IR 820clear films must be loaded in total darkness. Otherwise, light would leak into the cartridge even through the felted mouth, fogging the film inside. If you can't avoid handling one of these films under subdued light, expect the first frames, up to number 15 to be more or less fogged. So buying not to small a light-tight changing bad is recommended.

BUYING IR FILMS ABROAD:
Obtaining fresh IR films that the right prices from distributors you know, or from special mail-order companies is mostly not a problem. However, the photographer often fears not get optimal service when abroad. Be it that he has doubts about the freshness of the films, or be it that he fears excessive prices. In this context, refer to the introductory remarks at the beginning of this section. Particularly in countries like Australia, New Zealand, the United Kingdom, all of the Nordic countries, in the USA, and in Canada, MACO IR films will be available with relatively little, if any, problems. When in doubt, refer to the manufacturers' hotlines prior to travelling to ask for details. It may be more difficult to obtain LABOR PARTNER photo chemicals in these countries. Chemicals are heavy, and transport is expensive, unlike with films, which are lightweight. We are working to make LABOR PARTNER chemistry available in all countries as soon as possible.

MACO IR 750clear with filter Heliopan 715
Gran Canaria

IR-FILME: Bereits belichtete IR-Filme sollten unverzüglich entwickelt werden. Das latente Bild bei IR-Filmen ist vergleichsweise sensibler als das latente Bild bei ›normalen‹ Schwarzweiß-Filmen. Bei Flugreisen werden die Filme heute mehr geröntgt als in früheren Zeiten. Diese Strahlung ist eine sehr harte Strahlung, die insbesondere bei den hochempfindlichen IR-Filmen (KODAK HIE) zu Verschleierungen führen kann.
Wenn Sie sich nicht sicher sind, ob Sie ein Risiko in Kenntnis Ihres persönlichen Reisezieles eingehen, dann denken Sie bitte daran, ob Sie nicht doch

- einen grossen Wechselsack
- eine Film-Entwicklerdose
- Film- und Gewichtsklammern
- Thermometer

je eine Flasche

- LP-SUPERGRAIN
- LP-FIX SUPRA
- LP-MASTERPROOF

sowie einen Ordner für entwickelte Negative mitnehmen? Mehr benötigt man nicht, um direkt vor Ort seine IR-Filme zu entwickeln. Ein Thermometer und eine Uhr sollten sich doch sicher vor Ort finden lassen. Das Risiko, belichtete Filme erneut durch die Röntgen-Anlagen zu schicken, ist vielleicht größer, als die Filme vor Ort selbst zu entwickeln
Wenn Sie keine Lust oder Gelegenheit haben, die Filme zeitnah ›vor Ort‹ zu entwickeln, dann nehmen Sie zumindest auf Ihren Reisen den vergleichsweise sehr robusten MACO IR 750clear. Dieser leistet noch gute Arbeit, wenn andere Filme bereits verschleiert sein mögen.

IR-FILM-ENTWICKLERDOSEN:
JOBO und PATERSON Filmdosen sind bewährt. Das Autorenteam bevorzugt die von PATERSON, weil sich auch Polyesterfilme sehr gut in PATERSON Spiralen aufgrund der Kügelchen einspulen lassen.

IR-FILM IN ENTWICKLUNGSLABORS:
In den meisten Ländern gibt es sicher ein Labor, das dem Fotografen schnell und in guter Qualität IR-Filme entwickeln wird. Diese Adressen sind zumeist recht schnell über das Internet zu ermitteln. In diesem Buch finden Sie auch die E-Mail-Adresse von LABOR PARTNER. Nehmen Sie dahin Kontakt auf, wenn Sie erfahren möchten, welches Fachlabor Ihre IR-Filme mit LABOR PARTNER Fotochemie verarbeitet.

PELLICOLE IR CON IMMAGINE LATENTE:
Le pellicole IR esposte devono essere sviluppate al più presto. L'immagine latente di pellicole IR in confronto a quella di pellicole ›normali‹ è molto più sensibile. Durante i viaggi arerei le pellicole vengono oggi radiografate molto di più rispetto al passato- Questa irradiazione è una radiazione molto potente, che particolarmente con le pellicole IR sensibili (KODAK HIE) provoca delle velature. In caso di dubbi perché non munirsi

- di sacco nero di caricamento,
- tank di trattamento,
- pinze e termometro

e di una bottiglia di

- LP-SUPERGRAIN,
- LP FIX UPRA e LP-MASTERPROOF?

Non serve di più per trasportare e trattare le tue pellicole IR ›sul posto‹. Un orologio o cronometro all'occorrenza lo puoi trovare sul posto. Il rischio di trasportare e far passare nuovamente le pellicole esposte dalle radiazioni è di gran lunga più rischioso che sviluppare le pellicole in loco. Se ti manca la voglia o la possibilità, di trattare le pellicole sul posto, ti consigliamo di scegliere la robusta pellicola MACO IR 750clear. Questa pellicola compie bene il proprio lavoro, quando altre pellicole rischiano già di essere velate.

TANK DI TRATTAMENTO PER PELLICOLE IR:
Le tank di trattamento JOBO e PATERSON assolvono bene il loro compito. Il teAm di autori preferisce le PATERSON, per le loro spirali, che grazie al sistema di sferette permettono di caricare egregiamente anche le pellicole su base di poliestere. L'optimum è rappresentato dalle tank e spirali inox della KINDERMANN, Sì più costose, ma assolutamente sicure.

PELLICOLE IR IN LABORATORI FOTOGRAfiCI:
Nella maggior parte dei paesi sono presenti laboratori specializzati, che sviluppano velocemente e bene le pellicole IR. La maggior parte degli indirizzi li puoi cercare su Internet. In questo libro troverai l'indirizzo E-Mail della LABOR PARTNER. Prendi contatto se vuoi scoprire quale laboratorio specializzato utilizza la fotochimica LABOR PARTNER.

IR-FILMER og det latente bildet. Eksponerte IR-filmer bør framkalles med en gang. Det latente bilde i IR-filmer er forholdsvis mye mer sensibelt enn det er i ›normale‹ filmer. I tillegg blir filmer i dag oftere utsatt for røngten enn det var vanlig før. Denne formen for støling er spessielt hard og påvirker høyfølsomme IR-filmer og kan derfor sløre disse filmene (KODAK HIE).
Hvis du ikke er sikker på hvor stor risiko ditt reisemål innebærer, så kan det vær verd tanken å ta med seg

- en vekslesekk,
- en filmtank,
- film klyper,
- termometer

og en flaske av hver

- LP-SUPERGRAIN,
- LP-FIX SUPRA og LP-MASTERPROOF.

Mer tregnes ikke for å kunne framkale filmene sikkert der du er. En klokke har du sikkert med deg.
Risikoen med å la filmene gå en gang ekstra gjennom et røngtenapparat er større enn å framkalle filmene på stedet. Ønsker du ikke å gjøre dette , så kan du velge den relativt robuste filmen MACO IR 750clear. Denne virker godt der andre filmer blir sløret.

IR-FILMFRAMKALLINGSTANK:
JOBO og PATERSON har gode produkter. Vi benytter PATERSON, da spolene i disse er egnet for polyesterfilmer.

IR -FILM I PROFflAB:
I de fleste land finnes det laboratorier som kan framkalle IR-filmer med god kvalitet. Et søk på internett gir ofte et raskt svar

I denne boken finner du også emailadressen til LABOR PARTNER. Ta kontakt med oss og vi sier hvor du kan få filmen framkallt i LABOR PARTNER kjemi.

EXPOSED IR fiLMS

Exposed IR films should be processed as soon as possible. The latent image on IR films is more sensitive than that on conventional b&w films. When travelling by air, films are x-rayes more than used to be the case. The radiation used for this is very ›hard‹ radiation which, particularly with fast films (KODAK HIE) may result in fogging. If you are not sure whether your travels will take you to a region where your films are at risk, consider taking along

- a big changing bag,
- a film developing tank,
- hanging and weighting clips,
- a thermometer,

one bottle each of

- LP-SUPERGRAIN,
- LP-FIX SUPRA, and
- LP-MASTERPROOF,
- and a folder to store developed film.

This is all you need to develop your films wherever you are. You will certainly find a watch somewhere.
The risk involved in taking yet another round through the x-ray machine might be greater than that involved in developing your films abroad.
If you don't want to develop your films abroad, or there is no opportunity to do so, use the relatively robust MACO IR 750clear, at least when travelling. This film will continue to work fine when others are already fogged.

TANKS FOR IR FILM PROCESSING

JOBO and PATERSON tanks are proven in practice. The authors prefer PATERSON, because the balls facilitate the inserting of polyester-based films in the reels.

PROCESSING OF IR FILMS IN SERVICE LABS

In many countries, there will be a lab that can provide speedy and high-quality processing of IR films. The pertinent addresses can be easily found on the Internet.
This book also lists the address of LABOR PARTNER.
Contact us when searching for labs that can process your IR films in LABOR PARTNER chemicals.

MACO IR 750clear with filter Heliopan 715
Rhinestadium, Düsseldorf, Germany

© Marcus Schwier

Marcus Schwier was born in 1964 in Düsseldorf, where he first studied architecture before enrolling at the Art Academy there. Since the year 2000 he has also taught architectural photography at the Düsseldorf University of Applied Science.
His own photographic work, which today can be found in both public and private collections, has been included in numerous exhibitions at home and abroad. In 1999 Marcus Schwier received the prestigious prize photography of the DG Banken, accompanied by an exhibition at the Sprengel Museum in Hannover.

LABOR PARTNER

Home page
www.laborpartner.info

E-Mail address for dealer
sales@laborpartner.info

E-Mail for support
doc.darkroom@laborpartner.info

Address
LABOR PARTNER GmbH
Geesthachter Str. 66
D-21502 Geesthacht / Hamburg
GERMANY

Bibliography

Herbert Graewe, *Die physikalischen und chemischen Grundlagen der Fotografie*

Jost J. Marchesi, *Handbuch der Fotografie – Berufskunde, Band 2*

Udo Raffay, *Sammlung fotografischer Rezepte*